SEPT '94

MODERN COMPETITIVE ANALYSIS

MODERN COMPETITIVE ANALYSIS

Second Edition

Sharon M. Oster

New York   Oxford
OXFORD UNIVERSITY PRESS
1994

Oxford University Press

Oxford   New York   Toronto
Delhi   Bombay   Calcutta   Madras   Karachi
Kuala Lumpur   Singapore   Hong Kong   Tokyo
Nairobi   Dar es Salaam   Cape Town
Melbourne   Auckland   Madrid

and associated companies in
Berlin   Ibadan

Published by Oxford University Press, Inc.
200 Madison Avenue, New York, New York 10016

Oxford is a registered trademark of Oxford University Press

Library of Congress Cataloging-in-Publication Data
Oster, Sharon M.
Modern competitive analysis / Sharon M. Oster.—2nd ed.
p. cm.   Includes bibliographical references (p.   ) and index.
ISBN 0-19-507579-X
1. Competition. 2. Strategic planning. I. Title.
HD41.O85   1994
338.6′048—dc20   93-9826

1 3 5 7 9 8 6 4 2

Printed in the United States of America
on acid-free paper

To my mother
Karin Oster
for many reasons

PREFACE

This is a book about competitive strategy by an economist. Thus the book's organization reflects that orientation. I believe that some of the fundamental ideas in microeconomics are very important in understanding strategic planning. But I have also learned while exploring the issues of organizational strategy that much exists outside of economics, and that material too has found its way into this book.

Three overarching themes are carried through the text. First, following the economic tradition, I focus quite heavily on the *competitive* nature of competitive strategy. Strategy is developed in an environment in which organizations are in continuous contact with one another and in which the results of organizational choices depend on what other people do. In this book, we spend a good deal of time looking at how interactive forces inside and outside the market affect the strategic choices available to organizations and the outcomes that result from those choices.

A second theme of this book is the importance of change. A strategy is a plan to get us from here to there. Change is essential to movement, and we can thus think about strategic planning as a way of creating and managing change. We will deal in some detail with the kinds of opportunities created by the changing nature of the market.

A final theme is that the choices involved in developing a strategy are inevitably made in the context of limited information and market frictions. Strategic planning is a way of informing the choice-making process of an organization. Decisions are typically made both in large organizations and in small for-profit and nonprofit organizations without full knowledge of all the relevant facts. Timeliness and human limitations make it so. Indeed, these information holes create interesting possibilities for managers and make the management process both more interesting and less certain. Strategic planning is a way of informing and improving the choices made in organizations, but such planning must recognize that uncertainties will inevitably remain.

Although the economics perspective is manifest throughout, the text also tries to move beyond economics into marketing, finance, organizational behavior, and other applied management fields, for I believe that work in these areas is vital to the art of strategic planning. Only the reader can judge how successfully these diverse fields have been represented in this book.

The second edition has been revised in a number of ways. Of course, the data and examples have been updated, wherever appropriate. Early chapters on industry structure have been reorganized and expanded. A chapter has been added on global competition. Interest in this area has blossomed even in the few years since the first edition, as the economy has opened up. An interesting literature has developed asking such questions as why are some industries global, while others remain local, and how is management different in these industries. Chapter 6 deals with these issues. Chapter 8, in which implementation problems are first discussed, has been reworked to reflect very thoughtful comments by early adopters of the first edition of this book, as well as my own expanded reading in this area. While the agency theory included in the first edition remains, it has been augmented by a discussion of critiques and alternatives to that model. Throughout the book, I have reworked and added material from both the organizational literature and the strategy literature to give this edition of the book more breadth than the first edition. The discussions of corporate diversification and mergers have particularly benefited from recent work in the strategy area on these topics.

> This book grows out of a course on competitive strategy that I began teaching at Yale in 1982, a one-semester, second-year course. But the structure of courses in which material on competitive strategy is taught varies a good deal across institutions. Here too we have seen evolution over time. As a result, the book might be used at different levels in other schools. The material has also been used at Yale for an advanced undergraduate seminar in economics. Finally, we have used some of the chapters in the Yale Executive Program, a program designed for upper-level managers interested in broadening their backgrounds.
>
> When I teach a course using chapters from this book, I usually use cases as well. I believe, as I think most people do in the field, that cases are a helpful way to see both the lessons and limits of theoretical ideas. The appendix lists cases that I have used in conjunction with various chapters of the book. Many are Harvard Business School cases and are available from the HBS Case office. Others are cases that have been developed at the Yale School of Management and are available from me on request. Of course, these are only a sampling of the cases that might be used.
>
> Though I wrote the book for a course I was teaching and hoped that it would be useful in similar courses in other institutions, I see no reason the book cannot be read profitably by practicing managers. The tools of competitive analysis in the book should be of significant help to them in solving the strategic problems they face.

I have benefited from comments from a number of people who have used the book in this revision. Several years of SOM students have been especially helpful in pointing out infelicitous phrasing or downright errors in the first edition. I also received a number of helpful comments from faculty who used the first edition of the book. Joseph Mahoney was especially helpful in recommending literature for me to look at jn preparing the second edition, as was Gordon Walker. I think the revised edition is a significant improvement over the first. I hope the reader will agree.

New Haven   S.M.O.
April 1993

CONTENTS

MODERN COMPETITIVE ANALYSIS

1

Introduction and Overview

The American industrial landscape is marked by incredible variety. Multidivisional organizations with sales of hundreds of millions of dollars coexist, often even in the same industry, with family-owned firms with sales of less than $1 million. In any given year, some firms thrive, earning high profits and experiencing rapid growth in their sales. Other firms languish, sometimes suffering losses and growing not at all. Still other organizations operate deliberately as nonprofits. In any given industry, entry of some firms may be accompanied by the exit of others. Indeed, whole industries spring up as other industries decline and die.

The variety of the landscape is further intensified by a complex and sometimes bewildering array of business strategies. One firm may spend a large fraction of its profits on research, while another is content to imitate the innovations of others. One firm produces a wide product range, while a second mass produces one variety of its good. The Coca-Cola company, for example, has a wide and expanding range of soft drink brands, while Dr. Pepper has remained almost a one-brand firm. In another industry, relief services, Oxfam focuses all of its funds on long-term development efforts in recipient countries, while a second well-known agency, the Red Cross, focuses almost entirely on short-term relief efforts. The steel industry provides another example in which the old-line industry participants are for the most part well integrated into all facets of the business, while many of the new entrants operate exclusively in the final product end. Throughout the economy, we see evidence of a great diversity in business strategy.

In short, there are large differences both in the results achieved by organizations and in the ways in which those organizations operate. Of course, some of these differences are a matter of serendipity: New product development is sometimes more a function of luck than of concerted research effort, and managerial personalities may determine corporate behavior—and hence results—in unforeseen ways. In some cases, as Mintzberg suggests, strategies form gradually, without a cohesive world view,

3

as CEO's make decisions one by one.[1] Increasingly, however, a substantial portion of the behavior engaged in by organizations is the result of deliberate *strategic planning*. Moreover, in large measure the results experienced by those organizations can be explained by the quality of that planning and the basic economic conditions under which those organizations operate. It is a major theme of this text that an understanding of economic and managerial principles can make a striking difference in the quality of the strategic planning of an organization and in the performance of that organization.

Organizational strategy begins with the desire of an organization to outperform the market. A strategy is a set of concrete plans to help the organization accomplish this goal. Sometimes that strategy is articulated; in other cases, it reveals itself only slowly over time. But at the heart of any strategy is a set of choices confronted by the organization. Fundamentally, *a strategy is a commitment to undertake one set of actions rather than another* and this commitment necessarily describes an allocation of resources. But it is precisely the question of resource allocation and trade-offs that lies at the heart of economics. In part this helps to explain the new interest in the study and practice of economics in numerous organizations. Economics is a central ingredient in strategic planning, although by no means the only ingredient.

There has been a great deal of recent work in economics, and more specifically in industrial organization, that is relevant to managerial decision making, and this text uses some of this material to illuminate situations faced by modern managers. For example, though many questions remain, considerable progress has been made in understanding why some firms earn high profits while others fail. Even more progress has been made in understanding why some industries earn high profits, on average, while others do less well. Recent work on **evolutionary economics** has provided us with considerable insight into the ways in which organizations adapt to changes in their environments and how the selection process works in a marketplace. Recently, we have begun to understand more fully why some organizations are structured in one way, while others seem to thrive with quite a different structure. **Transaction-cost economics** has given us a new way of understanding organizational structure and its functions, with its view that contractual relations within and among firms are themselves the result of efficiency-seeking behavior in a world of limited information. At the same time, there has been an increased interest in the human side of strategy, in understanding the role of leaders in setting and implementing strategies, and in understanding how organizational power is both created by strategic choices and how it influences those choices. And we have begun to see the ways in which the techniques of decision theory may be helpful in structuring managerial problem solving. Finally, work in the subfield of game theory has proven quite fruitful in forecasting and diagnosing the intricacies of interactions among organizations, ranging from warring countries to feuding firms. In this text, work in all of these areas is pulled together.

The strategic-planning process is an experiment in directed evolution. The CEO of Emhart, a $2.5 billion Connecticut metal products firm, defines strategic planning as the "management of change."[2] And, indeed, change is fundamental to the planning process. Change creates new opportunities for organizational growth and development and sometimes threatens the way firms have traditionally run their businesses. Planning provides not only a way to manage change, but a way to *create* change.

Figure 1.1 is a schematic of the ingredients in this process of planning for new directions.

We begin in the lower box, with the organization itself. Organizations consist of a set of assets and liabilities. Some are carried on the balance sheet, others are less tangible but no less important. The firm has some production facilities, a brand reputation, a distribution network, and so on. The organization also has a structure and some goals. Some organizations are highly formal; others emphasize participatory management. Some firms stress short-run profits; others focus more heavily on growth.

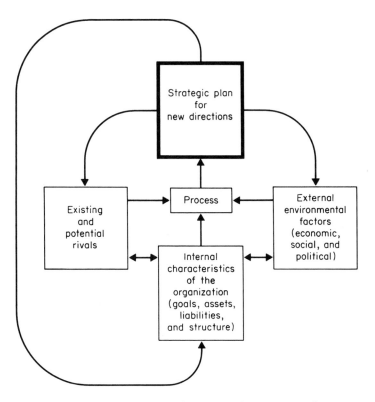

Figure 1.1 Forces contributing to the strategic plan

This set of internal characteristics will determine, in part, what options are available and attractive to the firm. One of the lessons we have learned in the strategy area over the last several decades is that the attractiveness of particular strategies is highly *contingent* on the history and characteristics of the organization in question.

All organizations operate within a broad community, represented in the right-hand box of Figure 1.1. The laws and customs of a society will help to determine the viability of new strategic directions, as will more mundane factors like the overall level of economic activity in a society. Firms are governed by antitrust laws and labor laws. They are affected by demographics and educational policy. But organizations themselves can sometimes influence the external environment in profound ways. Firms influence labor laws and trade policy, for example. So we have drawn a two-headed arrow between the firm and its environment in the schematic.

One very important part of an organization's environment is its rivals, real and potential. In Figure 1.1 we have isolated this component to highlight its importance. Here, too, the arrow is two-headed: a proliferation of rivals certainly will influence a firm's ability to enter a new area, but at the same time new strategic actions of that firm might influence the number and condition of those rivals.

Based on these three ingredients—the internal characteristics of the firm, an analysis of its environment, and a detailed consideration of its rivals—the organization can begin to put together a plan to move in a new direction. Thus, in the central box of the schematic we have placed the planning process. This process varies considerably across organizations. At some firms, strategic planning is done by the CEO alone without any strategic planning group. This was the case at Polaroid, for example, before 1982. In other organizations, strategic planning is done by a fairly large group of staff people, abetted by teams of consultants. Xerox works in this way as does Procter & Gamble. In some organizations planning involves many forms and lots of paper work. In other places, planning offices resemble war rooms at the Pentagon. In other firms strategies emerge piecemeal and there is no long-range planning. But no matter how strategies are developed, their success will be profoundly influenced by these three industry and organizational characteristics.

Any new plan, indeed any new process, potentially alters each of the various boxes in the exhibit, and thus gives the organization a new strategic-planning problem for the next round. Planning—done well—creates the momentum for change. Indeed, improving the capacity of an organization to react quickly to a changing environment was early suggested as one of the central advantages of a planning process.[3] One role of the planning process is to organize equipment to be used when fires need to be fought. Indeed, the firms which seem to rely most heavily on strategic planning are those with vulnerable core technologies.[4]

Improving organizational response time is one objective of the planning process. A second function of planning is to integrate the organization.[5] In successful organizations, managers have some reasonably well-articulated vision of the future direction of the organization. Sometimes that vision is very concrete. Seymour Cray, the founder of Cray Research, once the leading manufacturer of the super computer, articulated a very precise goal: "The purpose of my company is to design and build a larger, more powerful computer than anyone now has."[6] For several decades, this concrete vision served Cray extremely well. In other organizations, future direction is less well specified. In either case, the planning process can provide both input into the development of a vision and a way of disseminating that vision throughout the organization. Planning can also help in revising a mission when markets change.

The strategic-planning process also affects the control function of an organization.[7] As the complexity of the modern organization increases, this function takes on a more important role. Decision making in large and small organizations inevitably occurs with limited information. Control of the large organization is often not lodged in the owners of that organization, making these functions both more difficult and more important. As Jeffrey Pfeffer suggests, organizations typically consist of coalitions of individuals, with different preferences, power, and information. When resources are allocated, as part of a strategy, so too is power and this fact complicates our discussions of strategy. Here planning may on occasion be of help, as it allows us to monitor functions and perhaps alter the incentives of various members of the organization in its uncertain environment. Reginald Jones, the CEO of General Electric in the hey day of its strategic-planning effort, commented that the G.E. planning system provided "a strong discipline for differentiating the allocation of resources."[8] Control across areas was key to the planning process of this large diversified organization.

This text has four broad sections to reflect the ingredients in a dynamic planning process. Part I focuses attention on the environment faced by an organization, including the characteristics of the industry of which it is a part. In the U.S. economy, some industries appear to earn relatively high profits over substantial periods of time; other industries limp along year after year. What accounts for these differences among industries? The evidence is examined on the performance of various industries and some theory is developed to explain the persistence of these differences among industries. In this section of the text, we examine the factors that lead some industries to globalize, while others remain local. Part I also considers the effect of industry-wide forces on organizational strategy. Material in this section is primarily drawn from the discipline of economics, using work from industrial organization. Chapters 2 through 6 carefully look at what has traditionally been called **environmental analysis** in the strategic-planning literature.

Part II narrows in on the organization itself. Within a particular industry environment, some firms do well and others poorly. Is this a matter of chance alone, or are there some systematic forces which determine firm performance? How do we tell if one organization is performing well relative to a second? What kind of an economic accounting can we make of the assets and liabilities of an organization? Does strategy play a role? Why are there differences in the structure of organizations, and what difference, if any, does management structure make? How does an organization decide on issues of scope? These are difficult questions and Part II draws on a wide range of work in economics, sociology, psychology, and finance to provide some of the answers. In these chapters, the **implementation** questions of strategic management are treated.

In Part III, I consider the relationship among organizations operating within an industry. In some industries aggressive price competition is rare, and marketing is the prime competitive arena. In other industries, price wars are common. In some industries, research and development is often undertaken with joint ventures, and patents are commonly cross-licensed. In other industries, R&D is closely guarded and the subject of much litigation. How do we explain these differences? Is it the personality of the players that accounts for most of the difference among industries or is it economic factors? Or, a bit of both? Why have strategic alliances increased over time? Can we systematically learn anything about competitor behavior to help make it more predictable? Part III concentrates heavily on some of the recent and fascinating work in the area of game theory as applied to management.

Part IV deals with the planning process. As I indicated earlier, organizations differ substantially in how they plan or even whether they plan. Part IV describes some of these differences and looks at the way the principles we develop in the body of this book can also help us to understand differences in the planning process itself.

Throughout, many of the examples used will be drawn from the corporate world. Others are taken from small businesses, from the nonprofit sector, and some from the public sector as well. Economics as a discipline has been as interested in the public side of organizations as it has in the private; so, too, has sociology. Increasingly, the field of strategy has broadened to include the so-called independent sector. Many of the tools and ideas developed will be useful for the public manager as well as the private manager. In many ways, analyzing the strategic options of the Port Authority of New York is not so different from looking at the choices of Rouse, a private development corporation. Competition between the Whitney Museum and the Guggenheim over both art masterpieces and funding can be as intense as the Pepsi–Coca-Cola soft drink war. Differences, of course, exist as well, both in the kinds of objectives nonprofits and public sector organizations have vis à vis their private counterparts, and in the opportunities they face. When the time comes, I will try to illustrate these differences as well.

The Dynamics of Industry Structure

Before going into the main body of the text, I want to look more closely at some themes to be developed in it. As we indicated in Figure 1.1, the planning process is intended to bring the possibilities of change to the front of the organizational consciousness. In part, the evolution over time of an organization results from its own efforts. In most industries, however, there are also general forces operating to affect the selection environment in which the organization operates. Different strategic issues will come to the foreground as an organization moves through various stages. The sources of opportunities for creating new value will also change over the life cycle of the market. Seymour Cray's vision of the super computer market referred to earlier was a source of extraordinary profits for Cray in the 1970s and 1980s; increased competition and changes in the research area made it less attractive in the 1990s. Learning to adapt to fundamental changes like these is very difficult for most firms, and yet such changes are inevitable. We will use a stylized recital of a common path of industry evolution to set the stage for our organizational analysis and to highlight the theme of strategic interaction that will be carried throughout the text.

The early history of an industry or a product market is often characterized by considerable upheaval. Typically as the industry progresses, more stability sets in: The number of new exits and entrants into the industry begins to slow, profit and growth rates stabilize, and so on. Indeed the general pattern of industry evolution follows the path in Figure 1.2.

The industry begins when a new product is introduced by a firm. Typically, the initial production capacity of the innovator is below what the market will support. Growth and profit opportunities in the new industry appear to be very attractive and new entry occurs. This period is often

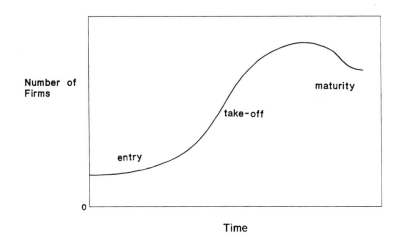

Figure 1.2 A typical industry

marked by experimentation around issues of production technique and sometimes around product style. In this period of the industry's development, uncertainty is rampant and learning rapid. At this stage in development, there are substantial payoffs to fleetness and flexibility.

The attractive and exciting initial period is not, however, destined to last. In many industries, as shown in Figure 1.2, the initial opportunities in the industry attract entry. In many cases, too many firms enter: Now firms find that there is more capacity than the market can profitably support. At this point, too, some firms turn out to have made production choices which, given demand conditions, are less costly than those of their rivals. Some product designs turn out to be superior to others. As many industries evolve, a dominant design begins to emerge.[9] All of these forces lead to a shakeout in a kind of Darwinian process of survival of the fittest in which prices fall and profit margins follow. Finally, stability sets in as only the most efficient survive.

This idealized pattern has occurred in a great many diverse industries, the automobile industry, for one.[10] Between 1900, when the automobile was first introduced, and 1910, demand for autos mushroomed. Demand exceeded the capacity of early producers and new entrants were abundant. Between 1902 and 1909, 47 firms entered the market. By 1921, there were 88 auto firms in the U.S. This period in auto history was marked by a high failure rate and considerable experimentation, particularly in the production realm. By 1931, however, consolidation had occurred, with General Motors controlling about one-third of industry sales. By this time, much of the early experimentation in the production area had fallen away and production methods used by the various firms in the industry had become standardized.

A more recent example of the same pattern is provided by the biotechnology market. The first biotechnology firm, Genentech, was founded in 1976 and pioneered in the production of human insulin and human growth hormone. By the early 1990s, there were dozens of biotechnology firms, exploring products in a wide range of human, animal, and plant applications. There were also a significant number of joint ventures and alliances between small biotechnology firms and their larger cousins in the pharmaceutical industry. As the 1990s have progressed, we have seen the failure and exit of many firms.

The general pattern of industry evolution shown in Figure 1.2 characterizes many diverse industries. But within this general pattern there are large differences among industries. Some new products compete from the outset with relatively close substitutes already in the market. Tylenol, for example, faced pricing pressure from aspirin even in its early stages. Biotechnology firms producing animal vaccines competed from the start with conventional pharmaceutical companies. Fiber optics producers, on the other hand, faced few substitutes in the entry period. In some industries, the development of a new product is rapidly followed by large-scale entry. The curve in the initial takeoff period is quite steep. The biotechnology industry is a good example of this pattern, as is the market for personal computers. In other industries, entry by new firms is quite slow. The copying industry is an excellent example of this pattern, with Xerox remaining almost alone in the industry for a considerable period. The instant-photography market similarly exhibited slow entry for a variety of reasons we will explore later in this text.

Industries differ not only in how fast entry occurs, but also in how much entry we eventually see. In many industries, sufficient capacity will enter the industry to drive prices down and eliminate any extraordinary profit opportunities that existed early in the industry's history. The smoke detector industry is a relevant example. In the mid-1970s the price of detectors was $50; by the 1980s the price of the average smoke detector had fallen to $15, despite some overall rise in the general price level. We see a similar pattern in the prices of chips in the semiconductor industry. While part of this price decrease undoubtedly reflected cost reductions associated with technical progress, most of the decrease simply reflected the pressure on margins caused by substantial entry. In other industries, while entry occurs and capacity grows, the new capacity is not sufficient to eliminate the high profits of the industry.

As a result of differences in the rate and magnitude of new entry, industries differ substantially in their profitability. One element in an organization's strategy is figuring out which industries are likely to be characterized by slow and difficult entry—thus yielding favorable profit opportunities for it for a protracted period. In the next several chapters of this text, we concentrate on identifying industry-wide factors that influence profitability rates. This will be the central thrust of our **environmental analysis.** (Of course, identifying potentially profitable industries may be easier than actually entering them. We all know that being a star pitcher for the Mets is a lucrative profession, but few of us are credible entrants into that profession.) But identifying lucrative areas is at least a start.

Figure 1.2 shows the evolution of an industry as a whole. That evolutionary path has clear and substantial influences on the fortunes of the individual organizations within that industry. But industry-wide patterns do not tell the whole story. In a number of industries, the average performance of the industry is no better than the average of industries as a whole, but particular firms or groups of firms manage to do considerably better than average. In these instances, the high-performing firm or subgroup has something special and hard to imitate that allows it to outperform its rivals. Porter refers to such special assets as the firm's **competitive advantage.**[11] A firm's competitive advantages are those characteristics that allow it to do well even in the face of mediocre industry-wide performance and free entry into the industry as a whole. In many cases, superior performance in a market requires a complex package of mutually supporting **complementary assets.**[12] Sometimes these assets are physical. In other cases, it is aspects of the organizational structure or corporate culture that results in superior performance. The oft-cited success of Japanese firms in many markets is as much a result of organizational factors as economic ones. Often it is market frictions that allow advantages to be sustained over a long period of time, frictions created both by nature and by governments. To some extent these advantages result from choices made by those organizations. And, we recall, one of the fundamental jobs of the planning process is to inform the choice process.

The Connection Between Economics and Strategy: A Theme to be Repeated

I have suggested that strategic planning is a way of creating and managing change. Ultimately the responsibility for developing a strategy belongs to the chief executive officer of that organization. Indeed the early strategy literature focused heavily on the role of top managers in shaping their firms.[13] In some organizations, particularly small ones, strategic planning is done by the chief executive officer without the support of a formal planning staff. Indeed the planning itself may be highly inchoate. In other organizations, planning staffs not only exist but are quite powerful in the development of the corporate strategy. Even within particular organizations, the role of the planning group typically varies over time. Formal strategic planning has had a checkered history in many organizations. In the 1970s planning groups emerged at most major U.S. corporations. By the late 1970s, 75 percent of the Fortune 1000 firms used strategic-planning methods.[14] These groups began with formidable agendas and high ambitions. Unfortunately, the early history of strategic planning at many large organizations rapidly degenerated into a formulaic mode as did some of the management literature. Firms *en masse* articulated and attempted to follow strategies like "Go for share," "Sell off low-growth businesses," or "Acquire businesses in high-margin, high-growth areas" as a way to increase the value of their organizations. The results of trying to apply these rules were often disastrous and in many organizations the strategic planners took the blame. People responsible for running operations soon learned that there really was no magic formula for making money in corporate America. And in many organizations the formal planning function declined. More recently, we have seen a cautious rebuilding of planning groups in numerous organizations.

Interestingly, one of the fundamental principles of economics, which we will explore in this text, easily predicts and explains the failure of a slogan-following brand of strategy.

If everyone can do it, you can't make money at it.

This principle contains a profound message for strategic decision making. Strategies must be formed in a competitive context, with an appreciation for how the market will react to those strategic moves. If a firm decides to pursue market share, it needs to determine if its rivals are also likely to go for share at the same time. If a firm decides to acquire a high-growth business, it needs to ask: Why does the owner wish to sell that business? And, what price will be asked? In short, planning must take place in an integrated, interactive context. And this brings us right back to the role of economic analysis in planning, for economics is essentially a study of the playing out of choices in a variety of marketplaces.

Traditional economics looks at phenomena using **equilibrium analysis.** By this I mean that we examine the results of particular choices after all of the salient reactions to those choices have occurred—that is, after the market has settled down. In various diverse markets we ask ourselves what the reaction of all the other actors in the market will be to the behavior of a particular actor. And those reactions affect our expectations about the results of initial decisions. More recent economic thinking, particularly in the area of **evolutionary economics,** has stimulated our interest in situations in which equilibrium has not yet occurred, when markets are still moving and adjusting. Work in **organizational ecology** similarly looks at lessons to be learned from growth, survival, and death patterns within evolving industries. And, as we will see, it is in evolving markets that much creative strategic decision making occurs. But even in these markets we will generally be able to discern the germs of a movement toward equilibrium, and seeing and understanding these movements is a vital part of planning.

The study of actions and reactions of players in a situation is relevant to our understanding of what goes on both inside an organization and outside the organization in formal marketplaces. If senior managers design a bonus plan, for example, we need to ask how this influences the work behavior of current middle managers? Does it change the number and quality of new middle managers? Does it influence how each of these managers performs his or her job? How do actions by middle managers feed back into the design of the next bonus plan? How does the current organizational structure of a firm influence the constellation of power within that firm and then go on to affect corporate reorganization plans? If an organization earns higher returns than its rivals, we need to examine how this influences rival behavior before we can build a strategy. Are rivals likely to imitate a successful firm? If so, what happens to that firm's performance? Actions and reactions are fundamental to economics and inform its influence on strategy. *A strategy must be devised and implemented with an appreciation of these second-order effects. Again, we recognize that there is no magic in planning.*

The argument that a successful planning effort should take into account wide-ranging reactions undergirds Chapter 2 and indeed the remainder of this book. The analysis which follows covers a wide range of strategic issues: pricing, marketing, research and development, decisions about organizational scope. But the common thread we weave is that in devising a strategy in any of these areas an appreciation for the reactions of other actors in the system is essential. This approach further leads us to conclude that strategies are specific to circumstances. Recently, this observation has been termed the **contingency theory** of planning: The right strategy is contingent on the specific circumstances of the organization.[15] Thus, no one strategy works for all organizations. The contingency theory has a strong, often unappreciated, economic base, for economic analysis too tells us that optimal behavior depends in predictable ways on antecedent conditions. For example, unless there is some reason that you alone can increase your market share or purchase a particular high-growth business, these strategies are not likely to deliver high margins over the long haul. Strategies that are able to help an organization move forward in response to changing times and integrate and disseminate the corporate vision are necessarily conditioned by the circumstances of the organization, its history and assets, and its environment.

> **While there are no generally successful strategies, some general principles of strategic planning can improve performance.**

In this text, I offer little in the way of generic strategies, useful to all causes. Instead, I focus on developing some tools and principles that *can* be used by any organization in trying to understand the unique problems and opportunities it faces in allocating its resources. As a result, the text has rather little to do with formal strategic planning, and much more to do with understanding the interplay between the economic conditions faced by an organization and its strategy.

I

THE COMPETITIVE ENVIRONMENT

Strategic planning is an integrative activity, pulling together information produced throughout the organization and, in its best form, helping to create a cohesive vision of where the organization is going. As indicated in the introduction, the planning process has several pieces.

I have reproduced below the planning schematic introduced in Chapter 1. In this section of the text, we take a closer look at the right-hand box of the schematic, the external environment facing the firm. In Chapter 2, I sketch the economic forces which constrain the kind of choices organizations can make and argue that in most markets there are pressures which eventually erode extraordinary strategic opportunities. One

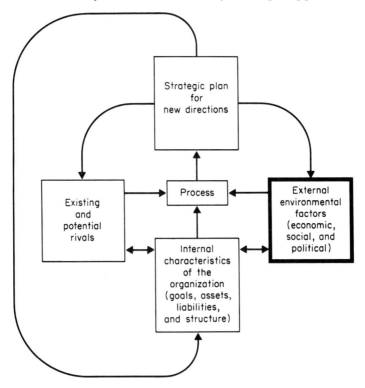

Figure I.1

of the lessons in Chapter 2 is that there are gains to be made from swift and flexible decision making, for major strategic opportunities are generally short-lived.

Chapters 3 and 4 focus on another element of the competitive environment: the forces that allow *some* markets to offer extraordinary opportunities for extended periods of time. If Chapter 2 tells us how markets work, Chapters 3 and 4 focus on frictions that impede their operation.

Chapter 5 continues our discussion of the external environment with a closer look at strategic groups. This is our introduction to the analysis of industry substructure, an analysis we will retain throughout the text as we look at the other elements of planning in our schematic.

Finally, in Chapter 6 we look at some of the special features of organizations that operate as global firms. What makes some industries global, while others remain local? And how do we explain the location of particular global industries?

2

Efficient Markets

The Broad Principle

When the Van Gogh exhibition opened in New York city in 1987, the staff at the Metropolitan anticipated that more people would want to see the exhibit, particularly on weekends, than the museum had room for. To ration the existing space, the Metropolitan decided to sell tickets that allowed an individual to see the show at a given time and date. Many people found, however, that on the particular day they wanted to see the Van Gogh show, they were without tickets. Were they in fact left out in the cold unable to see the show? Quite the contrary. People who were without a ticket simply went to the steps of the Metropolitan and loitered for a few minutes, with a certain interested look on their faces. Before too long, someone would approach them, often clutching a handful of tickets. In the case of the Van Gogh exhibit, and in many other sports, music, and cultural events generally, *scalpers* buy tickets in the hopes of reselling them at a profit later on. Generally speaking, **secondary markets** develop at these events, in which tickets are bought and sold. In fact, such secondary markets are so common that in some parts of the country potential buyers are outraged when they arrive at an event and find that scalpers have passed it by.

If we explore the scalping market further, we find that it has some interesting features. First of all, different scalpers operating at the same time and at the same event offer tickets at about the same prices. And yet there is clearly no central planning bureau setting scalping prices. Rather, the quick working of the market pushes prices together. If prices differed substantially, only the low-priced scalpers would sell their tickets. Higher-priced scalpers would find themselves with a supply of outdated and useless ticket paper. Anticipating this disaster, the high-priced scalpers lower their prices, thus closing the original price gap.

Of course, I do not want to argue that no one has ever bought a scalped ticket at a price higher than that offered by the majority of scalpers at the

17

same event. As the old adage tells us, there is a sucker born every minute and one can be found at most events. But the propensity of a reasonable number of people to ask around about the price and to direct their purchases accordingly has the effect of driving prices together, at least after a period of time.

Another feature of the secondary ticket market is the ratio of scalped prices to original prices on weekdays versus weekends. Suppose scalpers are not limited to the number of tickets they can buy. Of course, overall, more people want to see Van Gogh on weekends than weekdays. In response, scalpers typically want to buy more tickets for Saturday than they do for a typical Tuesday in order to meet the demand. The result is that, in these kinds of markets, the profits that scalpers make on Saturday tickets do not tend on average to be higher than profits on Tuesday tickets. More tickets are scalped on Saturday, but not necessarily at higher profits.

This is not to say that scalpers' margins remain constant at all times. On rainy Saturdays more people come to the museum than on sunny ones. On these days, prices of scalped tickets soar, as demand bids those prices up. The critical difference is that while scalpers can anticipate the coming of a Saturday, they cannot foresee the rain. Since the rain was unanticipated when the scalpers bought their ticket supplies, scalpers cannot adjust purchases in the way they do in anticipation of the known differences between weekdays and weekends. So on rainy days scalpers do rather well. An unanticipated strike by the Long Island Railroad, however, might wipe out any profits the scalpers see by leaving them with many unsold tickets.

The market for scalped Van Gogh tickets just described operates in large measure as an **efficient market.**

> **An efficient market is one in which prices reflect information instantaneously and one in which extraordinary profit opportunities are thus rapidly dissipated by the action of profit-seeking individuals in the market.**

In ways which will become clear shortly, it is the efficiency of markets that organizations do battle with in designing and implementing their strategies. Given the absolutely fundamental character of the efficient market principle for understanding the performance of an organization and for designing its strategy, we will stay with this idea a bit longer.

One of the primary areas in which economists have examined the efficient markets idea has been in the stock market. When you buy a share of stock, you are purchasing the rights to a portion of the stream of earnings that the firm earns over its lifetime. Of course, many people who buy stock don't really think of it this way; they are simply trying to make a profit on their investment. But the fact remains that buying a share does confer ownership. The value of the stock, therefore, should reflect the earnings ability of the firm, since the stock is nothing more than a right over a share of these earnings. If we hold the number of shares constant, then firms with high-earning potential should have stocks with high val-ues and those with low potential should have low-stock values. Under-standing this relationship between stock prices and the underlying char-acteristics of firms has led some analysts to use the earning potential of a firm to guide stock market purchases. By this reasoning, firms with high-earning potentials are thought to be better stock market buys than those with low potential. Investment advice based on this model is common. For example, an analyst's report might argue: "New tariff barriers which will protect the domestic steel industry make steel stock a good bet for the future"; or "Kimberly-Clark's excellent marketing ability make it a fine stock prospect"; or, more recently, "Increased competition in the per-sonal computer market makes IBM a bad bet for the future." We have all seen similar investment advice.

Unfortunately, making money on the stock market is not so simple as the purveyors of this kind of advice suggest. What complicates our efforts to earn money in the market is the two-sided nature of that market. In order to buy stock I have to find someone who wants to sell it. And in buying that stock, I must compete with all the other potential buyers of the stock. That competition will bid up the price of the stock. Of course, the buying and selling in this market is carried out by brokers, and so much of it is less apparent than what goes on at the steps of the Metro-politan. But the market principles are exactly the same. If I own stock in a firm with a high-earning potential, I will expect to sell it for a high price and competition among buyers who have investigated the firm's fine po-tential will keep up those prices. You may wish to buy stock in a com-pany that has a good earnings potential, but unless you're the only one who knows about that good potential, you will have to pay handsomely for the privilege of owning that stock. Investors' actions create an efficient market out of the stock market. In the stock market, the efficient-market principle is also known as the **random-walk theory**. Here is one version of the theory.

> **"Fundamental analysis cannot produce investment recommendations that will enable an investor consistently to outperform a buy and hold strategy in managing a portfolio."**[1]

On average, high-quality firms have high-priced stock and firms with poor prospects will find their stock selling at a discount. From the point of view of the buyer, there is no goose that lays a golden egg. Or, if there is one, it carries a high price.

This is not to say that no one ever makes money on the stock market. Sometimes scalpers are blessed with rain, and sometimes investors make lucky guesses. Indeed, on average over time the winners will just balance out the losers, although there are clearly investment strategies that will cause investors to perform considerably worse than the market average.[2] In some cases, investors may outperform the market by using information about a firm that few other people know.[3] Insiders can sometimes buy stocks for less than they're really worth or sell them for more than the true value, since they know something the seller or buyer does not. But for most of us, beating the market is quite difficult.

We should also be clear that efficiency in markets comes only with the passage of time. Until a sufficient number of investors learn of new investment opportunities, stock prices may not reflect true value. Until new competitors learn of the lucrative returns to be made in a particular market, firms can do extremely well. Taking advantage of these periods in which markets are off balance is one of the difficult tasks of a management team, and a task that requires both speed and flexibility. Increasingly, American business has focused on improving its response time or cutting product development time as a way to enhance profitability. Speed becomes important because the market is so powerful.

We have seen now two quite different examples of efficient markets. A belief in the force of efficiency in markets is central to the way economists think about markets, so much so that one of the classic jokes in economics centers on the idea. And, indeed, the spirit behind the principle of efficiency as well as its limitations are quite well reflected in the joke: Two economists, one an eminent efficient-market type and the second a bright young assistant professor, are walking down the street. Suddenly the young economist bends down and reaches, trying to pick up something from the sidewalk. "What are you doing?" asks the older professor. "There's a $20 bill on the ground," replies the young assistant. "Nonsense," retorts the older man. "If there were really a $20 bill on the ground, someone else would have already picked it up."

The efficient-market principle suggests that if there is a good opportunity for higher than average profits to be made, there will be a strong tendency for many of the participants in that market to try to exploit that opportunity. And, just as important, as more people try to exploit a good opportunity, the quality of the opportunity diminishes. The $20 bill doesn't last long on the ground. Prices of scalped tickets tend to converge. Stock prices quickly change to reflect changes in the assessment of experts on the earnings potential of different firms. Good things are inevitably ephemeral. It is not hard to see why economics has been termed the *dismal science*. In practice, the $20 bill does not always disappear instantaneously, despite the views of the older professor in the classic joke. And so there is sometimes gain from speed. But any $20 bill or apparently golden opportunity that persists for a long period of time perhaps deserves some skepticism.

We can now turn to try to understand the determinants of differences in the profitability of various industries using our understanding of markets as a base. The story we wish to tell is a simple but powerful one. In the typical industry, in the early period of that industry, there is too little industry capacity. This dearth of capacity allows high profits to be earned by firms lucky enough or clever enough to be in the industry. Indeed, we can think of the high returns of this period as a reward for **entrepreneur-**

ship. And one function of creative strategic planning is to arm an organization to take advantage of opportunities rapidly when they arise. As Eisenhardt has suggested, "the best strategies are irrelevant if they take too long to formulate."[4] In most circumstances, high profits induce new entry, just as potential profits on the Saturday scalped tickets induced scalpers to purchase more Saturday tickets. In some industries, this new capacity comes in fast and in large amounts, and profits fall dramatically. In other markets, entry is restrained, but entry pressures may nevertheless be substantial. Thus the possibility of entry is fundamental to patterns of profits in an industry.[5] A second function of strategy is to alert the organization to new entry and prepare it to meet that new entry and compete. Jack Welch, the current CEO of General Electric, describes the markets in which he competes as "brutally Darwinian." It is entry that produces that brutality.

If we are to understand what causes the differences between those industries characterized by rapid entry and falling profits, and those for which high profits are sustainable, it is useful to begin by examining more formally the **competitive model.** To do this, we will return to the period in which a new product has been developed, and industry capacity is inadequate to meet market demand. It is useful to start this analysis by looking at a simple stylized picture of the industry at this period to see what changes we are likely to observe as time passes. Some markets will move rapidly and easily toward this competitive position; others will move in fits and starts. But in virtually all markets there is some tendency toward the competitive position, and it is in the context of this tendency and indeed, in part, in opposition to this tendency that much strategic planning operates.

The Competitive Ideal

To facilitate the discussion, we will begin with some simple graphs. Figure 2.1 depicts two graphs representing the static situation affecting a firm. The graph on the right is a *Supply and Demand* diagram which represents the situation affecting the industry as a whole. At lower prices more of the product will be *demanded* by consumers. The downward slope in the demand curve is created by both the larger volume per customer and the larger consumer base typically expected for lower prices of an item. The typical producer's willingness to sell a given item, however, *increases* with the price level. The upward rising supply curve reflects the greater willingness of producers to introduce new expensive production methods if the output of that production can be sold at higher prices. The price for which the quantity demanded by consumers is exactly equal to the quantity supplied by producers can be found at the intersection of supply and demand and is known as the **equilibrium price.** At this price there is no pressure on either the consumers' part or the producers' part to change the price.

> **The equilibrium price in a market is one at which the quantity demanded by consumers exactly equals the quantity supplied by producers.**

There is neither excess demand, nor excess supply at the equilibrium. In Figure 2.1, let us suppose that P* is the prevailing equilibrium price in the early period of an industry's evolution.

What kind of margins are produced by this price. At P*, is the typical firm in the industry doing well or poorly? In order to answer this question, we need to know something about the firm's costs. Let us look at the costs of a firm operating with a fixed set of plant and equipment. The difference between the price a firm receives for its product and its unit costs constitute its profit. In the graph on the left in Figure 2.1, the **average costs** (AC) of the firm have a U-shape; the average costs are also thought of as the per unit costs of operating at various volumes. The U-shape is a common one for cost curves, though by no means the only one. In this instance, average costs fall initially as the firm increases volume and is thus able to spread overhead. At some point the difficulties of squeezing more output from a given plant increase. This accounts for the later rise in average costs.

The left-hand graph also represents the **marginal costs** (MC) of the firm producing the new product. Marginal costs are the incremental costs of producing an additional unit of the good. Marginal costs rise with increased volume because with a fixed plant it becomes increasingly expensive to produce additional units of a product.[6] The firm will find that it earns the highest profits if it produces at a volume for which the incremental costs are exactly equal to incremental revenues, here price. This point is marked as Q* on the graph. At this point, the firm is earning profits on all the units produced with lower marginal costs.

How well is the typical firm shown in Figure 2.1 doing? The answer to the question depends in part on what we have included in the costs

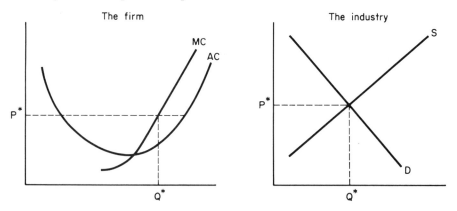

Figure 2.1 Firms earning excess profits

shown in the figure. Suppose we include, as is usual in economics, though not in accounting, the costs of capital in calculating the average costs drawn in Figure 2.1. Then, the situation drawn represents one in which the firm is earning revenues in excess of all costs, *including the cost of its capital.* Suppose the firm has entered this industry using entirely debt capital financed at 10 percent. In the circumstances of Figure 2.1, the prevailing market price is adequate to cover all operating costs, the debt on capital, and still leave something left over. In Figure 2.1, the firm has entered the market, been recompensed for the time and energy of its founders, and received a kind of bonus. The accounting profit will be in excess of the capital cost. Clearly this is a very appealing situation.

Remember now the efficient-market principle: Appealing situations do not in general last very long. In the above example we would typically expect other firms to observe the high returns earned by the firms in the industry and attempt to enter. Other firms will try to borrow capital to build production facilities to serve this market. Indeed, as long as returns in the market exceed the cost of capital we would expect there to be entry pressures in the industry. Of course, the existing firms in the industry, including the one represented in Figure 2.1, will continue to reap excess returns until new entrants appear. Again, these are the rewards to a swift-footed entrepreneur who sees opportunities early.

What happens in this situation if entry occurs? As new firms with new capacity enter the market, the supply curve in Figure 2.1 moves to the right. More output is supplied at any given price, since there are more firms with plant and equipment available to supply that market. Unless something has coincidentally occurred to increase demand in this market, price will begin to fall. At some point, price will fall to a level which is just sufficient to cover costs, again including the all-important cost of capital. Firms with inefficient production or distribution technologies or inferior products will be forced to drop out of the market. At this point, the elusive $20 bill has disappeared. All excess returns have been dissipated, and the industry proceeds with firms earning *normal* returns. This is the brutal Darwinian process.

In practice, the role of entry in reducing profit and prices may be dramatic. In the airline industry, large-scale entry occurred in 1981 with the first moves toward deregulation. Entry by newly certified carriers was estimated to have reduced fares by an average of 26 percent in just a few years.[7] It has been estimated that the structural changes associated with deregulation in the industry reduced fares in 1986 by $11 billion.[8] Deregulation has also affected the dispersion of profits considerably, and we have seen some winners and some losers among the carriers. Long-time air carriers like Braniff and Eastern have left the market and considerable consolidation has occurred throughout the industry.

As the airline example suggests, the passing of time in an industry is not always smooth. In many cases, too many firms enter in quest of excess returns, only to find below-normal returns from excess capacity by the time their production facilities are ready for operation. When there were more regulatory controls on entry, the air shuttle route between New York and Washington was quite lucrative. Once entry was permitted, new carriers like N.Y. Air entered the market (offering free bagels and the like), and drove margins down for other carriers, although air traffic congestion has even now restricted entry below its competitive level. In other instances, the ability of new firms to enter the market and instigate the process that eventually erodes excess profits is hampered. In this latter case, firms may be able to earn excess profits over quite protracted periods of time. In Chapters 3 and 4, we will focus on these cases and the conditions which allow relatively long-term earning of excess profits. Here, it is essential to keep in mind the great power of the entry force, the appeal of the $20 bill. In all situations in which excess profits are being earned, we begin with the presumption that entry pressures will eventually occur and ask ourselves what forces are likely to stop such entry. Many organizations that thrive in the early entrepreneurial period find themselves unable to continue their momentum through more settled times.

With this background on the principle of the efficient market and the rudiments of industry evolution, we now turn to some of the actual differences across industries in profitability.

Industry Profit Differences and the Opportunity Cost of Capital

Every spring, *Fortune* magazine publishes a list of the top 500 industrial companies in the U.S. economy. For each firm, *Fortune* gives a variety of data including various measures of its rate of return. In the same spring issue, *Fortune* publishes a list of returns by industry in the economy. Taken as a group, these indexes provide a useful snapshot of the relative positions of the firms and industries in the U.S. economy. Many organizations use one or another of these measures of return to evaluate managerial performance and to direct resource allocation within the organization. Most traditional strategic plans rely on these measures in one way or another. It turns out, however, if we rely too heavily on these figures to help direct our strategic analysis, we will find ourselves uncomfortably placed, again because of the force of efficient-market operations. Let us take a closer look at a sample *Fortune* list in Table 2.1 and see what we can and cannot learn from the data.

In Appendix 2, the various financial ratios typically used to describe firms are catalogued and discussed. In the discussion here, I focus on the lessons of these financial data for market-efficiency theories.[9] Again, my focus is on the usefulness of these indexes for strategic, forward-looking decision making.

Let us for a moment analyze the column marked Return on Sales (ROS). This is a commonly used index of a firm or industry's performance cre-

Table 2.1   Return differences among industries (1990 industry medians)

	Return on stockholders' equity (ROE) %	Return on sales (ROS) %	Total return to investors %
Tobacco	3.9	1.6	22.5
Publishing, printing	4.8	5.5	15.1
Furniture	4.4	2.7	14.3
Beverages	7.0	7.8	27.6
Pharmaceuticals	13.1	13.6	20.5
Food	6.2	3.1	27.1
Motor vehicle and parts	2.2	1.9	11.8
Transportation	3.7	2.9	9.4
Scientific and photographic equipment	5.7	4.9	.5
Aerospace	4.6	3.5	8.4
Metal products	4.8	3.9	18.3
Soaps, cosmetics	8.7	6.3	23.1
Apparel	4.2	3.3	19.9
Mining, crude-oil production	4.5	8.7	2.2
Computers (includes office equipment)	6.4	5.7	2.9
Electronics	4.4	3.2	10.0
Building materials	2.1	2.4	16.4
Petroleum refining	5.0	4.0	7.7
Rubber products	5.2	3.6	25.5
Forest products	4.3	4.4	13.2
Chemicals	5.8	5.5	13.6
Industrial and farm equipment	3.9	3.1	6.1
Textiles	.1	0.0	11.7
Metals	4.4	4.4	4.0
All industries	4.8	4.1	11.8

ated by dividing the earnings of the firm or industry by its sales. As we see from the table, there are wide differences among industries in their ROS's. In 1990, the pharmaceutical industry was high, earning an average of 13.6 percent on sales as contrasted with earnings of 0.0 percent in the textile industry.

Similar large disparities across industries are revealed in the return on equity (ROE) column. ROE is another common measure of performance used within firms. It is equal to the earnings of the firm divided by the book value of firm equity. In 1990, pharmaceuticals were high with an ROE of 13.1 percent, while textiles lagged with a value of .1 percent. Nor is the order of industries invariant with respect to the two indexes. Rubber products, for example, performed better than average using an ROE measure and worse than average based on its ROS.

A third index of firm performance calculated by *Fortune* is provided in column 3 of Table 2.1. The return to investors is calculated to include the price appreciation and dividend yield from a stock held for a one-year period, here 1989 to 1990. Here too there are large differences among industries, with beverages heading the list at 27.6 percent and mining experiencing more modest returns. Notice that textiles, our low performer on both ROS and ROE measures, does above average on this measure.

What sense do we make of these large differences among industries? The competitive entry story just used to illuminate the efficient-market idea would seem to imply that returns would tend to equalize across industries. Does the evidence above dispute this? Do the differences we see in annual rates of return suggest that in most markets the leveling process is not very effective? Should strategic planners put the high-return industries first on their lists of new fields to enter? Do return differences reflect real differences in the attractiveness of various industries? In short, what implication do these common indexes have for strategy?

Our first task in making sense of the industry median figures in Table 2.1 is to disentangle what we really mean by the proposition that rates of return tend to equalize across industries. How does the efficient-market principle play out in sectoral choices we see in strategic planning? In order to answer this question, we must begin by examining the idea of the **opportunity cost** of capital.

Whenever an individual takes one dollar and invests it in a venture he or she is giving up the opportunity of using that dollar elsewhere. Similarly, whenever an organization takes a dollar and invests it in one venture, it is foregoing the opportunity of investing that dollar elsewhere—either in or outside the operation. The cost of giving up that opportunity is known as the **opportunity cost** of capital and is an important ingredient in an individual or organization's decision to invest. For many organizations, the idea of an opportunity cost is embodied in the requirement that projects make a certain hurdle rate. A hurdle rate is the internal rate of return an organization requires that a new project make before it will be funded. By requiring that all projects from diverse parts of an organization go over the same hurdle rate, some organizations are attempting to recognize the fungibility of capital. Other organizations look at a project's **pay-back period,** or the length of time it will take a project to repay the cash invested in it as a way of comparing disparate projects. Both hurdle rates and pay-back periods recognize, imperfect though they clearly are, that a dollar tied up in one project cannot be used in a second. Alternative investment opportunities provide a useful reference for the cost of capital determination. Indeed, since strategy fundamentally involves making choices to allocate organizational resources one way rather than another, the idea of an opportunity cost of capital should be fundamental to strategy formulation.

Investments differ not only in the expected returns they have, but on the risks they manifest. The cost of capital will be higher, the higher the risk of the investment. Only by paying a premium can an organization induce people to risk their funds in an uncertain venture. On average, people are **risk averse:** They don't like to take risks and must be paid to do so. If offered one opportunity to earn $10, and a second opportunity to earn $20 half the time and nothing the other half, most people would prefer the first, certain deal. Although the average amount received (or the **expected value**) is the same in the two cases, most people don't feel equally about the two instances. The opportunity cost of capital, then, is equal to the return which that capital could earn in its next best use, holding risks constant. In practice, we think of the opportunity cost of capital as being equal to the return on long-term Treasury bills, plus a component for the risk of the venture. In the last section of this chapter, we will see that strong forces exist to equalize risk-adjusted returns across industries.

How do we reconcile the lesson of movements toward equalization of risk adjusted returns with the figures in Table 2.1? As we indicate in the Appendix 2, none of the return indexes tell us very much when viewed in isolation about the performance of either particular industries or particular firms.

Consider ROE first. To what extent do the differences we see in these returns really indicate superior performance by one industry over another? We first note that the numerator of the index—earnings—can be manipulated by accounting legerdemain. The denominator of the index is also suspect. Equity is typically valued at book, which will not generally reflect its true value. For mature firms, with relatively old assets, differences between book value and market value are likely to be substantial. The return on equity is also highly sensitive to the debt-equity ratio of the firm in circumstances in which firms can borrow at relatively low rates. Industries are known to differ widely in the amount of leveraging they do. The sensitivity of ROE to the debt ratio is one of several reasons that U.S.–Japanese comparisons of industrial performance are often so misleading. Firms with substantial debt relative to equity, like Japanese firms, generally look better in terms of ROE. But, in a real sense, of course, they are not better; they are simply financed differently.

What about return on sales, ROS? Is ROS any better than ROE as a measure of the relative attractiveness of one industry over another? I think the answer must be no, although some of the ways in which ROS is a bad measure of the performance of a firm are different. Here the problem is wide differences in the use of capital among firms and industries. In some firms, sales are generated using very little capital. A small amount invested yields high sales. Return on sales would look small, but return on investment would be high, and it is return on investment we are most concerned about. In other words, as long as **asset turnover** (ratio of net sales to average total assets) differs among firms, comparisons based on the ROS of industries or firms will not be very illuminating. In general, in the case of capital-intense firms, such as auto manufacture or steel, ROS will systematically overstate performance, while firms which use little capital—supermarkets, for example,—will find ROS understates how well they're doing. As in ROE measures, earnings manipulation is also possible.

The first general observation we can make is that the differences across industries seen in these indexes reflect many differences that have little to do with the underlying earnings potential of firms in those industries. This has come to be recognized as firms have increasingly turned away from a reliance on ROE or ROS for strategic directions and performance evaluation.[10] Differences across industries in these indexes reflect differences in the capital structure of firms in those industries, the age distribution of assets, accounting practices, and the like.

The return-to-investors column is a bit closer to the mark as a relative performance measure keyed to investors' valuation of a firm, but here too there are problems. These figures tell us how much investors earn on a stock in a given year. But stock prices rise not because firms are well managed, but because new information about the quality of the organization's management or opportunities is revealed. If a firm has been consistently earning extraordinary profits, this good performance has already been capitalized into its stock price, and current stock price changes would not be expected to be substantial. The return to investors then can be a reasonable measure of changes in the expected earnings profile of an organization, but not in its overall level.

But there is a second pitfall associated with using any performance measure taken from a single year as an indicator of performance. In our theories, we have described a tendency over time toward equalization of risk-adjusted returns across industries. At any one point in time, of course, some firms or even whole industries may do well, while others do badly. In the scalping industry, there were rainy Saturdays when all scalpers flourished, and sunny ones in which they did not. In the stock market, sometimes we guess right and make a killing, at other times we lose our shirts. And, in industry, sometimes an unexpected increase in demand or change in the regulatory environment catches an industry unaware and leads to high profits, or to low profits. Indeed, a function of good planning is to try to anticipate change and either exploit it or minimize its damage. The efficient-market principle simply says that good times have a tendency to go away, not that they never come. Indeed, creative entrepreneurial activity is in large measure the ability to see where new lucrative opportunities are likely to arise, as we will explore later in the text.

Even a cursory look at the data confirms our story about the variability of profits. In 1990, as we have seen, the tobacco industry performed rather poorly based on either ROS or ROE. In 1987, however, it was one of the best performers in the group. Beverages, on the other hand, which generated high returns to investors in the 1989–90 period, delivered almost no returns in the 1986–87 period. In short, as we would have predicted, many of the extraordinary gains and losses of industries are ephemeral.

Having said all of this in praise of market efficiency, the glory of entry, and the difficulty of interpreting data, I must now suggest that all industries do not perform equally well, even over long time periods. In some industries, over quite long periods of time, excess returns seem to be generated even if we appropriately account for risks. In the market for advertising in the Yellow Pages, for example, margins appear to be on the order of 50 percent, well above anyone's estimate of the opportunity cost of capital. In the Alaskan pipeline, tariffs per barrel in the 1980 period were around $6.00 per barrel, with operating costs of $1.50, and a thirty-year life to the capital stock. Rates of return in this case also appear to be well above market rates. For many years, the U.S. automobile industry was able to earn returns that once again most observers believed were consistently above market rates. How do we explain these departures from the free-entry model? What forces are there in some industries which impede entry and allow for long-term excess profits? We also see some industries in which returns are average, and yet there are one or two firms that consistently perform extremely well. Levi Strauss & Company produces jeans, earning consistently high returns in an appeal industry with notoriously low average earnings. Ben & Jerry's is an extremely profitable company in the fragmented ice-cream business. The 3M Company, operating a panoply of businesses in mostly quite competitive industries, also thrives. How do we explain this performance?

In the next several chapters we explore the reasons some industries and some organizations regularly outperform the market. As we will see, there are three principle sources of superior performance:

- Companies earn excess returns when they operate in protected environments where entry is difficult.

- Companies earn excess returns when they anticipate market changes and rapidly exploit new opportunities.

- Companies earn excess returns when they possess a sustainable competitive advantage over potential and actual rivals.

Most economists working in the strategy area in the 1970s focused their attention on the first source of advantage. All of the work by Porter and his followers in the industrial organization area looked to industry forces and particularly entry conditions as the main source of excess returns. Work in the general management literature, on the other hand, has traditionally looked to the latter two sources of advantage. Increasingly, firms too have focused on competitive advantage and particularly speed as a way to outperform the market. Wheelwright and Clark argue that, in the manufacturing sector, the speed of the development process is a major source of company success.[11] Jack Welch, CEO of General Electric, writing in 1991 emphasized the importance of speed of corporations as a way "to propel ideas and drive processes right through functional barriers, sweeping bureaucrats and their impediment aside in the rush to get to the marketplace."[12] In markets such as the ones General Electric competes in, where the overall level of competition is high, time to market is critical. So, too, is the ability of firms to develop and sustain an edge over real and potential competitors. In 1991, Robert Allen, CEO of AT&T, focused on AT&T's research and development as the source of their "powerful competitive advantage," the advantage which would deliver returns even in the face of substantial competition. In these two firms and in firms throughout the world, we see managers struggling to identify the right strategic path to superior performance.

But in this struggle for profitability and growth, the power of new entry and the lure of the $20 bill serve as a constant backdrop. Managers must constantly ask themselves in testing out alternative strategies the fundamental market question: What protects my strategy against encroaching entry and imitation by existing rivals? And if I am not protected and imitation does occur, what can I do to maintain good performance in the new era? We turn to these questions in the next several chapters.

3

Industry Analysis

As we saw in Chapter 2, the natural trajectory of a market is toward a point at which the risk-adjusted returns to that market are the same as those earned in the market as a whole. Nevertheless, in some markets, over some periods of time, most of the firms in the industry seem to do better than the market as a whole. In these markets, the overall environment is less hostile than average. This is the first source of superior performance outlined in Chapter 2. In this chapter we explore some of the reasons for industry-wide high profitability and the factors that contribute to a more forgiving environment. An analysis of these forces forms an essential part of the environmental analysis task of strategic planning.

Porter's Five Forces Model of Industry

One way to organize information about an industry that shows us the potential attractiveness of that industry is the **Five Forces Model** developed by Michael Porter and reproduced as Figure 3.1.[1] Taken together, the five forces shown in the figure help to explain the overall level of profitability one might expect in a given industry. We look to these forces to help explain why one industry is profitable while another is not. Why, for example, the disposable-diaper industry is highly profitable, while the pulp and paper industry is not. Porter's model suggests that, to a large extent, these industry differences can be explained by five factors: the current intensity of competition, the presence of substitute products, the power of buyers, the power of suppliers, and new entry. In this chapter, we explore the first four of these factors. Since entry is so vital to understanding industry dynamics, as we have already seen in Chapter 2, we will leave that topic for separate coverage in Chapter 4.

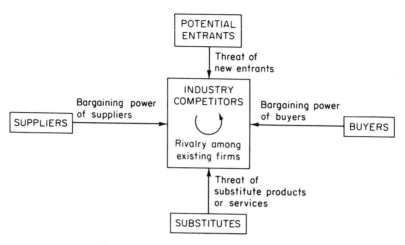

Figure 3.1   Porter's Five Forces Model

PORTER FORCE I
Intensity of Competition

We begin the industry analysis by looking at existing relations within the industry or the level of rivalry among firms. This is represented by the center box in the diagram. In 1992, the branded disposable-diaper market was dominated by two firms, Procter & Gamble (P&G) and Kimberly-Clark (KC). These two firms controlled approximately 80 percent of the market. But the market shares of these two firms were extremely unstable, as was the relationship between them as they warred via research and marketing. In 1982, for example, P&G controlled 65 percent of this $2 billion a year market with Luvs and Pampers, while KC, with its Huggie brand, had a modest share. By 1985, P&G's share had dropped to 52 percent and most of the difference had been taken up by KC. In 1985, in response to its market share decline, P&G introduced a new "thin" version of diapers and its share again rose. By 1986, KC had developed its own thin diaper and was recovering market share. Further product innovations followed in the next six years and market shares responded. In short, the competitive positions of the two industry participants were highly unstable. Moreover, despite the large size of the market and the relatively lucrative margins, a number of large firms had been forced to exit with large losses from the industry since the mid-1970s: Scott Paper, Union Carbide, and Johnson & Johnson. In 1992, a consortium of Weyerhauser, Johnson & Johnson, and Unicharm, a large Japanese firm, also failed in their bid to sell a premium disposable diaper. By almost any measure, the rivalry in the disposable-diaper business was and is intense.

In contrast, the educational book publishing market is a highly *fragmented* one. Approximately 60 to 70 major publishers compete in the elementary and secondary school market, with the top five in the industry accounting for only 40 percent of the sales in the industry. All of the major players in the market—McGraw-Hill, Simon & Schuster (Prentice Hall), Harcourt Brace Jovonovich, and Macmillan—have been important influences in the market for decades. Market shares are reasonably stable, and exit of major players has been rare, except for some recent mergers. Editors from the various publishing houses, as well as many of the people on the "business" side of the operations, frequently socialize with one another and larger publishers support and encourage smaller operations. Consider the following observation from Winthrop Knowlton, former president of Harper & Row: "Small presses often come to us for advice and help and sometimes marketing services. We are happy to oblige because we cannot cover the editorial waterfront ourselves."[2]

By most measures, rivalry in the book-publishing industry is modest and cooperation among the staff of various publishing houses is fairly common.

What accounts for differences in the levels of rivalry among industries? The question is clearly of interest both to potential new entrants in an industry, seeking to understand what lies ahead, and to current market participants involved in changing environments, because differences in the levels and variance of profits are explained in part by differences in the levels of rivalry.

Intense rivalry among firms in an industry reduces average profitability.

It is easy to demonstrate that, in any given industry, some measure of coordination is to the *collective* good of industry participants. Total profits in an industry are greater with coordination than without. In the pricing area, for example, perfect coordination would allow industry participants to avoid costly price wars, and in the extreme even to practice monopoly pricing as a group. In the area of branding, coordination would allow firms to avoid duplicating each other's products. In the area of research, coordination would permit firms to avoid costly duplicate research efforts.[3] Nevertheless, while the collective interest is served by coordination, the self-interests of the firms in the industry may not be perfectly consonant.[4] A few examples will help to clarify the seeming paradox.

Suppose we start with an industry characterized by pricing coordination among firms and above normal profits. That is, in this industry, prices exceed long-run marginal costs. Collectively, we would say that the industry is doing very well. Now let us take the perspective of one of the firms within that industry, perhaps one of the smaller firms. This firm, too, is doing well. On the other hand, the fact that prices exceed marginal costs is quite seductive to the firm. By lowering prices just a little, the firm can increase its market share and increase its own profits, since the incremental production can be sold at prices in excess of their costs. The firm may well believe that it can cut prices in this way without upsetting the overall industry pricing consensus. But, of course, if enough firms yield to this temptation, the market price will drift down, and industry coordination will be threatened. Similar stories can be told about the advantages to the individual firm of shading just a bit on other areas of industry coordination.

In an industry in which firm coordination yields excess profits, there are incentives for individual firms to shade prices.

We see then that there is a tension within an industry. Coordination increases the collective good, but individual cheating on that coordination may increase the individual good, as long as not too many other firms cheat at the same time. One way of analyzing the level of rivalry in an industry is to focus on the costs and benefits of coordination versus cheating from the perspective of the industry participants. We will adopt this perspective in our discussion.

From this perspective, we find that there are a number of characteristics of an industry that help determine the level of rivalry in the industry and should be considered when we look at the center box of the Porter model. Principal among them are the number of competitors, the size distribution of those competitors, the homogeneity of competitors, the fixed nature of investment in the industry, and the stability of demand in the industry.

The Number of Competitors

When the number of competitors in an industry is large, all else equal, we expect more competition in the industry. Under these circumstances, each firm believes itself to be only a minor player in the industry, and thus will act as if its price cuts or marketing investments will have only a small effect on the industry as a whole. Thus, firms tend to act more individualistically when there are many firms in the market. Moreover, under these conditions, coordination among the players, even if sought, would be quite difficult to consummate owing to sheer numbers. The larger the number of firms in an industry, the greater the uncertainty there is likely to be about relative costs and other operating factors of those firms, and this, too, complicates coordination.[5]

Large numbers of firms in a market reduce coordination opportunities.

Interestingly, in industries with many players, there is often considerable competition but very little direct rivalry among firms. In dairy farming, for example, competition is intense in the sense that any individual farmer would find it difficult to charge a price higher than that of his neighbors, since the individual output of any single farm is small relative to the total market. And yet rivalry in the dairy industry is quite impersonal. Neighboring farmers, for example, will often cooperate in the lending of capital equipment, R&D expenditures, and so on. In other industries—like computers—rivalry is both intense and personal. Apple thinks of IBM as a rival and devises its strategy accordingly.

A commonly used measure of the number and relative power of firms in an industry is given by the **concentration ratio.** In the United States, the concentration ratio is generally calculated as the percent of the total industry sales or employment accounted for by the largest four firms in that industry. Higher figures represent more concentration. Data on the C4, as it is known, is calculated by the United States Census and printed in the *Census of Manufacturing.* Industries vary widely in their concentration. Logging, for example, is a relatively unconcentrated industry with a C4 of 18 percent, while cigarette manufacturing is relatively concentrated with a C4 of 85 percent. We should note that the concentration ratio is keyed to the position of the largest firms in the industry, given that it measures the combined share of the top four firms in an industry. For some situations, it is also useful to know whether any appreciable fringe firms exist, since fringe firms can sometimes have a substantial effect on the overall stability of an industry.

We have suggested that as the number of firms in an industry grows, opportunities for coordination diminish. Some feel for this relationship can be seen if we look at the history of antitrust litigation. Greer and Fraas gathered data on the 606 illegal price-fixing agreements prosecuted in the period between 1910 and 1973. They then determined the number of firms typically involved in the industry conspiracies and computed a frequency distribution.[6] Their results are given in Figure 3.2. As we can easily see, the typical price conspiracy prosecuted by the government involves few firms relative to the average industry. About 10 percent of the price-fixing cases, for example, involved industries with only four firms, while in toto only about 2 percent of U.S. industries contained only four firms. This numerical pattern may in part reflect government interest in concentrated industries, rather than actual price-fixing behavior, but the results are nevertheless interesting and broadly consistent with the gen-

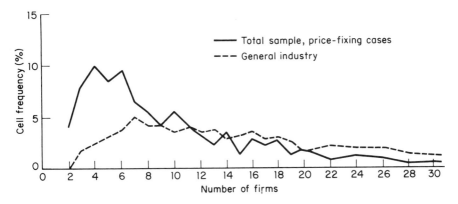

Figure 3.2

eral theme of small numbers providing more opportunities for cooperation.

The Size Distribution of Market Participants

The size of distribution of firms within an industry may be very important
in determining the intensity of rivalry. Are the top three or four firms in
the industry similar in terms of market share or quite different?

**In general, in industries in which the major firms are all similarly sized,
rivalry is more intense.**

In industries in which one large firm dominates the market, that firm
can often impose a certain discipline on the rest of its market, for its
relative size allows it to speak with some authority. In industries in which
several firms are equally sized more rivalry develops as each vies for the
leadership position.

An interesting example of the intense rivalry that can occur among
equal-sized rivals is provided by the European automobile market. There
are seven auto makers in Europe, with market shares in the range of 10
to 15 percent, among them Volkswagen, Fiat, and Ford. As trade barriers
across Europe have crumbled, the level of competition among these bal-
anced rivals has been substantial.

A convenient measure of the balance in an industry is provided by the
Herfindahl Index, which is used by government to help decide when
mergers among industry participants should be allowed. The Herfindahl
is equal to:

$$HI = 10,000 \sum_i S_i^2$$

where S_i is the market share of the ith firm. A simple example will be
helpful to show us how to calculate the Herfindahl. Suppose we have an
industry with three firms with market shares as follows: .5, .25, .25. The
Herfindahl would equal $(10,000)((.5)^2 + (.25)^2 + (.25)^2)$ or 3750. If the industry was configured .33, .33, .33, it would have a Herfindahl of 3267. The
unbalanced size distribution is associated with a higher index. With an
unbalanced distribution and thus a high index, the market leader can help
promote coordination.

The Herfindahl Index can vary from 0 (perfectly competitive industry)
to 10,000 (a monopoly). Generally speaking, Herfindahls (HI) in excess of
1800 are thought to characterize industries with reduced rivalry. Indeed,
at HIs of this level, the Department of Justice investigates merger activity
fairly carefully, since it believes that indexes in this range are associated
with markets in which collusion is more easily achieved. Thus, mergers
which increase HI's above this level are often challenged.

In January 1986, Pepsico proposed to acquire 7-Up from Philip Morris
for $380 million in cash. Pepsico argued that, unless 7-Up was bought by
a company with large marketing resources, it could not hope to survive.
A month later, Coca-Cola responded by announcing its intentions to ac-

quire Dr. Pepper for $470 million. Even before the two acquisitions were proposed, the concentration in the soft drink industry was fairly high. In 1985, Coca-Cola and Pepsico had 66 percent of the market, with a Herfindahl of 2362. If both mergers were to occur, the HI would have increased to 3258, a level far in excess of current federal guidelines. And, in fact, the mergers were blocked by the Federal Trade Commission. Indeed, the federal judge who ruled on an injunction in the case called the proposed acquisitions "a stark, unvarnished attempt to eliminate competition that totally lacks any apparent redeeming feature."[7] Dr. Pepper, we might note, was eventually sold in a leveraged buy-out. This is an excellent example of a case in which the antitrust laws and the use of the Herfindahl Index had a big impact on the industry structure.

Homogeneity of Firms

Industries with relatively few firms tend to develop at least some cooperative mechanisms in their dealings with one another. The more alike are those firms, the easier it will be for cooperative mechanisms to develop. If firms are very similar, the **symmetrical solution**—everyone behaves in the same way and reaps the same reward—becomes a natural solution. Then, too, if demand and/or technological forces perturb the industry, firms are more likely to be affected similarly than if they began in quite different positions. Thus, similarity among firms may dampen industry uncertainty.

> **The more similar are firms in a market, all else equal, the easier will be coordination of those firms.**

A classic example of the importance of similarity in starting points is provided by Schelling. In lecturing to a class of Harvard undergraduates, Schelling posed the following problem.[8] You are to meet a friend somewhere in New York at 12:00 noon. But your friend has neglected to indicate the meeting place. Choose the most likely place to meet.

There is one overwhelmingly favorite choice among Schelling's Harvard students: Grand Central Station. Students arrive at this choice without any direct discussion. Apparently, Harvard students typically travel to and from New York by train. For this population, Grand Central Station is a **focal point:** a solution to which similarly minded individuals converge without any discussion.

In our example, the focal point was a place. Other common focal points include prices—$3.95 not $4.01 is a common choice among price setters. We also see focal points among bargaining rules: Split the difference is a bargaining focal point. We tend to move to this solution unless there are good arguments to the contrary.

The ability to find a focal point depends in part on similarities among participants. Schelling's group consisted of undergraduates used to going to New York on the train. This common experience led to a common solution. In the same way, common management background and firm characteristics can ease the ability of organizations to find common ground. Even membership in common clubs can play a role in facilitating the search for commonality. Ouchi's work on "clans" suggests that homogeneity within organizations allows managers to act more or less autonomously because the organization's goals are congruent with their own.[9] So, too, homogeneity across firms allows for congruent behavior without explicit coordination. To the extent that firms in an industry differ significantly in the products they sell or the production processes they use, it may be harder for them to coordinate. In the same way, the entry of new firms into an industry, particularly foreign firms, often proves to be quite destabilizing. New players and new ideas often have an influence on the industry well beyond their direct one.

Asset Specificity
Virtually all organizations require some fixed assets to conduct their enterprises. But there is a wide variance in the extent to which fixed assets are used, or, stated alternatively, in the ratio of variable costs to total costs within the industry. In the consulting business, for example, the fixed assets employed are typically quite small relative to total costs. Most of the costs of the enterprise are labor costs. In heavy manufacturing, on the other hand, fixed costs form a substantial part of the total costs of the operation and, moreover, are quite long lived.

A second distinction among assets has also proved to be extremely important from a strategic perspective: the *specificity* of the assets used in a business.[10] One of the fixed assets of an airline is its airplanes. Moreover airplanes have no alternative uses: They can only be used to fly. In this sense, an airplane might be thought to be a specific asset from the perspective of the airline. On the other hand, if we think about the air market as having a geographic component, the specificity of the asset diminishes considerably. That is, an airplane currently used in the New York to Denver market could easily be transferred to the New York to Los Angeles market. This transfer could be accomplished either by the initial airline or through the competitive resale market. Contrast this example with that of the railroad and its track. The track between New York and Denver is a fixed asset quite specific to both use and market. It cannot be used to serve the New York to Maine market. In this example, track is clearly a more **specific asset** for a railroad than are airplanes for an airline.[11]

Organizations with large amounts of specific assets find exit from particular markets quite difficult. A brand name can be a valuable specific asset. Information about the way a particular market works can also be an important specific asset. High-asset specificity can be said to raise **barriers to exit** for an organization. These organizations find themselves with assets valuable only in the particular ventures to which they are currently committed. Lacking any alternative use for the asset, the organization will find it rational to continue deploying those assets in markets in which the accounting returns are exceedingly low. These assets can be said to have low opportunity cost. In the case of specific assets, there are few if any alternative opportunities for the asset.

Industries with substantial specific assets exhibit high barriers to exit and intensified rivalry.

Heavy reliance on specific assets encourages firms to stay in an industry even when times are bad, simply because there is nothing else they can do with these assets. Industries characterized by high-specific assets are typically also characterized by intense rivalry during downturns. Firms will fight hard for market share to help them cover at least part of their large fixed costs. Indeed, railroads, which are clearly an extreme in the high-asset specificity group, were regulated at least in part as a response to the fierce competition that arose from the operation of this market.

If we return once again to the comparison of diapers versus book publishing, it is clear that asset specificity plays a major role in distinguishing the two industries. The production of disposable diapers requires an extremely expensive, very specialized assembly line. Indeed, the equipment is so specialized that recent product innovations by Procter & Gamble required a major investment of hundreds of millions of dollars to put in a new assembly line. Book publishing, in contrast, uses a modest level of relatively unspecialized fixed assets. And, as we recall, the diaper market is considerably more rivalrous than publishing.

The extent to which a particular organization uses specific assets is in part under the control of the organization. In the case of airplanes, for example, I can lease a plane or buy one. In the case of a machine shop, I can buy a very effective, but highly specialized machine or a general purpose machine which is perhaps somewhat less effective. A railroad company could rent trackage rights rather than own them. The decision to use specific assets owned by the organization itself is a complex one and will be discussed in Chapter 11. The central point to note here is that the decision to use specific assets affects firm interaction in an industry, and thus looking at the extent of these assets is another part of our examination of the first Porter box.

Changing Conditions of Demand and Supply
One of the features that distinguishes the diaper and educational book publishing industries is the *stability* of the environments in which each industry is embedded. In text book publishing, demand has been relatively stable over time, paralleling school and college enrollments. Of course, there have been good years and bad, but variations have been relatively small and the growth rate on average only just above GNP growth. The market share of particular firms in the industry has also been relatively constant. The disposable-diaper industry, on the other hand, has exploded in the last twenty years as families switched from cloth diapers, going from a $20 million dollar business in 1967 to a $4.4 billion

business today. And, as we suggested, market shares have been volatile as well. In publishing, technological change has been modest; most changes have come from industries that supply publishing, for example, the printing-equipment industry. In the disposable-diaper industry, on the other hand, technological changes and product changes have been large and rapid, often involving complete changeovers in product design and assembly-line configuration. On many levels, then, publishing appears to be embedded in a considerably more stable environment than the disposable-diaper industry.

As a related matter, we also note that industries differ considerably in the extent to which they face cyclical demand. In the diesel engine market, for example, sales and production vary dramatically over time, largely in response to business cycle movements. In 1975, the United States economy was in a recession and sales of diesel engine suffered as a result. The recession of 1982 produced a similar sales decline as did the recession of the 1990–91 period. The diesel market is sensitive to GNP levels as diesel equipment is used in raw materials' industries such as housing construction. The cyclicity of the underlying user industry is thus reflected in the engine market. In this industry, variable demand is a fact of life, outside the control of individual firms. But it is a fact of life with substantial strategic effects.

Industries with unstable demand are often characterized by intense rivalry, in particular if this cyclical demand is coupled with high-fixed costs, a factor we will discuss below. In the five-year period between 1979 and 1984, one producer of diesel engines, Cummins, saw its market share of engines fluctuate over ten percentage points. Detroit Diesel, another major player in the industry, ranged in share from under 20 percent of the market to one-third of the market. Such instability carries with it substantial managerial and strategic costs. Indeed, several industries that early economists described as having "cutthroat" competition are precisely the industries that suffer from cyclical demand. In these industries when demand is high firms are led to increase capacity to serve that demand; in the subsequent slump, excess capacity encourages fierce battles for share. The identity of the market share leader changes over time, and the overall organization of the industry is fragile.

Variability in demand creates more rivalry within an industry.

But why does variability in demand and supply increase the level of rivalry in an industry? Increased rivalry occurs for several reasons. In the first place, coordination of pricing, branding, or research requires considerable agreement among the industry participants. Often, of course, agreement is tacit. Through the business press, for instance, firms make it known that modest price increases seem likely, and sure enough modest price increases occur. But such coordination, tacit or otherwise, requires agreement among firms as to what the desirable outcome might be. And such agreement is much harder to arrive at when the conditions of demand and supply are constantly changing.

Variability of supply and demand often creates additional uncertainty in an industry. This uncertainty will in turn influence the ease with which coordination can be maintained across disparate firms. We have already indicated that firms face some temptation to move away from a coordinated price. In part, firms resist this temptation because they realize that other firms will observe them and retaliate. If demand fluctuates in unpredictable ways, however, then it will be very difficult to detect departures from the common ground.

Demand fluctuations, even when predicted, may have a second impact on industry structure. When demand is variable, *flexibility* begins to play a more important role in the industry. Under these conditions, there is often an opportunity for technically diverse firms to compete. In particular, small firms may be able to use their flexibility in these industries to compete against scale advantages of larger firms. Thus, demand fluctuations may increase organizational diversity in an industry.[12] And diversity reduces the ease of coordination among firms.

PORTER FORCE 2
Presence of Substitute Products

Thus far, we have been discussing the effects on industry profits of the intensity of rivalry within the industry. But firms are also affected by competition from related markets. Air conditioners compete with fans, disposable diapers with cloth, opera with musicals and dramatic theater, and beer with wine. In each of these cases, the availability of substitutes influences the ability of a firm to raise its price or change the attributes of its products. These substitutes are especially important in markets in which there are few rivals in the narrow market or ones in which it is difficult to increase industry supply quickly. In these cases, we would normally expect some excess profits to accrue to firms in the industry. The presence of good substitute products limits those profits.

How do we identify those products and services which are substitutes for a given product? Here we wish to identify products and services that serve more-or-less the same function for more-or-less the same people as the product we are evaluating. Conceptually, we wish to ask: What set of products *constrains* the ability of firms in this industry to substantially raise their prices? Typically, when we ask this question we find a chain of substitute goods. Consider the market analysis done from the perspective of Kimberly-Clark, looking at its Huggies' brand disposable diaper. The closest substitute to this product is the other premium brand products made by Procter & Gamble, Luvs and Pampers. Next in line come the regional and generic brand diapers, made by Weyerhauser, Veragon, and a number of other small producers. Beyond these disposable diapers come the cloth diapers, provided by diaper services. Finally, we have cloth diapers laundered at home. For each of these products, we wish to ask: How much does the presence of this product influence Kimberly-Clark's ability to raise its price on Huggies? The **cross elasticity of demand** is one measure of this effect. It is the ratio of the percentage change in the demand for one good in response to a 1 percent increase in the price of a second good. Substitute goods have positive cross-elasticities: As the price of branded disposable diapers increases, we would expect an increase in the demand for generic brands. The higher the cross-elasticity, the closer the substitutes. Very close substitutes should be analyzed as part of the within-market competition which we covered in the last section of this chapter. Further away substitutes, while out of the market proper, may nevertheless have an effect on pricing behavior. In the case of Huggies, I think it is reasonable to include all disposable diapers as part of the market proper, while cloth diapers should be analyzed as one of the substitute products outside the market.

Substitute products play an uneven role in industry dynamics. In highly competitive industries or during periods of excess capacity, substitute products play a very modest role. All of the action in determining industry profitability is within the industry. But in times of rapidly increasing demand or in industries in which there are few competitors, substitute products may become quite important.

PORTER FORCE 3
Buyer Power

All firms need to pay attention to what their customers want. Nevertheless, there are considerable differences across markets in how powerful buyers are and in how able they are to force down prices or influence product quality levels. The steel industry sells a substantial amount of its output to the auto firms. Clearly this set of buyers has a lot more power than the individual consumers who buy from Coca-Cola. For Coca-Cola, on the other hand, the large fast food chains like Burger King and McDonald's wield considerable power.

The first factor to look at in determining buyer power is the number of buyers and the distribution of their purchases. The larger the number of buyers and the smaller their individual purchases, the less power each one will have. Second, there are some characteristics of the product itself. Standardization of products increases buyer power since it typically reduces switching costs of those buyers and allows them to more easily play one supplier against a second. Third, when buyers can integrate backward, producing the good for themselves, this also increases their bargaining power. Electric utilities, ostensibly regulated monopolies, have faced increased pressure in the last decade from customers who are able to *bypass* the power network and generate their own electricity. Finally, there are institutional factors associated with the way transactions are done

in the industry that are relevant to buyer power. The more open transactions are, the more power buyers have, in part because this reduces
their costs of search among producers.

PORTER FORCE 4
Power of Suppliers

In the same way that powerful buyers can squeeze profits by putting
downward pressure on prices, suppliers can squeeze profits by increasing
input costs. And, as we will see, the same factors that determine the
power of buyers also determine the power of suppliers.

First, we consider the number of suppliers available. The more suppliers, the better. Product standardization is also important: Standardized
products reduce a firm's vulnerability to supplier pressures. In the semiconductor industry, the government—an early large buyer of semiconductors—required firms to license other firms to serve as second sources
for government contracts. This practice ensured the government pur-
chaser against hold-up by suppliers. In the long run, it also reduced the
profitability of the semiconductor industry. If firms can pose a credible
threat to backward integration, this will further reduce supplier power.
Most of the major computer companies produce at least some chips themselves. This partial integration insulates them from pressure by sellers,
increasing the profitability of the computer industry at the expense of the
semiconductor industry. Finally, the more open information is in the industry, the less power will be held by suppliers.

The Role of Government in Determining Industry Profitability

Virtually all of American business is, in one way or another, influenced
by government. The government, while not explicitly one of Porter's Five
Forces, has an overarching effect on all of the other players in the market.
Government action affects levels of rivalry, buyer and supplier power, the
importance of substitutes, and the power of entry. In a later chapter, we
will explore some of the strategic implications of pervasive government
regulation. But at this point it is worth noting that heavy-handed regulation and antitrust laws may dramatically affect industry profitability.

Regulation

Regulation may have a dramatic effect on rivalry within an industry.

The banking industry provides an excellent example of the effect of regulatory changes on relations within an industry. Banking regulations affect virtually all facets of the bank's operations: where it can operate, what
prices it can pay suppliers (i.e., interest rates), and which businesses it

can enter. Originally, restrictions were imposed by Congress during the Great Depression in an attempt to limit the risks faced by banks and depositors and prevent certain conflicts of interests or abuses associated with the crash of 1929. The effect of the regulations was thus to dampen variability within the industry. And, for a long period, the industry was considered a relatively stable, cooperative one.

Since the early 1970s, regulations within banking have eased considerably. Interest rate ceilings were first raised and then removed; some limits on branch banking have been removed; some of the regulatory limits on diversification have been relaxed. The effect of deregulation has been to considerably increase the uncertainty in the industry since matters which were controlled by regulatory fiat are now under managerial control. And, as a consequence, the industry is becoming truly rivalrous for the first time.

For many banks these new pressures have created management concerns that were simply not present fifteen years ago. During the period of heavy regulation, marketing was the primary arena for competition among banks; now pricing is moving more to center stage. In the regulated period, mergers and outside growth possibilities were limited; since deregulation, all banks have had to adopt a much more external focus to their planning. State legislation, which has eased the rules on interstate banking mergers, has encouraged the development of super-regional banks, institutions often based in the hinterlands that now can operate across state boundaries. Banks like Fleet Financial in Rhode Island and Wells Fargo, based in San Francisco, are beginning to offer tough competition for the New York money center banks. The effect of deregulation on the relations among firms in the banking sector has been profound and has included both substantial mergers and many bank failures.[13]

Two useful additional illustrations of the importance of regulation are provided by the airline industry and the telecommunications industry. In the period before 1982, the United States airline industry was heavily regulated by the Civil Aeronautics Board (CAB). The CAB restricted entry and exit into markets and regulated fares as well. Aircraft type, frequency of flight, and service quality, on the other hand, were not controlled. As a result, airlines competed almost entirely on the basis of quality: flights were frequent, meals and movies elaborate, aisles wide.[14] The effect of deregulation in this case has been to change the *form* of competition in the industry, as well as its intensity. In many instances, it is easier to collude on service than on price; prices can be changed rather quickly in response to competitor action, whereas a change in service characteristics often requires a longer run strategic decision. Although an airline cannot widen its aisles overnight, it can decide, almost overnight, to change the quality of meals. As deregulation altered the possible arenas for competition, it had the effect of changing the level of intensity as well. We have all seen the results in terms of falling prices and changes in the product mix of the airline industry. We have also seen the failure of long-term industry participants: Eastern, Braniff, TWA, Pan American.

Regulation has had a rather different effect in the telecommunications industry. Throughout most of the history of the U.S. telecommunications industry, the long-distance market was serviced entirely by AT&T. Entry into the market was controlled by the Federal Communications Commission (FCC). This scenario began to change with a series of court cases in the late 1960s, until the market was completely opened up by the Modified Final Judgment settlement of an antitrust case against AT&T, separating long-distance telecommunications from local telephone operations. With one fell swoop, much of the protection afforded AT&T was removed, and Sprint, MCI, and numerous small competitors rapidly gained share. In just a few years, due in large measure to regulatory changes, the market has gone from one without rivals to an extremely rivalrous market in which the competitive weapons range from pricing and marketing to law suits.

Antitrust Laws

The main statute governing the behavior of firms in the United States on antitrust issues is the Sherman Antitrust Act. The Sherman Act was passed in 1890 at least in part in response to complaints by farmers and small consumers about the pricing practices of newly created trusts and big businesses. Virtually all of U.S. federal antitrust law rests on the Sherman Act, and its two later companions, the Clayton Act of 1914 and the FTC Act of 1914. The Sherman Act limits the ability of firms in an industry to coordinate their behavior.

Section 1 of the Sherman Act proscribes "every contract, combination . . . or conspiracy in restraint of trade or commerce among the several states." A reading of the case law in this area indicates that a variety of agreements among firms in an industry are *per se* illegal; in other words, these actions are intrinsically illegal, regardless of whether or not there is evidence as to negative social effect. Acts that are *per se* illegal include agreements among competing firms to fix prices, to share markets, or to restrict or pool output. Any express agreements among firms in an industry in these areas is a violation of the law, regardless of the ultimate effect.

In many situations it may be possible for firms to reach pricing or product agreement without express agreements or even direct discussion. Firms can at times send signals to one another through the media, for example. Information relevant to pricing decisions may also be disseminated by a trade association. At present in the United States, collusion without formal agreement, sometimes called **tacit collusion,** is in a grey area of the law. The *spirit* of the Sherman Act is clearly against such collusion, but in practice the likelihood of litigation in areas of tacit collusion is relatively small.

Antitrust laws attempt to increase firm rivalry.

In cases of tacit collusion, the Justice Department has two remedies that it can use under the Sherman Act. First, it can institute a civil case and seek, for example, an injunction against the prohibited act. Or it can institute a criminal proceeding, leading to fines and imprisonment for corporate personnel. In the well-known 1960 conspiracy case against electrical equipment manufacturers, seven senior managers were sent to prison as a consequence of a price-fixing agreement.[15]

The Sherman Act clearly imposes boundaries on the kinds of coordination that can occur in industries. It is interesting to contrast the United States situation with the situation abroad. While most other industrialized countries have some antitrust laws, "agreements" are not *per se* illegal. It is common for Japanese firms to work together on plans for industry cutbacks in depressed industries, with some firms compensating other, higher-cost firms for lowering production. Such coordination would be illegal in the United States. One explanation for the greater accommodation of the Japanese government is that, since many of the Japanese industries are primarily export markets, the world market is perhaps thought to provide sufficient discipline for firms.

History and Institutions

The Porter model outlines a way to structurally dissect an industry. But in many ways, it ignores industry history and institutions. Yet these factors may be very important in understanding the level of profitability in an industry. To the extent that firms have existed in an industry for long periods, confronting one another in many and varied submarkets, cooperative mechanisms have had time to grow and develop. A firm that anticipates being in an industry with a given set of other firms for some period will have quite a different posture than a firm only temporarily active in the same industry, even if the industry structure is otherwise identical. The knowledge that I will face the same rival tomorrow surely influences how aggressive I am likely to be today. Thus, history has an overarching effect on industry profitability, in much the same way that government does.

In some industries as time passes, institutional mechanisms develop that improve the ability of firms to coordinate. These institutional mechanisms are often referred to as **facilitating devices.** Facilitating devices may evolve as a result of government intervention in the market or through private initiative. They may at times be devised carefully to serve as facilitators or they may arise innocently to serve another purpose and have facilitation as a by-product. In either case, knowledge of the existence of these facilitators is an essential part of industry analysis.

Facilitating devices can help coordinate an industry through one of two ways: *information exchange* and *incentive management*.[16] An excellent example of an information-exchange device is the practice of preannouncing price changes, a practice common in the steel industry as well as in a number of other raw materials industries. By announcing a price change to take place six weeks hence, raw materials suppliers ease the transition for their buyers. They also eliminate some of the uncertainty associated with price competition in the industry and reduce any transitional gains from price discounts. In the absence of preannouncements, some firms can build share by underselling their competitors. By announcing price changes, firms make following those changes easier. Preannouncements also make it easier for firms to see if price increases will stick.

Trade associations are another institution that may improve industry coordination through information exchange. A **trade association** is an organization of firms in a given industry designed to promote the overall industry and collect and disseminate information about that industry. Often the information collected and published by these associations is extremely helpful; indeed this information is often used by industry analysts as they report on trends. But information disseminated by the trade association can also serve to improve industry coordination by reducing collective uncertainty about the future. Informal contacts made at trade association meetings can also help prepare the way for the kind of focal point agreements described by Schelling.

Facilitating devices also act to alter the incentives of firms. Consider the **most-favored-nation clause** (MFN) found in some sales contracts. Under this clause, the seller agrees that if the firm offers *any* buyer a lower price during a specified period of time for the particular item, that same price will be given to the firm with which the MFN has been signed. In other words, selective price discrimination is reduced. I cannot offer to sell jeans to Macy*s at one price and Bloomingdale's at another, if I have an MFN with Bloomingdale's. The MFN clause thus creates a penalty for price cuts, since cuts must be extended to more customers. If an entire industry uses the MFN, the effect will be to stabilize industry prices.[17]

Another facilitating device that operates through the incentive principle is **meeting the competition** clause. Under this provision, a seller offers to meet the price of any responsible rival. Such clauses, which are common in long-term contracts and even in retail-outlet advertising, perform different functions in different contexts. They protect sellers against losing a sale to a price cutter; alternatively they reduce incentives to cut prices, since such price cuts will be matched automatically by the firms operating with meeting-the-competition clauses.

Best price provisions combine the features of meeting the competition and most-favored-nation protection clauses. Sellers must meet the best price offered to a buyer by any rival *and* make this price available to any buyers with whom an agreement has been signed. Provisions of this form, which were found in the gasoline-additives market, also appear to reduce incentives of firms to compete on prices and stabilize prices at levels above competitive ones.[18]

Facilitating devices can ease coordination difficulties.

Summary

We have now reviewed four of the five forces explaining profitability within an industry as well as the overarching influences of government and history. These factors are summarized in Figure 3.3 and provide a guide to industry analysis.

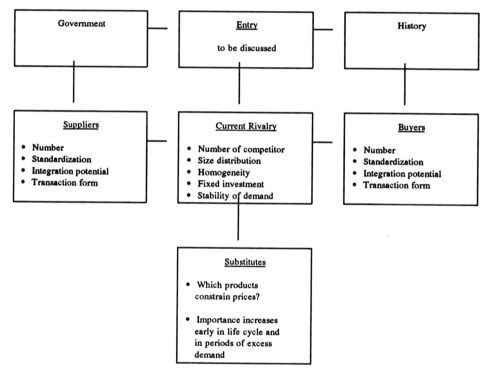

Figure 3.3 Schematic for determining intensity of competition

4

Understanding
the Impediments to Entry

In the last chapter, we explored four of the five factors that affect industry profitability as well as the overarching roles of government and history. Here we complete the analysis by looking at the final and arguably the most important force—the ease of entry into an industry.

The Entry Decision

Suppose we have a relatively new industry in which excess profits are being earned. What factors would influence a new firm's decision whether or not to enter this industry? What, in particular, would discourage entry given the presence of excess profits? Since, as we have seen, entry is a prime vehicle for reducing rates of return, factors that discourage entry will be viewed as favorable from the perspective of industry incumbents. Thus, the analysis of entry is a fundamental part of the environmental analysis of a strategic plan, the fifth force in the traditional Porter analysis. It is clear that in practice all possible entrants into an industry do not look the same. But for now, I will look at a so-called typical firm in the industry as a way of analyzing industry entry and leave differences among firms for a later chapter.

There are myriad ways a potential entrant might think about its entry decision, including simply tossing a coin. But here we will hypothesize a potential entrant who is more or less structured in its deliberations, and we will model that decision process. One tool a potential entrant might profitably use in structuring its entry decision is the **decision tree** (Figure 4.1). Decision trees have a long history in the area of operations research and have proved to be an extremely useful managerial tool, particularly in situations in which firms are developing strategies in complex and un-

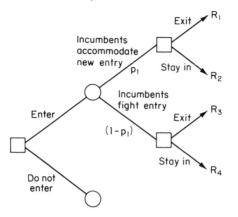

Figure 4.1   A decision tree for an entry decision

certain environments. The tree presents in an ordered form the *decision points* of the firm, and the *chance events,* not under its control.

Using the decision tree in Figure 4.1, the firm is able to track a strategy and its implications. At the outset (far left of the tree) the firm has two possible decisions, to enter or not. These decision points are marked by squares on the tree, the *decision nodes.* If the firm's decision is not to enter, we need go no further. None of the details of the industry history will be relevant, except insofar as they induce regret on the part of the firm. If the firm enters, there are two possibilities. The incumbents can accommodate that entry and thus the market price can remain stable, or incumbents can fight, causing prices to drop. In reality the possibilities are more complex, since rivalry can be muted or fierce. But here for illustrative purposes I have bundled a range of reactions together. The two possibilities concerning incumbent reactions are called *chance nodes,* noted as circles on the tree. These branches are out of the control of the decision maker, but of great importance. The first function of a decision tree is to focus the planner on what is and is not in his or her control. In constructing this branch point, the potential entrant must remember that the possibilities considered should be mutually exclusive and exhaustive.

> **Potential entrants should focus very clearly on important events that are out of their control as a way of understanding the danger areas of the market.**

In order to do some quantitative analysis, the firm can assign some probabilities to the chance events it faces. In the tree above, the decision maker could attach a probability of p_1 to the event that there will be accommodation and a probability of $1-p_1$ to falling prices. Note that the probabilities of these two events sum to 1, for the possibilities must be mutually exhaustive. Prices either fall or rise and cannot do both at the same time. As we observe what happens to prices, we come to a second decision node, and again we may either stay in the market or exit. If incumbents initially accommodate and we exit, we earn a payoff, noted as R_1. In this particular example, R_1 would typically be negative and represent our losses from the aborted entry. Exit following a fight is noted R_3. In general, R_3 is also negative and larger than R_1. If we stay in the market, after accommodation, we will earn a payoff of R_2 from the successful entry strategy or R_4 after a fight response. In a more elaborated strategy, one might continue the tree beyond this point. For example, if the firm decides to stay in at decision node 2, it will again face chance events of price movements. For simplicity I have terminated the branch at this point. Ideally, one would want to include in the tree all the decision moves critical in the planning period.

A strategy will consist of the predetermined set of moves along the branches of the tree.

Using the tree in Figure 4.1, one strategy might be to enter and, if prices fall, exit; or if prices remain stable, stay in. A second alternative strategy might be to enter and if prices fall, stay in for two periods and exit then only if prices do not recover; or if prices are stable, stay in. As we noted earlier, the essence of a strategy is that it involves a decision to choose one alternative over other possibilities.

As we have seen, the decision tree is a useful tool for setting out all logical possibilities associated with a decision. But in many instances, we will not have all or even most of the data needed to construct a fully blown decision tree. Trees have enormous heuristic power, nevertheless, for they force us to set out all of the options and ask ourselves the critical what-if questions. Indeed, we can view decision trees as simply a way to impose some discipline or structure on the strategic-planning process.

At times, we may be able to use the tree to help choose among the strategies laid out in the tree, particularly in situations in which our quantitative information is more refined. At each endpoint of the tree we have indicated the return associated with that path. Typically, this return would come from a more complex pro forma income statement associated with the scenario characterized in the branch. We can then find the expected value of a particular strategy by multiplying the probability of each of the chance events occurring in the strategy by the returns associated with the strategy-chance-event combination.

As an illustration, we can use the tree in Figure 4.1 to calculate the payoff to entry for this firm. The strategy of enter and stay in regardless of outcome, for example, has the payoff:

$$\text{Payoff} = p_1(R_2) + (1\text{-}p_1)\ (R_4)$$

On the other hand, the strategy of enter and then exit if prices fall has the payoff:

$$\text{Payoff} = p_1(R_2) + (1\text{-}p_1)\ (R_3)$$

The likelihood that a firm will enter will clearly depend on the particular payoffs it associates with entry strategies.

The higher the payoff, the more likely the entry, all else equal.

An Example: Poultry Operations among the Hmong

In order to illustrate the use of a decision tree in an entry decision I will draw on the experience of a group looking at small business opportunities for the Hmong refugees in Providence, Rhode Island. In the late 1970s, a number of Hmong refugees left the camps of Thailand and, under the aegis of the International Institute and Catholic Social Services, settled in Providence. Prior to settlement, the only contact the Hmong had had with Western society was through the military. The Hmong came with few resources, typically speaking little or no English. Moreover, the refugees were largely unfamiliar with the norms of industrial society. For instance, in Laos it is customary for a Hmong to send his brother in his place when he cannot attend work. American employers find this an unacceptable practice.

After moving to Providence, the Hmong found themselves in a major commercial, financial, and industrial urban center. In 1980, when the mass of refugees arrived, it was also a city with unemployment rates above the national norm, and relatively few jobs suitable for the new refugees.

Like many other immigrant groups, the Hmong formed a self-help group—the Providence Hmong Association (PHA). One of the primary objectives of the PHA was to find employment for its members. Again as with many other immigrant groups, starting their own businesses was high on the Hmong list of possibilities. Among the many business options discussed by the Hmong was the opening of a poultry shop. Interested Hmong approached the PHA for advice and help with funding.

For the Hmong, a poultry shop had several appealing features. First, the Hmong have a strong culinary preference for freshly slaughtered chicken. Moreover, the Hmong use the heads and feet of chicken in important religious ceremonies. For these reasons, the Hmong not only pay premium prices, but travel long distances to inconvenient locations to purchase fresh poultry. Second, the Hmong recognized that they had acquired some experience raising and butchering chicken in Laos. Finally, the capital requirements of setting up a poultry shop appeared to be minimal.

The target market for the new shop would be the Indochinese refugee population of Providence, including not only the Hmong, but other recent immigrants from Indochina, all of whom shared the preference for freshly slaughtered chicken. The prime competition for this segment of the market was Luigi's, a family-run butcher. Luigi's sold its freshly slaughtered broilers for $.85 per pound. Other competitors were the local supermarkets, which sold chicken at prices that were considerably lower ($.49 per pound), although the chickens were not freshly slaughtered.

From the perspective of the Hmong, the decision tree had one decision node. Do we enter or do we not enter the poultry market? The primary chance node involved the prices that could be charged. The optimistic view was that the Hmong could operate in the $.85 per pound price range, and sell at more or less full capacity. Two factors, however, threatened these prices. First, Luigi's might lower its price in response to the Hmong competition. Competitor reaction was thus one of the factors contributing to the chance element for the Hmong. Second, Hmong preferences for freshly killed chickens might diminish as the refugees assimilated into the American culture. Thus sociocultural phenomena also contributed to the chance node. In either case, these was a real possibility that the Hmong might be forced to reduce prices to the $.49 per pound level in order to stay at capacity.

The next task for the Hmong was to calculate the operating profits of the shop under the two price assumptions. This calculation required the Hmong to develop a *pro forma* income statement, which is shown in Table 4.1. The annual capacity of the shop is 200,000 pounds of poultry. The revenue stream depends entirely on which price regimen holds. Costs are independent of price regimen, since in both scenarios the best the Hmong can do is to operate at capacity.

As we see from Table 4.1, in the case of the poultry shop, the profits were likely to be modest but positive in the $.85 per pound case, but quite

Table 4.1 Hmong poultry shop, rough break-evens

	$.85/lb. scenario	$.49/lb. scenario
Revenues		
Volume (lbs./poultry)	200,000	200,000
Average	.85	.49
Sales	$170,000	$98,000
Costs		
Operating costs		
Cost/bird	.20	.20
Bird cost	60,000	60,000
Feed/bird	.05	.05
Feed costs	3,800	3,800
Labor	13,000	13,000
Transport	3,000	3,000
Total cost of goods sold	79,800	79,800
Total gross	90,200	18,200
Salaries	18,000	18,000
Rent and utilities	10,000	10,000
Depreciation	5,000	5,000
Interest	3,000	3,000
Total expenses	36,000	36,000
Net profit	54,200	−17,800

negative in the $.49 per pound situation. Clearly this was a case in which the chance node was important and would tilt payoffs one way or the other.

As a final exercise, the Hmong calculated the exit cost associated with the poultry shop. In this case, exit costs were modest. Fixed costs of operation included a truck and some butchering equipment, all of which could be fairly easily resold, at a modest loss.

The decision tree generated by the Hmong is given below in Figure 4.2 Note that it rests in part on the pro forma income statement. The tree format provides us with a convenient visual summary of the more complex data. In this example, the Hmong initially believed that there was an even chance that prices would be in the high versus low range, for cultural assimilation was proceeding slowly, and Luigi's was expected not to respond quickly to the new entry. In this instance, the payoff to entry would be positive:

$$.5 \ \$(54,200) + .5 \ \$(-10,000) = \$22,100$$

It is often useful in using a decision tree to calculate **critical chance values.** In other words, how high would the likelihood of an adverse event have to be in order to change the choice of the decision maker? Calculating a critical-chance value provides us with *sensitivity information,* for it tells us how confident we are in the soundness of a go-no-go decision. In the Hmong poultry example, as long as the odds were at least 4 to 1 ($p_1 > .22$), there would be a positive entry payoff. In this situation, largely because of the low exit costs, the Hmong decided to go ahead with the shop, and so far the decision seems to have been a sound one. But laying out the analysis in this way helped to pinpoint a potential problem—the price competition issue—and helped the Hmong focus on the costs of making a mistake.

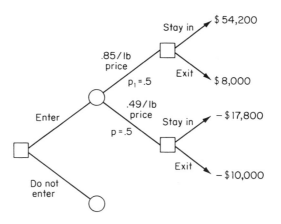

Figure 4.2   The Hmong decision to enter the poultry market

Decision Trees and Entry Barriers

In the Hmong example, I have indicated the ways in which the prospects of a new business start-up might be modeled using a decision tree. By using a decision tree to model how firms think about entering an industry, we can identify those factors that influence the rate of entry into an industry in which excess profits appear and those that keep out new entrants. In the traditional literature, factors that tend to impede entry have been known as **barriers to entry,** and in this text I will preserve that nomenclature. But it is helpful to organize those barriers and analyze them in the framework of the actual managerial decisions associated with entry.

> **Barriers to entry are industry characteristics which reduce the rate of entry below that needed to level profits.**

Such barriers are significant because they determine in large measure the friendliness of the environment in which the organization will compete, once the initial period in the industry evolution ends. These barriers determine what happens in the important adolescence and maturity of a market.

Several factors affect the expected payoff to the firm of an entry strategy. Of central importance are factors that affect the firm's expectations concerning the likely reactions of incumbents to a new entry. Evidence that post-entry prices are likely to fall will be a major deterrent to entry. A firm's expectations concerning prices that will hold once it enters, rather than current market prices, are relevant to the decision to enter and these prices in turn depend on how we expect incumbents to react.

> **Expectations of incumbent reactions influence entry.**

The second set of factors that will weigh in the entry decision of the firm are the size of the payoffs to the firm from a sustained entry. In the tree in Figure 4.1, the payoffs from sustained entry consist of the values of R_2 and R_4. As we will shortly see, the prevailing market price may allow for excess profits for the incumbents, even if the accounting is done right, and yet not be high enough to induce entry by new firms, given their cost structure. Several factors systematically reduce the payoffs of new entrants relative to existing firms, and these factors may be quite powerful in allowing existing firms to reap excess profits without encouraging entry.

> **The size of payoffs influences entry.**

A final deterrent to entry by new firms are the factors that lead to high losses from exit, or R_1 and R_3 in Figure 4.1. Entry is inherently a highly risky business, and all new entrants must reckon with the very real possibility that they may not survive in the industry. *Costs of failure* will be critical in determining whether or not entry occurs.

Exit costs influence the rate of entry.

Some analysts believe that an understanding of the costs of failure or exit costs tells us virtually the whole story of industry dynamics. To see this argument we return to the Hmong case just described. Suppose in the Hmong example that exit costs from the poultry business were zero. Then, no matter what probabilities we assigned to the chance nodes, or what payoffs we assigned to a successful start-up, the payoff value of entry would be positive. If exit costs are zero, the firm would enter no matter how dismal the chances of success or how low the rewards. In a poker game, if there's no ante, we begin every game. As it turns out, most games have an ante; most entry requires at least some irreversible investment and thus carries some exit costs. And once we have positive exit costs, even small ones, the full panoply of entry considerations becomes relevant. Thus exit costs are important, but they don't tell the whole story.

As indicated, many of the traditional barriers to entry can be understood as operating through one of these three factors. In tracing the entry barriers in each of these three areas, we will again see our analytical theme of equilibrium analysis. Our concern will be for understanding the results of strategic choices as the interactions of the various organizations work themselves through in the ever-changing market place. We will also see the critical role played by information. In all of the strategic decisions an organization makes, it proceeds with doubts and uncertainties about the real facts of the situation faced by itself and its rivals. This uncertainty is, of course, one of the things that makes the management process both more interesting and more challenging. Strategic management will invariably take some daring as well as some thought.

Expectations About the Reactions of Incumbents to Entry

In developing any of the *pro forma* calculations on the gains from entry in a market, a firm needs to make some assessment concerning the likely prices that will prevail in the market, just as we did in the poultry example. These assessments will naturally be made with limited data, and they will carry with them some uncertainty. Recent literature in the area of industrial organization has made clear the prominent role played by these expectations. Potential entrants into a market rarely know everything there is to know about that market and about how market participants will behave. These entrants take small clues from the marketplace and often use them to make quite large investment decisions.

But what influences expectations? What leads a potential entrant like the Hmong to optimism or pessimism on the future stability of prices?

The first factor of importance is the *technology of the industry,*—in particular the extent to which there are specific assets used by incumbents in serving the market, economies of scale, and/or excess capacity. The second important element affecting the formation of price expectations is the *reputation of the industry incumbents.* Both the technology of the industry and its history act as barriers to entry primarily by driving a wedge between the current market price and an entrant's expectations concerning the likely post-entry price.

Specific Assets

In serving a market, organizations require a set of assets. These might include some physical properties such as production facilities or a research lab. Most organizations also have a set of less tangible assets, for example, a cadre of experienced managers, complex existing relationships with suppliers and/or distributors, or a group of patents. For organizations in the service sector, intangible assets may be dominant. Investment banks, for instance, have few production facilities, but control considerable assets in the form of skilled labor, firm reputation, and customer relations. These assets, taken as a whole, enable an organization to serve its market and earn a rate of return for its shareholders. The specialization of an organization's assets will also help us to predict its reactions to an entry threat.

It has long been thought that an organization's commitment to a market increases along with the assets it has in that industry. Eastman Kodak, for example, has more than $10 billion in assets in its photographic equipment business. Threats by Fuji in this market are likely to be resisted in attempts to protect those assets. More recently, however, we have come to realize that it is not simply the size of the assets an organization has in an industry which determines its commitment, but the extent to which those assets are *specific* to that industry.[1]

> An investment is said to be specific to a market if it would neither increase value nor reduce cost when applied to a different market.

If Kodak's $10 billion in assets could be used relatively easily in another market, then its willingness to experience losses to fight Fuji will be diminished. If these assets are quite specific to the product and geographic market, Kodak's tendency to fight Fuji will increase. The broader an organization's options are, the less committed it will be to any particular market. In sum, to the extent that an organization's assets are specific to a market and thus primarily valuable only in that market, that organization is likely to fight harder to maintain its position in that market. Thus specific assets raise commitment levels by incumbents and reduce the attractiveness of entry. This is another side to the argument we made in the last chapter about the role of specific assets in increasing the intensity of rivalry among existing firms in an industry.

Economies of Scale

One of the central technological characteristics of an organization is the extent to which economies of scale exist. As an organization increases its volume by expanding its scale of operations, what happens to unit costs? If these unit costs fall, we say the organization is experiencing **economies of scale.** If unit costs remain stable, the organization is said to have **constant returns to scale,** and if unit costs rise with scale augmentation, the organization is said to have **decreasing returns to scale.**

The possible sources of economies of scale in an industry are many. In some industries, economies of scale occur primarily in the production area. This is particularly true in what have come to be known as the smokestack industries. A good deal of the machinery used in modern manufacture has fairly substantial capacity. Unless an organization can fully utilize this capacity, purchasing the machine will not make sense. Thus small organizations will find themselves with a higher cost technology than their larger neighbors. Then, too, as an organization's scale of operations increases, opportunities for specialization in the use of its inputs also increase. Gains from specialization with scale have played a prominent role in economic thinking since the descriptions by Adam Smith of a Scottish pin factory.[2] Borden's, one of the largest U.S. producers of pasta, buys 800 million pounds of durum wheat each year, which allows it to achieve considerable economies in purchasing. We have already talked about the way in which size increases buyer power. Borden's volume also allows whole plants to be dedicated to the production of odd-shaped pasta thus reducing plant changeover time. In the same way, Procter & Gamble can devote entire lines to one diaper size, thus increasing line speeds. In many of our service industries the prime advantages of scale are thought to be opportunities for increased labor specialization. Large investment banks can employ a specialist in each of many critical industries; smaller banks must rely instead on generalists to provide industry analysis. Inventory savings are also typically possible with scale increases, since the need for buffer stocks does not increase proportionately with scale. In the transportation and distribution area, scale advantages may also prevail, as firms can take advantage of full-truck load carriage and large shelf displays.

A concrete example of the magnitude of economies of scale is provided by the production of paper, a relatively capital intensive industry. In the production of uncoated paper for printing, for example, an expansion from 60,000 to 120,000 tons brings with it a 28 percent drop in fixed costs per ton. With this same expansion, labor costs can be reduced 32 percent as new technical opportunities for production open up.[3] Within this range of production, large-scale operations clearly have some cost advantage.

In Figure 4.3, I have constructed a cost curve in which unit costs decline for a period and then level off at Q^*. This L-shaped curve is rela-

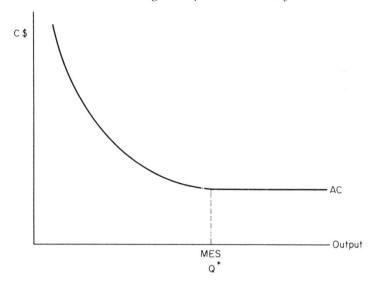

Figure 4.3 Economies of scale

tively common; the scale advantages described above often peter out over time, and coordination difficulties in large organizations begin to serve as a counter balance. The output level Q* is known as the **minimum efficient scale** of production (or the MES) for the industry, and plays an important role in determining entry patterns.

> **The minimum efficient scale of production (MES) is the *smallest* volume for which the unit costs reach a minimum.**

If a firm wishes to minimize production costs, it must enter at MES or larger.

Knowing MES will help an entering firm to figure out just what scale of operations is required, and hence what capital investment is needed to enter the industry. In the Hmong example, the small scale economies in poultry sales made this business attractive to new entrants. But understanding the likely industry dynamics requires more information. In particular, one would also want to know the ratio of minimum efficient scale to the overall size of the market. This ratio tells us the **market share** required for a low-cost entry into a market. In terms of understanding industry dynamics, the market share needed for entry is generally more important than the absolute size of the entry requirement. Estimates suggest, for example, that in the commercial aircraft industry the MES is approximately 10 percent of the U.S. market. In the long-distance telecommunications market, a 10 percent share is also thought to be necessary for cost parity. This information tells us that in these industries a new entrant, seeking to have unit costs as low as those of existing firms in the industry, should target its entry at a 10 percent market share or more. Even if the entrant assumed no complicated rivalrous response by industry incumbents in response to this high-share target, the simple industry supply increase suggested by an entry at this level would result in a post-entry price decrease, unless the entrant expects to replace the incumbent entirely. Of course, in some markets new entrants might hope to replace incumbents entirely, driving out the capacity of the incumbent and restoring prices to their earlier levels. But trying to completely replace an incumbent is quite a bit more difficult than entering as a small adjunct to the market. In practice then, economies of scale can influence entry by increasing the expectations of an aggressive price reaction by incumbents.

All else equal, the larger the MES is relative to the market, the greater is the expected wedge between pre- and post-entry price, and thus the less likely is entry to occur.

In practice, the size of MES relative to the market differs dramatically across markets. In Table 4.2, I have reproduced estimates provided by several different researchers. It should be noted that some of these estimates are relatively dated, and the index itself is likely to vary over time both in response to technical change and in response to demand growth. Nevertheless, the estimates provide a rough indication of the relative contribution of scale economies to industry structure in a range of industries.

We can see from this table that estimates of MES vary widely among industries. Typewriters, gypsum, steel, and tractors are all industries that have historically required large scale. The food industry has considerably smaller-scale requirements.

Focusing on the role of MES relative to the overall market as a major factor in entry conditions helps to explain some of the structural changes associated with the recent trends toward global business. Increasingly the relevant market for firms has become not the internal domestic market, but the world market. The effect of this trend has been to reduce the size of MES relative to total demand, essentially by increasing the demand figures. This has resulted in more markets served by firms that achieve their scale economies via sales in many different markets. The auto industry is an excellent example. The MES of the auto industry is quite large, and thus the domestic market will not support a great number of firms. On the other hand, the world market supports more firms, many of whom now compete in varied submarkets throughout the world, including the United States. The American auto market, which until recently included only four firms, is today served by numerous firms from all over the world.

The ability of firms to achieve production MES by operating in many diverse markets can also be seen in the U.S. motorcycle market. In the 1950s, the United States and British firms concentrated on the relatively small United States and European markets, which did not provide the scale needed to introduce high levels of machine and labor specialization. The technology of choice, given the market scale, was thus fairly labor intensive. When Japan entered the American market, it entered with a

Table 4.2 Minimum efficient scale estimates

Minimum efficient firm size as percentage of industry capacity	
Fruit and vegetable canning	0.5
Oil refining	1.75
Meat packing	0.2
Meat products	2.5
Fountain pens	10.0
Copper	10.0
Typewriters	30.0
Flour milling	0.5
Liquor distilling	1.75
Metal containers	3.0
Tires	3.0
Rayon	6.0
Farm machinery	6.0
Automobiles	10.0
Tractors	15.0
Shoes	2.5
Cement	10.0
Steel	20.0
Gypsum products	33.0
Soap	15.0
Cigarettes	20.0

Source: K. Lancaster and R. Dulaney, *Modern Economics: Principles and Policy* (Rand McNally, 1979), p. 211.

background of extremely large domestic markets, because many Japanese were using motorcycles as a work vehicle, whereas in the United States the motorcycle was primarily a leisure product. Japanese firms, with their large domestic markets, found it worthwhile to increase the capital intensity of their production and use the cost reductions associated with this mode of production to sell to the smaller U.S. market.[4] In the process, the Japanese firms with their low price and smaller bike design, expanded the U.S. market. From the perspective of the global market, the market share required to achieve MES in the capital-intensive production technique chosen by the Japanese was fairly modest; when viewed from the perspective of the U.S. domestic market in the 1970s, the market share was quite a bit larger. Thus the opening up of world markets has had the salutary effect of increasing the number of viable competitors in domestic markets. Of course, in many markets this foreign entry has put pressure on profit margins.

It is clear that if MES relative to market is high, the entering firm will likely have a large effect on prices by virtue of its entry. In this situation, however, there is another possible entry strategy. In particular, even if economies of scale are large, a new entrant may decide to enter at a small scale, suffer the higher unit costs, and try to compete on a basis other than price. In this case, even though MES/market is high, since the entrant does not come in at MES, its effect on the market price may be small. If new firms can profitably enter an industry at a scale less than MES, then large-scale economies will not protect the margins in the industry.

Under what conditions might a firm deliberately decide to enter at less than MES? First, we need to consider how much the small-scale entry handicaps the entrant in terms of its costs. This will depend on the shape of the cost curve. In Figure 4.3, if the L is quite steep, the cost disadvantage of small-scale entry will be high; if the vertical portion of the L is gentle, the cost disadvantage will be less. One measure of the shape of the curve is the increase in costs associated with production at levels of one-half MES. The higher the cost disadvantage of small-scale production, the less viable a low-scale entry strategy. For example, in the aircraft industry, the increase in costs associated with operation at levels of one-half MES has been estimated at approximately 20 percent. Home-laundering equipment, on the other hand, while it shares an MES relative to market of 10 to 11 percent with aircraft, experiences an increase in costs of operating at one-half MES of only about 8 percent. A new entrant must consider carefully the cost disadvantages with which it begins its quest.

The steeper the cost curve, the less likely is entry at smaller than MES scale.

Thus one side of the entry equation involves a calculation of the size of the cost disadvantage associated with small-scale entry. The other side of the equation is what the new entrant has to offer the market that might enable it to compensate for its high costs by charging high prices. In the Hmong example, the new lure to customers was freshly slaughtered poultry, and this product innovation would allow the Hmong to compete against larger, more efficient supermarkets. In the integrated steel industry, the MES of production has been estimated to be in the range of 6 to 7 million raw tons per year. In 1980, of the 28 plants run by the seven largest U.S. steel manufacturers, only seven plants had a capacity of MES or higher.[5] In this industry, small plants which operated with high unit costs were protected by high transportation costs. It was better to build numerous small-scale plants throughout the country to reduce transportation costs rather than to build more centralized, optimally scaled plants. Interestingly, when competition from the Japanese increased, a number of small operations on the West Coast found that their transportation cost barrier no longer protected them. Nevertheless, in many industries, transportation costs may protect less than MES-scaled operations. Products with high bulk relative to value often find that transportation cost considerations dominate the facility size decision.

In the automobile industry, the MES has been estimated to be in the range of 200,000 to 500,000 vehicles. Most United States domestic models are produced in volumes less than MES, including long time favorites such as the Corvette.[6] These products are expected to have such consumer appeal that they will be able to sell for high enough prices to compensate for the cost handicap associated with small-scale production.

Long-term survival at a scale less than MES requires some off-setting factors that permit the firm to charge a price premium. Product differentiation and locational monopoly are two possible offsets.

There are numerous examples of entrants coming into markets with plants of less than MES scale. John DeLorean's fiasco in the automobile industry suggests the difficulty in overcoming large cost disadvantages. DeLorean attempted to produce a high-end automobile, operating at small scale. The cost disadvantage in this example was large. In order to succeed as a niche producer in this market, considerable product differentiation and canny management are essential. In other markets, niche producers have an easier time. In these cases, small cost disadvantages may be offset by product design or distribution features that allow new entrants to charge premium prices to offset their higher costs. Once again, though, in industries characterized by large MES and very steep cost curves, niche strategies are less likely to work.

We have seen that a barrier to entry is created when the ratio of MES to market share in an industry is high, and small-scale strategies do not appear to be viable, either as a result of costs or consumer attitudes. The barrier to entry associated with scale works primarily by driving a wedge between pre-entry prices and post-entry prices. Scale economies affect the potential entrant's expectations concerning the likely path of future prices should it decide to enter the market.

The third major technological factor that influences a potential entrant's expectations concerning post-entry prices is the extent of excess capacity in an industry.

Excess Capacity

In discussing the role of economies of scale in affecting the relationship between pre-and-post entry prices, we focused on the effect of an incremental supply of the product on market prices. The size of gap between the two prices, however, also depends on any changes in behavior produced by the new entry among incumbent firms. To the extent that the new entrant expects incumbents to retaliate for the entry by cutting prices, entry becomes less attractive.

Under what circumstances is entry most likely to be met by price retaliation? We have already seen that the degree of specific assets used by an organization will affect its commitment to the industry. A second circumstance that has captured considerable attention both in the theoretical literature and in the courts has been the existence of **excess capacity** in an industry.

The argument is quite simple. Suppose an industry is already experiencing excess capacity, and a new firm enters. If the market demand remains stable, the new entry will induce even greater excess capacity on the part of incumbents. If there are economies to scale in production, the costs of idle capacity may rise with the degree of idleness. This suggests that incumbents will fight harder to retain market share under excess capacity conditions, and thus prices are likely to drop with entry.[7] If we return to our decision tree, we see that the existence of excess capacity, particularly if coupled by economies of scale, will increase the expected probability of post-entry price cuts, thus reducing the payoff to entry.

The role of excess capacity brings us to the notion of *strategic* versus *innocent* entry barriers as first introduced by Salop.[8] Firms may hold excess capacity for a variety of reasons. For example, if demand is cyclical, excess capacity is often called for. Large economies of scale, particularly if demand is expected to grow, also lead to the holding of excess capacity. Once firms build excess capacity, the result will be to deter entry. But the primary motivation for the excess capacity is an innocent one, reflecting usual business exigencies. The very fact that the excess capacity may deter entry, however, may create a second motivation for firms to overbuild. Firms may hold excess capacity, beyond that normally needed, in order to influence the expectations of potential entrants vis à vis their price-cutting tendencies. In this sense, excess capacity may be seen as a *strategic* entry barrier.

> **Excess capacity deters entry by increasing the credibility of price cutting as an entry response by incumbents.**

Holding excess capacity for strategic reasons involves some costs, and it is thus clearly not always advisable. Indeed, the holding of excess capacity to deter entry provides an interesting example of an economic problem known as the **free-rider problem.** In situations in which we cannot exclude nonpayers from enjoying the benefits of a particular good or service, no individual will wish to contribute to the purchase of it. They will all wish to *free ride* on the purchases of others. Actions that have the effect of deterring entry benefit all firms currently in the industry by restricting supply. Many entry-deterring tactics, however, including holding excess capacity, create costs borne by individual firms. Clearly a firm would have an incentive to wait and let the other firms in the industry hold the excess capacity and thus deter entry, giving the firm all of the benefits of entry deterrence without commensurate costs. But if all firms wish to be "free riders" in this way, no entry-deterring action is likely.[9]

Given the free-rider problem, we expect to see strategic excess capacity held primarily in industries in which the number of market participants is rather small. For example, one of the earliest cited examples of the use of excess capacity as a strategic entry barrier was in the 1945 antitrust case against Alcoa, which at the time dominated the aluminum market. Through 1940, Alcoa was the sole domestic producer of virgin aluminum ingot. In maintaining that monopoly position, Alcoa had no patents to rely on. Instead, the court found that Alcoa preserved its position by its production strategy: holding excess capacity. In particular, Judge Learned Hand argued in that decision: "We can think of no more effective exclusion than to progressively embrace each new opportunity as it opened and to face each newcomer with new capacity already geared into a great organization."[10] In the Alcoa case, since Alcoa was the only firm in the aluminum industry at the time of the alleged excess capacity strategy, no free-rider problem existed. Any entry deterrence effected by Alcoa only improved its own position.

In summary, we have found that if incumbents have specialized assets committed to a market, their tendency to fight entry will increase. Moreover, excess capacity, whether created in innocent or strategic ways, may serve also to deter entry by increasing the probability that incumbents will reduce prices in the event of new entry. We have further found that excess capacity, coupled with large economies of scale, is particularly likely to deter entry. The technology of an industry, however, is not the only industry feature that affects an entrant's expectation concerning likely responses of incumbents. In this sense, the pricing history of incumbent firms both in the particular industry and in related markets may influence a potential entrant's expectations. We turn now to this entry barrier.

Reputation Effect

Throughout this chapter, we have stressed the role of expectations in determining the entry behavior of firms. But how do potential entrants form their expectations concerning likely behavior by incumbent firms? We have already seen that the technology of the industry provides a new entrant with clues as to expected future prices in the market. How do outside firms factor in the effect of prior behavior of market leaders?

One approach to understanding how expectations are formed is to assume that the incumbent firms will meet any change in their environment posed by new entry by reacting in a rational, profit-seeking manner. Thus the potential entrant would estimate how much new output it plans to add to the market, and then calculate the "best" response in terms of the price and output of incumbent firms. The technology of the industry plays a role here in the sense that it helps to determine the profit-maximizing response of the incumbent to the new entrant.

As the entrant tries to understand the likely response of an incumbent to the threat of the entrant, it needs to have a good deal of information about the incumbent. The "right" response of a firm to entry depends, for example, on its costs. But entrants typically have rather poor information about the true costs of other firms. And this lack of information creates an opportunity for firms already in the industry. By engaging in certain pricing and marketing practices, firms may be able to mislead potential entrants about their costs, and thus about how aggressive their response to entry will be. This tactic may be a powerful weapon.[11] So the prior behavior of firms can influence public knowledge about the technology of the market.

Firms can also use other strategies to affect price expectations. Since expectations play such a large role in the entry decision, and since entry is vital for determining profit levels, one might think that incumbent firms would have great incentives to threaten to cut prices in the face of entry. Of course, out-and-out price threats are illegal, but subtle threats can make it through the antitrust filter and nevertheless be comprehensible to potential entrants. The problem with such threats is, as the old saw tells us, "talk is cheap." That is, if the incumbents threaten some action clearly harmful to themselves, it will not generally meet the *test of credibility*. Potential entrants simply won't believe a threat by an incumbent to cut its own throat. It is in adding credibility to seemingly irrational threats that the history of firms currently in a market may play a role.

Firms typically compete in many markets, over long periods of time. As a result, these firms develop reputations: Some are known as fierce competitors, liable to cut prices in response to even small entry attempts; others appear to be more conciliatory. Such reputations can play a powerful role in the entry decision of a new firm. If an entrant believes a firm to be irrational, it will be more leery of entering that industry. In some markets, for some time periods, a firm might find it worthwhile to employ what seems to be an irrational strategy in order to convince all future rivals of the ferocity of its interest in preserving its market share. Irrationality now and again will cost the firm in the short run, but may benefit it in other markets and other periods. In the instant-camera market, for example, the original CEO and founder of Polaroid, Edwin Land, had a reputation as a formidable defendant of his market. Land's reputation may have helped to protect Polaroid's market for a considerable period. Potential rivals may have been reluctant to test Land's determination. In other circumstances, it may pay firms to shade prices a bit to try to mislead potential rivals about their cost advantages. Hitachi, a leading Japanese electronics firm, can use its reputation for aggressive pricing to deter entry into the Japanese semiconductor market. We will be discussing at length the issue of firm reputation in determining the nature of interfirm competition in Part III of this book. At this point, it is worth noting that much information is often contained in the patterns of past industry behavior.

Occasional actions by firms that seem to violate their immediate profit-seeking incentives can be advantageous by increasing the credibility of a price-cutting response to entry and thus deterring entry.

Four factors that influence a firm's expectations concerning the stability of prices in a market in the face of an entry threat are (1) the existence of specific assets in a market, (2) the existence of economies of scale in the industry, (3) the existence of excess capacity in the industry, and (4) the reputations of existing firms in the market. Any of these factors can help to shield incumbents from new entry and allow them to earn excess profits over protracted periods. We turn now to the factors that influence the potential payoff from a successful entry into a market.

Entry Payoffs or Sources of Incumbent Advantage

Returning to the decision tree apparatus set up earlier, we now turn to the second factor which influences the payoffs to the entry option: *How much is a successful entry worth to a new entrant?*

We begin by remembering that we are dealing with entry into industries in which incumbents are earning handsome returns. Assuming that post-entry prices remain at pre-entry levels, new entrants might expect handsome payoffs from market participation. As we will see, however, this is not always the case. New entrants may find themselves at a disadvantage relative to incumbents due to the existence of *(1) precommitment contracts, (2) licenses and patents, (3) experience curve effects, or (4) a pioneering-brand advantage.*

All of these four forces have historically been regarded as barriers to entry. As we will see shortly, the way each operates as a barrier is to drive a wedge between the expected post-entry profits of the incumbents and those of the new entrant. In a number of cases, these factors protect incumbent firms because they increase the **transactions costs** that suppliers or customers face in purchasing from a new entrant.[12] Using another nomenclature, we may argue that each of these barriers comes into play because they create a **first-mover advantage** within an industry. Each allows incumbents to make profits where none exist for the potential entrant.

Precommitment Contracts

Many of the transactions that organizations engage in are made through long-term contracts. The organization signs a contract agreeing to produce a given amount of output or purchase certain inputs, and it is subject to large penalties if it fails to do so. Such contracts are extremely common, for they often are the most efficient way of transacting business. A refinery signs a contract with an oil-exploration firm in which the refinery agrees to buy and the drilling firm to supply a stated amount of crude for a fixed period of time. An aluminum company signs a contract agreeing to buy bauxite at specified prices and amounts over a given period of time. Electric utilities commit to purchases of uranium at specific prices. In each of these situations, there is typically a commitment both by the buyer and the seller, and there are often substantial penalties for nonperformance.

For a variety of reasons, organizations choose to transact by contract, rather than simply on the spot market. We will explore these reasons more fully in Chapter 11 as we investigate vertical integration. In some cases, however, whatever the reason for the initial contract, the *effect* of the precommitment is to deter entry. Once the contract is signed, an *asymmetry* is introduced between incumbents and potential entrants. A portion of the market is removed from the competitive arena, and a first-mover advantage is preserved by the use of the contract.

One example of a precommitment contract that serves as an entry barrier is one providing the incumbent with favorable access to an essential raw material. The Alcoa case is a prime example of this barrier. As we indicated earlier, Alcoa was the sole manufacturer of aluminum ingots in the United States until World War II. During this period, Alcoa managed to sign long-term exclusive contracts with all available high-grade bauxite producers, bauxite being an essential raw material in aluminum production. In part, Alcoa appears to have been able to sign favorable long-term contracts because it possessed more information about the nature of the industry and its prospects than either suppliers or other potential entrants into the market. Thus bauxite was not available to potential entrants on the same basis as it was to Alcoa, and entry into the aluminum industry was deterred, at least until the courts intervened.

A second example of an entry-deterring precommitment is an explicit or implicit contract between a producer and the retail agent providing distribution for the product. In the disposable-diaper market, for example, Procter & Gamble arranged contracts with hospitals for free distribution of disposables at a time when hospitals were less aware than P&G of the value of this promotional service. This distribution network may have given P&G an edge for a time over potential rivals in the disposable-diaper market. In many industries, shelf space is an important input and may be subject to contracting. It is important to note that the value of these contracts as entry barriers depends heavily on the uniqueness of the contracted supply. If retail space is readily available, long-term contracts governing this space will not deter entry, though they may well serve other functions.

A final example of an entry-deterring precommitment involves implicit contracts firms make with their purchasers. In theory a firm could deter entry perfectly simply by signing a contract with all of its customers to deliver its good at an extremely low price should entry ever occur. In terms of our earlier discussion, the incumbent has passed the hurdle of the test of credibility on its price response by committing itself contractually. An interesting aspect of this contract is that the potential entrant, seeing this contract, would never enter, and the incumbent would never need to carry through on the contract.[13] Elaborate contracts of this sort are rarely found, perhaps due to enforcement costs. But there are some provisions similar in spirit to these "entry-price threat" contracts, which have similar entry-deterring qualities. In particular, consider meeting the competition clause described in the last chapter in the discussion of facilitating devices. The seller agrees that if a second seller offers a comparable product at a lower price to the buyer, the original seller will either meet the price or release the customer.[14] In this way, the incumbent firm has precommitted itself to meet any price offered by a new entrant. To the extent that entrants hope to gain share through initial price concessions, such contracts can have severe effects on entry. A further discussion of marketing devices of the contracting form is contained in Chapter 14. For now, we simply wish to highlight the entry-deterring effects of such contracts.

Incumbents can create first-mover advantages and thus deter entry into markets through the use of contracts.

In each of the examples above, the entry-deterring firm had better information about its market than did its bargaining counterpart. In our examples, Alcoa and Procter & Gamble both knew more about the value of the bauxite and hospital distribution than did the bauxite producers or hospitals. This information asymmetry is essential if the benefits of entry deterrence are to accrue to the producing firm rather than the organization which controls the initial scarce resource.

In sum, the first set of factors that deter entry by reducing the potential payoff to entry for a firm are precommitments in the supply or final product market by incumbent firms. Again, these precommitments may well be undertaken for efficiency reasons; nevertheless, they do create entry barriers. The critical element in the use of precommitments as an entry deterrent is their ability to create asymmetries between the contracting incumbents and potential entrants into the market. Precommitments create frictions that slow down the efficient market forces.

Licenses and Patents Create Asymmetries

In a number of industries entry is controlled by government. Liquor stores in many states, for instance, require local or state licenses to sell their wares. In New York City as well as a number of other cities in the United States, taxicabs require medallions as a prerequisite to operation. Local telephone service is provided only by firms certified by the public-utility commission. Historically, cable television has also operated under local franchises. A decade ago, airline service was similarly restricted. In all of these cases, free entry in response to possible supernormal profits is prevented by government policy. In these cases, government policy acts as the barrier to entry. Even in instances in which licensing does not substantially decrease the number of entrants into an industry, the notification associated with licensing may affect the level of competition in the industry.

Another interesting example of the role of certification in deterring entry comes in the medical area. Under current regulations, only certified hospitals are reimbursed by federal payments for heart transplants. Certification, under the rules, requires facilities to have performed 36 prior heart transplants and demonstrate actuarial survival rates of 73 percent for one year and 65 percent for two years. Whatever the effect of this certification process on patient health, it clearly reduces the flow of new entrants into the heart-transplant market. Proposed regulations to govern the market for in-vitro fertilization will have a similar entry-deterring effect.

In industries in which government policy effectively deters entry, we often find that competition is displaced rather than eliminated. For example, in the N.Y. taxicab market, competition in the provision of cab service has been displaced in part by competition in the market for medallions, with the result that the price of medallions represents a substantial investment. In other instances, competition is displaced into the political arena, with organizations using resources to try to win the right to serve certain protected markets for local, state, or federal legislators. In the extreme, all of the potential profits associated with actually running the protected business may be dissipated in the quest for the right to serve the market. **Rent-seeking behavior** by firms is manifest in a number of regulated industries.[15] Rent seeking occurs whenever firms spend resources trying to secure for themselves a position in a market in which excess returns are being generated.

Patents have a similar effect in protecting incumbents from the threat of entry, though generally speaking the motive for granting a patent is rather different than the motive for using licensing. In creating an innovation, organizations and/or individuals typically expend some resources. Often the number of false starts per real improvement can be enormous, and enormously expensive as well. In the pharmaceutical industry, for example, the percentage of drugs that begin the clinical testing process that eventually make it to market is only 10 percent. But if entry is free, we can see that, once an organization begins marketing its new product, new entry would soon dissipate all excess profits from that market. In this case, there would be nothing left to pay for the costs of all the testing of the innovation or to cover the costs of all the failures experienced en route to the innovation. The patent system is intended to reduce entry into an industry by preventing product and process imitation. In the United States, the standard patent life is seventeen years; for this period other organizations are, in theory, not permitted to copy the innovation. The explicit goal of the patent system is to allow the inventor to reap some excess profits in the production stage to compensate for the expense and risk of innovating in the first place.

Patents and licenses can prevent free entry from eliminating excess profits in an industry and create asymmetries between existing firms and potential entrants.

While patents certainly act as a deterrent to entry, they are by no means an impermeable barrier in all cases. In some industries, for example, innovating "around" patents turns out to be relatively easy, and the effective life of patents is thus considerably less than the listed seventeen years. Recent interesting work suggests that there are wide differences among industries in the efficacy of patents: In the drug industry patents appear to be fairly effective, while in the semiconductor industry, they are considerably less so.[16] In some industries, like electronics and biotechnology, new regulations have increased the scope and importance of patenting. The causes of differences in the efficacy of patents and licenses and the strategic consequences of these differences are explored at greater length in Chapter 16, as we consider rivalry in the area of research and development.

Learning-curve Effects

In a number of industries, we have observed that as an organization gains experience in the production of a particular product, its unit costs for production decline. Early work in the field stressed the gains in labor experience over time. Workers were organized more efficiently over time and both the individuals and teams learned the ropes of production.[17] Later work, including that by the Boston Consulting Group (BCG), extended the application of the learning-curve idea to other costs of the firm as well. Machines could be fine tuned as experience with them increased. Distribution could be improved. Even input use might improve over time.

The typical learning curve can be cast either in terms of costs, as in the left-hand graph in Figure 4.4, or in terms of production efficiency, the right-hand graph. We will work with the cost graph. On the Y-axis, we have plotted the unit costs of the firm, corrected for inflation. On the X-axis, we have the *cumulative* production of the organization in units, over the full life of production. The experience curve represented in Figure 4.4 shows us that the costs of producing this product falls as our experience in making it increases. On the right hand graph, this translates into an improvement in productive efficiency over time. Typically, unit costs de-

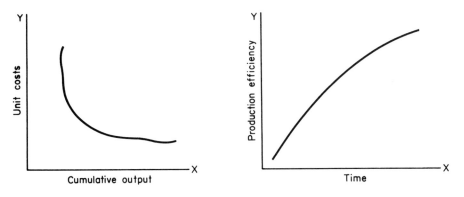

Figure 4.4 A typical learning curve

cline most in the early periods of production and then level off. Indeed, in the standard formulation it is assumed that costs decline by a fixed percentage each time volume doubles. Given this percentage relationship, if we were to convert our values to logarithms, as is frequently done by BCG, for example, we would have a straight line representation for the learning curve.

The magnitude of the decline in unit costs with the cumulative output of the firm differs dramatically among industries. In an 85 percent experience curve, for example, costs drop by 15 percent with each doubling of volume. In a 90 percent curve, cost reductions are less—only 10 percent, with volume doubling. In many industries, the experience curve can be approximated by an exponential equation of the following form:

$$C_i = C_o\left(\frac{P_i}{P_o}\right)^{-a}$$

C_i = cost now, deflated
C_o = cost at earlier period, deflated
P_i = current cumulated units
P_o = earlier cumulated units
a = constant, to be determined from the data

In general, as the capital intensity of an industry rises, so does the slope of the learning curve. Lieberman, for example, found that in the chemical industry on average each doubling of plant scale over time was accompanied by an 11 percent reduction of unit costs.[18] In other words, there was an 89 percent experience curve. Learning-curve effects in this industry substantially overshadowed scale effects, a result that has also been found in a number of other industries, including petrochemicals and electric utilities.

This last observation brings us to the important relationship between economies of scale and learning-curve effects. In practice, when we look at data on an organization it is often hard to distinguish scale and learning effects. If a firm grows over time, which is common, cumulative volume will grow both because of time passing and because of current scale increases. Unit costs may fall, both because current volume increases allow the firm to employ new methods, and because the firm has gained experience with particular methods. Ideally, we would like to distinguish the two, to concentrate on advantages from experience that could not be captured by a large new producer. It is experience effects that create first-mover advantage and not pure scale effects.

The existence of learning-curve effects in a number of industries, particularly capital-intensive ones, is well known. But first-mover advantages do not always come with learning-curve effects. In particular, the effect that such learning curves have on entry depends critically on the private appropriability of learning. If all of the gains of experience stay within the firm, the more cumulative output a firm has, the lower will be its costs, and the greater will be the wedge between that firm and inexperienced rivals, potential or real. In this sense, a market price which might yield profits for the experienced incumbents could simultaneously yield below market returns for potential rivals. In this circumstance, learning curve-effects create a first-mover advantage.

The situation is quite different if the gains from learning are not privately appropriable or, stated another way, if learning is subject to **spillover effects.** If new firms can enter the industry by "jumping" onto the learning curve of older firms, then no entry barrier or asymmetry is created. Everyone learns from the experience of a few. Ghemawat and Spence[19] and Stokey[20] both found that diffusion of new technologies has a profound effect on eroding entry barriers. Similarly, in a study of nine petrochemical industries, Stobaugh found that considerable new entry occurred through technology licensing, which is one way to appropriate the technology of other firms.[21] Similar results come from Lieberman who concluded that, because of diffusion of technology, learning-curve effects play only a small role in deterring entry in the chemical products industries despite the fact that learning is substantial.[22] If spill-overs are large, then even quite substantial learning-curve effects may not deter entry, since no real wedge is driven between the cost structure of the incumbent and that of the new entrant.

> **Learning effects which are appropriable by private firms may create asymmetries among firms and deter entry.**

Part of the competitive process involves an attempt to expropriate some of the learning effects of one's existing and potential rivals. New firms often hire labor away from existing players in the market, particularly in high-technology industries like computers, electronics, and biotechnology in which much of the process-innovation information is embodied in labor. When learning takes place in the equipment-supply part of an industry, these benefits are often available to all comers. Even consultants may at times serve as the conduit through which the learning of one firm spills over into the repository of a second.

As we can see from looking back at the equation on page 72, to calculate learning-curve slopes we require data on costs, both current and historical. For a firm already in an industry, its own costs may be used. But what about firms considering entry? How can they estimate the experience effects of the industry they seek to enter in order to see whether these effects create a first-mover advantage? In practice, learning-curve effects in particular markets are sometimes calculated from observations on pricing patterns. For example, in Figure 4.5, the evolution of the prices of integrated circuits has been traced, yielding a decline of about 28 percent with capacity doubling.

Unfortunately, while it is convenient to look at prices to determine experience effects, it is not always helpful. In particular, as we observed earlier, as an industry matures and entry increases, we see pressure on

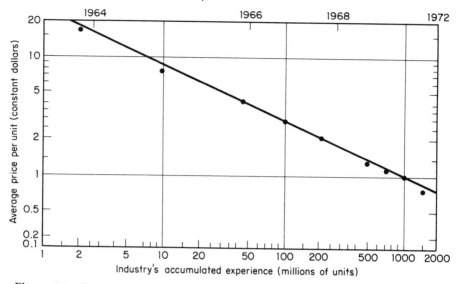

Figure 4.5 Learning curve in the microelectronics industry. *Source:* R. Noyes, "Microelectronics," *Scientific American,* September, 1977.

profit margins. The declines observed in price over time reflect both cost decreases and a softening of profit margins. Typically, these price patterns overestimate true experience effects.

We see then that experience curves are often difficult to measure. Nevertheless, where such effects are large and appropriable, they can serve as a first-mover cost advantage.

Pioneering-brand Advantages

In the discussion of barriers to entry, we have thus far focused heavily on the cost side of the equation. But as those involved in the marketing side of an organization can attest, there are often large advantages to being first in the market coming from the demand side as well.

As in the case of all of the barriers to entry thus far discussed, the efficacy of a brand identity barrier depends heavily on the industry. Long-lived advantages from being a pioneering brand appear to exist in the prescription drug industry,[23] the cigarette industry,[24] and the mainframe computer industry.[25] In examining IBM's position in the market for central processing units, one observer remarked that "most customers will not take the risk of leaving IBM for less than a 30 percent improvement."[26] This brand loyalty has made it quite difficult even for large, well-established firms like Hitachi to compete in the mainframe market. Notice this observer's emphasis on *risk,* an emphasis we will turn to shortly.

In some other markets, on the other hand, generic brands and johnny-come-lately's seem to do quite well. In the personal computer market, for example, established firms have had considerably more pressure from newcomers and customers seem quite receptive to new producers. Compaq, which entered the market for personal computers only in 1982, by 1992 was viewed as one of the two industry giants, with revenues over $3 billion. Sun Microsystems, the producer of computer work stations, has had a similarly meteoric rise in the few years since its birth, so that by 1992 it dominated the low- and mid-range work station market. Currently, both Compaq and Sun are being challenged by new companies like Dell and Steven Job's new company, Next, Inc. Indeed, in some markets, like high-end audio equipment, new products may have an edge.

Why should pioneering brands ever have an advantage over new products? Why should customers prefer old products to new? The answers to these questions seem to hinge on the problems of uncertainty and risk. For a number of products, we only see how good or bad they are only after we purchase and use them. Nelson has referred to this class of goods as **experience goods.** In contrast, some products can be judged fairly accurately through a simple inspection. These goods are known as **search goods,** since we judge them by search.[27] Tuna fish is an example of an experience good; roses might be considered to be search goods. New product success differs depending on whether the product is a search or experience good.

In the case of experience goods, consumers take a chance when they make a purchase. It is not clear by simple inspection whether a product is of high or low quality. Sometimes, when they make a "wrong" purchase, consumers simply lose their purchase price. In other cases—for example, medical products—losses from a bad purchase may be more substantial, even fatal. The problem faced by a potential entrant in an experience good market is to convince consumers to take a chance on a new product, when they already know the quality of existing goods in the market.[28] Remember here most customers' reluctance in the case of IBM to risk a switch to a second vender. Since most people do not like to take risks, convincing them to experiment may be difficult. In cases in which the losses from mistakes are large—mainframe computers and prescription drugs—and the existing satisfaction levels of consumers are already high, it may be quite difficult to convince consumers to take a chance. In some sense, the fact that there is already a tried-and-true product in the market reduces the willingness of consumers to experiment on a new product. However, in other markets, like the one for new restaurants, experimentation carries with it fewer costs.[29] It is no accident that the rate of new entry into the restaurant market is quite high, while the entry into the prescription drug industry is much lower, despite the fact that both markets provide experience goods.

What are the characteristics of industries in which pioneering brands have an advantage over incumbents? First, products should be experience goods, goods about which consumers are uncertain before purchase. Second, pioneering advantages are larger if the potential costs of making a product mistake are large. Finally, high levels of satisfaction with the existing product discourage experimentation. Under these conditions, product experimentation carries with it high transactions costs that protect existing brands.

Pioneering brands may have a first mover-advantage when product uncertainty is high and mistakes costly.

Of course, even if pioneering brands have an advantage in a market, this is not to say that entry is impossible. Many entry strategies, in fact, bear witness to the advantages of pioneering brands. New products offer free samples to encourage experimentation or at least introductory price offers. Endorsements by worthy figures are similar attempts to overcome the reluctance to try a new product. Government certification may at times reduce pioneering-brand advantages by providing quality assurances to customers. But in each of these cases, overcoming the pioneering-brand barrier requires the expenditure of resources. Thus, in each of these cases, the payoff anticipated by the firm from a successful entry will be lower if each of these structural elements had not been operative.

Increasing the Costs of Exit to Reduce Entry

We return now to the decision-tree analysis (Figure 4.1) and examine the exit branch on the tree. Every firm considering entry into an industry must simultaneously consider the costs of exiting that industry.[30] For small businesses, probabilities of exit are extremely high. In 1985, for example, one-half as many small businesses failed as started.[31] In the early 1990s, with the recession, failure rates increased. Mortality rates for larger concerns are lower, but examples of aborted entries into attractive markets by large firms abound. Johnson & Johnson lost many millions in an attempt to enter the disposable-diaper industry. Scott Paper entered and failed in the same industry as, more recently, did Weyerhauser and Unicharm, a Japanese company. General Electric finally abandoned its attempts to move into computers, after a substantial investment in a joint venture with Honeywell. Xerox also abandoned its efforts in this market, while numerous other new smaller entrants succeeded during the same period. Eastman Kodak was forced to leave the instant-camera market, though here the judicial system played a role as well as the market place.

Since each entry carries with it some probability of failure, the costs of that failure are clearly important for the initial entry decision. In thinking about entering a new business in which profits appear to be handsome, the organization has many incentives to proceed. In fact, one might argue that the main factor holding the firm back is the risk of failure with its attendant costs. Indeed, recent research maintains that in the absence of exit costs, excess profits will be very difficult to maintain. Should a profit-making opportunity appear, firms will enter quickly, earn temporary, but handsome profits, and then leave when the environment becomes less favorable. This possibility has come to be known as **hit-and-run entry,** and in some industries it may hold profits down very effectively. It is only exit costs that discourage firms from plunging into what appear to be high-profit industries.[32]

High exit costs discourage entry into an industry.

In the airline industry, for example, the threat of entry by a potential entrant with a price-cutting regulation has been found to have a substantial effect in holding air fares down.[33] Exit costs, then, can be an extremely high barrier to entry. But what factors are associated with high exit costs?

The primary determinant of high exit costs seems to be the extent and specificity of the capital required. If entry requires a firm to invest a large amount of capital, which is difficult to recover should exit occur, exit barriers are high.

It is important to remember that it is simply not how much capital is involved in the enterprise, but how easy it is to recover the capital invested. If capital can easily be leased or if there is a second-hand market for it, exit is likely to be relatively easy. Similarly, if capital is of a fairly general sort and can be shifted to other markets, exit is also easier. Just as highly specific assets encourage firms to fight harder to protect the markets in which they use those assets, they also discourage firms from investing in those markets in the first place. A few examples will prove helpful.

In the airline industry, capital requirements are high. But one major component of this capital is the airplanes used, and this capital, while substantial, is extremely mobile. In fact, Alfred Kahn, the head of the Civil Aeronautics Board during the period of airline deregulation, once characterized airplane costs as "marginal costs with wings." If the market between New Haven and Washington D.C. dries up, the planes can be moved to the New Haven–New York route. Other components of capital used in the airline industry, however, are less transferable. Informational costs in marketing are route specific, for example, as is control over gates and landing slots. Thus the airline industry is an intermediate case.[34] Entry and exit in the submarkets of the airline industry are only partially restricted and help to hold down profits in routes, even if they are served by relatively few carriers.[35] The possibility of some exit and entry keeps profits down, even if actual entry is small.

We can contrast this example with that of the Alaskan oil pipeline. The Alaskan pipeline carries oil from the ice-bound north of Alaska to the all-weather port of Valdez. The pipeline was built at a cost in 1977 of $10 billion, a hefty chunk of sunk capital. The pipeline is extremely task specific: it is large as pipelines go, with a diameter of 48 inches; and its design requirements included the ability to withstand Arctic winters. Moving the pipeline to another location or changing its use radically is extremely hard to imagine.[36] This is clearly a case in which exit costs are formidable, and entry is thus unlikely. In this instance, the pipeline has been regulated in part in recognition of the likelihood of there being excess profits earned in the industry.

Exit costs are largely determined by the irreversibility of capital investments in the industry.

In recent years, some economists have come to the view that freedom of exit is the crucial ingredient in determining the smooth working of a market or the absence of above-market returns.[37] It has certainly become clear that the performance of an industry depends on not only current structure but the dynamics of entry conditions.[38]

Summary

We began this chapter by looking at an entry decision and using this decision to observe the power of the entry force when profit opportunities appear. Three sets of factors impede such entry and prolong the period over which excess returns can be earned by firms in the industry. These factors are summarized in Table 4.3 below.

Planning to enter a new market is accompanied with much uncertainty, which dissuades some from entering markets. Occasionally, uncertainty can create a protective veil for organizations already inside the market. Within this uncertain decision-making mode, some factors influence an entrant's expectations concerning the likely price path in the industry, while others influence the entrant's expectations of its payoffs to a successful entry even if prices remained high. Finally, and in some minds most important, entrants face exit costs. Given the uncertainty of the decision-making process, these exit costs become very important.

To the extent that these factors are in strong evidence in a particular

Table 4.3   Impediments to entry

---

1. *Expectations of falling prices*
   Specific assets
   High MES / market
   Excess capacity
   Aggressive reputation of incumbents

2. *Large incumbent advantages*
   Precommitment contracts
   Licenses and patents
   Learning-curve effects
   Pioneering-brand advantages

3. *Substantial exit costs*

---

industry, incumbent firms on average will find themselves in favorable earning positions over a reasonably long period of time. In industries that are protected by one or another of these factors, strategic planning can occur in a less-threatened environment. Of course, even in hostile environments, some organizations may thrive at the expense of others. But in protected arenas, strategy is directed within the industry and less concerned with threats from without. In the many markets in which entry is easy, recognizing that ease of entry in the planning process can greatly improve the ability of organizations to adapt once that entry occurs. Going through an analysis of the entry issues summarized in Table 4.3 will help an organization plan its future.

5

Groups Within Industries

So far, we have focused on the industry as our unit of observation. We have sketched the forces that tend to lead to an equalization of risk-adjusted rates of return across industries, as well as the forces that impede this equalization process. In this analysis, we have considered homogeneous industries—industries comprised of firms that are more or less the same. In Chapter 5, we begin to focus on differences that sometimes exist among firms in an industry and on how these differences affect the competitive dynamic.

The Principle of Strategic Groups

In consumer goods industries, we often find brand-name firms operating side by side with firms producing unadvertised goods or so-called private label goods. Clorox produces household bleach, as do tens of other companies indistinguishable one from another. In producer goods industries, such as semiconductors, firms producing entirely for another organization in the same corporation (known as **captive production**) coexist with firms producing strictly for the open market (known as **merchant firms**). In some markets, like computers, highly innovative firms compete against firms that have no R&D group at all. In some sense, the firms in question are "in" the same industry: Their goods seem to be similar, and they serve more or less the same consumers. But it turns out that some of the differences in the ways groups of firms in an industry operate play a substantial role in the industry dynamics. In these cases, we will find the strategic group structure of the industry of use in understanding the sources of profitability.[1]

> Strategic groups are defined as clusters of firms within an industry that have common specific assets and thus follow common strategies in setting key decision variables.

A **strategic group** is part of the substructure of an industry that may play a role in understanding performance differences among firms. One group of firms in an industry may exhibit high advertising-to-sales ratios, extensive marketing efforts, careful attention to service, and wide brand ranges. Other groups of firms in the same industry may follow a quite different strategy, focusing perhaps on volume production of a single brand. Hitachi, the diversified Japanese electronics giant, is a very different competitor in the mainframe computer industry than is Amdahl, a small single-product American firm in the same industry. Veragon, a small western producer of generic disposable diapers, looks very different from the market leader Procter & Gamble. Thus our first observation is that large differences in operations may exist within an industry.

At times, different strategic groups may follow common strategies in situations in which their differences in assets and structure play no operational role. Amdahl and Hitachi have many similarities in their operating strategies, as they compete against IBM. In other situations, structural differences among groups become more important and strategies diverge. Veragon and Procter & Gamble compete very differently in the disposable-diaper market, with Veragon focusing on price and Procter & Gamble on marketing and research. Not only may groups in the same industry have different strategies, they seem to be differentially protected from the market, in part because of these differences in their assets and strategies. Brand bleaches like Clorox, for example, may have **pioneering-brand advantages** not shared by generic producers. Captive semiconductor producers, like Hitachi, may have **learning-curve advantages** and co-ordination advantages not fully shared by merchant firms. As a corollary of this, groups may react very differently to changes impinging on the environment. Foreign competition may hurt one group of firms and not another. Tariff barriers may protect only one group in the industry. Since strategic planning is a way of reacting to and helping to induce change, the differential sensitivity of strategic groups to changes in the environment is especially important.

In terms of analysis, the strategic group is a middle ground between the industry and the firm. In some industries, the group structure is obvious and very important. In other industries, some differences in strategies among firms seem to exist, but they play little permanent role in the evolution of the industry. We will develop the discussion of strategic groups by looking at two different industries and tracing the strategic group structure within each. We will then explore some of the consequences of segmenting industries in this way, by moving back and forth between our two sample industries.

The Steel Industry: A First Example

The steel industry is one of the major "smokestack" or basic industries in the United States. In its early years, the steel industry was vitally connected with U.S. industrial development. Recently it has found itself threatened by foreign competition and the focus of considerable regulations, some of which have helped the industry and others of which have resulted in losses. From the perspective of group structures, steel is a fascinating industry.

The six largest firms in the steel industry—USX, LTV, Bethlehem, Armco, National, and Inland—account for more than one-half of the U.S. steel production, with most of the rest being produced currently by minimills. If we had looked at these firms in the mid-1950s and early 1960s, these firms would have appeared on the surface to be quite similar to one another, except for differences in their relative size. All were principally one-product firms; all were integrated producers; all were investing fairly heavily in steel; pricing consensus was strong. Indeed, the industry was often cited as a prime example of a homogeneous product oligopoly, and levels of cooperation among steel firms were seen as quite high. Consider this 1970 description of the steel industry: "Price leadership is a pervasive characteristic of the steel industry. Typically, U.S. Steel sets the pace and the other companies follow in lockstep."[2]

But even in the early 1960s, the environment facing steel firms began to change. Foreign competition, first from Japan and later from firms in the less developed and in the newly industrialized countries, increased dramatically. By 1984, imports had increased to more than 25 percent of United States consumption, and in the years since then we have seen a continual trade battle between U.S. and foreign steel makers. Competition from substitute materials—principally plastics and aluminum—cut demand in the market, and minimills—small scale operations which use electric furnaces to convert scrap to steel—began to emerge as viable competitors in many product lines. Indeed, by 1992, in some areas of production like wide flange beams, minimills had captured the entire market. In the face of the resulting decline in demand and increase in competition, the major firms in the steel industry adopted new strategies.

A change in the environment can help to precipitate a major strategic change among firms in the industry.

When confronted with dramatic changes in their environment, firms can respond with changes in strategy in any of a number of areas: capacity, product mix, organizational structure, R&D, marketing, pricing, and so on. The steel industry in the 1970s focused on capacity and product mix strategies. The basic decision facing steel firms in this increasingly difficult environment of the mid-1960s was to invest further in new productive capacity in the steel industry or to put their capital into other industries.

Despite the capacity rationalization that was occurring in the industry, significant investment opportunities were still available to it. Between 1955 and 1965, two major process innovations, the basic oxygen furnace and the continuous caster, became available. The basic oxygen furnace was a method developed in Europe in the post-war period of producing raw steel more efficiently. The continuous caster allowed firms to produce steel forms more effectively by directly molding hot steel. Both innovations promised substantial cost reductions in production; both also required significant capital investment of an irreversible sort. On the other hand, steel firms could decide not to invest in the new processes, but to send capital into other industries. Considerable cash was still coming out of the industry and could be used to start operations elsewhere. Organizations faced a major strategic choice, one with implications for actions throughout the operating units.

As we look at the major steel firms today, we find that to a large extent they have taken different paths along this investment route. As a result, by 1980, steel firms were structurally quite different from one another, even to a casual observer. Group structure had evolved in the industry as a result of challenges posed by the environment. Figure 5.1 depicts a **strategic map** of the steel industry as it looked in 1960 with arrows to indicate how it looks today. The relative size of each firm in the industry is noted by the diameter of each circle. The central strategic distinction among the current major firms in the domestic steel industry is in the extent to which they are currently investing in steel versus other enterprises—that is, their level of diversification. Two of the firms, LTV and Inland, have been pursuing quite aggressive steel investment policies. LTV, for example, merged with Republic during this period to move into the number two position in the industry.[3] In 1992, despite the fact that it had spent the last years in bankruptcy, LTV still had aggressive plans to increase its steel capacity by more than 10 percent. Other firms, like Armco, have curtailed their steel investment considerably. Firms that sent capital out of the industry are currently saddled with old equipment in their steel divisions. As of 1980, Armco had a larger portion of its capacity in open hearth (an obsolete technique) than any of the other firms in our sample.[4] USX, another exporter of resources from the steel division, has also lost ground relative to its rivals in modern equipment.

A similar story can be told about these firms' speed of adoption of the continuous caster, the second major innovation during the 1960s and 1970s. Between 1980 and 1990, the share of United States production produced by continuous caster increased from 15 percent to 67 percent. But firms varied considerably on how fast they converted. USX and Armco, during this period, lagged behind the heavily steel investors like LTV and Inland in terms of percent of capacity in continuous casting. This lag was a natural consequence of their export of capital from the steel group, particularly in the early 1980s. Moreover, the differences among firms in the quality and age of their production capacity appears to be growing over time. Notice in Figure 5.1, the distance among firms is larger today than it was in 1960; groups are fleeing to opposite ends of the strategic map. Strategic differences among firms' capital equipment today are considerably larger than the historical differences among firms. Such investment

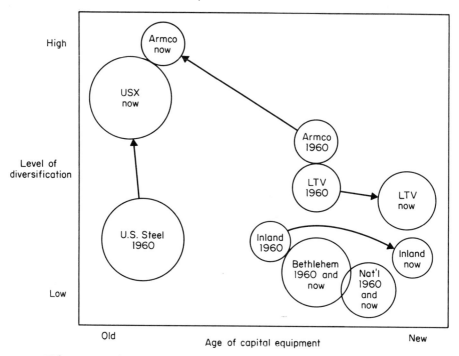

Figure 5.1   The steel industry: a strategic map for 1960 and today

differences translate into differences in the extent of specific assets or the exit barriers faced by the various firms. And, as we will see later, these differences affect the opportunities available to these firms and the threats that confront them.

What are the firms doing that are not investing in steel capital? A cursory look at the investment data suggests that they are heavily investing elsewhere. In our strategic map, some of the firms are rapidly moving up in the vertical axis. USX and Armco have both realigned their investments outside the industry. USX perhaps has been most notable in its oil investments (the Marathon acquisition). Prior to 1965, none of the major steel firms were diversified to any great extent. Today, the U.S. steel industry is headed by a firm, USX, that has dropped the word *steel* from its name! This change, too, alters the perspective and opportunities of the different players in the market.

There is some evidence that the patterns revealed in the data are the result of deliberate articulated firm strategies. In particular, the different firm strategies concerning diversification revealed by the 1970s data were set forth in annual reports and described by the trade press in the late 1960s. Republic, currently part of LTV and one of the single-product firms that has not aggressively pursued other investments, commented in 1968 that the firm was already very well diversified: "We're into iron ore. We're into coal. We have no immediate plans for any acquisition."[5] Indeed Republic later increased its commitment to steel by merging with LTV. Similarly, Inland argued: "We have high confidence in the steel business. . . . We have considered various forms of diversification and we haven't regarded any of them as attractive."[6]

On the other hand, USX in 1967 reported that it was "vigorously pursuing profit opportunities in the growing markets for ores, limestone, coal, coke, chemicals, plastics, fertilizers, cements."[7] By the early 1970s USX was even stronger. "We could conceivably get to the point where steel would be a minor instead of a major segment of our business."[8] Similarly, Armco asserted, "We're going to become a supplier of basic materials. . . . [Armco's Chairman] has persuaded the board to let him reshape Armco's top management in a way that would increase flexibility and make major diversification more feasible."[9]

In the steel industry, significant differences among current players, particularly in the level of diversification, affect in an important way the dynamics of that industry. But before we turn to that discussion, let us look at the pattern of strategic groups in a second, quite different industry, relief and development. Here the idea of strategic groups developed in the context of large industrial enterprises proves useful in the world of small nonprofits.

Relief and Development Agencies: A Second Example

In 1984–85, when the American public began to realize the extent of the mid-African drought and famine, a number of agents were in a position to help. In the United States, foundations, corporations and the government all contribute to international aid and were thus all potential agents of relief. Since World War II, however, the most significant group of organizations involved in international relief and development has been the private voluntary organizations (PVOs).[10] PVOs are nongovernmental, nonprofit organizations involved in voluntary foreign services. In 1992, there were over 180 of these organizations registered with the U.S. government, with revenues in excess of $2.5 billion, a rather sizeable industry.

Many differences exist among organizations in the relief and development market, but three appear to be most important in understanding industry dynamics. First, the extent to which an organization attacks the poverty problem by the use of relief versus development is critical. Relief aid focuses on the effects of underdevelopment through the supply of basic goods such as food and medicine. Development aid attempts to attack the structural *causes* of underdevelopment. The distinction is expressed by two slogans common in the industry. Development proponents say, "Give a man a fish, he can eat for a day. Teach him to fish and he can eat for a lifetime." Relief proponents say, "People don't eat in the long run. They eat everyday." Among professionals the debate concerning the use of short- and long-term aid has been a heated one.

Catholic Relief Services (CRS), one of the largest PVOs, with a budget of more than $500 million, does a considerable amount of relief, along with its development efforts. For example, in a recent annual report, CRS stated "quick reaction to emergencies has been our hallmark since our founding." CARE, another well-known agency, devotes even a larger portion of its resources to relief efforts. On the other hand, Oxfam, a much smaller organization, has as its foremost explicit goal "long term empowering development." Relief efforts are viewed by Oxfam as a second best alternative, and one that fosters dependency.

The second important distinction among the PVOs is whether they are primarily engaged in *field administration or grant giving.* Organizations involved in field administration typically have a relatively large labor force, often in part indigenous, and are themselves engaged in running the development efforts. CARE and UNICEF are both heavily involved in field administration. Other organizations focus more of their effort in giving grants to groups, usually indigenous, as a way of initiating development. Oxfam and Church World Service both fall into this category. All of the grant-giving institutions are small organizations; field administration is carried out by both small and large organizations.

The third and final substantial distinction among relief agencies involves the *source of funding.*[11] PVOs grew in stature after World II at least in part because they were perceived by recipient countries to be less political than government agencies. Food for Peace was the primary governmental precursor to current relief efforts, and strong links still exist between many PVOs and the government. From a strategic perspective, a central issue facing PVO is how heavily it should rely on government funding. Again, within the industry different strategies have prevailed. CARE is almost entirely government supported; Oxfam U.S. refuses government aid, although Oxfam U.K. receives considerable government support.

Figure 5.2 places the leading organizations in the relief and development industry on a strategic map that visually highlights the three distinctions among them.[12] Looking at the map, we can see that CRS is a large organization, using field administration, with moderate government aid, and an intermediate relief/development focus. Church World Service is a much smaller organization, pursuing relief efforts, through grant-giving, and accepting little government aid.

Just as we observed substantial differences among groups of steel firms, so too we see group structure in the relief industry. In the steel industry, group structure appeared relatively recently, precipitated by industry adversity. In steel, group structure was the result of different financial bets placed by players in the steel game; in the relief industry, ideological differences played a role in strategic grouping. In the next section of this chapter, we will explore further the *causes* of the emergence of this group structure in the two industries.

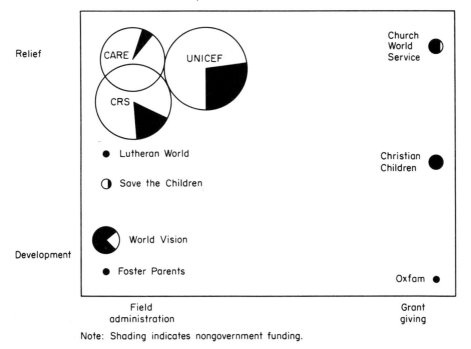

Relief

Development

Field
administration

Grant
giving

Note: Shading indicates nongovernment funding.

Figure 5.2 A strategic map of relief and development agencies

Causes of Strategic Differences among Organizations

We have now seen two quite different industries in which there appear to be substantial differences in groups of firms. What causes those differences among firms in the same industry?

To answer, let us return for a moment to our discussion of an industry in its early stages. In a new industry considerable uncertainty faces early entrants. Consumer preferences are perhaps not even well understood by consumers themselves. Experimentation with various production models is also taking place. In this uncertain environment, different industry participants make investments based on their assessments of the trends in the industry. One set of firms, deciding that consumers value variety, may develop a wide range of branded products. A second set of firms, emphasizing scale economies, may focus on high-volume production of a narrow line.

The investments made in an industry's early period create a set of strategic assets for firms that conditions their later choices.

Of course, some firms will make investment choices that do not survive in the environment. But in some industries, several different ways of doing business can exist side by side, even over long periods of time.

Thus group differences born of uncertainty in an early period in an industry's life can persist as the industry matures.

It is not only in the early stages of an industry's evolution that uncertainty is large. Any major environmental change will perturb organizational routines and create new possibilities for strategic groups to form. Moreover, in some environments demand fluctuations are a natural way of life. In these industries—like housing, for example—fluctuating demand creates rewards for flexibility and may create opportunities for small innovative, relatively uncapitalized firms to compete with larger scale operations. Thus demand fluctuation may create and sustain strategic groups.[13] Of course, only some of the strategic groups created will survive. Other firm differences will be weeded out by the environment. We will discuss the stability of strategic groups below. But first let us look at the causes of strategic group differences in our two rather different sample industries.

As of 1960 or so, the steel industry did not appear to have a very well-defined group structure. If we look back at Figure 5.1, we will see that the firms in 1960 were fairly similar in structure. Large adverse changes since that period gave rise to strategic groups, as steel firms undertook different investment strategies when industry decline set in. Differences in strategies in the 1980s do not seem to have been entirely serendipitous; rather firms seem to have placed their bets in terms of steel versus other investments because of the structural differences among firms found in the 1960s and 1970s. These differences occurred both on the hard side—in production—and on the softer management side. Differences that appeared rather modest and even inconsequential in the easy-going pre-1960 environment, took on more significance as the pressures in the industry grew.

Industry adversity can lead to strategic investments that accentuate differences among industry participants.

In the steel industry, the physical capital used to produce raw carbon steel is not in any practical sense adaptable to the production of any other product. Moreover, installation costs are large, so the capital is truly fixed. Capital costs are both specific and irreversible and thus play an enormous role in the industry. Even in the 1970s differences existed in the composition of the capital stock owned by the six firms being considered. In 1970, only 28 percent of USX's hearth capacity had been built since 1957. On the other extreme, 81 percent of National Steel's capacity had been built since 1957. These differences stemmed in part from the different entry dates of the steel firms. As a result, some firms owned primarily modern capital that had low operating costs; other firms had much older capital stock. Thus the potential profitability of the various firms in the steel industry varied somewhat even before the environment changed. As a result, firms' reactions to decline varied. And these reactions accentuated the initial difference.

In 1960, most of the large steel firms were functionally organized. Marketing was grouped in one area, research in a second, and so on. Product lines were not a structural focus. A functional structure makes diversification more difficult, as we will discuss further in Chapter 10. And as we have indicated, only three of the major steel firms were diversified in this early period: Armco, USX, and National. The multidivisional structure of Armco and USX reflected early interest in a broad product line and later helped them to engage in wide diversification—which in turn encouraged further organizational change. If we follow Chandler's terminology, strategy was affected by prior structure, which then further influenced strategy in a kind of circular dance.[14]

Armco and USX are similarly distinctive in the other characteristics of their managements. In both firms, the majority of their boards were from outside the firm and the industry, even in the early period. This is true of none of the other firms in our sample. Bethlehem Steel, in particular, avoided the use of outside directors until 1965, despite trends in this direction both inside and outside the steel industry. Thus board composition may have encouraged or discouraged an outward-looking strategic focus in several of the steel firms. It is interesting to note that Bethlehem Steel was the last of the major steel firms to form a joint venture with a Japanese steel firm, waiting until 1992 to join with NKK in a project to produce galvanized steel. Here, too, USX was early in allying with the Japanese and thus looking outside traditional industry boundaries.

Finally, one can look at the geographic scope and product mix of a firm as an indication of its ability and willingness to broaden its marketing base. USX and Armco have historically had broad product mixes within steel. Moreover, both firms, while heavily concentrated in steel, had made efforts quite early to broaden their bases. USX had very small, but viable, operations in chemicals, cement, and housing. Armco had a thriving international division. Similarly, the geographic scope of both firms was wide relative to the industry: Armco and USX have more plants than any other steel firms. This fact is particularly striking in the case of Armco, since it is only a medium-sized firm. Inland, Kaiser, and National stand out on the other extreme.

Thus we have seen that history seems to have played a role in directing the investment of the steel industry in its recent decline. Prior commitments both to physical capital and to organizational capital created firm differences. We see in this example that an understanding of a firm's current strategic decisions requires a look backward. The U.S. steel industry evolved under conditions of relative plenty. The environment was favorable and allowed a variety of management and production styles to coexist. When the environment became more hostile, firms' adaptations were conditioned by the particular kinds of capital they had developed in this earlier more favorable climate. Under these conditions, earlier rather modest differences among firms were accentuated by incremental strategic choices.

An interesting second example of the role of history in determining current strategy is provided by the global operation of the auto industry. Recent research in the British auto market finds that most entry from foreign firms has occurred in market segments stressed by those firms at home. Thus G.M. first entered the British market in the large-car segment, while Honda began its British production in the small-car segment. For these firms, entry strategy was clearly affected by domestic experience.[15] We see again the very important role of history in understanding present strategy. The tendency for global strategy to be heavily conditioned by domestic experience is an example of the importance of the **strategic predisposition** of an organization.[16]

What have been the root causes of the strategic differences we currently observe in the relief industry?

Ideology plays a substantial role in group structure in the relief industry. Mintzberg defines an organizational ideology as a "system of beliefs about the organization, shared by its members, that distinguishes it from other organizations."[17] Virtually all organizations have some ideology that conditions the kinds of strategic choices it can make. Ideology thus forms another of the strategic predispositions of an organization, inclining it to some actions over others.[18] But for some organizations, which Mintzberg describes as *missionary organizations*, ideology plays a very central role.[19] Oxfam, U.S., for example, is a highly "ideological" agency. Its liberal political philosophy makes it unwilling to accept government aid and simultaneously predisposes it in favor of development efforts over relief. Catholic Relief Services has a strongly ideological foundation, but a Roman Catholic one. It is a much more conservative organization than Oxfam, U.S. and rather more eclectic in its relief versus development stance.

Ideology can be an important strategic asset for an organization.[20] The case of Catholic Relief Services is a good one in this respect. As a result of its religious connection, CRS has a natural donor base not concerned about accepting government contributions. The Catholic tie also provides CRS with a strong international network, perhaps stronger than most of the other relief agencies. This has helped CRS maintain its focus on development, rather than grant-giving.

The role of ideology in focusing an organization is easily seen in the humanitarian world of relief. But it plays a vital role in determining strategic options in many for-profit firms as well. Like prior capital investment, ideology forms one of the antecedent conditions that helps to sort firms into strategic groups. Polaroid provides an excellent example of the power of ideology in directing the strategic choices of a for-profit firm. Polaroid is an organization with sales of approximately $2 billion, predominantly in the instant-camera market. For many years, Polaroid was run by its founder, Edwin Land, a man described by most as a visionary who imbued the organization with a sense of the technological mission of Polaroid. This vision influenced virtually all of Polaroid's choices and made some options—for instance, producing a high volume, relatively low quality camera—out of the question. Ideology, in this case and in many others, constrained the strategic choice set. Once Land retired, the new Polaroid management began making major changes in both the corporate culture and the product mix. Similar changes often occur when a charismatic founder dies or leaves a company.

The Effect of Strategic Group Membership on Strategic Options of an Organization

How much difference does strategic grouping make in the actual strategy of an organization? We can answer this question with reference to dramatic events in the relief area.

As a result of the widespread attention in 1985 to the famine in Ethiopia, the pool of potential donors to U.S. relief and development agencies expanded enormously and dramatically. Historically, annual growth rates for PVOs had been on the order of 8 percent. In 1985, the donor pools of a number of organizations doubled and tripled. This huge increase in donors was an important opportunity for PVOs. How did the strategic differences in the PVOs outlined earlier influence their abilities to take advantage of these opportunities? This same question might be asked in a for-profit industry when a large, exogenous demand shift occurs. Which players benefit most from the shift?

All organizations react to new opportunities in ways that reflect their goals. Typical for-profit firms usually pursue opportunities insofar as they are expected to be profitable, although, as we will see in Chapter 8, the issue of goals is more complex than this even in the private sector. In the nonprofit sector, given that earnings cannot be redistributed, it is difficult to model the organization as a profit maximizer. We have already indicated the possible role of ideology in relief agencies. Relief agencies often look upon new opportunities as a means to expand their programs. Growth, not profits, appears to be a goal for many relief agencies.[21] How did different groups pursue this goal in their new prosperous environment?

The first distinction we made among the PVOs was their focus on relief versus development. For the most part, professional workers in the field have come to favor integrated development efforts over pure relief efforts. Donors, on the other hand, appear to be heavily influenced by the images of starving children and the promise that their dollars can feed those children. In the case of the Ethiopian famine, the increase in support destined for Ethiopia was enormous. One relatively modest agency indicated that it had received money from 50,000 new contributors in 1985 as a result of the Ethiopian crisis. The ability of an organization to use new donations effectively, however, is highly dependent on its pre-existing service mix. For a variety of reasons, relief agencies found it easier to cope with the increased donor pool than did development agencies.

Funding development efforts is typically a long-term commitment, requiring considerable set-up costs to identify worthy projects and follow through over long periods. Locating credible investment and development projects that needed immediate funding in Ethiopia at the level of the new donations proved to be problematic. And yet the "rules" of donations make it difficult for organizations to set aside donations for future crises, or to divert them to areas in which development projects are more worthy. In mid-1985, for example, Catholic Relief Services was accused of misleading donors and misappropriating Ethiopian relief funds because it spent only $9 million of the $50 million raised for Ethiopia. CRS argued that it had withheld some of the funds to invest in longer term development efforts. But the brouhaha had a damaging effect on potential giving and points out the difficulty of matching resources and capabilities to needs in a crisis. In this instance, CRS's position on the strategic map affected its ability to take advantage of a large environmental change.

In the Ethopian case, the difficulty facing the development-oriented groups was exacerbated by the expected transient nature of the relief volume. The same agency head who reported an increase of 50,000 new contributors in response to Ethiopia, later found that only 20 percent of those new contributors continued to donate in subsequent years. Yet development efforts often require funding over a substantial period of time. Efforts in some projects can be front-loaded, but flexibility is limited. Finally, the Ethiopian famine was an emergency situation requiring large doses of near-term relief. Organizations committed primarily to development recognized the need for an immediate relief effort, but sometimes found it hard to shift resources toward relief. In other words, ideology sometimes got in the way of strategic responsiveness. (Many have argued that Land's vision had similar effects in the 1980s in the Polaroid organization.) Administering relief in large doses requires considerable coordination and control as well as excellent transportation facilities. Organizations experienced in relief efforts could shift apparatus from other areas to Ethiopia and thus were better able to deal with the sudden inflow of donations. Development-oriented organizations lacked the infrastructure to administer relief in large doses. Thus it appears that, in the context of country-specific increases in donations, relief-oriented groups may be able to respond more quickly than development-oriented groups.

How does the distinction between field administration and grants influence an organization's responsiveness to large unexpected increases in targeted receipts? The advantages here are less clear than they were in the relief/development dichotomy. In general, organizations with large field staffs often find it possible to shift that staff among countries in response to donor patterns. Finding viable grant recipients in an area, particularly when other agencies are similarly situated, may be more difficult. Oxfam, for example, which almost exclusively uses grants rather than its own project management, has on a number of occasions been unable to spend all the money allocated to a particular region due to a shortage of good projects. Fielding one's own good projects may in fact be easier.

Finally, we noted the distinction among organizations as to funding sources. Here the differences in the ability to exploit the new donor sources appear to be quite prominent. Agencies that have historically relied heavily on the government for funding appear to have been less able to benefit from the new private philanthropic increases. In the Ethiopian crisis, for example, Oxfam, which historically and by design has been completely privately funded, increased its revenues almost threefold. CARE, which is fairly heavily government funded, had a much more modest increase of approximately 30 percent. In this market, organizations appear to have developed a set of abilities and assets, which are specific to either private or public fund raising, and changing form does not appear to be easy, at least in the short run.

> **Strategic groups operating within the same industry may have quite different abilities to take advantage of changes in the environment. As a result, the relative profitability of particular strategic groups may change over time.**

Demand changes, regulatory changes, technological changes all may affect the relative position of groups within an industry, the market shares of those groups and their relative profitability. Some groups will improve their positions, while others will not. We see this pattern clearly in the relief agencies. In the steel industry, different levels of diversification have affected the relative vulnerability of firms to changes in trade policy and the like. This pattern is also revealed in data from other industries in the corporate sector, both domestic and international. In an interesting study of British firms, for instance, Cubbern and Geroski found that firms in nearly a third of the industries studied showed no common industry-wide response to dynamic forces.[22] Strategic groups responded quite differently to common industry events. The payoffs to particular strategic choices can vary considerably across groups. For example, high advertising budgets appear to be most efficacious for leading brands in a market.[23] Winston cigarettes and Coca-Cola earn higher returns from advertising than their rivals. From a strategic perspective, in these industries group identification dominates industry membership.

Barriers to Entry and Barriers to Mobility

In an industry that has fairly well-defined strategic groups, analyzing entry into the industry is more complex than in the homogeneous industries described in Chapters 3 and 4. Entering the bleach industry as a branded product, for example, may carry with it quite different potential exit costs than would entry as a generic. First-mover advantages may also differ, depending on which funding source a relief agency turns to. Learning-curve effects may protect R&D intensive pharmaceutical companies from entry into their industry segment, but play no role in deterring entry in the generic segment.

In some industries, barriers to entry may be specific to the group.

If entry conditions do differ significantly for groups of firms in an in-dustry, we might expect to see differences in the profitability of firms within those groups. Moreover, in looking at forces that push profits toward a common level, we will want to look at movement, or *mobility*, between groups, as well as entry into one or more of the groups. In some sense, in industries with substantial group structure we add a second layer of analysis that looks quite like the industry analysis described in the last few chapters.

We can return now to the efficient-markets idea: Suppose we have a group of firms that is following one strategy, and a second group follow-ing another. For example, one group of auto firms produces in the small-car segment and a second in the large-car segment. At any single point in time, we might well observe that the two groups will be earning dif-ferent risk-adjusted rates of return. This observation is comparable at a more micro level to the observation that two industries are earning differ-ent risk-adjusted rates of return in any given year. In the industry ex-ample, we were interested in whether these differences persisted over time. So, too, in the group case we are concerned with timing. In what way does entry from the outside move profit rates within either of the groups to an economy-wide level? And in what way does mobility *between* groups equalize within-industry returns?

The central distinguishing feature of a strategic group is that its differ-ences consist of differences in strategy, not simply in daily tactics, and that they persist in the face of different profit rates earned by other groups in the same industry.

In the case of relief and development agencies, the central question is: Do we see substantial funding and programmatic differences despite per-sistent disparities in the growth payoffs to these strategies? Similarly, in the steel industry, we want to ask about the robustness of differences in diversification strategies. If we see persistence, we must then ask why it exists. In the industry case, differences in profits are maintained across industries only if there are impediments to free movement. So too in the strategic group area.

Risk-adjusted profit differences will persist among strategic groups only if there are barriers to mobility among those groups.

The evidence suggests that the height of mobility barriers varies con-siderably across industries. The relief industry is one in which mobility barriers appear to be quite high. Ideological differences, in particular, seem to have an enormous impact on the mobility of various agencies. In Land's day, ideology played a similar role for Polaroid. The drug industry provides another example of an industry with quite persistent strategic groups. In this industry, some groups of firms emphasize marketing, including advertising, and others are more production oriented. Bristol-Myers, Smithkline-French, and Pfizer are all members of the first group; Upjohn and Lilly have historically been in the second. For marketing firms, first-mover barriers in the form of pioneering-brand advantages appear to be substantial. For the production-oriented firms, patents and capital investments have been major sources of protection. Moreover, in this industry, the movement among groups has historically been extremely low. Drug firms which began as marketing and advertising leaders have tended to remain so, while nonadvertisers have found it hard to change as well.[24] Among major drug firms tracked over an eight-year period ending in the 1980s, only three—Abbot, Searle, and Smithkline—changed strategic groups.[25] Moreover, the stability in the membership of strategic groups has persisted despite long-lived differences in the profitability of the groups, measured both in terms of average profit rates and the variability of profit rates. Marketing-oriented firms had significantly higher and more stable profit rates than production-oriented firms over long periods of time. Apparently, mobility among groups has not been easy and could not eradicate these differences, nor has entry outside the industry into the marketing group played a substantial role in reducing the profitability of this group. In this industry, differences in specific assets, rather than ideological differences, have influenced mobility. In the steel industry, as well, capital differences have created mobility barriers.

A recent analysis of mobility within the oil-drilling industry finds similarly high stability in strategic groups.[26] In the period 1973–81, of 109 occasions in which firms could change groups, only two changes occurred. This stability, too, existed in the face of substantial profit differences across groups.

A contrast to these examples is provided by the furniture and carpet industries. In these industries, in any given year, we observe some firms who advertise and market heavily and others who do not. However, in both industries, large changes occur over time in the kinds of strategies firms adopt. Firms move advertising and marketing budgets around substantially, in response in part to perceived profit opportunities. Firms advertise heavily relative to rivals in one year, and lightly the next. As one might expect, in these industries profit differences among strategic groups do not persist over time; in some years one strategy works, in another year, another dominates.

Can we explain which industries exhibit persistent cross-group profit differences and which do not? As we have indicated, profit differences persist when barriers to mobility exist. In the case of a group pattern based on marketing differences, the longevity of advertising and marketing efforts is crucial to forming mobility barriers. In industries in which current advertising is important, firms have an easy way to announce themselves and win customers. Barriers to mobility from pioneering brands are likely to be low. Carpet and furniture industries both exhibit very high elasticities of demand with respect to current advertising, and as we noted movement between groups is common.[27] On the other hand, if *past* advertising plays a major role in the industry in creating product demand, mobility barriers will be higher. It is interesting to note that the drug industry is one in which the effects of advertising appear to last a long time.[28] In this case, low advertisers have a lot of "catching up" to do in adopting a high-advertising strategy. At the same time, high advertisers have a large sunk-cost investment in their advertising strategies. Since the drug industry is one in which costs of choosing the "wrong" brand may be substantial, product reputation is often very important.

One expects a similar pattern in groups based on R&D. If the pace of R&D is rapid, and technological gains largely noncumulative, groups based on an R&D advantage are not likely to be stable. Large investments of R&D this year may soon pay off in a single innovation, but they do not affect the firm's *future* innovative opportunities. On the other hand, if R&D is more cumulative in nature, this might possibly form the basis for a first-mover advantage and create a mobility barrier. In this case, R&D payoffs will depend on the current stock of innovations *within* the firm.

In the oil-drilling industry, the cross-group profit differences are attributable to several factors. Customer power varies considerably across groups; segments which serve government and large companies with the ability to vertically integrate are less profitable. Moreover, the equipment needed to supply various market segments differs, and this equipment is very costly. So, in these industries, specific assets create mobility barriers and protect profit differences.[29]

In sum, we see that the existence of large specific assets—physical or organizational—can have a substantial effect on a firm's strategic choices. If, within an industry, firms differ substantially in their portfolio of these assets, they will also differ in their response to environmental change. And this difference will make the study of industry dynamics both more interesting and more complex.

A Return to the Beginning

Suppose we find some substructure in an industry, so that it appears that two groups of firms have quite different strategies for doing business and earn quite different profits as a result. How does this affect the kind of analysis we want to do? Should Oxfam ignore the actions of CARE and CRS as it designs its funding effort? Should USX track Inland or not? Does Forest Labs have any influence on Bristol-Myers? How should General Motors respond to Honda, when both are operating in the British auto industry?

The simple answer is that competition tends to be stronger within a strategic group than across groups. CARE would probably want to track CRS more than it tracks Oxfam, and Bristol-Myers should pay more attention to Warner Lambert than to Forest Labs. In the equilibrium analysis of strategic directions, firms will want to focus most heavily on members of their strategic groups and less on further-flung rivals. But just as firms want to consider the possibilities of entry into the overall industry, firms should also carefully look for any changes in the kinds of mobility barriers protecting them.

Strategic groups are a kind of middle ground between the industry and the individual firm. In some industries, strategic grouping turns out to be a helpful way to think about the opportunities available to firms. In others it is less helpful and one can proceed directly to the firm level which we cover in Part II of this book.

6

Competing in Global Markets

In the discussion so far, we have largely ignored the question of whether firms are competing in a domestic market, against other domestic firms, or in the international market place. Indeed, the frameworks introduced in the last several chapters are equally applicable to domestic and global industries. In both cases, a careful analysis of industry structure is clearly important as a way of understanding profit potential. In some industries, however, we apply our industry structure to what is going on in the domestic market: The rivals we look at are domestically based, as are the buyers, suppliers, substitute producers, and potential new entrants. In other markets, we need to look at what is going on world-wide in order to fully understand operations within any one country. These latter markets are known as **global markets** and form the basis of this chapter.

> **A global market is one in which the economics of operating in a particular market depend not only on what the firm is doing in that market, but on its activities world-wide.**

This chapter will focus on two central questions concerning global industries: Why are some industries global, while others remain domestic? And, how do we explain the national location of various global industries? In 1992, the auto industry would be considered by most to be a global industry, while consumer banking has historically been a domestic industry. What accounts for the difference? In the mid-1950s, the United States dominated the machine tool industry. It had the most advanced technology in the world and was the world's largest exporter. By 1986, the dominant position had shifted to Japan, which controlled one-half of the U.S. market and an even larger share abroad. The semiconductor industry started in the United States, but by 1992, Japan was emerging as the dominant player in this industry as well. How do we explain these locational shifts? Why does Germany dominate the chemical industry, while Denmark is known for its brewing industry? These questions are of concern both from a public policy point of view, as governments struggle to fashion effective industrial policies, and from a managerial point of view, as individual firms and industries learn to anticipate changes in patterns of international competition and locational advantage.

Competition in global markets also brings with it a number of interesting organizational structure questions. While several of these are touched on in this chapter, we will deal more directly with these issues in Chapters 8 and 9.

The Extent of Global Competition

It is apparent to anyone, even in the course of shopping for the goods and services we typically consume in a given week, that the economy has become more integrated in the last several decades. Both goods and capital flows across countries have increased dramatically. Private U.S. investment overseas increased between 1970 and 1988 from $10 billion to over $80 billion. Private foreign investment in the United States, over the same period, increased even more dramatically, from less than $1 billion to over $165 billion. There is hardly a country in the world where one cannot purchase an American soft drink or a German beer. The number of joint ventures between firms in different countries has also skyrocketed. Between 1980 and 1990, over 500 alliances were forged between American and Japanese firms alone. These joint ventures exist in industries as different as steel, semiconductors, computers, and pharmaceuticals. We see joint ventures between NEC and AT&T, Sharp and Intel, British Steel and Avesta of Sweden, General Motors and Toyota, Bethlehem Steel and NKK.

In the longer view, however, the perception that international integration is increasing is, as Krugman has recently pointed out, somewhat misleading.[1] In many ways, the world in the nineteenth century was considerably more international in terms of both capital flows and product flows than is today's economy. In the forty years before World War I, Britain invested a larger fraction of its savings abroad in an average year than Japan has ever invested.[2] Wars and protectionist government policies encouraged domestic production in the period after World War I in a process we are only now emerging from. There have always been strong forces encouraging the globalization of markets and it has largely been government policy that has curtailed that globalization. In this long view of history, there are important lessons for our understanding of the evolution of global industries.

Pressures for Globalization

There are two central reasons that global industries arise: **comparative advantage** and the existence of **economies of scale**. These principles help to explain not only why we see industries which cluster in some areas and serve many, varied markets, but also the location of those clusters.

The theory of comparative advantage forms the basis for most of the classical theories of trade.

The usual formulation of the theory is that, as a result of natural endowments, some areas are relatively more efficient at producing some goods, while others excel in the production of other goods. Under these circumstances, it will be of mutual benefit for countries to specialize along lines of their comparative advantage and then trade.[3] The United States, given its climate and land area, is highly efficient at producing certain agricultural products—wheat, for example. Australia, because of its natural endowments, is a highly efficient miner of uranium. Much of South America abounds in forests and this forms the basis of a comparative advantage in timber and paper supply. Krugman calls this "garden-variety resource driven" specialization, and it clearly forms the basis for a considerable amount of the trade we observe.

When we look at agricultural production and mining, the theory of comparative advantage based on natural endowments is quite persuasive. As an explanation for the location of modern manufacturing, however, it is somewhat less compelling. It is difficult to argue that semiconductor production began in Silicon Valley in the United States or that Detroit dominated U.S. auto production for years because of the area's natural endowments. In explaining these patterns, principles of scale economies and clustering effects seem to have considerably more power. Indeed, Hout, Porter, and Rudden, in their early work on globalization, argued that "potential for global competition is greatest when significant benefits are gained from worldwide volume."[4]

Krugman tells the following, persuasive story of the clustering of economic activities: An industry begins with the setting up of production in one particular area. We will discuss the choice of initial location in the next section; for now, we simply arbitrarily assert a location. If there are strong economies of scale in production, and transportation costs are not high, the producer will benefit from serving a large geographic market from that single location. By doing so, the producer can reduce its average costs of production. Now clustering advantages set in. Because of the location of the initial producer, a labor market will begin to be developed which has certain skills. Other firms that need similar skills will be attracted to the area because of the pooling benefits of shared labor markets. Firms which supply to that industry will also be attracted to the area to reduce the transactions costs of serving that industry. The existence of clusters of firms within the same broad area will also generate technological spill-overs. Indeed, Kobrin finds in an empirical study of globalization that technological intensity is the major determinant of global integration.[5] In industries with very complex technologies, scale economies and technological spill-over effects both favor global firms.

Scale economies and technological interdependencies create advantages to industrial clustering.

The result of economies of scale and industry connectedness will be to create industrial clusters with competitive advantages over firms that locate in other areas. Note that the competitive advantages in this case are *created advantages,* and do not stem from any inherent differences in natural endowments. In some sense, the existence of economies of scale and transactions costs have created a comparative advantage. They have also created global industries in the sense that the costs of serving various national markets will be interdependent. In much the same way, Ohmae describes the way in which firms in a number of industries have created global industries, rather than simply responding to natural endowments.[6]

It is important to note that the picture just painted depends heavily on the existence of economies of scale. Absent such economies, multiple clusters could develop all over, serving markets at each production site. Firms would not need the scale of multiple country markets to achieve low costs. Notice also that clustering will be most likely when transportation costs are low, particularly in cases in which the costs of transporting final goods are low relative to the costs of transporting intermediate goods.[7] Steel remained a domestic industry for many years not only because of protectionist government policy but because of the high costs of transporting steel. And it was improvements in transportation that opened up steel markets to world competition and put pressure on governments to reduce protectionism.

The semiconductor industry provides an excellent example of a global industry created by the joint conditions of scale economies and low transport costs. In this industry, American and Japanese firms produce semiconductors for the world. NEC and Hitachi, the two largest producers of semiconductors, produce their chips in Japan and ship them world-wide. High capital costs, research and development costs, and the complexity of production all suggest that both scale economies and learning-curve advantages are extremely high in this industry. Finally, transportation costs in this industry were extremely low. The entire production of the world's semiconductors in 1986 could be shipped in ten 747 jets.[8] No wonder the market has been a global one almost from its onset.

A contrasting example is provided by the case of white goods (appliances) in the European market.[9] The European market for white goods was originally dominated by the United States. In the 1960s, a number of Italian firms grew up, firms like Zanussi, Indesit, and Borghi. By the 1970s, the Italian firms had 40 percent of the European market, and a process of industry consolidation occurred. Electrolux and Phillips, both grown larger through this process of consolidation, looked to be the dominant global players in Europe. As we examine the European market in the 1990s, however, the trend toward globalization has been thwarted. In most markets, we find national players dominating, and the performance of those national players appears to be considerably better than that of the global firms. In fact, it has been argued that the trend toward globalization that began in the 1960s was frustrated by two features of the market. First, flexible manufacturing reduced the minimum efficient scale. Thus global firms did not gain cost advantages from their large-scale production. Second, increased diversity in national tastes, combined with the fact that retail markets in which appliances were sold are national, led to pressure on the demand side for responsiveness and local ownership over the integration advantages of global firms. In this case, the two forces leading to globalization—scale economies and taste homogenization—were reversed over time, and so too was the trend toward globalization.

If comparative advantage and scale economies encourage globalization, what factors inhibit it? Here we see the role of both economic forces and political forces. On the side of economics, both transportation costs and coordination costs reduce the thrust toward globalization. Perhaps even more important in explaining much of the pattern of local versus global industries is the role of government policy.

High transportation costs in the final product will reduce the extent of globalization.

With high transportation costs, the cost advantages of large-scale production are dwarfed by costs of reaching the final market. The strategy of building only a few plants and using those efficient plants to serve the world market will not be possible under these conditions. It should be noted, however, that while high transportation costs reduce some of the advantages of globalization, they by no means eliminate multinational operation. When transportation costs are high, the typical strategy for a firm wishing to enter new markets is to build multiple plants, sited around the world. The disposable-diaper industry provides a good example here. While there are considerable plant-specific economies of scale in the industry, the high ratio of size to value of the product makes transportation costs quite large. The optimal strategy is thus to locate plants near the point of sales, building smaller plants than would be optimal if shipping were free. Thus Procter & Gamble has not been able to exploit plant scale economies as a way to move itself into a dominant position in the world market, and the fact that it has plants in the United States does not help it compete in the German market. Unicharm and Kao, which dominate the Japanese disposable-diaper market, do not distribute their products at all in the United States. P&G, which sells in many markets including Japan, has historically operated as a multinational in this market and not as a global competitor. Its market share in Japan is principally determined by its production scale and operations in Japan and not by its American operations. But this may change: As research and development and marketing grow in importance in this industry, and, as their products are more easily transported across national boundaries, we may see the industry growing more global and the number of players in the industry may shrink to a few who then dominate the world market.

Coordination costs also play a role in limiting globalization. Moving into world markets requires a new emphasis on communication and control within the firm and the challenge of coordination, while maintaining flexibility and responsiveness, is considerable.[10] Globalization—inasmuch as it tries to capitalize on multinational production and sales—demands integration. But such integration can carry with it costs of lost flexibility in terms of dealing with local differences.[11] The experience of CS Holding, a large, international banking and financial services group based in Switzerland, is quite interesting in this respect. In 1989, CS Holding was put at the head of the large international agglomeration in an attempt to pursue a more global strategy in the banking business. Rainer Gut, the head of CS, while emphasizing the economies associated with global banking also acknowledges some of the difficulties in terms of managing across diverse areas, with diverse customs, regulations, and economies: "With the Swiss banking tradition, you can't conquer the American market or the German market or the Japanese market. . . . We have to blend our people with domestic talent and try to pick up as much of the other culture as we can."[12] The jury is not yet in on whether the advantages of integration will outweigh the costs of losing local flexibility in this industry.

Coordination costs reduce the gains from globalization.

At least some of the coordination costs associated with globalization come from consumer differences across nations. We saw this effect operate in our example of white goods in the European market place. But there is some indication that, at least in some areas, consumer tastes are converging. Ted Levitt, for example, argued that the increased homogenization of consumers across disparate parts of the world has made "the multinational corporation obsolete and the global corporation absolute."[13] Homogenization of customers has reduced the need for local flexibility and made the marketing lessons learned in Germany applicable to serving markets in France. In this way, homogenization increases the payoff to world scale.

Improvements in the technology of communication and coordination have also played a role in stimulating globalization. In the 1970s and 1980s, the technology of wire transfers, satellites, and computers and the emergence of more sophisticated foreign exchange markets have greatly reduced the transactions costs of buying and selling assets in multiple currencies. Capital has thus become more mobile at the same time that customers have become more alike. Both of these factors have reduced some of the inhibiting transactions costs associated with globalization.

Finally, governments have historically played a role in limiting globalization. Krugman provides a striking example of the role of government in a comparison of industrial patterns across states within the United States and across countries in Europe.[14] Within the United States across states, there are relatively modest governmental barriers to trade. There are no tariffs or quotas, there is a single currency, and regulatory differences pertinent to the operation of most industries are modest. In Europe, on the other hand, since World War I, there have been considerable barriers to trade, including tariffs, exchange controls, and large regulatory differences. In this context, Krugman compares the degree of specialization observed between the U.S. Midwest and South, on the one hand, and Germany and Italy on the other. Patterns of comparative advantage are quite comparable in the two instances. Germany and the U.S. Midwest, both have assets which give them an advantage in heavy industrial production. The U.S. South and Italy, on the other hand, have a comparative advantage in light labor-intensive production. In the United States, specialization has proceeded quite far. The South has "globalized" the textile industry completely in terms of the United States, and the Midwest dominates the machinery market as well. In Germany and Italy, some specialization has occurred, but it has been modest. The economic forces were quite similar in these two instances, and the performance differences that we see are evidence of the profound power of the government in limiting globalization. Of course, it is this kind of evidence and the corollary discussion of the efficiency losses from such governmentally induced fragmentation that has fueled the interest in Europe in creating a more cohesive unit.

Government policy often limits the extent of globalization.

Given the oft-times profound influence that government can have in inhibiting globalization, it is useful to ask whether there are any successful strategies available to private firms for loosening up government protectionism. In this respect, the experience of Coca-Cola and Texas Instruments in trying to move into the Japanese market are instructive.[15] Coca-Cola began trying to enter the Japanese soft drink market at the end of World War II. For a number of years, however, the Japanese Ministry of Finance blocked Coca-Cola's entry by denying it foreign exchange permits needed to import key Coke ingredients to Japan. Behind the government's position lay the power of three Japanese breweries, Kirin, Asahi, and Sapporo, firms that marketed a competing line of soft drinks. It was not until 1960 that the government finally issued the necessary permits, just after Coke awarded one of its most potentially profitable bottling franchises to Kirin. In a similar way, Texas Instruments' (TI) attempt to enter the semiconductor industry in Japan was thwarted by Japan's Ministry of International Trade and Industry (MITI) until TI agreed to license its key patents to numerous Japanese competitors. In a current turnaround, Japanese semiconductor firms are hoping to ease current U.S. entry restrictions by establishing joint ventures with American semiconductor firms. In all of these cases, government cooperation in the process of globalization is accomplished through cooperation with industry in the host country.

In sum, we have seen that comparative advantage and scale economies both encourage globalization, while high transportation costs, high coordination costs, and government interference all inhibit globalization. As we look at the world today, we see a push toward even more globalization from at least several of these areas. In many industries, minimum efficient scale is increasing over time; technical progress is typically scale-augmenting. Technological differences and social changes have both reduced coordination costs and probably increased the payoffs to worldwide research and marketing efforts. Finally, the principle of free markets and limiting government protectionism appear to be gaining strength across the world.

While many forces are pushing us toward increased globalization, the principle of comparative advantage may well be drawing us in the other direction. Modern industry is less tied to particular areas for reasons of resource-location than was industry a hundred years ago. Indeed, it could be argued that the free flow of resources has reduced some of the traditional gains to trade. Increasingly, patterns of comparative advantage are created, not only by governments, but more commonly by industry itself in the evolutionary path described by Krugman. This trend has made even more compelling our second question: How do we account for the location of various global industries? We turn now to that question.

The Location of Global Industries

Franko has recently done a quite interesting analysis of the location of headquarters of a number of different global industries during the period 1960 to 1986.[16] He examines fifteen industries: aerospace, autos, banking, chemicals, computers, electrical equipment, food and beverages, iron and steel, nonferrous metals, industrial and farm equipment, paper, petroleum, pharmaceutical, textiles, and tires. In 1960, U.S. firms accounted for over two-thirds of the world business in ten of these fifteen industries. By 1986, U.S. dominance remained in only three of these industries: aerospace, paper, and computers. Most of the slack had been picked up by Japanese firms.

Of course, the Franko data is limited in terms of the industries it samples. There is also a strong bias in the sample to relatively mature industries. It has long been argued that the United States has an advantage early in a product's life cycle and thus, in some sense, the erosion of U.S. market share in Franko's maturing industries is to be expected.[17] Nevertheless, the shift in comparative advantage across nations is striking and we turn now to look more deeply into the sources of change in advantage.

In his recent work, Porter has developed a framework for explaining the location of various industries among nations which he calls the **national diamond.**[18] This diamond is reproduced in Figure 6.1 and we will use it to organize our discussion. Much of the recent work that is more centrally located in the economics discipline, such as that of Krugman, can be described in the context of the Porter diamond.

The central question we ask is: What accounts for the national location of a particular global industry? The answer begins, as does all classical trade theory, with the match between the factor endowments of the country and the needs of the industry. In the diamond this is represented in the far left box. Industries thrive in countries which are either naturally endowed in the factors of production needed by that industry, or are easily able to obtain those factors elsewhere. Important factors of production can include physical resources, like climate and mineral wealth, human resources, including the knowledge and skills of the work force, infrastructure, and capital.

The strongest and most enduring competitive advantages for nations are created by those factors that have the least mobility.

In our earlier chapters, we talked about the role of diffusion and imitation in leveling industry profitability. When an industry is exceptionally profitable, new firms enter unless there are sizeable barriers to such entry. Similar diffusion and imitation occurs in the international market place. German firms copy French firms, Japanese firms imitate successful Amer-

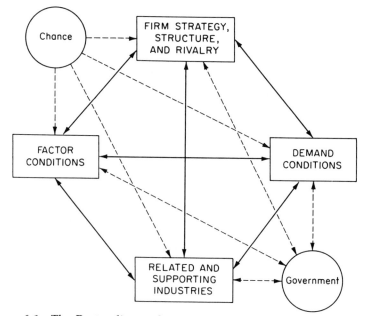

Figure 6.1 The Porter diamond
Source: M. Porter, *The Competitive Advantage of Nations* (New York, 1990).

ican strategies, Korean firms imitate the Japanese. In the last few years, terms like *just-in-time management, quality circles, kanban,* and *keiretsu* have entered management conversations throughout the world. Even governments imitate each other's successful industrial policies. The more difficult is the imitation or mobility of the factor on which a nation's industrial clusters are based, the more long-lived that cluster will be.

We can now look at the various factors of production and ask how mobile each is. At the extreme, we have climate. Unless we have more global warming than anyone expects, Sweden will never be a major producer of citrus fruit, no matter what government and industry do to try to change the rest of the national diamond. Mineral resource base and land quality are also relatively immobile, although iron can be moved and fertilizer applied. Infrastructure, both physical and organizational, is also relatively immobile and thus forms a strong basis for comparative advantage. Indeed, Kogut argues that a major source of persistent competitive advantage for nations is the technological and organizational capabilities of different nations, coming from the educational system, prevailing culture, and history.[19] These capabilities diffuse only very slowly across national borders.

One of the areas in which differences in country capabilities and infrastructure play themselves out is in the technologically advanced areas. As late as the mid-1980s, the world's 700 largest technologically active firms continued to perform 90 percent of their innovative activities at their home bases.[20] These home bases provide the educated labor force, communications networks, and technical and managerial structure to support technological innovation. Hence, while technologies themselves travel and diffuse, the capacity for generating new technologies is considerably more rigid.

Human resources, on the other hand, are somewhat more mobile. Historically, in much of the world, physical movement of labor across national borders in response to work opportunities has been limited, although in recent years we have seen loosening up in the case of intra-European immigration. As the European community develops, labor mobility should increase further. Even without physical movement of labor, however, we have seen a considerable increase in the diffusion of knowledge. This diffusion is one reason that as industries mature, even if they require labor with particular skills, they tend to spread out across the world. Industries diffuse as the skill base on which they are based diffuses.

Finally, we come to capital, probably the most mobile of the factors of production. In the United States, in particular, we have seen enormous increases in the inflow of foreign investment capital and in the flow of American capital abroad. In 1988, the U.S. foreign direct investment in Switzerland comprised 10.4 percent of its GDP; in Canada, the figure was even higher, at 12.2 percent.[21] The recent *Economic Report of the President* refers to the increases in foreign direct investment throughout the world as "part of a process of global economic integration."[22] Technology and the loosening of currency restrictions throughout the world have improved the flow of capital across nations and suggests that differences in capital availability is no longer likely to form a very stable competitive advantage for an area.

The second broad determinant of the location of industries is the nature and size of home demand. This is represented in the right-hand box of Porter's diamond. In his analysis of industrial location, Krugman emphasizes the interaction between scale economies, transportation costs, and the size of the home market. He argues: "Given sufficiently strong economies of scale, each producer wants to serve a geographically extensive market from a single location. To minimize transportation costs, she chooses a location with large local demand."[23] When scale economies limit the number of production locations, the size of a market will be an important determinant of its attractiveness. Large home markets will also ensure that firms located at that site develop a cost advantage based on scale and oftentimes on experience as well. Scott, Lodge, and Bower have also emphasized the role of large home markets in creating national competitiveness.[24] A particularly felicitous pattern is that of an early large home market which then becomes saturated, forcing efficient firms to look abroad for new business. In an earlier chapter, we described the way in which the Japanese motorcycle industry, with its large home market, used its scale advantages in the global market place after an early start in Japan.

Industrial location often reflects the location of early demand.

Porter, in his discussion of the role of demand in the location of industry, focuses more heavily on the composition of demand. He argues that "a product's fundamental or core design nearly always reflects home market needs."[25] In electrical transmission equipment, for example, Sweden dominates the world in the high-voltage distribution market. In Sweden there is a large relative demand for transporting high voltage over long distances, as a consequence of the location of population and industry clusters. Here the needs of the home market shaped the industry that later was able to respond to global markets. The sophistication of the buyer is also important. The U.S. government was the first buyer of chips and remained the only customer until 1964. The price inelasticity of government encouraged firms to develop technically advanced products without worrying too much about costs. Under these conditions, the technological frontier was clearly pushed much further and much faster than it would have been had the buyer been either less sophisticated or more price sensitive. Today, as electronics firms have come to dominate the market for semiconductors, the Japanese, who dominate this market, are influencing the shape of the industry and price issues have become more salient.

The third element of Porter's diamond is the presence of related and supporting industries. This is a locational advantage heavily stressed by

Krugman in his discussion of industrial clustering. In part, the advantages of clustering come from reduction in the transportation costs for intermediate goods. In many other cases, advantages come from being able to use labor attracted to an area to serve the core industry, but available and skilled for supporting industries. Coordination of technology is also eased by geographic proximity. Porter argues that Italian world leadership in gold and silver jewelry has been sustained in part by the local presence of manufacturers of jewelry-making machinery.[26] Here the advantage of clustering is not so much transportation cost reductions, but technical and marketing cooperation. In the semiconductor industry, the strength of the electronics industry in Japan is a strong incentive to the location of semiconductors in the same area, despite the fact that transportation costs are low. It should be noted that the clustering story is not independent of scale economies. If there were no scale economies in the production of intermediate inputs, then small-scale centers of production could rival the largescale centers. It is the fact that we have scale economies in both semiconductors and electronics, coupled with the technological and marketing connections between the two, that give rise to clustering advantages.

The fourth element in the Porter diamond is the firm strategy, structure, and rivalry in the home industry. One of the most compelling results of the Porter study of successful industries in ten different nations is the powerful and positive effect that domestic competition has on the ability to compete in the global market place. These results are particularly striking in the case of Japan. There are nine domestic automobile producers in Japan, as contrasted to the U.S. case of three. In 1987, there were fifteen producers of television sets, ten producers of videocassettes, fifteen producers of cameras. In Germany, the fierce domestic rivalry among BASF, Hoechst, and Bayer in the pharmaceutical industry is well known. Small Sweden has two auto companies, Volvo, and Saab-Scania. As we have suggested earlier in this book, the process of competition weeds out inferior technologies, products, and management practices and leaves as survivors only the most efficient firms. When domestic competition is vigorous, firms are forced to become more efficient, adopt new cost-saving technologies, reduce product development time, and learn to motivate and control workers more effectively. Research suggests that domestic rivalry is especially important in stimulating technological developments among global firms.[27] All of these lessons serve firms well when they enter the global market place. Moreover, the presence of fierce domestic competition also encourages firms to look to outside markets for growth, particularly in industries in which scale economies are important.

Vigorous domestic competition improves the ability of firms to compete in global markets.

When we look at the history of most industries, we also see the role played by chance. Perhaps the most compelling instance of chance involves the question of who comes up with a major new idea first. For reasons having little to do with economics, entrepreneurs and inventors will typically start their new operations in their home countries. Once the industry begins in a given country, scale and clustering effects can set in which cement the industry's position in that country. The births of George Eastman and Edwin Land in America had as much to do with the early dominance of the United States in films and instant cameras as any other patterns of factor supply. Krugman attributes the emergence of a carpet industry in Dalton, Georgia to the entrepreneurial efforts of a young woman, Catherine Evans, who in 1900, while making bedspreads, developed a technique of tufting, which was later adapted to carpet-making. What starts out as chance can have substantial economic consequences.[28]

The final determinant of location is government. We have already discussed the powerful role that governments sometimes play in inhibiting globalization while trying to encourage and protect domestic industry. But governments also play a positive role in encouraging the development of industries within their own borders that will assume global positions. One way governments do this is through their effect on other elements of the national diamond. Governments finance and construct infrastructure, providing roads, airports, education, health care, and a host of other public goods and services that affect factors of production. The German system of widespread, rigorous general and vocational education clearly provides a strong basis for their competitive advantage in engineering-related industries. Britain's decline in relation to Germany, the United States, and Japan, has been attributed in part to weaknesses in the British educational system.[29] Governments also construct laws and regulations that influence the degree of competition within their own borders and the ability of firms to compete outside those borders. It is clear that in this respect the influence of government is enormous.

Governments have also tried to influence industrial location and development more directly, in a process that some in the United States have come to call "picking winners." The idea here is that government should act much like a venture capitalist, identifying promising new technologies and ideas and funding those new ideas to produce industries which emerge strong enough to compete effectively in the global market. The evidence on the effectiveness of these more targeted or direct policies is less clear. It is clear that early American dominance in electronics and semiconductors was largely attributable to national security policies. Most analysts agree that MITI has had a profound and positive influence in helping Japan to catch up after the war. At the same time, France was quite unsuccessful in establishing a competitive electronics industry, despite considerable investment of public money. Nelson argues that the more general character of the Japanese and American efforts is in part responsible for its greater relative success.[30] The French program typically sunk investment into particular commercial designs. When governments attempt to be very narrow in picking winners, they are typically less successful.

In sum, we have identified six factors that influence the location of global industries: factors of production, home demand, the location of supporting industries, the internal structure of the domestic industry, chance, and government. We have also suggested that these factors are interconnected. As industries evolve, their dependence on particular locations may also change. High technology industries typically mature, and the research opportunities within those industries often decline. In some industries, technological developments reduce dependence on particular raw materials. In steel, for example, the strong emergence of minimills, which produce new steel from old, has reduced the need for steel mills to locate near iron and coal supplies. The composition of demand will often change as the product matures. The shift in users of semiconductors from the military to the electronics industry has had a profound effect on the shape of the national diamond in that industry. To the extent that governments and firms recognize the source of any locational advantages that they have, they will be better able to both exploit those differences and anticipate their shifts.

Some Strategic Implications of the Theory

We have now reviewed current theory on why industries globalize and how we can explain where those global firms locate. There are a number of implications of this theory for the way firms manage their global businesses. First, it is useful for firms to understand the sources of global advantages. In the present era, we see a reduction in the costs of coordination, and at least some reduction in government impediments to globalization. Even with these changes, however, not all industries will globalize. The European white goods industry we discussed earlier remains an interesting counter. By understanding the advantages of globalization we have discussed here—scale economies, comparative advantage, clustering effects—managers can better anticipate which industries will globalize and which will remain multidomestic. An understanding of the interconnectedness of industries is also a vital lesson of this chapter. Government barriers in one area are likely to be felt by other industries as well. Tariff barriers on tires will make it more difficult for a domestic auto industry to survive. Again, this is an important lesson for both government and industry. Finally, we have stressed the role of change in the global market place. The same forces of diffusion and imitation we see in the domestic market occur internationally, creating considerable competitive pressures. In some instances, there are barriers to such diffusion-immobile resources—for example, ones that maintain an area's dominance in a particular industry. These barriers are comparable to the entry barriers we described in the last chapter. But few of these barriers prevent diffusion forever. And one of the tasks of management is to be prepared as these barriers crumble.

II

INSIDE THE ORGANIZATION

In Part I, we looked at the overall environment in which an organization operates. Our principal focus was to describe the forces that influence organizations over time and affect the harshness of the overall environment in which they operate.

In Part II, we move inside the organization, to the box in the lower part of our familiar schematic.

Chapter 7 sets out the principles that allow organizations, at times, to outperform their rivals. As we will see, the two forces that permit exemplary performance are (1) speed and flexibility in exploring opportunities, and (2) taking advantage of those market frictions that prevent other organizations from imitating your successful strategies.

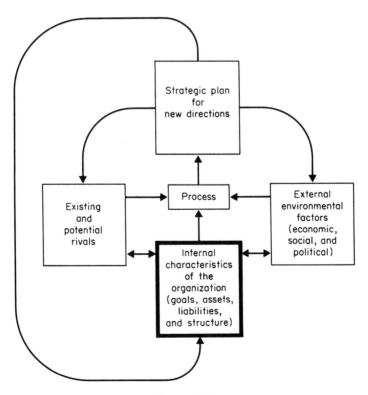

Figure II.1

Chapters 8 and 9 explore the issues of organizational goals, structure, and design and look at some of the complex implementation problems of strategic planning. Finally, Chapters 10, 11, and 12 move us into the diversified firm context and explore strategy in the important area of resource portfolio design.

7

Competing for Advantage

In Part I, we focused on the factors that enhance profitability by delaying entry into an industry or industry segment, and looked at factors that make the overall environment in which the organization operates relatively benign. But participation in an industry with impeded entry is only one of three routes to high performance for an organization.[1] In this chapter, we explore two other ways to earn higher-than-average returns, routes that depend more on the behavior of the particular organization than on the characteristics of its industry. These two routes are *entrepreneurial activity* and *relative organizational advantage*.

One way for an organization to earn higher returns than other similarly placed organizations is for it to see and seize new lucrative opportunities early, before entry has accomplished its leveling function. We will call this activity **entrepreneurship**.[2] One question we will ask in this chapter is what an organization, particularly a large, mature one, can do to promote entrepreneurial activity. Again, one of the fundamental roles of strategic planning is to help an organization thrust itself into favorable new positions, to take advantage of changes in its environment.

A second route to high performance, even within a relatively easy-to-enter market, is for an organization to develop and protect its **relative advantage**. Even in relatively hostile environments, some organizations thrive. Much has been written about the kinds of attributes that distinguish one firm from a seemingly similar neighbor. At times a firm earns rents not because of its unique individual resources, but because of its *distinctive competence* in using those resources.[3] In this chapter, we will explore some of the possible sources of relative advantage. A central theme of this discussion will be that sustained advantage is possible only when frictions exist in the market to prevent imitation. But before we explore the ways in which an organization can distinguish itself from its peers, we will try to get a feel for how much quantitative difference individual performance makes in the U.S. economy.

How Much Difference Does It Make Anyway?

In an earlier chapter, I indicated that despite the power of the efficient market, some industries seem to have persistent rates of return in excess of the market, even allowing for differences in accounting practices. Recognizing this, one might argue that firms should spend most of their managerial and strategic effort trying to enter those industries, and much less time worrying about what to do once they are actually in. If we adopt the metaphor of a poker game, we might say that the real trick to winning at poker is getting in the right card game, and not playing well once you are in the game. *A central strategic planning issue for an organization is how much time and energy should be devoted to identifying and entering attractive existing markets, and how much should be spent instead in cultivating entrepreneurial ability and high performance in the organization as it is currently structured.* This debate is played out in organizations throughout the United States economy.

One piece of evidence relevant to this debate is how much difference *individual organizational performance* makes in an organization's rate of return. Are organizations tightly bound by industry forces or is there room for exemplary performance? Unfortunately, the academic evidence on the role of industry effects versus firm-specific effects on profitability is not conclusive. On the one hand, early work by Schmalensee attempting to separate profits into industry, firm, and market share effects overwhelmingly identified industry effects as determining profits.[4] Schmalensee found that firms profitable in one market were not on average particularly profitable in other markets. Industry effects, on the other hand, were found to be quite important. Wernerfelt and Montgomery similarly found strong industry effects in their empirical work.[5] Systematic, long-lived differences seem to exist across industries, in all likelihood due to the entry barrier differences we discussed earlier. On the other hand, other work, both in Britain and the United States, has found that firm characteristics play a *substantial* role in determining profits, even if we account for industry membership.[6] One quite careful study using line-of-business data found that firm effects were large and significant.[7] In recent work, also based on line-of-business data, Rumelt finds that while corporate effects on profitability are modest, business-unit effects dominate.[8] It seems reasonable to suppose that there is some room for firms to outperform their industries, but the magnitude of that room varies from situation to situation and from industry to industry.

The external strategic planning orientation that focuses on getting in the right card game has fueled many of the diversification efforts of American corporations, both through mergers and acquisitions and through internal development. Profitable industries have been quite attractive to new entrants. For example, one acquisition strategy used by a number of firms has been to search for firms only in industries with persistent returns in excess of the market and then attempt to acquire them. Indeed, some firms have designed computer programs with search algorithms of this sort to use with large industry data bases currently available. Consider the following acquisition strategy described by the vice president for planning of Ciba-Geigy, a large chemical company:

> At Ciba-Geigy, we said our candidates should be in growing markets, should be able to benefit from our R&D know-how, should have sales of at least $50 million, [and] should be able to yield a return on investment of at least 15%.[9]

Ciba-Geigy, by looking at sizeable firms in growing industries, clearly hopes to gain advantage from the acquired organization, while sharing its own considerable research expertise.

This strategy is much easier to plan than it is to actually accomplish. *De novo* entry into an industry with persistent supernormal profits is difficult; if it were not, profits would have sunk to normal. Of course, it is possible that entry is difficult in general, but less so for one firm than another. All potential entrants do not approach with the same set of assets; some firms will find that large capital requirements and the need for a state-of-the art research staff are entry barriers, while others will find access to these resources easy. Nevertheless, even for the large and capable firm, entry into a new profitable industry may prove difficult. In 1992, the disposable-diaper market, for example, was a highly profitable one and also a very difficult one to enter. A consortium consisting of Weyerhauser, Unicharm, and Johnson & Johnson, attracted by the market potential, clearly believed their combined resources made them one of a few potential entrants into that market. Unfortunately, they discovered that, even with their excellent management and complementary assets, entry into the disposable-diaper market was extremely difficult. The consortium eventually abandoned the market, losing considerable investment in the process.

Another approach to entering a profitable industry is to buy one's way in through merger or acquisition as suggested in the Ciba-Geigy description. But implementing this strategy puts us right up against the efficient-market wall we described earlier. If an industry is generally known to be highly profitable, there will be many firms bidding on the assets already in the market. Moreover, few firms will want to leave the market. As a result of these two factors, the price of buying into a profitable industry will be quite high. Indeed, in general the price of these assets will be so high that once the firm finishes paying for the property, it will have consumed all expected supernormal profits from that property. And the situation may actually be worse, given the phenomenon of the **winner's curse**.[10] In most acquisitions, there are at least several potential bidders, each of whom has different expectations about the future profits of the acquisition target. The winning bidder is generally the firm with the most optimistic expectations. But, on average, the most optimistic bidder is in fact overestimating the true value of the firm. Hence, the term winners' curse. Often when you win in a bidding situation, you've paid too much. This theme will be pursued at length in Chapter 12. There are clearly some exceptions in cases in which specific synergies that exist among acquired and acquiring firms account for differences in bid values. The central point to note now is that entering profitable industries through acquisition is not easy.

In short, many organizations will find that they will not be able to move to a better poker game as a way to improve earnings. The external focus on planning options will simply not lead to substantial incremental gains for the organization. Instead, organizations will need to focus on improving the quality of the way they play the game they're already in. And indeed, the evidence suggests that there are some differences among organizations in how well they perform in any given industry.

In any given year, it is easy to find firms within the same industry with quite different earnings rates. For example, in 1990, IBM had an ROE of 14.1 percent, and earned -25.4 percent for investors who held its stock for one year; DEC, in the same year, earned for its investors 33.1 percent and had an ROE of .9 percent; Apple Computer yielded a return to stock market purchases of 23.5 percent and exhibited an ROE of 32.8 percent. All three firms are in the same computer market, yet in any given year large differences exist in the profits they earned.

For many of the firms earning high profits in a given year, however, the tide will soon turn. Much of the profit variance we see within a given industry disappears if we average returns over a longer period of time. Conditions which favored one firm over another in one year may change to favor a second firm in the next. For example, in the auto market, Ford lagged Chrysler in 1985, but outperformed it in both 1987 and 1990. We see this yearly variance even among the top performers in the field. In 1982, Peters and Waterman listed 43 companies in their hall of fame, at least in part because of their profit performance.[11] In the years since, a number of these firms have had unprofitable years. Levi Strauss, a well run, highly profitable firm in a relatively unprofitable industry—apparel—found the early 1980s much more difficult than earlier times. The 1990s, since Levi Strauss went private, seem to be more prosperous. Texas Instruments, one of the prominent members of Peters and Waterman's hall of fame, suffered huge losses in 1983 when its home computer business folded, but has since done well in other business lines. In the performance of any organization in a given year, in any one line of business, there is a considerable element of luck. Indeed, as we will argue in the next chapter, this is one of the reasons that managerial control is so difficult. A change of government leads to a new tariff barrier; sometimes the R&D team gets lucky; sometimes consumer tastes change unexpectedly in ways that favor the firm's product; at other times luck is less favorable. No organization can avoid all of the vagaries of the market, nor would management be very much fun if it could.

In short, all firms have good quarters and bad quarters, just as, I suppose, all poker players have good days and bad days. But there is some evidence, both anecdotal and formal, that some organizations *on average, over time* consistently manage their environments better than their rivals. While accounting data are often hard to interpret for reasons we discussed earlier, some organizations do seem to outperform their industries. Among the high performers in the past have been Campbell Soup, Bristol-Myers, Black and Decker, and Procter & Gamble.[12] Some of these high performers are in high-performing industries—for example, Bristol-Myers. Others, like Campbell Soup, are in industries with historically modest margins. Some of these organizations thrive through entrepreneurship; others do well by tilling the same field over and over again, but doing so better than anyone else. All of them have had disappointing years at times, and many have had failing ventures. But for these and a number of other firms, the poker game has yielded more wins than losses. The question is, why have these firms done better than the average in their particular industries?

The Returns to Entrepreneurship

The value of being first in a market was early stressed by Schumpeter in his classic treatment of the gains to entrepreneurship. Consider the following description of a textile entrepreneur, the first to introduce power looms where once only hand looms had served.

> If a worker with such a loom is now in a position to produce six times as much as a hand worker in a day, it is obvious that the business must yield a surplus over costs. . . . But now comes the second act of the drama. The spell is broken and new businesses are continually arising under the impulse of the alluring profit. Consequently, the surplus of the entrepreneur and his immediate followers disappears. Not at once, but as a rule only after a longer or shorter period of progressive diminution. Nevertheless, the surplus is realized . . . and constitutes, a definite amount of net returns, even though only temporary. Now to whom does it fall? The profit will fall to those individuals whose achievement it is to introduce the looms. What have these individuals contributed? *Only the will and the action.* (Emphasis added)[13]

Organizations that *consistently* maintain the vision to see the emerging market or the new way of producing in the old market and have the will to execute the new venture will reap entrepreneurial profit. Port, in a recent analysis, argues that in the electronics market, the first two manufacturers of a new product lock up 80 percent of the business, at least in the early stage of the market.[14] As Schumpeter tells us so eloquently, these profits will dissipate over time in the processes we have described in Chapter 2 of this text. More modern writers have found the same tendency for entrepreneurial rents to self-destruct.[15] But in the short run, such returns can well compensate for the risks of the new venture.

Let us return to the evolutionary metaphor we introduced early in the text.[16] We can think of an organization as being embedded in an environment in which new ideas are constantly developing. Some of the new ideas are technical and may come from the basic sciences. Developments in recombinant DNA from the area of biology and superconductivity in physics are two recent examples of technologies that have fueled new industrial developments. Some ideas have management theory as their source: Frederick Taylor's writing on scientific management and, more recently, theoretical ideas of risk in finance theory are good examples of powerful management ideas that have shaped business operations. Changes in laws and regulations produced in the political arena similarly introduce variation into the environment.

The central task facing an organization which has entrepreneurial aspirations is to take advantage of the opportunities from change that appear in its environment.

In order to accomplish this, the organization needs three abilities: a sensitivity to the changes available; the ability to sort through those changes and select viable ones from among the many; and the Schumpeterian will and action to execute change.[17] But how do organizations develop and maintain such capabilities? In considering this question, we are likely to be most interested in organizations with *repeated* entrepreneurial successes in a range of areas, for the gains from a single success generally dissipate over time.

Companies that meet with relatively rapid early success soon face the pressures for a repeat performance. Consider the case of Sun Microsystems. Sun is the largest domestic producer of mid-priced computer work stations. Sun began operations in 1981 as a joint venture of three novice businessmen all under thirty years of age. By 1992, its sales were over $3 billion. But despite its successes, the forces for creating something new at Sun became clear in the first decade. Scott McNally, the CEO at Sun, asserted as early as 1987 that his goal was for Sun to become a "broad-based, general purpose computing company."[18] This transition in the quest for new entrepreneurial success has proven to be a rocky road for Sun. Nevertheless, the pursuit of continual entrepreneurial activity is one important way for a firm to outperform its rivals.

Most of the work on entrepreneurship has tended to be of the case-study variety, but a few general principles have emerged. First is the observation that it isn't easy to be entrepreneurial: Organizations, particularly large ones, tend to be characterized by considerable inertia.[19] In large organizations, in fact, there are almost inevitable pressures *against* entrepreneurship. Kanter, in her provocative book, *The Change Masters*, argues that much of the recent loss in competitive position of American firms can be recouped by new attention to broad-scale innovation and entrepreneurship.[20] And yet, despite the difficulties, a number of large organizations do seem to be able to maintain an entrepreneurial spirit, to move into new areas, and adapt new ideas with relative ease. What, if anything, do these organizations have in common?

Organizational structure appears to play a large role in promoting or suppressing entrepreneurship. Kanter refers to the "elevator mentality" of organizations resistant to change. In these organizations, very tight vertical relations are coupled with poor lateral relations. Information flow is up and down, with no possibilities for the often fertile cross-fertilization across areas. Such organizations are sometimes described as having mechanistic structures.[21] If entrepreneurship is in large measure combining existing resources in new ways, lateral communication across previously separate boundaries is clearly essential.

Alderfer similarly focuses on organizational structure as one of the indexes of an organization's resistance to change.[22] Alderfer refers to organizations with restrictive, monolithic authority relations and precisely detailed role definitions as **overbounded systems.** In overbounded organizations, goals are typically very clear, and stress and confusion tend to be minimized. Unfortunately, the energy levels in the organization also tend to be reduced, and open communications are rare.

Some positive strategic gains are associated with overbounded systems, particularly clarity of goal and direction and unity of purpose. But resistance to change also exists, and if change is critical, such structures will be seriously dysfunctional.

Structurally overbounded systems tend to be resistant to change.

A number of well-managed U.S. companies have tried to put in place structures explicitly designed to overcome the narrow focus and conservatism of their bureaucracies. Eastman Kodak, for example, instituted a Venture Board, consisting of managers drawn from a wide radius in Kodak, dedicated to fostering and reviewing new ideas in the organization.[23] The 3M corporation, another repeated entrepreneur, has similar structures designed to cut across functional and product lines in the organization.

> **The structure of an organization helps to determine how sensitive it will be to changes in its environment. Structure thus can play an important antecedent role in organizational change.**

Most organizations rely heavily on decision rules as ways of directing their operations. Decision rules constitute routinized ways of doing things that reduce an organization's decision-processing time. Gersick and Hackman have recently called these routines the "habits" of the corporation.[24] Rather than deciding *de novo* how much to spend on research or advertising each quarter, for example, many organizations simply follow a fixed percentage rule.[25] Employment practices are also typically established over time. But large changes can upset decision rules, even well-established ones. Adverse competitive conditions caused both Eastman Kodak and

Levi Strauss to abandon long-standing policies on not terminating employees, for example.

Large changes in the environment tend to unseat existing decision rules and pave the way for internal change.

Examples of how environmental changes encourage organizational changes are prevalent. The YMCA, for instance, was founded as an evangelical organization, devoted to Christian salvation; in the century since its founding, it has been transformed into a fee-based organization concerned with health, athletics, and (perhaps) character development. Changes in the religious environment of U.S. society clearly played a large role in this change.[26] In the corporate sector, new market entry by competitors or systematic declines in consumer demand can precipitate organizational change. At Xerox, the end of its patent protection in the copying industry created a new environment for strategic change. In the case of Kodak, the entry into the film market by Fuji, a Japanese competitor, has also had profound effects on normal operating procedures. IBM, once well-known for its conservative management style, has been pushed by domestic firms like Apple and international rivals like Hitachi and Fujitsu to adopt new, faster-moving entrepreneurial management techniques.

Of course, it is clear that the inside and outside forces for change are not really so distinct as we have made them out to be. As Kanter points out, some organizations tend to be more responsive to crises than others. Miles has examined the response of U.S. tobacco companies to the 1973 Surgeon General's report and found widely varying reactions—reactions that in large measure reflected the style of the various organizations.[27] Some organizations foresee an incipient crisis; others need to be hit on the head. Nevertheless, both internal and external pressures help create opportunities for entrepreneurship within organizations and increase the likelihood that an organization will anticipate opportunities and threats before they materialize. And a well-managed organization can take advantage of opportunities rapidly. Again, improving organizational reaction time is a fundamental goal of planning, for in the competitive market place, the race is to the swift.

Although seeing opportunities early is important, even highly sensitive organizations can find themselves in markets with competitive pressures. Unless entry is completely blocked, organizations will find early environments growing less hospitable over time. The process of competition is one that Schumpeter early identified as a process of creative destruction. What kinds of assets can firms rely on once the early stages of a market have passed and the forces of competition emerge?

Relative Advantage: What Is a Likely Source?

We turn now to a final way in which an organization can earn high returns: by acquiring and tending to some advantage that allows it to outperform its peers. In the remainder of this chapter, we will explore a number of possible sources of relative advantage. In the traditional language of strategic planning we can think of this exercise as a search for the **key success factors** in a market.

The key success factors in an industry are those assets that allow a firm to outperform its rivals for a sustained period of time.

In looking for key success factors, researchers working in the resource-based tradition of strategy have focused on the firm's portfolio of different core skills and routines, use of complex tactics across skills, and unique and appropriable know-how.[28] For example, in the auto industry, Rockhart has identified style, costs, dealer efficiency, and ability to deal with regulators as the key success factors.[29] Underlying these success factors are two fundamental principles: Doing well *relative* to the market and preventing imitation. The acid test of whether a particular asset gives advantage is in whether it can easily be imitated, traded, or purchased. What protects firms from competitors, then, is the existence of **transactions costs—** costs that prevent competitors from imitating successful strategies. Transactions costs create frictions in the market place, and frictions allow for exemplary performance. Rumelt calls these market frictions "isolating mechanisms" and argues that they explain considerable intraindustry differences among firms.[30] Following this line, we can articulate several broad principles underlying a firm's ability to create advantage.

Playing Against the Market

Firms make money when their prices exceed their costs over a long period of time. Thus the prices a firm can charge are critical to its future. But what determines the price a firm can charge? For some firms, like the local telephone company, government regulations help to set prices. For most firms in the U.S. economy, however, prices are kept down not by the efforts of public policy but by the movement of the market. Firms set prices based on what the market will bear.

This observation recalls our earlier discussion of efficient markets. In setting prices, firms must consider the alternatives facing consumers. It is unlikely that a local dairy selling milk to a retail chain of 7–11 stores can sell that milk for any more than the other dairies are charging. When IBM markets its personal computers, its ability to attract customers depends on prices charged by Apple, Compaq, Leading Edge, and a host of other firms. Of course, in the strict sense, sellers always set their own prices, but in fact sellers often have very little control over prices. In a number of cases, *the market sets the price.*

The milk case is an easy one to analyze, since there are many dairies— all operating in the same market—as there are many firms in the personal computer market. What role does the market play in the case of a new product? When Coleco introduced the Cabbage Patch Doll in the early

1980s, what constrained the prices it could charge? There were no other Cabbage Patch dolls available to retailers and consumers. Nevertheless, while Coleco had some price discretion, it faced some constraints as well. If it set prices too high, customers might well change to Rainbow Brite or even Barbie. So in the case of a new product, the market also imposes some discipline on the pricing policy of a firm, at least after a time. Entrepreneurship, as we have seen, will contribute temporary returns. But more sustained returns require either continual entrepreneurship or a sustained advantage over the market.

Any firm then, in trying to make money, is playing the game against the market.

A central consideration in designing a strategy is to do well relative to the other players in the market.

The poker analogy is again useful. In poker all that matters is relative performance. Sometimes a simple pair will win the pot, while at other times even a flush will end up a loser. Thus focus on relative performance is a natural outgrowth of the equilibrium principle.

The observation that excess profits are attained in conditions under which a firm has an advantage relative to the rest of the market has long been held in economics. Consider the following explanation taken from David Ricardo's *Principles of Political Economy and Taxation*, written in 1817:

> The exchangeable value of all commodities, whether they be manufactured or the produce of the mines, or the produce of the land, is always regulated, not by the less quantity of labor that will suffice for their production under circumstances highly favorable . . . but by the greater quantity of labor necessarily bestowed on their production by those who have no such facilities, by those who continue to produce under the most unfavorable circumstances.[31]

The market price is set by the marginal producer. Firms which are on average more productive than that marginal producer will earn supernormal profits; those less productive will be driven out of the market.

What makes one organization special relative to its competitors is scarce resources, for assets gain value in proportion to their scarcity.

Limited Resources Create Specialization

A firm has limited resources to allocate. Of course, if a firm has a good investment, the capital market will generally make new capital available. And labor can be hired as well. But real management problems of coordination and control appear to limit the size and extent of an individual firm.[32] Thus the typical firm has a limited number of things it can do, and it must constantly choose among them. In making resource-allocation decisions, the firm should consider the principle of **relative advantage**. The price a firm can charge in a market will depend on the prices charged by other firms in that market or in nearby markets. If a firm is excellent at producing something that everyone else is excellent at producing as well, the market price will be low, and no one will make very much money. On the other hand, even if a firm is mediocre at producing a good or service, as long as everyone else is poor at the same job, the mediocre performer will make money. One is reminded of the advantage of the one-eyed man in the land of the blind. It is a firm's performance relative to the market that determines the profitability of its ventures.

Specialization should follow an organization's advantage relative to the market overall.

Of course, there are some exceptions to this general principle. At times, an organization may be interested in growth and size more than in profit rates, for reasons we will discuss further in Chapter 8. Under these circumstances, the firm may prefer to earn modest margins on a large volume business, rather than higher margins on a smaller operation. Then, too, if the firms' only area of relative advantage lies in a dying industry, a concern for the future might suggest that it broaden its focus. But to the extent that an organization is targeting return, the principle of relative advantage is a very powerful one.

The Ability to Defend Against Imitation Is Central

Suppose a firm finds that it has an advantage in a particular market. Perhaps it is able to produce its good at a lower cost than its rivals; perhaps its marketing costs for given levels of penetration are lower than average; perhaps the firm has a better R&D team than its rivals. For a time, the organization may find that it outperforms the market. But market pressure on this firm will in all likelihood soon start to build. Other firms within the industry, and perhaps without, will observe its performance results and *may observe the strategy as well.* Successful strategies breed imitation, and imitation, if successful, will increase the average performance of organizations in an industry—thereby reducing any advantage held by the firm. Thus ease of imitation is a key element in the strategic development of a high-performing firm. The firm will need to understand not only the source of its advantage, but the *defensibility* of that advantage.

Successful strategies are prime targets for imitation, and imitation tends to equalize returns.

Pressures toward imitation in our economy are apparent on many fronts. We begin by examining the pattern of techhology transfer among firms.

Extensive research has traced the path of imitation of technological innovations. A careful look at a wide range of quite different innovations suggests that, as a general rule, the path of adoption of an innovation has an *S* shape, as shown in Figure 7.1.

Under the standard *S* or **logistic curve,** adoption begins slowly, picks

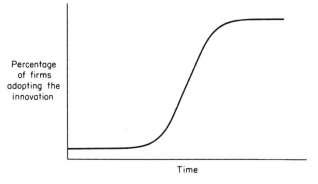

Figure 7.1 The S-shaped innovation path

up speed, and then levels off. The history corresponding to this logistic might resemble the following: One firm discovers a new way of doing something. For a few years, it is alone in its use of the new process. Soon, other firms begin to observe the positive results of the innovation, but at first many of the firms may be uncertain about its nature and effectiveness. An adventurous few try the innovation, and learning about it gradually spreads as uncertainty diminishes. In the middle period, adoption is extensive. As the number of firms in the industry using the innovation increases, the probability that a nonuser will follow also increases. Finally, we reach the top of the S curve: All firms who intend to shift over to the new process have done so.

The first observations that the path of imitation of an innovation tends to assume an S shape were made by looking at the use of hybrid corn in U.S. agriculture.[33] Since then, the pattern has been observed across a wide range of private-and-public sector projects. The S curve reflects the way learning occurs in our society: The more people there are who know something, the easier it is to find out about it. Let us look at the diffusion of innovation in several different instances.

The Basic Oxygen Furnace (BOF), along with continuous casting, is one of two major innovations in the steel industry since World War II. The BOF was developed by an Austrian firm, Linz-Donawitz, in 1949. The first U.S. adopter was a rather small firm, McLouth Steel in 1954.[34] By 1960, industry usage was still modest: Of the top 23 firms in the industry, only 4 had converted *any* of their plants to BOF. In these early years, there was considerable uncertainty about just how cost effective and how reliable the new technology would be. The investment was a substantial one and largely irreversible. Thus firms moved slowly in the initial period. By 1968, however, 17 of the 23 firms had at least one BOF plant. In the intervening years, as costs and reliability information about the BOF accumulated, its superiority over the open-hearth furnace had become clear. Today, virtually all integrated firms have BOF capacity.

Similar patterns of diffusion of innovation can be found in the building industry.[35] The path of technical innovation has been rather slow in this industry, but some material and technique innovations have emerged. In the United States, the use of building innovations is governed by local building departments. In order to implement a new construction technique or use a new material, approval from the building department is necessary. We can thus examine the diffusion of a *regulatory* innovation: How fast building departments permitted an innovation to be used in their jurisdictions. A study of acceptance by local building departments of four innovations revealed again the S-shaped diffusion curve (Figure 7.2).

The four innovations studied were (1) preassembled plumbing, (2) substitution of 2×3 studs for 2×4s, (3) use of nonmetallic cable, and (4) wider placement of studs. All four innovations were described by a major federal commission in the late 1960s as yielding cost savings in construction without quality decline. Scattered localities in the period before 1930 had used these four building techniques. Usage picked up in the 1950s; by 1973, usage had begun to slow. Diffusion seems to have proceeded among public-sector officials as among private-sector firms. Early on, the reliability of cost data was unclear, and many officials knew little about the innovations. As time passed, information and hence usage diffused through the regulatory jurisdictions.

Imitation works in the area of management innovations as well. Per-

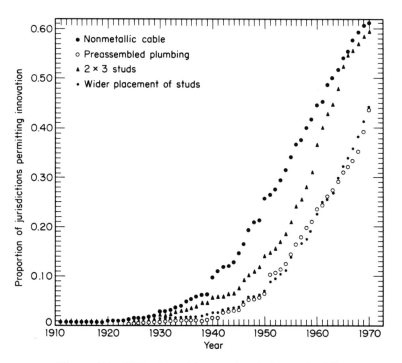

Figure 7.2 Diffusion of innovation in house building

haps the best example of this is the diffusion of the **multidivisional structure** throughout the American economy.[36]

In the 1920s a few large U.S. firms began to experiment with a new
organizational structure. In each case, firms moved away from the functional form and toward a more decentralized divisional form. For example, rather than have one group in charge of marketing for an entire
company, under the new structure each division would have its own
marketing arm. Divisional heads would be responsible for a wide range
of the resource allocation decisions within the division, and they would
be held responsible for the performance of that division.

The initial innovations toward the multidivisional form came from Du
Pont, General Motors, Sears, and several other large firms. Chandler argues that, in the initial period, each firm discovered the organizational
innovation *de novo*. As it turned out, the new structure appeared to be
especially useful, given the greater diversification firms were undertaking. In Chandler's terms, strategy and structure supported one another
as firms began to search for new ways to deal with diversification. And
they began to follow the example of the pioneers—that is, to *imitate* the
organizational innovation. As Chandler tells us, this imitation opened up
strategic options for the imitators as well:

> Once the new type of structure became known, as it did during the 1930's,
> its availability undoubtedly encouraged many enterprises to embark on a
> strategy of diversification, for the ability to maintain administrative con-
> trol through such an organizational framework greatly reduced the risks
> of this new type of expansion.[37]

Even in the area of a complex organizational change, firms eventually
learn of an innovation and, if the innovation is a good one, imitation
occurs. As we suggested in the last chapter, imitation occurs even across
national boundaries. Moreover, to the extent that the imitation occurs,
the advantage of the innovator is no longer unique. And, of course, the
profit edge produced by the initial advantage begins to decline.

For the initial innovator, two features of the *S* curve are of central
importance. First, how long will it be before the first few rivals imitate?
In Figure 7.2, this is translated into the length of the flat part of the curve.
The second question involves the slope of the curve: How fast does new
imitation occur once it starts? If imitation occurs quickly and *en masse*, the
innovator will find its advantage quickly dissipated, and its high profitability will fall as the average industry performance rises. The combination
of these two factors helps determine the **appropriability** of profits from a
new idea. When diffusion is slow to start and proceeds slowly, the innovator will be able to *appropriate* the profits from its innovation. This appropriability occurs because the bulk of the market—which is determining
overall price—lacks access to the new product or process. When imitation
occurs rapidly, society benefits from the innovation as prices fall for the
new product, but the innovator does not benefit.

The ease of imitation of an innovation is affected both by institutional factors and by economic factors. Again, one way to look at this issue is to identify the transactions costs associated with imitation. One important source of transactions costs is the patent. In most countries, firms may apply for patents on innovations. In theory, patents protect innovators by prohibiting other organizations from copying the innovation, thus increasing the costs of imitation. In some industries, for example, pharmaceuticals, the patenting system appears to work fairly well, at least in the sense that new chemical entities are difficult to copy. In other industries, like electronics, patents are less helpful. For organizational innovations or changes in management styles, it is hard to even imagine a protecting patent.

Other institutional factors influence the ease of imitation as well. In order for firms to imitate one another, they have to learn about one another. Trade journals improve the spread of information across industries, as do consultants and even business schools. A major channel for communication is provided by the movement of personnel across firms. In the electronics industry, this movement appears to be very large and is one cause of the quite rapid imitation of innovations in that industry. And many institutional factors affect the mobility of labor. Some—like compensation packages, firm location, and the development of corporate culture—are under the control of the firm. Others are socially determined or determined by the laws of the land. In Japan, labor mobility is quite small relative to mobility in the United States. Contracts that prevent an employee from using specialized knowledge gained in one firm for the advantage of a second may impede mobility and reduce imitation, although some argue such contracts simultaneously increase the rate of innovation itself.

Economic factors that influence the speed of imitation of an innovation are essentially its profitability and its riskiness.[38] Excellent ideas are copied faster than good ones, and good ideas faster than mediocre ones. Some innovations look profitable, but carry with them considerable failure risks. These are less likely to be adopted than less risky ventures. Nevertheless, if payoffs are large enough, imitation may be fast indeed. In the $3 billion per year disposable-diaper market, for example, Procter & Gamble developed a new "thin" diaper in 1985, and invested $500 million in a new plant and equipment to produce the diaper. This was a huge capital investment, and for the most part completely specific to the new diaper. Nevertheless, Kimberly-Clark imitated the innovation within 18 months. The risk was large—due to the large specific investment—but the potential payoff in this hotly contested market was high as well.

In practice, some firm advantages appear to be much easier to imitate than others. Let us consider some examples of ostensible advantages and judge them against our two principles of comparative market performance and defensibility. We will look at five often-cited sources of advan-

tage: market share, learning curves, corporate culture, marketing and research expertise, and asset ownership.

Market Share

Among high-performing firms, a substantial number are market leaders
in their industries. Caterpillar Tractor, Black & Decker, Procter & Gamble
are only a few examples of high-performing firms that hold the highest
market share in their respective industries. Statistical work, both old and
new, similarly points to the strong relationship between market share and
profitability.[39] In the typical attempt to use regression analysis to explain
variations in profits across a range of firms, market share has historically
been found to play a dominant role. In some fairly recent work using line-
of-business data collected by the PIMS groups, a market leadership position was associated with approximately a 10-point premium in ROI.[40] Other
work also suggests that, on average, firms with high market shares seem
to earn profits in excess of the market.

The observed relationship between market share and profitability has
played a prominent role in strategic planning. Managerial practice and
literature strongly emphasize the role of market share in firm performance. "Competition is inherently the struggle for dominance," we are
told by Robert Schapiro, vice president of G. D. Searle, a large pharmaceutical firm.[41] Many top managers believe that only if a firm is one of
the largest two firms in a market can it hope to succeed. The belief that
share is one of the vital weapons in the competitive game underlies some
of the planning techniques popular in the field. Consider the **growth/
share matrix** formulated by the Boston Consulting Group, as depicted in
Figure 7.3.

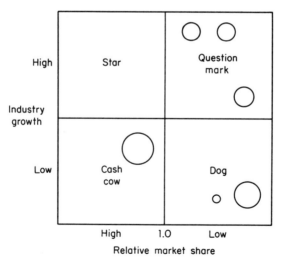

Figure 7.3 The growth/share matrix

On the horizontal axis we measure the relative market share of the business unit. Typically, the market share is given relative to the firm's largest competitor. If a firm has sales of $10 million and the industry leader has sales of $50 million, then the firm's relative share on the BCG matrix would be 20 percent, or .2. Thus, to be on the left-hand side of the matrix, requires that the business unit be the market leader. On the vertical axis, we place the unit's real market growth, that is, the market growth correcting for inflation. The area of the circle represents the dollar sales of the unit. "Star" business units are defined as those with dominant market shares and high-growth rates. The expectation is that stars will yield high profits precisely because of their dominant positions in high-growth industries. Low-share business units in slow-growth markets are "dogs," generally to be avoided.

Numerous other **Business Attractiveness Screens** relied on by major U.S. companies also use market share as a criterion for judging a business unit's worth. And, indeed, for some organizations, investment decisions are made in part on the basis of a profile of the BCG variety. Firms fight for market share in the hopes that share will eventually yield profits. Unfortunately, in many cases those high profits never materialize.

We are all familiar with the successful dominant firms. What about the firms with dominant market shares and unremarkable financial performances?

The computer market is an excellent example of the lack of correspondence between market share and profits. IBM is the clear market leader in sales, with six times the sales of its nearest competitor. But in recent years IBM has had only middling profit performance relative to its rivals. Cray Research, a tiny operation relative to IBM, over the decade of the 1980s, took the honors in return to investors, although recent years have been more difficult. The 1990s may well belong to the smaller niche players. In this industry, and in many others, high market share is no guarantee of success.[42]

In other industries, we find the traditional high margin–high share pattern, but a strategy of pursuing share may still be unprofitable. In order to understand why, we need to turn back to our statistics. Suppose we observe in the data on firm performance that high profits are often associated with high market shares. There are at least two explanations for this observation. First, perhaps high shares *cause* high profits. This hypothesis clearly underlies strategic reliance on the growth/share matrix. But it could equally well be that there is a third factor, unobserved by us, that causes *both* high profits and high market shares. In this case, we would see a *correlation* between profits and market share, but no causal relationship.[43]

An example is easy to construct. In the pharmaceutical industry, a successful innovation can lead to high profits for a number of years. At Upjohn, for example, one product—Motrin—was responsible for a third of the firm's profits in the early 1980s as well as a substantial portion of its sales. In the anti-inflammatant market, Upjohn had both high share and high margins. But the high share and profits both resulted from a successful and defensible R&D effort. Upjohn's successful strategy was not to price and market so as to win share, but to launch an intensive R&D effort and use patent protection. Thus, while we would observe statistically a high share–high return relationship, it would not be a causal one. New entrants into the market would be mistaken if they thought they could duplicate Upjohn's success simply by building share through pricing cuts, for example.

Another example of the dangers of confusing correlation and causality can be found in the diesel-engine market. Caterpillar Tractor is a world-wide leader in the sales of earth-moving and construction machinery, one of the major end-use markets of diesels. It is also widely thought of as a high-performing firm, based on long-term financial performance relative to its industry. But it is not at all clear that market share is the base on which Caterpillar's strong financial performance rests. Rather, there is some evidence that Caterpillar's strength lies primarily in its distribution and service network, and that this asset has led to both high share and high returns. If Caterpillar Tractor is successful because it has good service capabilities, then it might be more appropriate for a new entrant to attack on the service side rather than to try to directly threaten share without inquiring as to the *cause* of the share dynamic.

Is market share never causally related to profits? Does it never make sense to pursue share as a way to make money in a market? This is too strong a statement. Rather, market share is one factor which, under certain circumstances, in some industries, may generate excess returns for a firm. (Further discussion of the statistical modeling needed to identify the role of market share is given in Appendix 3). In practice, careful recent analysis suggests that when we appropriately correct for all the factors that vary across firms, market-share effects are relatively trivial.[44] And it is certainly clear that among the top 1000 firms in the U.S. economy, share differences have little effect.

In what sense might market share meet our general principles for a possible advantage? The issues here are two: Does the factor create advantage for a firm, and can it be easily imitated? If an industry has large economies of scale, the dominant firm in that industry will have a cost advantage. Our first criterion is thus met. But the appropriate strategy a firm would need to use to challenge the dominant player is also clear: Competitors and potential entrants can see that if they too grow large, they will have low costs as well. If prices are high, the new entrant or small current competitor may well be tempted to shade prices a bit in an attempt to grow large rapidly and steal the market from the current dominant player. Of course, this aggressive strategy is a risky one. But the potential for high payoffs encourages such challenges. In this example, imitation is easy, and share not defensible.

If, on the other hand, scale economies are accompanied by the existence of large and highly specialized assets in an industry, the dominant firm is in a more favorable position. In this case, in order to challenge the dominant player for the market, the new firm must invest heavily. Moreover, if the investment is highly specialized, the challenger stands to lose substantially should the dominant player successfully respond to the challenge—that is, by price cutting.

Scale economies combined with high exit costs may make market share a defensible advantage.

Learning-curve Effects

To what extent can learning-curve effects create relative advantage for large, established firms in an industry? To the extent that a firm is first in the market, it may, through the operation of the learning curve, have lower costs than newer rivals. Thus learning-curve effects may meet our first criterion of giving initial relative advantage. What about the imitation issue? A large survey of R&D managers discovered that, in the case of process innovations, secrecy was viewed as important primarily as a way of exploiting lead-time and attendant learning-curve advantages.[45] As Ross points out, the cost advantage of a dominant firm that has moved down a learning curve, allows it to inflict losses on its newer rivals while still earning profits itself.[46] The dominant firm's "asymmetric power of annihilation" improves the market outcome for that firm.

But learning-curve effects, even if large, do not always lead to a defensible advantage. If learning-curve effects are not firm specific, the advantage of the dominant firm disappears. In this situation, new firms can "jump on" the learning curve of the dominant firm and past experience again becomes less relevant. Then, too, if technology is moving rapidly, experience gains may become rapidly obsolete, and cost advantages disappear.

Learning-curve effects that remain within the firm and persist in the face of technical change can create a competitive advantage.

Corporate Culture and Structure

An organization's culture is a complex set of beliefs and ways of doing things that influence the organization's perspective on itself and the world around it. One element of a corporate culture is the set of formal rules and structures that govern the way in which people relate to one another at the workplace. Another is the set of myths and traditions that help define the **ideology** of the organization.[47] The style of the organization's leader also contributes to its culture.

Different organizations have quite different corporate cultures. Champion International and Cummins Engine, with their strong traditions of participatory management and social responsibility, are a long distance from United Technologies with its more centralized tradition. Nucor Steel, with its emphasis on lean management and a flexible, incentivized work force, is a far cry from bureaucraticized USX. But to what extent can an organization's culture be a source of competitive advantage.[48]

An organization's culture creates value because it allows that organization to strike deals with its suppliers, customers, and employees that are not available to other firms. Thus culture is an organizational asset. An organization with a culture that stresses management stability can ask for greater specific investments by its managers than an organization with high manager turnover. An organization with a tradition of social responsibility may be able to strike a better deal with a local community in a location decision than a rival with a reputation as irresponsible. Examples of the value of a corporate culture in facilitating transactions in our complex environment abound.

Finally, corporate culture is hard to imitate. The formal structure is only one small piece of corporate culture. Even the leader of an organization embodies its culture only to a limited extent. Thus an organization's culture—because it is hard to emulate—may produce a competitive edge. Indeed, Itami argues that invisible or intangible assets like corporate culture are often the only sustainable source of competitive edge, primarily because such advantages are so difficult to imitate.[49]

Marketing and Research Expertise

Most industry analysts argue that IBM historically derived much of its comparative advantage in the computer industry from its marketing expertise. How is it that IBM could maintain an advantage in this area? Why didn't other firms copy it or hire away its marketing staff? The answer seems to reside in the very complexity of the advantage itself. If a marketing advantage simply meant that IBM ran more interesting advertisements, one could hire IBM's advertising agency. If a marketing advantage simply meant having a good distribution network, one could develop a similar network. The fact is that IBM's marketing advantage came from a complex combination of a variety of management practices, along with perhaps a dash of unique and elusive spirit. The very complexity of the advantage makes it difficult to imitate. It is interesting to note that if much of IBM's competitive edge still lies in the marketing area, its 1992 decision to move into the mail-order computer business is difficult to justify.

One might argue that 3M has the same kind of advantage in its creative research department. We can see some of the elements of the advantage: the practice of allowing scientists to use some of their time on pet projects; permitting scientists to manage projects if their ideas are successful; the wheeler-dealer atmosphere of 3M. But the combination of these elements has an indefinable bit of mystery about it, and this makes imitation hard. Again we return to the Schumpeterian idea that "new combinations" can generate rents.[50]

In the same way some technological innovations may be easier to imitate than others. For some innovations, the fundamentals of the change may be accurately and well captured in a set of blue prints, easily transferred across firms. For other innovations, the blue prints contain only a fraction of the story; implementation requires much art and practice as well. Clearly innovation proceeds faster in the former case.[51]

Winter has argued that an organization's knowledge or expertise can serve as a profitable strategic asset if it meets three criteria: (1) the knowledge is tacit rather than articulable; (2) the knowledge is not observable in use; and (3) the knowledge is complex rather than simple.[52] If a particular organizational expertise meets these criteria, it will be difficult for rivals to fully identify and thus to copy that advantage. Again, the asset becomes invisible in Itami's terms. Since imitation is reduced, the value of that asset is preserved.

A second way of gauging how easy an innovation is to copy is to examine the number and scope of **cospecialized assets** associated with the innovation.[53] Winter stresses the inability of rivals to fully *identify* the innovation as a barrier; Teece focuses on implementation of the innovation as a barrier to imitation. Most innovations are supported by other parts of an organization: marketing, distribution, service, and so on. Commercializing an innovation requires other specialized assets in the areas of marketing, production, and sales. These assets may be specialized to the particular innovation. In some real sense, the diffusion of the innovation may be impeded by the complexity and number of cospecialized assets needed to put the innovation to work. Firms may find it easy to copy the innovation, but much harder to put together the organizational supports needed to bring that innovation to market. A complex set of cospecialized assets may thus protect the innovation and allow it to continue to yield value.

If factors that create complex relative advantages are hard to imitate, from the firm's point of view, this is all to the good. On the other hand, such advantages are also hard to manage and hold on to. Since the firm's advantage is not something tangible, like a patent or a hill of bauxite, there is often no formula for maintaining that advantage. Apple Computer, which built its early lead on a core of creative efforts, and People Express, which used chutzpa and a spirited labor force to surge ahead, both found it difficult to preserving their edge. Apple with a change in management now seems to have overcome its midlife crisis. People Express was less fortunate. IBM, which found its marketing expertise to be a valuable entry barrier in the mainframe computer market, has had less success protecting itself in the personal computer market. After IBM introduced its Personal System/2 line in 1987, redesigned clones were available just over one year later, as Tandy entered the market.

Asset Ownership

A relatively common source of comparative advantage for a firm lies in its ownership of some specialized physical asset. A viable patent over a process or product can confer an important cost advantage; similarly, ownership of a key input may provide the basis for a comparative advantage. Long-term contracts that tie up the most favorable distribution network can confer an advantage on a firm as well, for other organizations cannot gain access to the favored resources. Ownership stymies imitation.

But the ownership of an asset or even a long-term contract that gives an organization an advantage in a market does not necessarily mean that organizations should pursue that advantage. The organization must also consider how to use its assets, in particular, whether to *sell them* or to *use them.*

Let us return for a moment to the poker metaphor introduced early in this chapter. In the game of five-card draw, if I am dealt three aces I can build my game strategy around those three aces; it is part of my endowment. If I choose to fold, no one else can use those aces. In managing an organization, however, I have an additional choice. Instead of keeping my three aces and trying to draw for a full house, I can sometimes sell my aces to someone else. If I find someone who already has a pair of kings, my aces may be worth more to him than they are to me. This is one reason that a careful definition of property rights has become important in the strategy area: only by defining such rights can we tell what assets are transferable and which aces we have to hold on to.[54]

The fact that many assets are transferable in the market plays an enormous role in strategic considerations. If I own a truck, I can use it to run a delivery business; on the other hand, I can also sell it to someone else to run a delivery business. If I own a patent, I can exploit it myself by opening a production facility, or I can license it to another firm. In fact, in the case of patents, firms often do both. If I own both a semiconductor manufacturer and a computer company, like Hitachi and IBM, I can produce semiconductors solely for my own computer firm, or I can sell the semiconductors to another firm and buy my supplies elsewhere.

The number of examples one could cite on the transferability of assets is large and varied. The fact of transferability carries with it two related propositions.

The firm should keep its specialized asset inside the organization only if it is better able to exploit that asset than any other organization.

In making a decision to use an asset or sell it, firms should always keep in mind the opportunity cost of assets used internally.

The first proposition implies that firms should maintain control over their own specialized assets only if they have or can get control over the complementary assets needed to effectively use those assets. In the absence of needed complementary assets, organizations will maximize earnings by selling off or licensing their main strategic assets.

The second proposition is an example of one of the most fundamental laws in economics. The importance of keeping in mind the opportunity cost of assets has by now been fairly well internalized in multidivisional firms with vertical links. In many organizations, if part of the firm supplies to another part, the transfer is done at prices that reflect the value of the transferred input to the firm as a whole.[55] This is known as the principle of **transfer pricing.** It is a formal way of recognizing that in the absence of the internal trade, the firm could have had an external trade that would have realized revenues for it and that external trade is one consideration of the value to the firm of the transferred input.

The principle of paying attention to opportunity costs in transferring inputs across boundaries within the firm is fairly well established, although in practice it is not always easy to do. Tracking the opportunity cost of other assets is even more difficult. In the case of patents, cross-licensing and patent sale are sufficiently well established that firms are often aware of the market value of the innovation for use outside the firm. On the other hand, the physical assets of a firm are generally carried on the books at historical cost, and the opportunity cost of these assets may generally be unappreciated. Some items of critical importance to organizations are not carried on the books at all—for example, corporate systems, corporate culture, and monitoring systems. In the case of airlines, ticket-counter location may be an important advantage, but since location is not formally owned by the airline, it would nowhere appear on the books. It is most often in the acquisition market that the true market value of the assets of an organization are revealed, and here it is generally the bundle of assets being valued rather than individual assets and that makes it difficult to identify the value of particular assets.

Nevertheless, the organization should keep in mind the possibility of moving the asset into the market place should that prove more profitable. Even asset values which do not appear on an organization's books should remain in its plans and thoughts.

Some Final Thoughts

In this chapter we have explored two ways an organization can achieve exceptional performance even in relatively unforgiving environments: entrepreneurship and developing a relative advantage. In the case of entrepreneurship, we have seen that both organizational structure and environmental pressures have a role to play. In the case of relative advantage, we have seen that protection against imitation is critical.

We have also explored some of the technical and economic issues associated with various strategic choices: pursuing market share, exploiting learning-curve effects, developing a unique culture, playing on one's strategic control of some asset. In all of this it is useful to remember that strategy is a path-dependent process. The optimal choice today, for a firm, often depends on yesterday's decisions. History creates, in Nelson and Winter's terms, a genetic endowment for a firm and that endowment begins to determine the extent and sources of its competitive advantage.[56] Sá and Hambrick in a study of six different industries, for example, found strong evidence of both the importance of key success factors and of predictable differences in those factors.[57] A knowledgeable sales force and product R&D were found to be vital in the machine tools industry, while location of reserves and purchasing infrastructure dominated in the coal and iron ore industries. As customers and technology change, so too may key success factors in an industry. Consequently, firms which, because of their endowments, are well placed to compete in one decade may fail in the next. It is one of the tasks of strategy formulation to anticipate these changes and trace their consequences.

8

Organizational Goals: Politics and Power in the Organization

So far, we have looked at the environment within which organizations operate and at the characteristics that allow firms to outperform their rivals. Our orientation has been largely economic, as we have looked at the literature on markets, entry barriers, and so on. In this chapter and the next, we switch gears somewhat and turn our attention to the internal organization of the firm.

Traditional neoclassical economic models treat the firm as a kind of black box, producing profit-maximizing outcomes through a process largely cloaked from observation and hardly even seeming to involve people. Organizational theory and more modern work on the economics of organizations, on the other hand, move the people inside organizations much more to center stage. Organizational theorists like Pfeffer, for example, model organizations as coalitions of individuals, with different preferences, power, and information.[1] March describes firms as business coalitions, consisting of a collection of interest groups each with different goals.[2] Perrow, looking at the issue of goals from a political perspective, focuses on the importance of differences in goals within the organization for the search for power inside those organizations.[3] Each of these perspectives argues that there is typically a gap between strategies formulated in accord with the rational, economic principles outlined in the last seven chapters of this book, and the implementation of those strategies by the managers within organizations. A similar view that problems in organizations may arise because the individuals inside of them, charged with the responsibility for a variety of tasks, may not always agree on either goals or methods comes from behavioral economists like Cyert and March and more recently from agency theorists.[4] In this chapter we will use these varying perspectives to look at the way the internal structure of the organization mediates in formulating and implementing strategy.

The importance of the internal workings of the firm in strategy and performance cannot be overemphasized. Recent work by Hansen and Wernerfelt suggests that organizational climate—the broad organizational and perceptual variables that reflect individual and organizational inter- action—explains a larger share of the variance in the firm profit perfor- mance than the more traditional economic variables we have thus far fo- cused on.[5] In earlier case-study work, Lorsch reports on a number of organizations in which the implementation of a strategic change followed the more rationally based diagnosis of a specific problem by more than a decade. In each of Lorsch's cases, resistance from the existing corporate culture and the coalitions of individuals charged with implementation, proved to be the stumbling block to agreeing on solutions to manifest problems.[6]

In this chapter, we will look in particular at the issue of goal congru- ence in organizations and on the role of managerial leadership. In Chap- ter 9, we turn to organizational structure and design and examine their role in implementing strategic change.

Implementing Goals: A Look at the Problem

The modern American corporation is one wherein there is widespread separation of ownership and control.[7] The owners of the firm are its stockholders; they are the **residual claimants** of the firm. Any value not owed other creditors belongs to these stockholders.[8] But in the typical corporation only a fraction of these stockholders have any managerial function. The managers of the corporation make most of the decisions that determine how well the corporation performs. Yet many of these managers have but a small ownership share in the firm. The nonmana- gerial work force also has discretionary influence on the well-being of the organization, and for these workers the firm ownership stake is indeed typically small.

The disciplinary power of stockholders in this typical corporation has received considerable attention in recent years. But while the stockholder has power, he or she often lacks the specific knowledge needed to take action. Without detailed information about the complexities of daily man- agement, it is hard for stockholders even to learn whether or not their objectives are being pursued by the firm. Is the poor performance of the firm due to managerial negligence or bad luck? Nor does the single, small stockholder have strong incentives to discipline management to pursue his or her objectives. The single stockholder receives only a fraction of the benefit of any improvement stimulated by managerial performance.[9] Firm managers have better access to information than do stockholders, but often fewer incentives to purse profitability.

The power-knowledge problem plays itself out in a parallel way as we move down in the organization. The senior manager in a firm may know what it is he or she hopes to do in the next year, but actually accomplishing those goals requires the aid of a large number of middle and lower managers, as well as nonmanagerial labor. In a typical management situation, top managers depend on their subordinates not only to implement strategy but to provide the data and advice used to generate that strategy. A fundamental organizational question is how superiors can elicit accurate information from their subordinates and motivate the kinds of strategic responses they need.

As Arrow tells us, managers in the modern, complex organization face either a "hidden information" problem or a "hidden action" problem as they go about their jobs. Both problems are made critical by the typical lack of goal congruence among the individuals in a firm. The modern theory of organizations, described earlier by Pfeffer, takes as its central thrust the proposition that organizations are staffed by individuals with often conflicting interests, and that **subgoal pursuit** by those individuals is ubiquitous. Even when subordinate managers are truly interested in pursuing global profit maximization, they typically lack the information necessary to do so.[10] Thus we have a conflict between local and broad interests in organizations and it is a conflict that manifests itself quite profoundly in the area of strategy.

> **A critical task of an organization is to recognize the presence of subgoal pursuit within the organization and to manage conflicts between local and broad interests.**

In organizations, the subgroup identification and loyalty that give rise to subgoal pursuit have a number of sources, and they are often quite strong. First, as Alderfer and Smith point out, subgroups are often fairly homogeneous with respect to the personal characteristics of group members.[11] Younger people are in lower management jobs, somewhat older people in upper management. At least up to now, blacks and women have not penetrated deeply into upper management jobs. Similarity of personal characteristics make organization subgroup identification more likely.[12] Subgroup identification is also reinforced by cognitive factors—that is, members of subgroups often have selective exposure to environmental cues.[13] Finally, the economic incentives in the organization may encourage subgroup loyalties if compensation and resources are divided up in a competitive way among groups in the organization.

Another perspective on the lack of goal congruence among individuals in an organization comes from agency theory.[14] **Agency theory** begins from the proposition that individual actors in an organization have different goals, and asks how the owner of the firm (the principal) can configure the organization so that the managers and workers (the agents) in it will align their interests with those of the owner. In the usual model, the principals have well-defined preferences and the "problem" is that they cannot observe the behavior of the agents in sufficient detail. Under these circumstances, the members of the organization are likely to behave opportunistically.

Opportunism occurs whenever an individual takes advantage of information asymmetry to pursue his or her own goals at the expense of a less knowledgeable partner.[15] Such opportunism can include shirking (the usual alternative in simple economic models) or pursuit of subgoals.[16] A recent survey of several hundred middle-level managers points to the importance of opportunism for the strategic-planning process.[17] This survey found substantial tendencies for managers to intervene in organizational decision processes to protect their own self-interest, even in decisions with wide-ranging strategic impact. At times, pursuit of narrow interests by managers may seriously jeopardize the overall movement of the organization. Sloan, writing decades ago, observed the same phenomenon at General Motors in the 1950s: Some of the top managers "had no broad outlook, and used their memberships on the Executive Committee to advance the interests of their respective divisions."[18] Subgoal pursuit is obviously not a new managerial concern.

Perhaps the most important contribution of agency theory to organizational literature comes from its focus on the role of uncertainty and information. Shirking, subgoal pursuit, and opportunism are possible because of information problems. As we have seen in previous chapters, industry-wide factors may bolster margins even when management is inept. Shifts in demand, new entry by foreign and domestic rivals, unexpected cost increases—these all influence earnings and are to a large extent out of the control of the manager. As a result, there are limits to the kinds of inferences stockholders can make about managerial effort based on organizational performance. The emergence of multidivisional structures, with their product-line financial reports, reduces that uncertainty and thus helps reduce agency problems. But as much of modern accounting theory emphasizes, we can make only limited inferences about either individual or firm performance from financial data. Thus uncertainty and goal divergence in the modern complex organization make new strategies difficult both at the formulation stage and the implementation stage.

Goal Congruence: Two Examples of the Conflict of Local and Broad Interests

In order to explore the ways in which conflicting interests and subgoal pursuit among managers occur in the real workplace, we will study two quite different organizations, one a nonprofit and one a for-profit. Both are **multidivisional organizations.** This will allow us to see not only the individual-organizational relationship but also the conflict between local and broad interests at the divisional level.

The Waverly Community House (WCH) was formed in the early 1940s as a social-service agency focusing particularly on the needs of children in the urban Northeast. Over the years, the agency has grown, both in scope and in size. Much of this growth has occurred in the last ten years, during which time the budget of the organization has increased sixfold.

By the early 1980s, there were considerable tensions in this social-service organization. Senior staff believed that growth was putting pressure on both the facilities and staff, that the growth was proceeding higgledy-piggledy, and that the agency was in danger of forgetting its mission. Finally, the staff, which had once seen itself as a close-knit family, was beginning to feel competition among themselves for resources. The parallels between the feelings of staff in this small nonprofit and those of staff in growing entrepreneurial ventures are striking.

In the early 1980s, WCH ran four divisions: a Children's program; an Adult program; TEAM, a program for the retarded; and Emergency Food. The Children's program was a large one, the oldest and best-established division at WCH. It consisted of an after-school recreation program, a latch-key program, a summer camp, and an outreach program taking special educational and recreational sessions to the community schools. In any given year, the Children's program served over 600 children. The after-school program was extremely popular in the community and was consistently oversubscribed. On the other hand, the Children's program was the least well funded of WCH's four programs. In conventional economic terms, the Children's program was a high-volume, low-margin operation.

The fastest growing part of the WCH agency was TEAM, the division responsible for programming for retarded adults. TEAM started in 1978 as a one-evening-a-week social program. In 1981, it expanded into vocational training, running a daily program for several dozen retarded adults. Most recently, TEAM has opened several group homes that allow some retarded adults to live more independently than they had been able to previously. The TEAM division is funded primarily by the State Department of Mental Retardation, and is the best funded of the WCH divisions. From the organization's perspective, this part of the operation was a relatively profitable high-growth opportunity.

WCH has also traditionally served as a gathering place for local adults to pursue various educational and social activities. Indeed, this is one of the fundamental services associated with traditional settlement house agencies, of which WCH is an example. In 1984, approximately 100 adults used the WCH facilities. Fees charged for these services are set in an attempt to cover direct costs, although, as in most for-profit operations, calculating direct costs is not a simple matter.

Recent public concern with the homeless led the agency in 1980 to begin an emergency food program. WCH provides food and some emergency counseling for the indigent and homeless in the community. It serves primarily a walk-in population and coordinates with the clergy in the community. Emergency Food is the fourth and final division of WCH.

WCH is run by an executive director, who has been at the agency since 1970. The Children's program is also run by an old-timer, a woman who has been at the agency since 1971 and has strong ties to the local community. The other three directors have all come to WCH in the last three years and are young social workers.

This is a sketchy outline of the divisional structure at WCH, but we can already see some potential organizational tensions. WCH is a nonprofit organization and thus has no stockholders to serve. Nevertheless, the agency has a number of **stakeholders,** people who believe that WCH is responsible to them. The explicit mission of the organization is to serve the community. Thus the community is one stakeholder. Funding agencies are also concerned with strategies pursued by WCH, as are the staff and clients. The potential for conflict in interests among these constituents is substantial.

Perhaps the biggest direct conflict in the objectives of the agency and the community in this case came from a direct consideration of the target audience for WCH. The explicit mission of the agency was to serve the *local* community. But consider the following concerns. The Children's program runs a summer camp in a lovely idyllic spot. But camp enrollment is under capacity, and in recent years WCH has been accepting Fresh Air children to bring it up to capacity. Indeed, in one recent year, almost one-half of the camp population was comprised of Fresh Air Fund kids. But these children were not from the local area; most came from another state. Many people in the community think the camp should be shut down, and the resources of WCH redeployed, since relatively few local children actually use the facility. The WCH executive director wishes to keep the camp open, in part because as a social-service professional, he sees the client base as considerably broader than the local community. In short, the director believes the larger community has some residual claim on the agency. The Children's program director also wants to keep the camp open, in part because it constitutes a third of her program budget, and she is concerned that any resources released by the camp closing will be allocated to another program in the agency. The Children's director also believes herself to have some claim on agency resources. Her feeling is not unlike that of a divisional manager asked to shut down a piece of his or her operation. Budget size confers power in all organizations. Here we see a conflict in objectives both between the community and the executive director and between the director and one of his subordinates.

A similar conflict played itself out in the program for retarded adults. At first the TEAM program served local adults by providing a social evening. When the WCH introduced vocational training, the client base expanded to serve those outside the local community, in part because there are some scale economies in the provision of vocational services and there were simply not enough retarded adults in the local community to fill to capacity the program. The group-home project reaches out even more to outsiders, since the funding agency *requires* that one-half of the home spaces be allocated to individuals currently in institutions, not in the community. Again, the professionals inside the agency are interested in the expansion of what they believe to be a needed and valuable service; the community in part is concerned about the agency moving away from local services. The TEAM director wishes to protect her growing share of agency resources, while other areas of the agency are threatened by that divisional growth. In this instance, the natural tendencies toward subgoal pursuit are reinforced by the strong professional identity of individuals in the TEAM division. As Mintzberg suggests, professionals, particularly in nonprofits, often derive their goals more from their professions than from the particulars of the organization in which they practice that profession.[19] We see that tendency operating strongly at WCH.

There was also ample room in the WCH situation for opportunistic behavior. The WCH director controlled the budget process and had wide discretion over the allocation of the fixed and shared costs of operation. Thus information about how much cross-subsidization was occurring was not widely held. Budgeting was not done on a program basis, thus allowing the executive director to shift resources across budgets without being explicit. In this way, the accounting system played a role in fostering particular constellations of power within WCH. Program directors had the best information about details of enrollments in the camp and the group homes and about future potential growth in these areas, but no agency-wide financial information. Here, too, subgoal pursuit was possible.

Cross-group tensions were also manifest in the agency. As a result of the rapid growth, both the Children's program and the TEAM program needed the van for client transportation. The TEAM director in particular was very committed to the needs of the retarded and resented any suggestion that any of the resources from her well-funded program in any way cross-subsidize the rest of the agency. The executive director, on the other hand, was committed to a full-service agency and needed some flexibility to move money around to accomplish this goal. The Department of Mental Retardation—principal funder for the TEAM program— opposed cross-subsidization, but was almost helpless to find out if there was any going on, given the arcane allocation rules followed by the agency and the almost total lack of program budgeting. Again, one is reminded of the tensions in multidivisional private corporations in which cash flow from one operation is used to fund a start-up in another.

It is easy to explain the rising stress levels in the WCH agency. As the agency grew, the subgroup structure began to take precedence over the organization itself. Directors began to see themselves as committed to their particular constituencies, and not to the rather large social-service agency WCH was now becoming. As we saw from the earlier comments by Sloan, similar patterns appeared at General Motors when divisional managers began to concentrate on the fate of Chevrolet or Buick and neglected the fortunes of G.M. as a whole. Subgoal pursuit is almost inevitable in a large organization.

We will return to the WCH agency later to explore some of the ways organizational structure and compensation at the agency exacerbated the problem of conflicting objectives. Now we will turn to an organization in the for-profit sector that exhibited many of the same problems as WHC.

Electron Industries is a moderately sized multidivisional organization operating in the area of scientific instrumentation.[20] The scientific instruments industry is highly dependent on the state of scientific research. Instruments are demanded when research funding is high. The instrument industry is thus highly dependent on government, which funds most research. The industry has grown dramatically in the post-war period, but appears to be now approaching a more mature slow-growth phase.

Electron Industries, a moderate player in this industry, is composed of three divisions. Able Electronics is the oldest and largest part of the firm, with sales of approximately $40 million. It produces a broad line of electronic lab equipment. In 1970, the organization acquired its second division, Beacon, which has sales of approximately $22 million, in a narrower line of high-priced, high-quality equipment. In 1978, the organization acquired its third division, Atlas, which presently has sales of about $5 million, in instruments used in environmental monitoring. Thus all three divisions produce scientific instruments, although they operate in rather different niches of the market.

Up until recently, each of the three divisions operated as an autonomous unit, with the central organization providing direction in terms of resource allocation. But apart from the requirement that each division provide plans and budgets, little direct supervision was done. Each division undertook its own marketing, research, and planning. No coordination of a formal sort across the three divisions was done.

In part stimulated by discussions in the management literature about synergies and the value of cross-pollination among divisions in an operation, the president of Electron Industries hired a management-consulting group to try to promote divisional coordination. The task turned out to be more formidable than he had imagined, largely because of the kind of human-resources problems we have been discussing.

The first task outlined by the consulting team was for divisional heads to develop strategic plans for their own operations that had a set of common elements: first, an environmental analysis of the basic conditions of supply and demand in the industry submarket served by the division; second, a broad statement of the current direction of the division and its strengths and weaknesses; third, a plan for the new directions of the division, including a discussion of possible overlaps with the other two divisions. The objective of this exercise, as articulated by the team, was to coordinate activity among the divisions and to "rationalize" the resource-allocation process.

In terms of Electron Industries, the most interesting application of theory lies in the way it can help us understand the conflicts between the organization as a whole and its three divisions. The president of Electron

Industries was interested in the overall growth and profitability of his own organization. But the division heads were not similarly motivated. Each divisional head was concerned about his operation; all the more so, since in each case, the head was once the successful entrepreneur who established that business. Divisional heads worked hard and creatively; there was no shirking here. But they worked for their own purposes, not necessarily for the organization as a whole. There had been no history of coordination, and there were no economic or social incentives for coordination. In this case, the corporate culture of autonomy proved to be a large stumbling block to integrated strategic analysis.

In fact, the consultants found that they received almost no cooperation from the two largest divisions. Both of these divisions were sizeable, and their investment needs were modest relative to their cash flows. In the case of both, the submarket served was a fairly mature one. Both divisional heads believed that cooperation and coordination would likely diminish their own organizational control, and resource rationalization might well divert funds from the mature part of the business to the "upstart" part of the business, the newly acquired Atlas. Both of these divisions saw themselves in the unenviable position of "cash cows," and neither wished to cooperate in the milking process. In this case, the subgoals of the organization were at conflict with the overall goal of the organization. Atlas, a small division with big ideas for the future, produced a careful and ambitious plan. From its perspective, coordination and resource reallocation were likely to be beneficial. But Electron's consulting and planning effort was blockaded by the conflict in objectives with the other two groups of the organization.

We will return to both of these organizations shortly to see how they faced some of their problems. But first let us turn to a more general look at some of the ways in which organizations try to gain cooperation to accomplish their goals, in the face of differentiated interests within the organization.

Improving Cooperation: Motivation

Given this picture of the organization, how do we begin to resolve some of the potential conflicts we see? How can we limit opportunism or harness subgoal pursuit in the broader interests of the firm? One of the ingredients that helps provide an answer to this question is a better understanding of what motivates people. Social psychologists in the organizational area have developed a number of theories about human motivation that are of relevance here. My goal is to try to draw from the various theories some of the broad principles that might be of relevance to motivation in the workplace.

Expectancy theory, developed by Vroom, suggests that a worker's job performance is directed toward obtaining a particular outcome.[21] If we asked workers to rate the importance of work outcomes like wages, prestige, security, friendship, professional satisfaction, and then to trace for us the ways in which job performance led to high outcomes on these various scales, we should find that workers perform in ways most likely to lead to the kinds of outcomes they most value. For example, if workers value wages most highly and believe that the major determinant of high wages is alternative job offers, then we should expect to see heightened attempts to sell oneself on the external job market. And, indeed, the empirical literature has some modest support for expectancy theory.[22]

What practical, managerial suggestions emerge from expectancy theory? Most important, organizations should be clear on just what the links are between performance and outcomes. This clarity serves at least two functions. First, it provides better motivation for existing workers. Second, it allows efficient sorting of workers; thus individuals who are most concerned with wages move to one industry, while those more interested in working conditions flock to a second. In the face of substantial differences in worker preferences, such sorting is clearly optimal. Hence, organizations do not try to mold the preferences of their workers, but find workers who already have the "right" preferences.

The evidence is substantial that setting goals is important in motivating people. We are less clear on just why this is true. Salancik, for example, argues that it is in part the process of goal setting that is central and not the goals themselves.[23] Indeed, Japanese management style reflects this same focus on process. To the extent that goal setting requires substantial meetings focused around questions about what the organization ought to be doing, the culture of the organization can be more effectively diffused through the organization.

We are also less clear on what specific kinds of incentives truly motivate people. As we will see, the central focus of economists in this area has been on compensation and promotion schemes as motivating devices. Organizational theorists are less sanguine about the power of economic rewards to solve problems of opportunism or subgoal pursuit. Pfeffer, for example, argues "the evidence is ambiguous concerning the extent to which compensation systems based on returns to owners are actually effective in motivating managerial behavior that is in closer correspondence with ownership interests."[24] Lane, in his critique of agency theory, argues that compensation plays only a very modest role in motivating people to work.[25] On the other hand, the widespread reliance on compensation schemes as a way to motivate individuals in the modern corporation suggests that such schemes are not without effect. Thus we will look at a wide range of ways to understand and moderate the problems of opportunism and subgoal pursuit.

While there is considerable uncertainty among academics about precisely what motivates individuals in a work situation, there is less debate about the profound effect of group structure on work performance. The classic study of the power of subgroups in an organization was done in coal mining in Tavistock, Great Britain.[26] Initially, coal miners were organized in small groups of about six to eight miners. Groups were homogeneous and socially close, inside and outside of work. After a technological change in industry production methods, old groups were reformed into much larger units, with members numbering about 50. The new technology required interdependence just as the old method did, but the configuration of larger, newer groups was much less conducive to such cooperation. Productivity deteriorated dramatically, along with worker satisfaction. The fact that the organization designed its work in response to technology alone, without regard for the dynamics of group structures imposed considerable costs on the firm. The resulting productivity decline reveals something of the power of the group even in economic terms.

Group loyalty is easier to develop in small groups than in larger organizations.[27] The psychological ties binding small groups are further buttressed by the economic incentives facing individuals. The smaller the group, the more each individual's efforts matter to the success of the organization. As the organization grows larger, the individual sees his or her contribution to the group diminishing proportionately. As a result, the connection between individual action and group consequence is perceived as diminishing, and individuals typically invest less in actions that aid the whole. This effect is known in economics as the **free-rider problem.**

A free rider is an individual who enjoys the result of a particular collective action without fully contributing to the achievement of that action.

Many organizations have seen the free-rider problem in action as their members have reduced their commitments to the collective in response to organizational growth. Indeed, many organizations have tried to design systems to preserve a small-firm feeling precisely to avoid free-rider problems that often come with size.

The existence of subgroups in an organization is a powerful tool for promoting strong goal orientation. It can also serve to divide complex organizations. Thus organizations look to both economic and organizational techniques to harness the power of subgroups.

Economic Incentives

Economic incentives include two broad tools: salaries and wages, and promotion policy. Among Fortune 500 firms, more than half of the compensation of most top executives consists of bonuses that are based on the performance of the firms they operate. Walt Disney's chief executive, Michael Eisner, earned a salary of only $750,000 in 1986, but received a bonus of $2.6 million based on Disney's high return on equity. Even in relatively small firms—like the several hundred sampled by *Inc.* magazine—bonuses tied to performance measures are ubiquitous.[28] The form of performance payments differs substantially among firms. Some are short-term earnings-growth bonuses; others are longer term payments; still others are in the form of stock options. Often such payments are a relatively small fraction of total compensation. But all share the characteristic that one goal of the payment is to try to better align the objectives of management with the objectives of the owners of the corporation.

One type of performance compensation that highlights the issues we have been discussing is when workers are paid precisely in proportion to the output they produce. Piece-rate work and sales commissions fall into this category. If workers shirk, their pay diminishes. Consider the following description of the contracting process involved in laying hardwood floors in Hong Kong.[29]

> A landlord who wants to build a high-rise finds a building contractor. This contractor subcontracts with a hardwood floor contractor on an agreed price per square foot—a piece count. The subcontractor, who imports the wood materials and adds finishing work to the wood on a piece-rate basis, in turn finds a sub-subcontractor, provides him wood, and offers him a price per square foot laid. Finally, the sub-subcontractor hires workers and again pays them per square foot laid.[30]

In this industry, piece rates clearly dominate wage rates. Workers vary considerably in speed and skill, while the job itself is quite standard. Square footage is a standard measure, and quality is easily assessed.

Under some piece-work systems, including the well-known putting out system of early industrial England and much of the current work in Hong Kong and other parts of East Asia, it is common for workers to own their own piece of the production process, and it is the role of the entrepreneur to buy and sell the pieces to put the whole together. Each worker faces the right incentives because, despite the complexity of production and the variety of steps in production, each worker is simultaneously an owner. Thus there is neither a problem of shirking nor of divergence of goals between local and broad interests.

Why not apply performance-compensation schemes across the board in the large, modern corporation? Performance-compensation schemes provide workers and managers with the right incentives to serve stockholders, since paying the people precisely in proportion to their output eliminates the incentive problem. Why not, then, go all the way and organize all compensation in this way?

There are two fundamental impediments to the full use of performance compensation. First, the natural **risk aversion** of individuals makes them reluctant to work for firms with pure performance compensation. Second, the very complexity of work performance in most areas makes strict performance schemes impracticable.[31]

Risk aversion discourages excessive reliance on performance compensation.

Since performance compensation schemes do not guarantee a fixed wage, but rather link wages to some measure of job performance, uncertainty is introduced into employees' compensation. But most people do not like uncertainty, particularly in something as important to them as their daily wages. Thus, for most people, a job with a 50 percent probability of earning $75,000 and a 50 percent probability of earning $25,000 would be distinctly inferior to one which pays a steady wage of $50,000, even though the **expected value** of the two wages is the same. Given that most people are risk averse, an employer offering an uncertain wage needs to improve the terms in order to be able to hire any people. In the above example, one might have to pay $90,000/$25,000 instead of $75,000/$25,000 to compete in the labor market with the steady wage firm. But of course this offer will, on average, be more expensive to the firm.

Now, you might ask, don't the terms that I have to offer depend on the source of the uncertainty in the job? The answer is, Very much so. Suppose in the first place that the uncertainty is out of control of the individual worker. For example, a textile worker is paid on a piece rate which varies with market demand. When demand is high, the price per piece produced rises, and when demand falls, so does the piece rate. Here uncertainty created by the market affects the individual's wage. Another source of wage variation is if the sewing machines used by the textile workers break down through no fault of the sewers. In either of these cases we might expect the natural risk aversion of individuals to discourage them from taking piece-rate wages unless there was some sweetener involved.

Now suppose the uncertainty in wage payments is completely within the control of the worker. If you work hard and carefully, you earn the larger sum, but if you work shoddily and slowly, you will earn the smaller. In this circumstance, hard careful workers will be attracted to the firm paying performance rates, and sloppy slow workers will not. Here the wage structure will serve an additional role as a **screening device,** sorting out for the firm the good and bad applicants entirely on the basis of whether they find the job offer attractive. Shy people will find commission-based sales jobs unappealing, and only the nimble fingered will work for piece rates in manufacturing. In this case, performance compensation performs two admirable functions: It screens the workers, to raise the overall level of those workers, and it improves the work effort incentives of the workers hired. This is quite a different story from the case in which the performance measure varied dramatically as a function of exogenous forces.

The objective for the organization, then, is to identify a performance measure on which compensation can be based that reflects as much as possible only the effort and contribution of the individual being compensated. To the extent that this can be done, the performance measure can serve its beneficial screening and incentive roles. On the other hand, using a performance measure that has a great deal of noise in it, outside the control of the worker, will prove to be quite unmotivating for the worker.

Performance-related compensation measures should screen out, as much as possible, factors unrelated to individual performance.

This principle of trying to minimize outside noise can be seen in practice in the way many organizations currently organize compensation. Textile workers, for example, are typically compensated based on the number of units sewn, not on the gross profits of the organization. Thus demand fluctuations in the textile market do not influence wages. Salesmen are paid a commission based on the number of units sold, and are given exclusive, fixed-boundary territories to shield them from some of the outside forces that might otherwise thwart the success of their selling efforts.

A simple **principal-agent model** of the problem of compensation in an organization with conflicting interests and uncertainty helps to illustrate some of the points just raised. We begin with a simple firm, with an owner who wishes to maximize firm profits. We have a representative worker, and we are concerned with designing a compensation scheme to motivate that worker.[32] There are two possible "states of the world"— that is, either the climate is favorable for the firm or it is not. Call the favorable climate s_1 and the unfavorable s_2. Suppose further that there are two possible kinds of behavior for the worker: working hard *ah*, and working less hard *aL*. Finally, we assume that the employee likes wages, but does not particularly like working hard. This situation is the classic "worker as shirker" model that characterizes simple agency models. While it is clear that in practice not all workers are shirkers, the simple model does illustrate a point. To make the problem concrete, let us suppose that the employee's utility function can be written as $U = z^{1/2} - v(a)$, where z is income and $v(a)$ an index based on how hard the employee works. Thus income is positive and working is negative and the worker is risk averse. Finally, the worker has available an alternative job that yields a utility level of 150. This situation is depicted in Table 8.1.

The numbers inside the matrix represent the revenues that could be realized by the efforts of the worker under various states of the world and different levels of effort. We see here that sometimes hard work pays off and sometimes (state 2) it does not.

Table 8.1 A simple agency model of compensation

		State of the world		Loss of utility from work
Level of effort	ah	s_1 $500,000	s_2 $100,000	v(ah) = 40
	aL	$100,000	$100,000	v(aL) = 20

Revenues of the organization given in matrix

Suppose the firm could perfectly observe both states of the world and the employees' level of effort. In that case, the first best solution to this problem is to offer the employee a wage in which he or she is required to work hard. Since the employee has a wage offer at present that yields a utility level of 150, and since working hard causes a loss of 40 $v(ah)$, the owner will have to offer the new worker $36,100. In this case, the worker earns utility equal to $36,100½ − 40 or 150. If the two states of the world are equally likely, the expected cash flow from this hiring strategy will be $263,900 (.5(500,000 − 36,100) + .5(100,000 − 36,100)).

The typical organization, however, faces a harder problem. In particular, the firm owner is unlikely to know for certain either the state of the world or the level of effort of the worker. Of course, the worker will know his or her own effort level and may well know the state of the world. But, in this model, he or she has no incentive to truthfully reveal this information. The compensation package is one way to achieve the end we wish here—hard work—in the face of uncertainty.

Suppose we offered the potential employee not a fixed wage but a contingent contract. In particular, we might offer the employee a base salary with a bonus if revenues exceed a certain level. In the example given here, we could offer the employee a base salary of $28,900 and a salary of $44,100 if revenues rose to $500,000. It is easy to verify that this wage offer satisfies the following criteria: First, the offer yields an expected utility to the worker of 150, equivalent to his or her alternative offer. Second, the offer provides enough of a bonus to induce the worker to work hard. Finally, the combined wage offer leaves the organization better off than it would be offering a flat wage and ending up with a shirker. It is also easy to see that the organization would be better off still if there were no uncertainty, and it could simply offer a flat wage to the employee and demand hard work. Thus the uncertainty in the environment coupled with the natural risk aversion of the potential employee has some costs to the organization.

Of course, in practice, problems are likely to be somewhat more complicated than the one described here. In particular, there is typically a continuum of effort levels and states of the world, rather than two of each, and utility functions are not so easily found out. Many workers are not shirkers, but have more complex goals that also may not be congruent with owner goals. Oftentimes performance on the job depends on team effort, rather than individual effort. Nevertheless, the model provides a formal way of understanding the lure of bonus systems, and the situations in which they are most attractive.

Bonus systems are a way to motivate behavior in situations of goal conflicts and unobservable behavior.

As we see in the simple model, bonus systems serve as a partial alternative to monitoring and rules. The typical organization will use both monitoring and some form of bonus, depending on their relative efficiency.

So far, we have not attached a precise meaning to performance measure. Our stylized example keyed compensation to the organizations' profits and this is a commonly used measure. At Walt Disney, for example, CEO Michael Eisner's contract calls for a share of net income over a base 9 percent return in equity.[33] There is some surface logic to the focus on profits in compensation schemes. Stockholders are, after all, focused on profits. And, in practice, most bonus schemes applied at the management level are tied to some version of profits. It is no small matter, however, just how one defines this performance measure. Incentives keyed to short-run profits will encourage short-term strategies; longer term profits may be harder to track and provide less immediate motivation. All incentives schemes keyed to accounting measures encourage creative tinkering with accounting systems and interfere with other corporate use of these systems.

The main long-term performance compensation method used in the United States has historically been the **stock option.** A stock option is the right to purchase stock at a below-market price. The option increases with the value of the stock of the firm. Thus options have been thought to provide a greater link between stockholders and managers.[34] There are, however, drawbacks to the use of options. First, the market price of a stock is only partially related to the performance of any particular manager, however highly placed. Market demand, foreign entry, even the weather can influence stock prices. Second, stock options have unfortunate properties in terms of risks to the manager. If a manager holds large stock options, he or she is doubly at risk when the firm does badly. Thus extensive use of stock options may conflict with managerial needs for financial diversification.

The prime alternative to stock options has been the use of bonuses tied to the earnings growth of the organization. For many organizations, the critical measure is the annual earnings growth of the firm. Others, like Koppers Co., a $1.5 billion Pittsburgh mining firm, use multiyear plans in an attempt to encourage managers to adopt longer range horizons.

Bonuses based on single year performance or multiple years' earnings are still quite imperfect, again because the earnings of an organization are only partially the result of managerial efforts. Considerable variability in performance is unrelated to effort variability. One attempt to get around this problem has been the use of **filtering,** a method by which management bonuses are keyed to the performance of the organization *relative* to other similarly placed organizations. For example, U.S. Trust bases its executive bonuses on growth in earnings per share relative to 17 other banks with similar characteristics. Similarly Phillips Petroleum pays off only if Phillips does better in earnings than at least 4 of the other 10 oil companies in a similar position. Phillip's vice president for human resources explained the policy as follows: "Before 1974, we set absolute goals for earnings. Then things like the OPEC price hikes started making those goals obsolete. It was just too easy for us to make our goals, so

now we measure ourselves against our competitors."[35] In the more competitive 1980s and 1990s, filtering protected managers on the down side.
The effect of filtering is to remove some of the variability in an organization's performance caused by outside forces. By putting the performance
measure under the control of the organization's management, managerial
incentives can be improved. Work by Antle and Smith suggests that a
number of firms are moving toward the use of filtering bonuses.[36]

**Compensation tied to the performance of an organization relative to its
competitors may provide better-focused incentives for managers.**

Another approach to the problem of defining performance measures
has been taken by companies like Mead Corporation, a large paper maker.
At Mead, bonuses are tied to the division's ability to "make its plan." As
a Mead vice president explained, "Our focus here is to attain the approved plan. That means it is entirely possible for a unit, during a period
of expansion, to have a lower return on net assets and yet meet its plan
and get a bigger incentive pay off."[37] In this way, if a group anticipates
some dire event in the market to sour earnings, it can account for that in
its plan and not suffer the consequences. The plan plays a role both in
informing the center of likely future events and motivating managers.
Again, as in the filtering scheme, the attempt is to weed out some of the
system variability before applying the performance criteria. Of course, bonuses tied to meeting plans have their own difficulties, not the least of
which is some tendency on the part of managers to "low-ball" plans to
ensure reasonable bonuses. But the attempt to remove some of the exogenous variability is clearly a move in the right direction.

Filtering also occurs in compensation plans designed for low-level
management. Very often managers as well as workers are judged not in
terms of some absolute standard, but in terms of their relative ranking.
The best performer in a sales operation receives a bonus, for example.
The most creative suggestion by a production worker earns a prize. **Yardstick competition** can be quite useful when the individuals being com-
pared face similar uncertainties produced by outside influences. Bonuses
or higher salaries can then be paid to individuals based on which one
outperforms the others, all of whom operate in a similar environment.
Again the effect of yardstick competition or ranking methods is to try to
remove some of the exogenous variability from performance measures.[38]

Yardstick competition as a way to rate individual performance also
mitigates the well-known problem of different standards among supervisors. It is well known that some supervisors tend to rate everyone high,
while others are uniformly critical.[39] If supervisors are required to rate
employees relative to one another, perhaps by having to allocate a fixed
quota system of points, these cross-supervisor differences will diminish.

One reason organizations do not rely more heavily on performance
compensation is that variability in performance is in most instances partially exogenous to the individual, and most individuals are risk averse.

We can begin to see the kind of trade-off an organization faces. To the extent that the individual's effort determines actual performance, the organization will do well to rely at least in part on a performance-compensation scheme. But the use of performance measures when those measures only imperfectly reflect managerial or worker effort will often violate the individual's sense of fairness. Moreover, the more narrow performance standards are set, the more likely managers will pursue narrow subgoals, albeit with zeal. Under these circumstances, reliance on performance measures may be counterproductive. If other factors play a prime role in performance results, then a straight salary will be preferable.

> **Compensation programs that vary in ways which do not reflect individual effort or ability violate a fundamental sense of fairness essential to employment relations. Narrow performance-based compensation programs may also reduce cooperation within the firm.**

Let us return for a moment to the two organizations described earlier to see the role played by compensation schemes. In the case of WCH, the social-service agency, the agency had historically compensated its directors on the basis of seniority. Poor performance could result in termination, but this threat was the only instrument used to discipline managers. The director, four or five years ago, realized that this system was not an effective compensation scheme. The directors of the various divisions by this time had quite different responsibilities, and they performed quite differently. A new compensation design was thus introduced in which managerial compensation varied according to the size of the division's budget. The director reasoned that successful divisions would grow and that this compensation scheme would thus ensure the right incentives for his managers. (A great many for-profit organizations similarly key compensation to growth. In the *Inc.* survey, fully a third of the firms paid bonuses to managers based on sales goals.[40]) The WCH director also argued that the incentive schedule would be "fair," since directors with larger budgets and staffs did more supervisory work. In fact, this compensation scheme only exacerbated the tensions already in the organization. As Porter, Lawler, and Hackman warn, "Organizations tend to motivate the kind of behavior they reward."[41] Directors who were already inward looking from an organizational perspective became more so. The economic incentives now reinforced social incentives. Moreover, the rapid growth of the organization was further fueled by the overly ambitious plans of directors who had come to see growth as the central goal of the organization. In an attempt to reduce problems of shirking, the WCH director had exacerbated problems of subgoal pursuit.

Similarly, in Electron Industries, each divisional head was paid a fixed salary plus a bonus based on the performance of the particular division. The argument in favor of this bonus was clearly that each head only controlled his area. But the effect of the bonus was to encourage a further narrowing of objectives. Subgoal pursuit was again increased in an attempt to reduce shirking.

Can we control both shirking and subgoal pursuit at the same time through the compensation scheme? Some organizations try to broaden the management perspective of divisional managers by offering bonuses partially keyed to the group's success and partially keyed to the overall organization's success. The problem with these broad incentive plans, however, is that insofar as individuals see themselves as contributing only on the margin to the larger organization it will be hard to really motivate them to push harder in that area. Again, the free-rider problem arises.

We have thus far focused on the use of financial compensation as a way to motivate employees. But organizations can also influence behavior via their promotion strategies. Indeed, many organizations offer fairly homogeneous, nonperformance-based salaries to individuals at the same managerial rank, but use the possibility of promotion to a higher rank as a way to induce effort. In a wide range of organizations, internal job promotions are one of the most important rewards available.[42] One of the advantages of the promotion system may lie in its ability to encourage effort while not simultaneously narrowing the manager's perspective. In this way, promotion incentives may at times dominate narrow compensation schemes.

Very often the president of a large corporation is chosen from among the ranks of the numerous vice presidents. It is also generally the case that the president is paid considerably more than the vice presidents. Surely it is hard to believe that the vice president chosen to be president suddenly gains so much in his or her productivity as to warrant a doubling of salary. It seems much more reasonable to view the large salary increase accompanying promotion as a kind of prize for the individual who wins the contest among vice presidents to become the new president. Thus the president's wage "is settled on not necessarily because it reflects his own current productivity but rather because it induces that individual and all other individuals to perform appropriately when they are in more junior positions."[43] The promotion policy of many organizations serves to create competition, where the tournament prize is a higher position and salary. Such competition may at times have a salutary effect on earnings.

Thus organizations can use promotion policy as a complement to performance-compensation schemes as a way to induce better performance by managers. This is not to say that in most firms narrow productivity is the only or indeed the optimal basis for promotion. In a survey of almost 400 firms in the private sector, Abraham and Medoff found that in 60 percent of the organizations senior employees are favored for promotion over more productive junior employees.[44] In a number of these organizations, it was corporate policy never to promote junior employees, regardless of how good they were. Promotions may in these organizations serve the role of transmitting and preserving corporate values and culture. Promotions can also be used politically; supervisors "act politically to place strategically those loyal to their aims."[45] Perrow has argued that the widespread nepotism observed in firms has as its principal product loyalty.[46] This same theme about the use of promotions to promote loyalty recurs in DeLorean's description of his time at General Motors:

> [They] developed what I call the "promotion of the unobvious choice." This means promoting someone who was not regarded as a contender for the post. Doing so not only puts your man in position, but it earns for you his undying loyalty because he owes his corporate life to you."[47]

Social Incentives

The economic model works on developing goal congruence, including reducing shirking, by designing incentive systems. But economic incentive systems take us only part of the way, even in the ideal managerial case. When superiors are dependent on subordinates not only for performance, but for the judgment and data needed to design policy, when individuals work on complex problems in teams, when ideal performance is multifaceted, simple agency models are limited. And more complex agency models, with their predictions about complex fee structures, seem very different from systems of compensation we observe.[48] In these areas, organizational theory provides some interesting insights that both complement and, in some cases, supplant the economic models.

In the general discussion thus far, we have focused on the two problems of reducing shirking and increasing goal congruence. We have seen that economic incentives work most powerfully and simply on the problem of shirking. In dealing with goal congruence, the organizational literature is more salient. In that literature, perhaps the most influential current organizational theorist is Ouchi.[49]

Ouchi focuses his attention on what he calls **clans** in organizations. Clan members, because they have a "shared social understanding" of the organization and the way it operates, also share the organization's goals. This allows them to operate more-or-less autonomously, reducing both monitoring costs and the need for novel incentive systems. Organizations in which clans develop thus have efficiency advantages over their rivals. Developing clans is Ouchi's organizational alternative to agency theory's emphasis on compensation schemes.

How can an organization in its drive for efficiency promote clans? Ouchi and Wilkens argue that clans develop when there is a stable population within a firm that has broad interaction and relatively nonspecialized career paths. Corporate cultures and a belief in the uniqueness of the organization further reinforce clanishness. Most organizations that have been in existence for any time have a collection of myths or stories about the birth and operation of the organization. Bolman and Deal refer to these set of myths as the "symbolic frame" of the organization.[50] Mintzberg calls them the "ideologic goals" of the organization.[51] For Ouchi, such stories play a role in holding clans together. A vivid example of the kind of story that carries with it a message of the strategic vision of an organization is provided by Akio Morita, the CEO of Sony:

> Two shoe salesmen find themselves in a rustic, backward section of Africa. The first salesman writes back to his office. "There is no prospect of sales since all the natives are barefoot." The other salesman reports: "No one wears shoes here. We can dominate the market."[52]

Morita's marketing focus is more clearly reflected and disseminated in this story than it might be in a dozen business memos. Indeed, the function of a symbolic frame or ideologic myth is to provide a way for the organization to transmit a set of shared values—to create a clan—so that individuals, acting autonomously, move the organization forward.

The clan is created through culture in two ways. First, there is the screening role of the corporate culture. When an individual considers taking a job in a new organization, almost the first thing he or she will confront will be the many manifestations of the corporate culture. How do people dress? Is there a common cafeteria? What are the office arrangements? The culture of larger, older corporations may already have been conveyed to recruits through the media. We all share quite different images of IBM, with its myth of the uniform blue-suited manager, and Apple, with its different myth of the wide-eyed innovator. These public personae can serve an important role in attracting like-minded individuals to the organization, and they can make the later job of socialization considerably easier.

But the corporate culture can play a role beyond screening. Organizations can also *socialize* individuals so that they adopt a perspective closer to that of the organization. In its ideal form, the socialization of individuals that begins with their entry into an organization acts to internalize the goals of the organization, and thus reduces the need for either extrinsic rewards or careful monitoring of the individuals.[53] Here, Ouchi argues, we see the efficiency gains from the clan.

Socialization or clan creation can occur in many ways. There is some indication that it is most easily accomplished through the use of symbols, stories, and myths and that an emphasis on the dominant position in the area of the organization is an important part of the socialization process.[54] In some organizations, extensive meetings and broad interaction among managers from different areas serve as an opportunity to transmit the culture of the organization.[55] Some evidence suggests that moving individuals into foreign or alien environments may help them develop a more organization-oriented frame.[56] Similarly, Ouchi argues that an absence of viable alternatives outside the firm encourages the development of clans. The weight of the evidence taken from the area of psychology and management seems to be that socialization can greatly enhance internalization of the goals of the organization. In describing the use of socialization by organizations, Schein writes: "The speed and effectiveness of socialization determine employee loyalty, commitment, productivity and turnover. The basic stability and effectiveness of organizations therefore depends upon their ability to socialize new members."[57]

Not all observers are so enthusiastic about the advantage of strong goal congruence in organizations. One of the more interesting critiques of the emphasis on goal congruence as a way to increase organizational efficiency comes from Weick.[58] Weick argues that while conformity increases an organization's effectiveness in accomplishing particular tasks, it greatly reduces its ability to adapt to change. Effective organizations, according to Weick, are "garrulous, garrumphing, superstitious, hypocritical, monstrous, octopoid, wandering and grouchy." Loose coupling inside these organizations allows individuals to act independently, and this greater internal diversity makes the organization more adaptable, albeit less efficient in dealing with a concrete, well-specified problem.

The politics literature also emphasizes the costs of goal congruence. It has been suggested that as a group develops very strong ties, and socialization works well, groupthink may develop.[59] **Groupthink** carries with it a variety of symptoms especially troublesome to organizations trying to engage in creative, forward-looking strategic planning. These symptoms include an illusion of invulnerability, a tendency to ignore incipient troubles, a stereotyped view of others which can blind an organization to new actions by rivals, and strong pressures to conformity.[60] All of these characteristics, while promoting static efficiency in Ouchi's framework, fare less well in the dynamic, more confused world described by Weick and others.

The costs of groupthink, from the perspective of an organization and society, were described by Arthur Schlesinger in his failure to oppose the Bay of Pigs invasion plans:

> In the months after the Bay of Pigs I bitterly reproached myself for having kept so silent during those crucial discussions in the Cabinet room, though my feelings of guilt were tempered by the knowledge that a course of objection would have accomplished little save to gain me a name as a nuisance. I can only explain my failure to do more than raise a few timid questions by reporting that one's impulse to blow the whistle on this nonsense was as simply undone by the circumstances of the discussion.[61]

We see an interesting trade-off here. For short-term efficiency, in stable environments, developing a cohesive and homogeneous group with congruent goals may be preferable. For changing environments, where adaptability is important, a more heterogeneous organization may perform better. Murray, in a thoughtful and ambitious article, tried to test this hypothesis in a sample of food and oil companies. While Murray's results are clearly tentative, he does find some support for the proposition that managerial heterogeneity improves long-term adaptability while reducing short-term efficiency.[62]

Summary

In this chapter we have examined the human and organizational problems that face an organization attempting to allocate scarce resources. All organizations are characterized by uncertainty and peopled with managers who depend on one another both to set goals and to accomplish those goals. In this setting, the development of a cohesive, functioning organization is a formidable task. Indeed, Stinchcombe has argued that the high mortality rate of young organizations reflects in part the difficulties they face in dealing with the mutual socialization of organizational participants.[63] The fragility of new organizations in managing diverse workers has been described in industries from newspapers[64] to retail markets[65] to social-service agencies,[66] in the United States and abroad.

In this chapter, we have been discussing various elements of human resources strategy. It is difficult to overemphasize the role of human resources management in strategic planning. Jack Welch, CEO of G.E., one of the leading corporations in the strategic planning area gave his views: "I am the ultimate believer . . . people first, strategy second."[67] In many organizations, seemingly well designed technical plans are developed and then never make it off the ground. In the early 1980s, Xerox underwent a massive planning effort, resulting in a several hundred page planning document of great technical quality. For the most part, the document gathered dust, until the planning group rethought *its strategy* for creating a cohesive, viable strategic vision for Xerox. In this case and others, the new effort has been to make planning rewarding to all those who must contribute to its success. In the absence of this kind of effort, strategic planning will never become strategic management.

9

Organizational Structure and Strategic Planning

The senior management of an organization plays a central role in the strategic planning process, for it is these managers who ideally embody the strategic vision of the organization, and who have the ability to see the organization as a whole.[1] But the vision of senior management is an imperfect one, typically obscured by a lack of complete information about the workings of the operation to be managed. Indeed this lack of information is one factor impeding goal congruence in an organization, as we discussed in Chapter 8. The complexity of the modern organization makes it unlikely that senior managers will ever have all the information they might need to make perfect judgments about the strategy of the organization.[2] Thus strategic planning inevitably goes on in an environment of uncertainty, and indeed part of the function of that planning is to reduce uncertainty.

In almost any strategic planning process, some information flows toward the decision-making center. In theory, this information is intended to improve the decision-making process. Information is also essential to help *monitor* the result of the strategic planning process.[3] As Pfeffer suggests in his description of the role of organizational design: "It is not only tasks that are allocated and distributed throughout organizations. Control over resources, legitimate authority and control of decision making are also distributed."[4] In part because information has a monitoring function, it is likely to be distorted as it moves through the organization. Even the choice of the structure or channels along which information flows will bias the information available to managers.[5] If the head of a division in a multidivisional firm expects his or her assessment of the future prospects of that business unit to influence capital allocation (surely a reasonable expectation), then managerial incentives to overstate those prospects will be strong. In this way, managers may behave *opportunistically* in the information they provide as part of the planning process.[6] Even nonopportunistic managers may provide misinformation to the center as a result of **cognitive distortion.**[7] Finally, environmental uncertainties impinge on the planning process. Thus strategic planning goes on with gaps in knowledge and, in some instances, with distorted information.

How does senior management obtain the kind of broad information, however biased and imperfect, it needs to direct resources? The *structure* of an organization helps to determine how that information moves to senior management, as well as how the vision of those senior managers feeds back down the organizational ladder. It defines who is responsible for what activity, how people and tasks are grouped in organizational subunits, and who can give orders to whom.

Thus organizational structure is one of the instruments that senior management can use to influence the strategic planning process. At the same time, the organizational structure typically reflects both the personality and values of its top managers.[8] Thus structure has both economic and socio-psychological antecedents. Decisions about the way in which work units are structured, the degree of hierarchy, the extent of discretion and levels of monitoring all have important effects on the way in which an organization implements a planning process and ultimately how well it performs. In this chapter, we discuss some of the central issues involved in the design of organizational structure.

Dimensions of Structural Differences

Considerable differences exist among organizations in the ways work is divided and tasks are coordinated, but three features of organizational structure remain salient: *the principle governing the division of tasks (i.e., functional versus multidivisional versus matrix); the depth of the hierarchy used; and the extent of authority delegation.* We briefly outline the major differences among organizations in each of these dimensions, and then inquire in the next section as to the principles governing structural choice.

In 1919, in the process of a major reorganization, Du Pont Corporation provided one of the earliest articulations of a principle of organization:

> **The most efficient results are obtained at least expense when we coordinate related effort and segregate unrelated effort.**[9]

But which efforts in an organization are naturally related and which are not? Most operations in an organization are, of course, somewhat related to one another, and so important relationships must be distinguished from unimportant ones.

Early industrial enterprises in the United States (before 1870 or so) engaged in essentially one function: They manufactured goods. Middlemen accomplished most of the rest of the functions we normally associate with the modern enterprise: purchase of inputs, sale of outputs, and so on. As enterprises began to expand, they developed a need for more elaborate structures.[10] The first distinctions most organizations made among their internal groups were functional in structure. Individuals engaged in marketing were placed in one group, those in research in a second, purchasing in a third, and so on. In dividing work and forming units, the principal criterion was technical efficiency. Coordination of the various functional units was expected to occur via senior managers.

As enterprises grew, they began to expand their product lines. The large electric companies, like G.E. and Westinghouse, which had traditionally produced generators, began to move into mass-consumer markets; steel giants entered the building industry; rubber companies began to produce plastics. But this expansion of the products of many organizations created new problems for the organizational structure. In particular, the conventional functional differentiation now became muddied by a product-line differentiation. And it was not at all clear which of these differentiations was more important. Is the marketing of generators for electricity producers *related to* the marketing of consumer goods? If so, one marketing group for both product lines might make sense. Is research for rubber *related to* research for plastics? Or are the differences so substantial that merging the functions across product lines serves no goal? Monitoring issues also arose with the increased size and complexity of modern enterprise. If the central organization needs to make some judgment about the relative prospects of plastics versus rubber in order to allocate a capital budget, can they do so when functional areas merge the two divisions? Or would a new structure make more sense?

During the 1920s, the product-line expansion created considerable strains on existing organizational structures, as some of the original efficiency reasons for merging functions were reduced by the product heterogeneity. Out of the welter of product-line expansions came a new organizational form: the **multidivisional organization.** This new form was first introduced by Du Pont, a firm which by the 1920s was struggling with the organizational difficulties of producing goods as diverse as paints, vegetable oils, and sulphur mines. In these early days, General Motors was perhaps the most successful at implementing the new multidivisional structure. In these and other enterprises new divisions were formed, representing broad product categories, and then each of these divisions was subdivided by functional category. Reorganization into product-line divisions placed most coordination decisions in the hands of divisional managers who were more knowledgeable about the products involved. The growth of the multidivisional structure, traced by Chandler in the United States, occurred as well throughout the world.[11] In Figure 9.1, we have represented simple examples of a functional versus a multidivisional firm.

In the traditional multidivisional form, as we can see from Figure 9.1, there is little formal contact between the marketing group of one division and that of a second. But if the markets served by the two divisions are related to one another, this lack of contact can create coordination diffi-

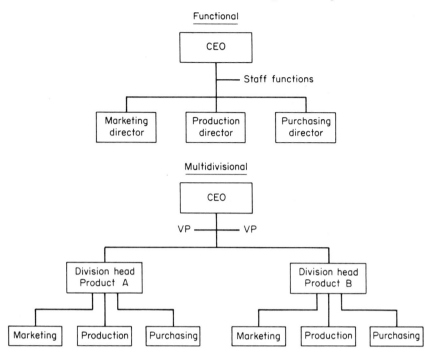

Figure 9.1 Comparison of functional and multidivisional organizational structures

culties. Philip Morris markets both cigarettes and soft drinks, through its control of 7-Up. Clearly these are quite different product lines. Nevertheless, one of the reasons Philip Morris acquired 7-Up was to capitalize on the marketing expertise it had developed in the tobacco market. Running two completely distinct marketing divisions will clearly make this coordination process more difficult. Sears, which runs geographically based divisions using the multidivisional model, nevertheless has a central purchasing department, a functional unit.[12]

In recent years, largely in response to the need for coordination in several directions, we have seen the development of *matrix structures* in a number of organizations.[13] A **matrix organization** contains two lines of control, one through the functional area and a second through the product line. Figure 9.2 is a schematic of a matrix organization.

As we can see in this type of organization, the marketing manager of product A is connected to the product A division head and to the vice president of marketing for the overall organization. In the ideal, this manager can learn from the marketing ideas of the rest of the organization, while simultaneously maintaining a strong product focus. Matrix organizations were designed in part to exploit relationships that cut across product lines, while preserving some of the informational efficiency of the

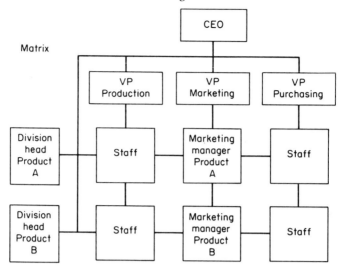

Figure 9.2   A matrix organization

divisional structure. The matrix form was thought to improve information flow and project integration. In complex, high-technology organizations, this innovative form has received a good deal of attention.

G.E., Dow Chemical, and Texas Instruments have all experimented with the matrix form. As one might expect, the matrix form turns out to be rather complex to manage and this complexity has in some cases overwhelmed the coordination advantages of the structure.[14] Texas Instruments and Xerox, for example, both abandoned the matrix form in despair at the complexity involved. The complex form has been described as a "battle scarred spider."[15] Another description of the matrix structure by Roger Schipke, a vice president at G.E., is also instructive:

> In the early 1970's we got ourselves in trouble with matrix management. . . . By the late 1970's we had 13 corporate VP's in major appliances, and they all had different agendas. We were paralyzed. No one could make a decision.[16]

In some circumstances, the matrix structure may provide too much cross-flow of information. Other common complaints include the tendency of the matrix to create power struggles, as a consequence of there being less clarity in authority lines, and to slow the decision-making process. In fact, Pfeffer—who favors the matrix form—argues that one of the reasons for its effectiveness is its legitimation and institutionalization of conflict.[17] Again, we see that organizational structure allocates power as well as information.

Modern enterprises, in their choice of organizational structure, thus turn to three archetypes: the functional firm, the multidivisional structure, and the matrix organization. One strategic choice of the firm is which of these structures to adopt.

A second consideration involved in structuring a firm is how deep to make the hierarchy. A hierarchy is a set of authority relations and information flows. It consists of a set of positions that occupy some reporting and authority relation to one another. Organizations differ dramatically in the number of steps between the lowest manager and the CEO, for example, even if we hold organizational size relatively constant. Figure 9.3 depicts examples of a short versus deep hierarchy. Typically information flows primarily between adjacent stages in a hierarchy; thus the deeper the hierarchy the more stages through which information and decisions must flow.

The number of subordinates under an individual is often called his or her **span of control.** If we take a fixed number of people and organize them in a short hierarchy, as in (A) in Figure 9.3, each of those people will have a wide span of control relative to a similar sized group organized in a deep hierarchy (B). The optimum span of control and how deep the ideal hierarchy should be is of central interest to organizational sociologists and, more recently, to economists.[18]

A final characteristic of the organizational structure of a firm is the degree of autonomy possessed by each of the working units in the organization. All organizations operate in environments characterized by un-

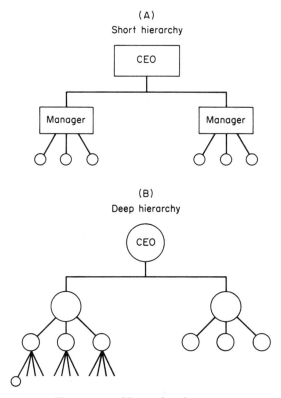

Figure 9.3 Hierarchical structure

certainty. Thus it is not possible to specify what a particular manager should do under each and every contingency. One very central characteristic of an organization is how it deals with unexpected events. How much discretion does the manager at various levels of the hierarchy have in dealing with the unexpected? What levels of decision can middle managers make on their own, and what levels need to be approved by authority?

In *hierarchically controlled firms,* decisions about unexpected events are generally bumped up to higher level managers. In *horizontally controlled firms,* semiautonomous decision making and coordination at relatively low levels in the hierarchy are emphasized. It should be clear, however, that it is possible for a firm to have a very deep hierarchy and yet allow individual managers substantial discretion. Thus the depth of the hierarchy is not necessarily coincident with the level of discretion allowed managers.[19]

In sum, there are three decisions which need to be made about the structure of an organization:

1. What principle should we use to subdivide units?
2. How deep should the hierarchy be?
3. How much centralization of decision making should there be?

Principles Guiding the Choice of Organizational Structure

Let us turn now to explore the general principles that can guide decision making on these three issues. The right organizational structure for a firm to adopt depends on a number of factors. In what environment does the organization operate? In many cases, internal reorganizations are undertaken to make organizations isomorphic with their changing institutional environments.[20] Firms in stable markets have different organizational needs than those in more dynamic ones.[21] What are the current characteristics of the firm? Larger firms may have different needs in terms of structure than smaller firms, for example.[22] A firm that wishes to grow rapidly may require a different set of authority relations than its more mellow rivals. And, finally, what is the firm trying to do? The strategy of the firm has a substantial impact on choice of organizational structure.[23] In what follows, I will outline the broad principles an organization should use in designing structure. In the discussion, we should keep in mind the two dimensions along which structural choices will be important: Structure influences our ability to collect and process information in order to make decisions, and it affects our ability to monitor and motivate behavior once particular decisions are made. Organizational theorists like Galbraith echo the view that a well-designed bureaucracy has value because it allows organizations to process tasks that would be impossible to accomplish in any other way.[24] Structure influences both strategic choice and strategic implementation, and does so both by affecting the distribution of economic resources and the distribution of power within the organization.

In recent years, **transaction-cost economics** has had a good deal to say about organizational design.[25] Transaction-cost economics argues that governance structures are chosen in response to the kinds of transactions—with customers, suppliers, and its own labor force—that organizations are engaged in. Transaction-cost economics rests on two assumptions that play a fundamental role in organizational design: **bounded rationality** and **opportunism.**

According to the assumption of bounded rationality, there are strict cognitive limits on one's maximizing possibilities. Managers *cannot* know everything relevant to a decision before making that decision. The second critical assumption is that opportunism is present in most situations—that is, people will take advantage of informational asymmetries to pursue their own ends. In transaction-cost economics, then, organizational structure is chosen so as to best limit the possibilities of opportunism in a world of bounded rationality. Incentives and information are two of the drivers of organizational design.

Consider again the Du Pont quote given earlier. The proposition that we want to group together all units that are related to one another is a very appealing one. But, in practice, most operations within a complex organization have some relation with each other. We need to focus, therefore, on the relationships that are most critical. Which kind of relationships among units would one most like to be able to exploit? And what turns out to be central is the way in which uncertainty in one area influences decision making in a second.[26] These two principles help to govern the choice of organizational structure.

The organizational structure should be chosen to reduce the amount of uncertainty that affects decision making in an organization.

Suppose we have two units in an organization that are very closely related to each other, in the sense that to operate department B you need some physical input from department A. For example, department A might produce a good that is an input in the production process of department B. If department A can supply its input with relative certainty, there is no need to consolidate the two units or even to provide good information flows between them. The two departments can simply precontract for the supplies. Department B can order what it needs from A, and A in turn can design its production to meet B's needs. In designing a strategy for the organization as a whole, we can simply count on the precommitted supply flow between the two units; on judging results from the two divisions we can have a similar reliance.

Unfortunately, as we indicated earlier, in many situations considerable uncertainty exists about the elements in the environment in which an organization operates. Production in department A may depend on an input from outside the organization that is subject to shortages. Department A may use a production process that breaks down irregularly. If department A can, by reason of its expertise and familiarity, make a sound prediction about its output flow, that information will be of considerable use to the downstream production department. In particular, knowing there may be bottlenecks in the flow of materials from A, how serious they will be, and when they will occur may influence the design of the production process in B. Under these circumstances, the organizational structure should exploit the ability of the people in department A to reduce the variance faced by the downstream production people. Group A can thus inform the strategic choices of group B.

If we look at the example above, we can see that a need for coordination between two units in an organization resulted from the existence of two factors: first, an underlying relationship between purchasing and production; and second, a particular form of uncertainty in the operations of the two units.[27] In particular, the uncertainty we see in this example necessitates coordination, in the sense that it has an effect on the behavior of one of the units of the firm. In this way units in an organization are interlinked or, stated another way, there are **externalities** from one part of the organization to another.[28] Moreover, in order to induce us to consider merging or coordinating the units of the organization it must be the case that the uncertainty can be resolved in part through organizational restructuring. One critical fact in the earlier example was that department A knew more about its variable production than did B. Moreover, A's information had a potential impact on B's optimal strategy. There are many uncertainties facing an organization, but only some of them have substantial effects on decision making, and only some of them are reducible. Thus, to the extent that an organization can take action to hedge against an input shortfall, for example, or redesign production to accommodate the shortfall, it is more important to be able to predict that shortfall. Unless the improved information has decision consequences, there is little point in using the organizational structure to improve the information flow.

The growth of the multidivisional firm in the U.S. economy can be understood in part as a response to perceptions about where the critical uncertainties reside, as an example of the kind of analysis we have been describing. For the multidivisional structure to make sense, most critical uncertainties must occur within the product chain, rather than within the functional unit. Because the critical uncertainties occur where they do, transactions costs are minimized by using a multidivisional firm. Thus, in Williamson's view, the multidivisional structure is preferable to the functional in part because it reduces information overload problems for the manager. Moreover, subgoal pursuit by managers in multidivisional firms is more easily monitored than is similar behavior in the functional organization, an issue which is accentuated as levels of uncertainty in an operation increase.

An interesting example of the role of uncertainty in motivating organizational design can be found in the structure of transportation plan-ning.[29] Many transportation planning organizations house under one roof bus transport, train transport, and air traffic. Day-to-day management is typically the responsibility of individual transportation modes, despite the overall integrated structure of transportation planning. This allocation of responsibility makes sense because, at least in the short run, a problem in one of the transportation areas is not resolvable via action in a second mode; in our earlier terms the information has no decision content. Ex-cess demand for train service in one area can be taken care of by a switch of cars and personnel from a second area of train service, but not by a shift in air traffic patterns. In the long run, when capital planning occurs, shifts across modes become more practicable and, indeed, long-range planning in the transportation area is often done in an integrated fashion.

Our discussion of the role of uncertainty in promoting particular or-ganizational structures can help to lend perspective to discussions of the importance of technology for organizational design. It has long been noted that high technology plants with automated continuous-process opera-tions often have particular organizational structures: high hierarchies, small spans of control with supervisors acting as group leaders, and participa-tory decision making.[30] In plants of this sort, there are substantial inter-dependencies across parts of the organization, and thus a more flexible, free-flowing information exchange may play an important role in decision making. Recent work in the operations area on concurrent engineering also emphasizes the importance of early information exchange between research units and production units in winnowing out good from bad designs.

Our first principle of organizational design recognized the importance of providing salient information across intrafirm boundaries in order to aid in strategic decision making. In our second principle, we recognize the costs of information flow.[31] Consider the following description of the most important attributes of a manager as described by Andrall Pearson, former president of Pepsico:

> A primary skill of a manager is to pick the specific area where his involve-ment will have the greatest impact on business results. . . . The scope of the job is such that a general manager nearly always faces many more problems and opportunities than he or she can possibly deal with person-ally. . . . Knowing what *to emphasize, when to emphasize it, what and when to delegate and to whom to delegate are crucial decisions.*[32] (Emphasis added)

Given the limited ability of a manager to process information and the costs of acquiring information, it is clear that many decisions will have to be delegated and others undertaken with imperfect information.[33] When we delegate authority, we allow managers who have good, but localized information, and strong but perhaps narrow incentives to make deci-sions. When we centralize authority, we undertake costs to gather all of the pertinent localized information and make our decisions with a more global perspective, albeit a less detailed one. The inflow to the center of localized information enables the kind of strategic vision senior managers must have. Ideally, the organizational structure should be such that the "right" information filters up to senior management to inform the "important" decisions in a cost effective way, while other decisions are made at lower levels in the hierarchy.

Organizational structure should economize on information time.

This focus on the costs of decision making allows us to better understand the relationship between organizational size and structure. Increased size in an organization leads to increased bureaucratization of that organization.[34] As an organization grows, some hierarchy is needed in order to expedite the information-collection and decision-making processes. The creation of hierarchy generally reduces the planning time needed by an organization, holding constant the amount of information collected. This is because, within a hierarchy, subordinates can work concurrently on several aspects of a problem.[35] If an organization is considering launching a new product, the marketing group can investigate the demand side of the product, while production looks at the optimal manufacturing configuration and the purchasing department investigates input supplies. All of these activities can be carried out more or less simultaneously, although clearly some coordination will be needed.

Hierarchies also influence the degree of control managers have over their subordinates. As we increase the number of people under a given manager, he or she loses the opportunity to closely supervise each of them. Increasing the degree of hierarchy thus increases control. Hammond and Horn develop a model along these lines in which increasing the complexity of the hierarchy reduces the scope of the individual for opportunistic, strategic behavior.[36] This argument again speaks to the advantages of hierarchy.

The importance of a large enterprise creating some hierarchical structure and delegating authority to it is well illustrated by the example of Henry Ford and the Ford Motor Company.[37] Ford built the motor company into one of the largest and most profitable in the world. By the late 1920s, however, Ford Motor was in a shambles, largely due to Ford's unwillingness to delegate any authority. Without some viable hierarchical structure, decisions simply could not be made wisely or expeditiously enough. By contrast, General Motors, which had adopted the new multidivisional structure and had spent considerable time concentrating on matters of organizational design, was functioning smoothly.

Increasing hierarchy has costs as well as benefits. Some argue that increasing hierarchy creates rigidity and timidity, although the evidence is by no means all in on this point.[38] Pfeffer argues that increasing the number of levels in a hierarchy can lead to obfuscation of information flows, in much the same way that messages become garbled in the familiar children's game of telephone.[39] Williamson similarly notes that the information distortions are likely to be biased in particular ways by members of the hierarchy who "divert the communication system to their own uses."[40]

A second cost of increased hierarchy are the resulting delays in decision making.[41] As information is gathered from subunits in the organization and processed by the center, time inevitably passes and so too do many opportunities. In some cases, these delays may be critical. The Chinese general Sun Zu, writing in 514 B.C. reminds us of the importance of implementation:

> Weak leadership can wreck the soundest strategy; forceful execution of even a poor plan can often bring victory.[42]

A modern-day description of decision making in an organization with a very deep hierarchy and highly centralized control sounds a similar note:

> It's so hard to get a decision that I think of this as a glass, forty-story graveyard. Impediments in the decision-making process affect the morale of the whole organization.[43]

Planning delays will be created when we attempt to gather the information collected and processed by various members of the hierarchy and use it in centralized decision making, instead of allowing the subunits which collect the data to make the decisions. At times, the more informed vision created by centralization of information will be less important than an ability to move quickly in the market. It is in part for this reason that firms in rapidly changing technological environments are enjoined to decentralize.[44] As Eisenhardt suggests, "more than ever before, the best strategies are irrelevant if they take too long to formulate."[45]

Rapid decision making is enhanced by decentralization.

Among other advantages, decentralization encourages the building of multiple, simultaneous strategic scenarios which speed decision making.

An additional cost of centralization involves what have been termed **influence costs.**[46] In central planning in either a private or public organization, we take information gathered by subunits and use it to make decisions that typically affect the well-being of the people in those subunits. A common exercise, for example, might be to use the project evaluations of an R&D department to help decide how many new projects to fund. Demand projections made by a marketing department might help to determine how fast to roll out a new product or how much advertising support to provide. Thus the subordinates in any hierarchical system will have an interest in how their information is used. As a result, these subordinates will have an incentive to behave opportunistically.

As we discussed earlier, this opportunistic behavior typically results in some distortions in the information provided. Williamson's preference for the multidivisional structure comes from his view that subordinates in these structures are less prone to opportunistic behavior than their counterparts in functional firms, in part because a product-line structure allows managers to collect profit data to better monitor those subordinates. As a result of opportunism, individuals in all organizations will spend some time trying to influence the central authority's decisions. Individuals, for example, will write memos on subjects of concern to them. Likewise, in the public sector, lobbyists will spend considerable resources trying to convince legislators of their views. As Perrow suggests in looking at a variety of different organizations: "The resources and goals of the organization are up for grabs, and people grab for them continually."[47] Organizational design creates constellations of control and induces efforts to both cement and change those control patterns.

We can see then that organizations may wish to spend some time thinking about ways in which influence activity might be discouraged. On the other hand, of course, some information flow is clearly important to an organization and it is not always easy in practice to distinguish influence activity from information provision. One important instrument to reduce influence costs is the degree of decentralization. If we remove the power to make a decision from a senior manager, then there is no point in trying to influence his or her views.

In order to reduce influence costs, organizations should decentralize in matters which are of considerable importance to the individual relative to their importance to the organization as a whole.[48]

A classic example of this principle occurs in the teaching procedures at most universities. Typically, instructors can use their own discretion in choosing their teaching assistants. This choice is delegated because it has as its prime consequence the welfare of the instructor—a poor assistant creates more work for the instructor. The instructor generally cares more about the choice than does the institution as a whole. On the other hand, in most universities faculty have less discretion about which courses they teach, since this is a matter of paramount concern to the university administration. And, of course, we see considerable faculty time engaged in influence processes in this area.

In the discussion thus far, we have focused on the role of organizational structure in improving the flow and use of information in a firm. But the organizational structure also influences the level of satisfaction workers associate with their jobs and may profoundly affect corporate performance via this route. In designing the structure of an organization, it is important to consider the values and motivations of the individuals who will occupy the various positions in the hierarchy. In general, structural changes that increase the degree of discretion of individual managers simultaneously increase job satisfaction.[49] The power to make decisions is one of the most sought after managerial perquisites. The ability of a wide group of people to participate in a range of decisions in an organization can often carry with it considerable symbolic force in helping to define the culture of that organization.[50]

Decentralization generally increases job satisfaction.

The effect of hierarchy on job satisfaction is more ambiguous. On the one hand, very deep hierarchies are often associated with quite small spans of control by managers, and this is generally a negative characteristic. Sharper hierarchical organizations also often lack participatory decision making, another important criteria for job satisfaction.[51] On the other hand, elaborate ranks in an organization can allow more opportunity for a sense of advancement and this may increase job satisfaction.[52]

Particular facets of organizational design may have symbolic value for the organization.[53] Organizations may be able to limit the opportunistic behavior of managers by designing the organization in such a way as to create a more cohesive corporate culture. We have already seen in Chapter 8 some of the trade-offs associated with the creation of single-minded organizations. As we will see later in our discussion of U.S. versus Japanese organizational design, the choice of structure may also be contingent on the culture in which the organization is embedded.

The organizational structure should complement the social and corporate culture.

Another link between culture and structure relates to the discussion in Chapter 8 of the principal-agent problem. One of the functions of an organizational structure is to allow information to travel to the center of the organization to be used as a way to monitor the performance of the rest of the organization. The further the objectives of the owners of the firm diverge from those of the various managers in that firm, the more critical such monitoring becomes. But the degree to which organizational consensus on goals obtains varies dramatically across organizations and across cultures. In situations in which consensus is high, more delegation is possible. Of course, even here some centralization will be needed to achieve the broad vision needed for some decisions. Nevertheless, if monitoring is not of prime importance, delegation becomes a more attractive alternative for many kinds of decisions.

Delegation of decisions is made easier if there is goal consensus.

What role does the CEO play in influencing organizational structure? Small organizations can be dramatically influenced by the personalities of their leaders, as were Polaroid and Apple by Edwin Land and Steven Jobs.[54] CEOs who score high on psychological tests in "need to achieve" tend to promote structures for their organizations that are quite formal and rather centralized.[55] Henry Ford comes again to mind. If we think of the hierarchy and delegation rules as being in part an instrument used by the CEO to improve his or her decision-making ability, the potential effect of the character and preferences of that leader on structural design becomes manifest.

We have now explored several principles that inform the design of an organization. They tell us that an organization should be structured with an appreciation of

1. the relationships among units in an organization with a particular focus on how information in one area would improve decision making in a second;
2. the costs of information processing within the organization;
3. the effect of structure on the constellation of power within the organization;
4. the cultural environment in which the organization is embedded.

In the next section of this chapter, when we look at some differences in the typical organizational structure in Japanese versus U.S. manufacturing, we will discover that many of the differences we observe in these two settings can be traced to one or more of the principles described above.

Japanese versus U.S. Organizational Structure

The substantial success of the Japanese economy in the post-war period has given rise in the West to considerable speculation as to its causes. In the manufacturing sector, attention has focused on the role of organizational structure in helping to explain the fine performance of the Japanese. As a consequence, some U.S. firms have adopted Japanese organizational style, but with mixed success. U.S. companies, for instance, have attempted to democratize the decision-making process along Japanese lines, but the long-run viability of these methods is still very much in question. What differences between the United States and Japan in organizational structure might reduce the effectiveness of Japanese style management in the United States?

The major differences between Japanese and U.S. organizational structure appear to be the following:

1. The typical Japanese firm has taller hierarchies than its U.S. counterpart.
2. The typical Japanese firm has greater apparent centralization and more formalization than its U.S. counterpart.
3. The typical Japanese firm has more delegation of decision making and less de facto centralization than its U.S. counterpart.
4. Japanese decision making is more consensus oriented than U.S. decision making and there is less job specialization in Japan.[56]

These differences in organizational structure appear to hold even if we look across firms in the same industry.[57] Thus they cannot be explained by the different mixes of business in the two countries. To what instead might we attribute these differences?

An important factor in explaining U.S.–Japanese differences in organizational structure is the Japanese employment system. The typical Japanese firm hires its employees after they leave school with the intention of retaining them over their lifetime. Movement by workers across firms is thus uncommon in Japan, whereas mobility within the firm in Japan is quite high. In manufacturing firms, rotations in the production area typically occur every two months. Also most Japanese firms follow the **nenko** seniority system, in which promotions are virtually guaranteed in exchange for steady service and employment, and **seniority wages** are common practice. A worker joins a firm at a low entry wage, but his wage rises over his lifetime employment even if his job does not change.[58] Finally, within most Japanese organizations, considerable emphasis is placed on team spirit: *Wa*—harmony—is a central part of the philosophy of many Japanese organizations. The idea of *wa* is to promote teamwork in an organization.[59] The U.S. system is typically more individualistic in orientation. As we will see, these society-wide differences in labor relations play a large role in the design of the typical organization.

A second important distinction between Japanese firms and their U.S. counterparts that plays a role in organizational design is the relatively greater degree of vertical integration in the United States. The automobile industry provides an interesting example. In the United States, approximately 45 percent of the value of an auto is created in-house, with the remainder supplied by outside venders, such as tire makers. In Japan, only 25 percent of the value of the car is made in-house.[60] This difference is common across many industries and may reflect the tendency of large firms in Japan to subcontract to lower wage, nonunion operations. In part, as a consequence of the large distance between union and nonunion sectors, Japan has relied more heavily on elaborate long-term contracts than U.S. firms and less on vertical integration.[61] The resulting lower complexity of the Japanese firm also contributes to differences in optimal organizational design.

As indicated above in items (1) and (2), Japanese firms are characterized by relatively tall hierarchies with considerable formal centralization. This pair of attributes seems to derive from the *nenko* seniority system. If the organization "owes" promotion opportunities to its workers, within the firm and over their lifetimes, then a tall hierarchy with a large number of ranks is essential in order to supply the sequence of positions to which people can be promoted.[62]

Interestingly, along with their relatively steep, formal hierarchies, Japanese firms are also characterized by considerable real delegation of authority and participatory decision making (items 3 and 4 above). Formal hierarchies are thus partly symbolic. The extent of real decentralization is well captured by the prominence of the **kanban** or just-in-time system in Japanese manufacturing. A kanban is a card which orders particular inputs from the upstream department to be delivered at a given time to a downstream group.[63] It is a physical device for facilitating discussion across horizontal units without the need for supervisory intervention. Indeed, consensus and working together to solve problems is a prime characteristic of the Japanese manufacturing system. **Quality circles** in which workers meet to resolve problems or suggest improvements that cut across various areas of the firm are also a manifestation of this cooperative decision-making style.

What accounts for the delegation of decision making in Japan? Again, the employment relationship seems to play an important role. Decentralization becomes more attractive when there is goal consensus, and the lifetime employment relationship common in Japanese firms helps to create goal consensus. The seniority wage system further reinforces the identification of the worker with the firm. If you plan to work for one firm for your whole career, your interests will become more aligned with that firm's interests, than if you are planning a career across firms. Decentralization becomes more attractive under these circumstances, because the subunits are likely to have the same objectives as the center of the organization.[64] The central role played in Japan by *wa* or harmony also contributes to an integration of objectives, as does the fact that corporate life in Japan involves extensive socialization that further creates a cohesive corporate culture.[65] The decreased sense of competition among individuals as a result of the seniority wage system and career-long identification with one firm may also reinforce collective decision making.[66] Finally, Japanese workers and managers are also typically rotated among jobs more frequently than are their American counterparts. This creates *within* individual workers and managers a broader perspective that may decrease the need for formal coordination via supervisors.

Decentralization in Japanese firms is further supported by other mechanisms available to the firm for coordination. Here the Japanese have created some management innovations (like the *kanban*) that have made decentralization more efficacious. Quality circles reinforce a sense of collective decision making as well.

The smaller degree of vertical integration of the Japanese firm also plays a role in encouraging more decentralization within the firm. On average, the Japanese firm is *less complex* than its American counterpart because a number of its functions are located outside the firm. This lower complexity permits the Japanese organization to engage in more delegation of authority and to use the formal control mechanisms of its hierarchy somewhat less. Here the market has replaced the hierarchy.

In sum, it appears that the particular organizational structure we see in Japanese industry may work in part because of the way in which it is embedded in the institutions of the community. Labor practices and cross-firm contractual relationships both help to support the participatory, decentralized Japanese management style. Implementing this style in the U.S. context would thus require attention to a wide complement of features of the organization. Moreover, the American social and political environment may not support the new organizational structure as well as it is supported by the Japanese system. We see from this comparison an excellent example of the broad-ranging issues associated with the choice of an organizational structure and the way in which that choice may be conditioned by the environment.

Conclusion

Strategic planning can be thought of as a process by which a broader perspective of the organization is developed and shared by members of the community. The way in which an organization is structured clearly affects the way this process can occur. In this chapter we have explored some of the central differences in structure across organizations. In Chapter 10 we will expand our vision to examine strategic choices faced by diversified organizations.

10

Corporate Diversification

Discussion thus far has focused on strategic management of an organization within a given industry. We have examined a wide range of issues pertinent to the running of a business within a particular industry. We have looked at the forces that explain the relative performance of various industries and asked, for example, why pharmaceutical firms on average outperform steel firms on conventional return measures. Within a given industry, we have asked why it is that some organizations do consistently better than others. How, if at all, can we explain the long-lived success of Bristol-Myers and 3M? We then turned to explore some of the central implementation issues facing a firm. Why do we see the pursuit of subgoals inside organizations, and how should we try to mold this process? What principles should govern the choice of organizational structure or the degree of hierarchy? These issues were addressed with reference to firms operating within particular markets. But many organizations operate in numerous markets, some related, some not. These organizations face not only the question of how to manage resources *within* each of their segments, but also how to allocate those resources *across* various segments.

Studies of diversification are one of the mainstays of strategic management literature.[1] The literature covers a diverse set of topics: How much diversification is there among businesses and what are the forms of diversification? When should firms diversify and what goals are served by diversification? How should firms diversify, through internal growth or through mergers? Finally, how well do diversified firms do relative to single-product firms? We explore this rich set of issues in the next three chapters.

What Is Diversification?

A diversified firm is one that operates in a number of different markets. But not all diversified firms look alike. Some operate in a cluster of highly related markets, also known as **concentric diversifications.** Others operate in markets that have buyer-supplier relationships with each other. Still, others operate businesses in widely different markets. Our first task is to explore the dimensions of diversification.

One way to begin our inquiry is to imagine that we are at the helm of an organization currently operating in one particular market—say as a producer of tires. Of course, we will be concerned with trying to manage our tire business as well as we possibly can. But we may also be concerned with determining whether or not our organization should be making something in addition to tires, or even possibly an alternative to tires.

There are numerous possible ways the firm can begin to think about broadening its portfolio of businesses. A common question that most organizations face is whether or not to *lengthen the vertical line of the firm.* That is, the firm might consider producing materials currently purchased from suppliers outside of the firm. Or the firm might consider distributing its own product or increasing the amount of finishing done in-house. Hitachi has traditionally distributed its mainframe computers in the U.S. market through U.S. distributors. Its current plans to distribute its own computers represents a **vertical integration** move in the U.S. market. Such vertical moves could be accomplished either by building new facilities or by purchasing one of the organization's former suppliers or buyers. The tire company, for example, might purchase or create a rubber producer. This would represent *vertical integration in a backward direction.* Another possibility would be to purchase a tire distributor or create a new distributor. This would be *vertical integration in a forward direction.* In either of these cases, the company would be lengthening the vertical chain of its operation.

> **Vertical integration involves an extension of the stages of production and distribution in which a firm operates.**

Another important dimension of an organization's portfolio is its breadth. How many different related and unrelated industry segments is the organization operating in? For a variety of reasons, an organization that has previously produced in only one segment may decide to broaden its offerings and, indeed, may decide to move horizontally into quite different fields. Here, too, the change in the corporate portfolio could be effected either through purchases of existing ventures or by investing in the construction of new facilities. A strategy involving a broadening of the corporate portfolio would involve **conglomerate diversification.**

> **Diversification involves moving into new lines of business.**

Within the category of conglomerate diversification, we can further distinguish related versus unrelated moves.[2] Related business units support or complement one another, typically in marketing, research, or production, whereas unrelated businesses typically have few opportunities to exploit joint skills or assets. Motives for diversification, the results of diversification, and the optimal management structure of the firm all depend in part on the type of diversification followed.

In the modern organization, portfolio issues absorb a considerable amount of the attention of upper management. The recent history of Armtek, a moderate-sized Connecticut company operating in the auto supply industry, provides a nice illustration of one organization's management of its product portfolio. As recently as 1980, Armtek, which was then known as Armstrong Tires, realized virtually all of its sales in the tire industry. For a variety of reasons, having to do both with foreign competition and changes in the nature of the product, the tire industry fell on hard times in the 1970s. Margins fell, as did growth rates in sales. As a result of the poor performance and projections of dim future prospects, the management at Armtek began to look for other fields to till. The company's first efforts were to deepen the vertical chain of the organization, to try to bring more of the value associated with tire production into the firm. During this period, Armtek engaged first in backward integration, acquiring majority ownership in Copolymer, one of its synthetic rubber suppliers. The firm then consolidated its relationship with Sears, its primary distributor, in a move toward partial forward integration through stock transactions.

In the 1980s, as the tire situation worsened, management began to change its portfolio of businesses in another way, by broadening the scope of the business via diversification. During this period, a full-fledged planning group was established to help focus the diversification effort. In the mid-1980s, Armtek moved aggressively into auto parts via acquisitions of an operation producing heat exchange units and a second unit producing hoses. By 1987, Armstrong Tires had changed its name to Armtek and had well less than half of its sales in the tire industry. As Figure 10.1 indicates, Armtek had experienced in less than a decade a major change

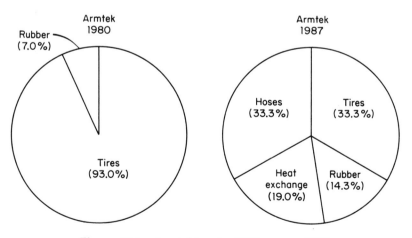

Figure 10.1   Armtek's sales 1980 versus 1987

in its mix of activities. Indeed, in 1988, Armtek completed its restructuring by selling off its tire assets completely!

We see in the Armtek example many of the themes echoed in the planning literature. Diversification often accelerates under environmental pressure. In the tire industry and in many of the traditional "smokestack industries," the pressures to move at least some resources out of the home industry have been substantial. Early moves often occur in what firms see as related industries, in attempts to use firm assets in another venue.[3] The resource profile of a firm is very important in explaining the subsequent direction of diversification. Finally, diversification often occurs, as it did with Armtek, in a mix of acquisition, internal expansion, and strategic alliances.[4]

Why Do Firms Diversify?

In 1988, a former CEO of a medium-sized diversified New England company was asked to explain the history of the organization's portfolio. In the 1960s the firm, along with many others throughout the economy, broadened its scope considerably, moving out from a mature, slow-growth home industry. Through mergers as well as new capacity construction, the firm moved into an increasingly wide range of activities. Then, beginning in the 1970s, the firm started to shed segments, sometimes at the rate of two or three in a given month. At present, the firm operates in only a few related segments. In explaining this accordion-like history, the CEO made the following argument:

> In the 1960s, I listened to my finance people. They were all worried about slow growth and risk. My goal was to diversify as fast as possible, to remove the corporation from the swings of the market. In fact, my goal was to acquire companies in a diverse enough group to ensure the company would have a Beta of 1. In the 1970s and recently, my planners and consultants gave me another message: "Stick to your knitting." Now it seemed clear that the only way to succeed was to specialize. And so, I looked at my various units, and sold many of them off, looking for customers who would see synergies in them.[5]

We can see in this CEO's arguments the germs of four of the most powerful motivators of conglomeration: the desire to exploit **economies of scope** or **synergies,** interest in stablizing profits, the desire to exploit efficient internal capital markets, and cash management for rapid organizational growth. In the last twenty years, these principles have underlined much of the diversification of organizations that has occurred. We also see from our CEO's remarks some of the pitfalls of following fads in designing the corporate portfolio. In what follows, we will examine the soundness of the various motives for diversification and try to sort out the smoke and mirrors from the realities.

Economies of Scope and Synergies

The strategic management literature emphasizes the role of diversification in creating synergies. Two business units have **synergies** if their union allows for opportunities not available to either separately. **Economies of scope** are a more specific expression of synergy, usually thought of primarily in the cost context. Economies of scope exist when it is less costly to do something when two units are joined than when they existed separately.

Economies of scope create efficiencies from diversification.

Common sources of synergy are thought to be marketing operations, research operations, and distribution outlets. In each of these cases, the perception is that the organization has a relatively fixed operation that can be used to service a related product without needing appreciable expansion.

The marketing area provides us with a good illustration of potential gains from expanding a product line. Take Levi Strauss & Co., a firm widely perceived as producing a high-quality line of blue jeans. In its early history, it made jeans only for men. But it soon found that it had an asset that was perhaps not being fully utilized—its name. Levi Strauss found that by producing women's and children's jeans it could piggyback on the advantage of its name recognition in men's jeans. Thus it could add lines of women and children's clothing without facing the kind of brand development costs new entrants would experience. Much of Levi Strauss's early diversification represented attempts to exploit the value of its brand name in this way.

The health-care area provides another example of attempted synergy. Humana, a leading health-care firm based in Lexington, Kentucky, developed a network of health maintenance organizations and hospitals in the 1980s. Part of the strategy for this diversification was to channel patients from the HMOs into the Humana hospitals, thus extending the value to the firm of knowledge about patients and access to patients. In 1992, David Jones, the CEO of Humana, proposed a spin-off of the two operations, arguing that the channeling approach "is not the strategy for today."[6] We see in this example that synergies are sometimes difficult to maintain.

In another case, for many years, IBM made only mainframe computers and peripherals. In pursuing this market, IBM developed two valuable assets: consumer confidence and a marketing network. In moving into the personal computer market, IBM has attempted to use its investment in the mainframe market. This approach has worked only in part. It is clear that IBM has great name recognition as a result of its long and successful performance in the mainframe market, and it is also clear that some consumers will pay a premium for a brand-name computer, although the value of a brand name in this market appears to be diminishing. But the mainframe marketing network did not appear to be equally effective in the personal computer market. Indeed, IBM currently uses mail-order merchandising to sell personal computers, a far cry from its traditional reliance on personal service. In this case, it appears that the new market is sufficiently different from the old that existing marketing and distribution operations cannot be vertically extended. In the IBM case, there were some economies of scope between mainframes and personal computers, but perhaps not as many as initially appeared.

In the nonprofit area, the Boston Symphony Orchestra has for many years sponsored the Boston Pops, a popular concert series, two ventures with many costs in common. The Orchestra and Pops use the same concert facilities and some of the same musicians; they share a distribution network for performance tapes, and pool a variety of employee benefits.[7] Economies of scope in this case cut across a variety of functions.

To the extent that an organization extends its product line to take advantage of synergies or economies of scope, it will look for products that are related to its current offerings. Firms will identify their distinctive competencies and use those in a new market. Thus the diversification that we see occurring will be among related products.[8] At times, marketing assets will be used (men's and women's jeans); at other times, it will be research capability (fiber optics and glassware); at still other times, it will be distribution that links the units. Southwestern Bell purchased Metromedia's cellular phone division for $1.2 billion in 1987 in the belief that its distribution network would provide links to this operation. TW Services, a food service company, spent close to $1 billion on a coffee-shop chain in a similar quest in 1987. Many international acquisitions are also motivated by a desire to capitalize on underutilized parent firm skills.[9] But in some cases, synergies have been hard to find. The less related are the new units to the old, the less likely it will be that any true synergies will exist. In the Levi Strauss example, moves into related jeans products have been quite successful; broader moves into high fashion clothing have been less so. It appears that the name recognition asset is not extensible across too broad a product line. Product line connections often motivate acquisitions, but subtle differences in those product lines often prevent synergies from being realized.

Similar efficiency-promoting motives for diversification come from Williamson's transactions cost approach.[10] Here firms decide to broaden or lengthen their product lines as a way to deal with critical and uncertain interdependencies in their environments. Here it is transactions costs that are being reduced as we combine units, rather than the production or marketing costs we see more commonly discussed in the economies of scope literature. The evidence suggests that diversification for transaction costs savings is principally relevant in the case of vertical diversification and we will discuss it at length in Chapter 11.[11]

In many industries, we observe that the push to find new areas in which to apply firm assets increases as the firm ages. This diversification is to be expected given the usual life cycle of most products. In the early stages of a product, investment costs are typically high; firms must advertise heavily, engage in research on product specifications, and build new capacity. Since supply is typically low relative to new demand, prices and margins will be high. Managerial resources are strained, simply trying to keep up with activities in the core market. As the industry develops, however, investment needs fall and prices and margins follow. In the late stages of a product's life, price competition is typically intense, but many of the managerial structures are already in place.

This life cycle model has some implications for an organization's portfolio. We expect, for instance, that the type of organizational infrastructure needed in the various parts of the life cycle changes. In the early stages, research and advertising needs are high, and the organization will be heavily involved in establishing organizational routines. Later in the evolutionary stage, more emphasis is placed on cost management skills, as prices become more sensitive and industry supply increases. This growth suggests that as organizations age, they often develop excess capacity in particular functional areas. Diversification is a way to use that excess capacity.

Of course, as they age, organizations have a second choice: They can shut down excess capacity. But there are transactions costs associated with changing the infrastructure of an organization, and those transactions costs will limit the flexibility of the organization somewhat. Exiting an industry is a very difficult matter and done with considerable reluctance by most management.[12] Rapidly changing the balance among functional areas of management is also a difficult task. Thus we often see instead a pattern of diversification as organizations age.[13]

Market Power

A second motive that is sometimes suggested for diversification is to increase the market power of the diversifying firm, beyond any increases associated with enhanced efficiency. The observation that large diversified firms may have strategic options not available to their more specialized rivals has been in the literature for a considerable period of time.[14] Firms that have multimarket contacts with one another in theory have an enhanced ability to collude.[15] Thus a firm which faces the same rival in two industries will be more cooperative because such cooperation pays off in two places. As a result, we might expect to see more shared monopoly and higher profits as a result of diversification. In fact, the literature provides only sketchy support for the view that diversification increases market power, once efficiency gains are excluded.[16]

Profit Stability

Most business units, regardless of how well they are managed, experience some fluctuations in their returns over time. Sales of most products respond, at least to some extent, to changes in the overall level of economic activity in the nation, the **gross national product.** Some products—like automobiles and housing—are quite sensitive to fluctuations in GNP. Other products—like food and apparel—are less so. Some products, like new pharmaceuticals, require investments that yield returns only over a long time period, so that their costs and returns are not always well matched in the time frame. Changes in the level of competition in an industry can cause its returns to fluctuate over time, perhaps in response to changes in trade policy. And so on. One possible gain from diversification might be its potential for reducing the variation of a firm's returns.

The earliest work in diversification emphasized the advantages of combinations for reducing the variance of returns of the organizations.[17] As long as the earnings for two lines of business are not perfectly correlated, combining the two lines will reduce the variance to total earnings for the organization. If one business unit does well in the sunshine, and a second thrives in rainy weather, the organization as a whole will find itself with rather even seasonal returns. If one of an organizations's units produces tires for original-equipment manufacturers, and a second specializes in parts for used cars, the overall returns experienced by the firm will be relatively steady, regardless of the mix of new versus used cars that consumers purchase.

We can see then that diversification is a plausible way for an organization to reduce the variance of its earnings or to even out its earnings path. It has been argued that diversification into unrelated areas is often used by R&D intensive firms as a way to hedge against technological surprises.[18] To the extent that earnings stability is a goal of the firm, it should seek new acquisitions or investments with return streams different from those of the existing units of the firm. Notice this strategic prescription is very different from the one emerging from the discussion of economies of scope. There, related diversification held the most promise; for profit stability, on the other hand, unrelated diversification is useful. Indeed, Caves has argued that international diversification creates profit stability, inasmuch as economic and political conditions affecting firms are uncorrelated across countries.[16] And indeed in the 1960s, many acquisition-minded CEOs looked for new ventures in fields very distinct from their current businesses in the hopes of evening out earnings fluctuations. In 1968, for example, Pepsico bought North American Van Lines. Uniroyal Tires in the late 1960s bought a fabric company and a laser firm. General Tires bought a chain of independent theaters. Indeed, the view was widespread that diversification was an important way to achieve stability. In a 1969 statement to the Antitrust subcommittee of the House of Representatives, Harold Geneen, then President of the high-growth firm, International Telephone and Telegraph (ITT) stated:

> Diversification is therefore a necessary type of corporate insurance which sound management must achieve on the behalf of its stockholders, so that the risks of separate sectors are pooled.[19]

The New England CEO cited earlier used the same theme, insurance, as a metaphor for diversification. His desire to attain a "Beta of 1" was simply a shorthand way of expressing the goal of acquiring businesses to replicate a diversified stock portfolio.

Why should a firm be concerned about the variance in its returns? In what sense might diversification protect investors? Does a reduction in the variance of a firm's returns improve its ability to attract new capital to a firm, and thus reduce capital costs? Are there some other gains to earnings stability?

When an organization enters the capital market to find new funds for expansion, investors typically look at two elements of the performance of that firm. All else equal, firms with *higher average returns* will find it easier to attract new capital than will those with low returns. Investors will also be concerned about the *volatility* of returns. Indeed, risk averse investors (of whom there are many), will sacrifice some returns in order to avoid variability in their investments.[20] But this does not necessarily mean that investors will look only for firms which themselves have stable returns. *Investors can allocate their own funds across various firms to reduce the variance of their portfolios.* By doing so, investors can limit the unsystematic risk in their portfolios. But neither the individual nor the diversifying firm can avoid systematic or market risk. **Systematic risk,** which accounts for approximately one-third of a security's total risk, is the covariability of the firm's returns with the aggregate market. In the above example, investors do equally well buying stock in two disparate companies, one of which produces tires and the other auto parts, as they do by investing in the single diversified unit producing the two lines. Indeed, most investors do seek some balance in their portfolios, looking for stocks that complement one another. Since investors can engage in diversification themselves, they will not pay a premium to buy a firm that has done nothing more than engage in financial diversification.[21]

> **Diversification to reduce the variance of a firm's returns is not necessary to attract capital to that firm, as long as investors can engage in their own diversification.**

Thus there is no reason that *by itself* diversification would reduce the costs of capital to the firm. But there is more to the story.

The individual investor may be indifferent to the diversification needs of the organization, but the same cannot be said of the managers within the organization. Diversification may provide a needed "insurance" for the managers of an organization. When a firm is producing many products in a wide range of areas, there is less likelihood that a turn for the worse will destroy the entire organization. As we indicated earlier, expanding lines of business does reduce volatility. Thus diversification increases the expected life of a firm. Managerial compensation is typically tied in part to the stability of returns of the organization, as well as to the overall level of those returns. More important, if a firm fails or substantially contracts, many managers will be terminated from the organization. Diversification is one way to protect managers against the high costs of termination.

Diversification also increases firm growth and this may further improve managerial incentives. Most organizations find that it is difficult to stimulate and encourage management unless some growth opportunities are available. It has been argued that the tall hierarchies associated with Japanese organizations reflect the need to provide managers with promotion opportunities. Since most firms reward managers via promotions rather than bonuses alone, this creates a further organizational growth bias.[22] In larger, more diverse organizations, managers can grow and change within the operation and may feel less need to move elsewhere to thrive.[23] The potential for *job advancement* is generally thought to be one of the prime motivators of managers.[24]

But why should stockholders want to protect managers against termination costs? If managers are able, could they not move to other positions if their original firm failed? We wish to protect managers against termination to reward them for the commitments they have made to the organization. As we indicated in Chapter 8, managers typically share the risk of doing business with the owners of a firm. For example, managers learn specialized ways of accomplishing tasks that are beneficial for the firm for which they work, but perhaps not for other firms. They do this in part because they expect to have long careers with their firms. If the risk is very high that the organization will flounder, then managers will have little incentive to invest in their own specific training. The manager of a very specialized firm might well find that he or she had spent ten years building a sound career with this firm only to have it go under just as he or she is reaching middle age, when it is more difficult to relocate. In a more diversified firm, opportunities to move individuals across business units in case of a failure in one area protects managers and encourages them to develop closer ties with the firm in the first place. We can thus think of diversification as a way that managers can reduce the risks they face of working for a particular firm and investing in that firm.[25] Based on a number of case studies, Donaldson and Lorsch argue that managers of diversified firms have stronger motives to invest in the long-run survival of their firms.[26] Diversification is one of the instruments managers have available to protect their investment in their organizations. Indeed, surveys indicate that managerially controlled firms do diversify more than owner-controlled firms.[27]

It is important to note that stockholders as well as managers will gain from the firm's diversification. To the extent that diversification encourages able managers to join a firm and invest time and energy working for it, stockholder interests may be served. (In much the same way, the Japanese system of lifetime employment encourages Japanese managers to identify with the needs of their firms). By influencing managerial choices, diversification can positively influence the overall earnings of the firm.

Diversification may increase the value of an organization by reducing managerial risk and thus encouraging managerial commitment.

Diversification by an organization may play a similar role in reducing risk for stockholders with a controlling interest.[28] In a large sample of Fortune 500 firms, almost 80 percent had at least one stockholder owning 5 or more percent of the stock of the firm. In smaller firms, ownership concentration is generally higher because stockholders may be descendants of the firm's founder and locked by tradition or tax rules into large block-ownership positions. Alternatively, such stockholders may value the monitoring powers conferred by large block ownerships.[29] In either case, capital constraints may prevent these stockholders from individually diversifying and cause them to seek organizational diversification.

Thus far we have been looking at organizations for which bankruptcy is not an issue, and we have seen that even for these stable firms, diversification may be advantageous. More recent work on diversification has emphasized a second gain from diversification: the reduction in the risk and costs of bankruptcy.[30] Since cash flow is stabilized as the scope of the firm increases, the probability of bankruptcy also falls with expansion in scope. It is interesting to note that if a firm broadens its scope in order to reduce the variance of its earnings, it may be inducing a transfer from stockholders to bondholders.[31] Bondholders do not gain from very high earnings, since their payments are fixed. They do, however, lose if earnings are low enough to induce bankruptcy. Thus bondholders are often willing to forego the small chance of high returns in order to insure against bankruptcy. And this is precisely what is accomplished by masterful diversification, since it may reduce the risk of bankruptcy.

Thus we can see that there is some argument for diversification to protect against wide swings in the financial position of an organization, to reduce bankruptcy costs, and protect managerial interests. Nevertheless, the case for diversification as a way to increase profits by stabilizing earnings is considerably weaker than the case for expansion driven by economies of scope.

Diversification to Improve Financial Efficiency

Large established firms are sometimes thought to have an advantage over newer firms in terms of access to capital. Firms generate cash from operations that they can reinvest in new projects. This process of reinvestment is called the **internal capital market.** There may be times in which the internal capital market works better than the outside capital market because of transaction costs considerations. Just as product transactions are sometimes more efficiently organized through a hierarchy rather than a market, so too with financial investments. In cases in which advanced technology is involved, inventors may find it difficult to convince investors of the worth of a product without disclosing valuable information to a rapacious set of potential competitors. Under these circumstances, the market will not perform well and worthy projects will be underfinanced.[32] Thus in some circumstances, the cost of information may encourage the development of a more extensive internal capital market.

Diversification can allow a firm to take advantage of an informationally efficient internal capital market.

It is interesting to look at diversification in the nonprofit area as an example of the working of an internal capital market. Many nonprofit organizations run profitable side ventures as a way of funding their core activities, as well as cushioning against revenue fluctuations. In one large-scale survey of nonprofits, 65 percent of the surveyed organizations were found to generate substantial revenues from activities outside their normal missions.[33] The Smithsonian publishes *Smithsonian* magazine and also sells products through its mail-order catalogue. The Boston Symphony Orchestra supports the Boston Pops concert series. The Children's Television Network, using the merchandising power of Sesame Street and the other shows, generates substantial revenues for funding new projects.[34] In each of these cases, one venture is deliberately run in order to provide funds for a second. This practice has been termed **strategic piggybacking,** since the core venture rides on the back of the money-making operations.[35] Nonprofits, because they face tax and regulatory limits both on profit redistribution and on capital accumulation, may need the internal capital market more than the typical firm in the for-profit sector.

Diversification for Growth

In the 1960s, Smithkline engaged in a number of new acquisitions and new ventures in the areas of electronics, skin care, veterinary medicine, and related health areas. Its strategy, similar to many other firms in the pharmaceutical industry and elsewhere, was "to invest corporate resources in business areas of sufficient diversity and potential to assure continuous growth."[36] For many organizations, particularly those in mature home industries with forecasts of slow growth, diversification has been seen as the only way to promote growth, and growth is often hypothesized to be highly valued by managers. If a firm consists largely of slow-growing operations, it may generate more cash than it requires for internal projects. Paying this cash back to shareholders (i.e., via dividends) reduces the resources controlled by managers. Instead, the managers of these large established firms may wish to acquire smaller, high-growth partners as a way to *use* excess cash from operations. Thus organizations diversify to accomplish the growth aims of the managers that control them and not to maximize profits for shareholders.[37] Indeed, this excess desire for growth is one of the problems that the takeover market is supposed to help remedy, as we will see further in Chapter 12.

One popular embodiment of the use of the corporate portfolio to promote organizational growth is the growth share matrix developed by the Boston Consulting Group and discussed in Chapter 7. If a business unit is a market leader in a slow-growth industry, then it will often be the case that the unit is throwing off more cash than it needs to serve that particular market. In mature industries, cash needs typically fall because requirements for investment in plant and equipment, research and development, and advertising normally decline as an industry matures. The BCG analysts refer to these operations as cash cows. They argue that cash generated by these units can provide resources for growth in other parts of the organization. Organizations with business units primarily in the cash-cow category typically find themselves faced with the prospect of either shrinking the organization by returning funds over time to the stockholders, or finding new investments to make in other fields. Organizations with most of their resources in the mature end will find themselves looking elsewhere—perhaps to diversification—to meet the growth objectives of the firm. They will search for high-growth units—stars—to meet those objectives.

In the 1960s and early 1970s, a number of large organizations used one or another version of the growth share matrix in this way to direct a strategy for realigning their operating units. Since then, it has become evident that this rather naive use of the matrix is not very helpful, and firms—including BCG—have moved away from this approach to **portfolio management.** It has become clear over time, for example, that simply siphoning off cash from mature operations to fuel growth elsewhere in the firm is not always a successful strategy, even as a way to generate growth. When an industry reaches maturity, competition within it often accelerates. In this period, careful and creative management of scarce resources is essential. But if the overall organization has cast a unit in the role of cash cow, managers of that unit are unlikely to have very strong incentives to exercise careful and creative management. It is more likely that the best managers will be casting about for new opportunities for themselves. We see again the power of subgoal pursuit within organizations. In this situation, the mature operation may soon find itself in a precarious financial position. The sensitivity of mature markets to correct handling is noted by Anthony O'Reilly, the CEO of Heinz, the highly profitable food giant: "It is a mortal sin punishable by instant death at Heinz to say a market is mature."[38]

We have now reviewed a number of different motives for diversification: the search for synergies, market power, stabilizing profits, using the internal capital market, and pursuing managerial goals of growth. The evidence suggests that there is no single explanation for diversification. In an interesting survey of merger and acquisition professionals, Walter and Barney found that no single goal dominates the push to diversification.[39] For vertical diversification, managing critical interdependencies—an example of scope economies—predominated. For related diversification, synergies were also important. On the other hand, finance and growth motives were more powerful in explaining conglomerate diversification.

The Effect of Diversification on Performance

A number of the motives for diversification just described are linked to profitability. That is, firms are assumed to seek diversification to exploit synergies, for example, because this strategy will improve the profitability of the firm. Reducing profit variance through diversification is also justified as a way to increase overall profits. To the extent that diversification allows a firm to use the more efficient internal capital market, profits should rise. What evidence is there that diversification in fact has this effect on profits?

Answering this question is complicated by several problems. First of all, it is difficult to measure firm performance. Financial measures, such as return on equity or assets, are at best imperfect proxies for true firm performance, for reasons we have discussed at length in Appendix 2. Stock market value changes are more helpful if the diversification occurs through a single, distinct event (such as an acquisition), but are much harder to use for evaluating diversification that occurs slowly, over a long period of time. Moreover, there is considerable variety in diversification efforts. Some are vertical, others horizontal; some efforts are primarily in related areas, others are more conglomerate in nature. Some diversification occurs through acquisition, while other product expansions occur through internal efforts. It is difficult to take all of these differences into account in measuring the effects of diversification. Finally, a more subtle and even more difficult problem has been raised by Chatterjee and Wernerfelt.[40] There is strong evidence that the resource profile of firms in an early period helps to explain both the extent and type of diversification they engage in later. Thus, in more economic terms, there is a **selection bias, if** we simply try to compare the performance of diversified and undiversified firms. One of the reasons we see differences in diversification strategies is that the diversifying firms differ in other ways, many of which may be unobservable to the analyst. This bias makes it very difficult to draw strong inferences about the effect of diversification on profits from a cross-sectional performance study.

Nevertheless, considerable evidence has been gathered on performance differences and, given the importance of the issue, it is worth reviewing, even in the face of the problems suggested. The evidence itself is quite mixed. In general, holding industry constant, firms which follow a pattern of related diversification have better performance than those which follow a more conglomerate strategy.[41] Single-product firms have typically been found to outperform diversifiers, although here the selection bias issue is especially acute, since firms that remain in single-product areas for a long period of time often have profound and invisible assets in those markets. As a result, firm strength may lead to low diversification rather than the reverse.

Summary

In this chapter, we have begun to look at issues involving firm diversification. We have seen there are a variety of motives for diversification, some of which are connected to firm profitability, and others to firm growth. We have also looked at the evidence on the results of diversification. We turn now, in the next two chapters, to examine more closely how organizations go about broadening their portfolios. In Chapter 11, we concentrate on vertical integration, where we will look extensively at the work stimulated by Williamson. In Chapter 12, we turn to the area of mergers and acquisitions, one of the principal vehicles for diversification.

11

Vertical Linkages

In Chapter 10 we explored why organizations might wish to diversify. A second and increasingly important way a firm can change its scope is by lengthening the vertical line of its organization—that is, by adding to the stages of production and distribution in which it operates. We explore this option in this chapter.

The typical firm engages in many transactions as it goes about its business of producing a line of goods. The way in which the firm organizes these transactions helps in large measure to determine its relationships with its buyers and suppliers. It buys raw materials alternatively from long-time suppliers, from another division within the same organization, or in the market place. Similarly, in transactions involving its capital equipment the firm may buy equipment ready made from one of several suppliers; it may have it made to order by an outside firm; it may produce the equipment in a joint venture; it may even rent its capital equipment. And in the same way, firms sell their products in various ways: anonymously, in stores, through franchises, or even, in vertically integrated firms, directly through firms' own channels of distribution.

Every organization has a set of strategic decisions that involve some consideration of how many of the usual transactions of that organization will be *internalized*, or how far it should *vertically integrate*. Some firms characterize this set of decisions as the "make-or-buy" decisions. But, in fact, as the examples above suggest, the possibilities are really much richer than this simple distinction suggests. Firms can in practice carry out their transactions wholly within the firm, outside the firm, or in the grey area between the firm and the market place. Nor need the make-or-buy decision be a rigid one. Coca-Cola, for example, bottles some of its soft drinks through franchised bottlers; a growing fraction of its product, however, is bottled by bottlers owned by Coca-Cola itself. American TV and Communications, a multiple-systems cable operator, buys some of its programming from Home Box Office, its subsidiary, but buys considerable other programming from nonaffiliates. Indeed, mixed cases of **vertical integration** seem to be particularly efficacious.[1]

Decisions about how to organize transactions can have widespread strategic importance to the organization, for such decisions are crucial to the structure of production, distribution, and marketing within a firm. They may influence the appropriate organizational structure and mode of compensation. New decisions about the level of internalization of transactions may lead to strategic initiatives in the area of acquisitions. How does an organization decide whether to deepen its vertical integration? Recent work in the economics of organizations will be central to the perspective adopted in this chapter. Broadly speaking, we will ask ourselves how conditions in the market place and within the firm affect the appropriate degree of vertical integration.

Some Broad Principles

Figure 11.1 outlines the vertical chain associated with the production of the ubiquitous cartons in which our nation's "fast food" is sold. These cartons are fashioned from polystyrene, a natural gas derivative. Polystyrene, a plastic, is used widely in the construction and packaging industries. Major producers include Arco Chemical, Dow Chemical, Huntsman, Fina Chemicals, and Polysar.

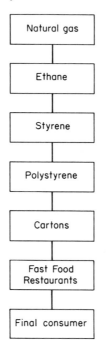

Figure 11.1 Steps in the production of plastic food cartons

The producers of polystyrene have taken quite different approaches to drawing the bounds around their operations. Dow Chemical invented polystyrene in 1925 and remains one of the industry leaders in its production. In terms of sales, Dow is the number two player in the chemicals market, behind the behemoth, Du Pont. Relative to its major rivals in the polystyrene market, Dow is fairly highly integrated. In particular, virtually all of the styrene monomer needed in the plastics group is produced internally at Dow by its basic chemicals division. In this sense, Dow has vertically integrated in an upstream direction at least to some degree. In other words, some of the suppliers of the polystyrene division are other divisions within the same organization. The pattern in which firms acquire their suppliers is also known as **backward integration.**

An organization that begins to produce its own inputs is said to have vertically integrated in the upstream market, or, equivalently, to have engaged in backward integration.

Some of the buyers of polystyrene are also located within the Dow family. Thus Dow is also integrated downstream, or in a forward direction.

An organization which begins to market its own goods has vertically integrated downstream, or in a forward direction.

Approximately 20 percent of the polystyrene produced by Dow is converted to end use by the company itself—for example, the styrofoam cups and containers made in the consumer-products division. Thus Dow is vertically integrated into three elements of the line shown in Figure 11.1. As a result of this pattern of integration, for Dow as a whole, operating in the polystyrene market, the suppliers of interest are the ethane producers (typically petrochemical firms), while the buyers facing Dow are the restaurants and retailers who purchase the styrofoam products. The plastics division within Dow has as its suppliers the chemical division within the same firm. Its customers include outside fabricators as well as its corporate sibling, the consumer division.

Dow's strategy of relatively heavy reliance on vertical integration can be contrasted with that of Huntsman, the current leader in terms of industry capacity of polystyrene. Huntsman was formed through leveraged buy-outs of the polystyrene capacity of Shell and American Hoechst. Huntsman is partially integrated upstream, owning several styrene monomer plants, but still buys much of its styrene in the open market. Moreover, Huntsman has no end-use markets. Thus, for Huntsman, operating in this market requires it to deal with styrene as well as ethane producers on the supplier end and with fabricators of styrofoam in the end-use market. At least up until now, Huntsman has drawn the market boundaries quite differently from Dow.

Our first observation, then, is that the *degree of vertical integration is one of the decision variables of an organization.* Firms have a choice about which of their inputs they buy in the outside market and which they produce internally, either through a process of acquisition of an existing producer of the input or through the internal development of a new venture in the input area.

We also observe that vertical integration does not exclude other possibilities. Huntsman, for example, produces some of its own styrene, but buys the rest of it. Dow uses some of its polystyrene internally, but sells the rest of it. Firms may be in both the **captive market**—that is, the market in which the firm produces for its own internal use—and in the **merchant** or outside market. Indeed, as we will see, firms sometimes participate in the captive market in a modest degree simply to improve the kinds of deals they can strike in the merchant market.

Finally considerable variation exists in the kinds of supplier and buyer relationships characterized as captive or merchant types. In some organizations, sales are made across divisions, but they are very much "arm's-length" transactions, with scrupulous attention to transfer pricing issues. In these organizations, though we think of the selling division as having a captive market, the market may be rather free. The merchant market, too, is complex just beneath the surface. East Asia, for example, relies heavily on subcontracting as a middle ground between vertical integration and purchases of inputs on the open market. Joint ventures between suppliers and customers also occupy a middle ground between the open market and the internal market. Networks of organizations thus play a role between the market and the internal organization. Some market transactions are governed by contracts, long or short term, explicit or implicit. In each of these examples, transactions ostensibly in the merchant market may take on some of the characteristics of the captive market.

What governs the choices made by Dow and Huntsman about whether to buy more ethane suppliers or fabricators? At first blush, there appear to be many advantages to integration. By integrating backward, a manufacturer can gain an assured source of supply, lessening his vulnerability to suppliers. Integrating forward would seem to have the potential of assuring an outlet for one's product, and perhaps a profitable one at that. As we will see, however, these advantages are often overstated; they sometimes amount to nothing more than moving money from the firm's right pocket to its left. Moreover, integration involves certain costs that are often overlooked, for integration increases the scale of an operation, putting pressure on both capital and managerial resources. Integration also reduces the flexibility of a firm, while at the same time requiring it to learn a new, albeit related business.

Let us consider the apparel industry. In this industry, as in many others in the United States, competition from abroad has increased in recent years. The result has been some reduction in the operating margins experienced by apparel firms. Since fabric constitutes 40 percent or more of the costs of many of the apparel firms, many of these firms have considered vertical integration as a survival strategy. Is this wise? Suppose an apparel firm is paying $1 a yard for fabric that it knows is being produced at a cost of $.75 per yard. If the firm purchases the textile manufacturer, it would appear that it could reduce its fabric costs by 25 percent, simply by transferring the fabric across divisions "at cost." This would clearly increase the profits of the apparel manufacturer. The difficulty arises because, while the transfer may be increasing the profits of the apparel manufacturer, it may also be reducing the profits of the textile division by a comparable amount. The firm has simply transferred textile profit into the apparel industry, with *no* increase in profits of the overall entity.

Of course, as we indicated earlier, the appropriate price the apparel manufacturer should charge itself for fabric transferred within the firm is whatever price maximizes the sum of profits obtained from the two divisions taken as a whole.[2] In particular, the apparel division should pay a price that reflects the "opportunity cost" of the fabric. If the opportunity costs are fully considered, the economic accounting in the case of a vertical integration will be more helpful. Some of the most successful vertical integrations have been in firms that recognize that owning an input does not necessarily mean the firm should use that input internally.[3]

In considering vertical integration, an organization should consider costs and benefits netted across units, reflecting fully on opportunity costs.

Unless the organization considering integration considers the opportunity costs of resource transfers, it may end up simply deluding itself about where its profits are coming from and thus creating harm rather than good. So our first observation in this area is that, in considering the potential benefits of vertical integration, the firm needs to look at the whole picture, the plight of the new entity as well as the core business. If it does so, it may still find some profit opportunities from integration, as we discover below.

Incentives for Vertical Integration: Taxes and Regulation

Now, sometimes shifting profits around through vertical integration *can* increase those profits, typically by avoiding taxes. If an organization is paying very high taxes on its profits, it may be able to avoid some of those taxes by consigning profits to a relatively less-taxed product line. A good example of this is provided by the oil business. Alaska taxes oil by collecting a fraction of its well-head value. The well-head value is determined by the market price of oil minus its transportation costs, which, in Alaska, consists primarily of the rates charged in the Alaskan pipeline. Now it happens that the pipeline is owned mainly by the same firms that drill the oil and thus pay the well-head tax. Since pipeline profits are not subject to high state taxes, oil firms have an incentive to "take their profits" in the pipeline, by charging themselves high transportation rates, rather than in the heavily taxed extraction end. In this instance, the shifting around of profits can actually increase them; thus vertical integration enhances the possibility of avoiding taxes. Similar opportunities are sometimes created by integration that spans country boundaries, given that different countries have rather different corporate tax rates.

Vertical integration can, on occasion, reduce an organization's tax burden.

A second incentive for integration related to tax avoidance is **regulatory evasion.**[4] Consider an organization subject to rate-of-return regulation in one of its markets. Under rate-of-return regulation, a commission (usually state) sets an allowed return on capital that constrains the earning ability of the regulated firm. In general, we expect the allowed rate of return to be less than the return the organization could earn unconstrained. Now suppose this organization purchases supplies from a freestanding agent. It will normally pay the market price. If the regulated entity purchases that agent, it may begin to charge itself very high prices for the input. The costs of the regulated division will rise and, since rate-of-return regulation simply passes costs on, the prices the regulated entity can charge will also rise. For the regulated division, revenues have just risen to cover the new, inflated costs. The rate-of-return constraint is still being met. But, if we look at the earnings of the input division, they will have increased due to the inflated prices! The regulated unit has effectively shifted profits around through the use of vertical integration.

In a regulated industry, vertical integration can expedite regulatory evasion and lead to higher profits.

For most businesses, however, operating as unregulated units within a single country, tax avoidance and regulatory evasion are not prominent by-products of vertical integration. Are there other, less institutional motives for vertical integration?

Incentives to Integrate: Transaction-Cost Savings

When we think about an organization vertically integrating, the first image most of us have is of closely connected physical units. Technology seems to drive traditional ideas of integration. Consider, for example, the process of integration in paper manufacture.

Paper pulp is produced by extracting moisture from wood and isolating the cellulose fibers. Since wood is about 90 percent water, pulp manufacturing involves considerable drying with its attendant energy costs. Thus it is most efficient to make paper directly from the pulp, so that the paper is made as the drying takes place. If a manufacturer instead must buy pulp from another source, it will be delivered in large dry rolls to reduce transport costs. Water must then be added to the dry pulp to introduce it into the paper-making machine. The water is then extracted out again as the paper is made. In effect, the pulp is dried twice—once by the pulp manufacturer and once by the paper manufacturer. As we can see, pulp and paper manufacture are most efficiently located side by side to avoid duplication of effort. With side-by-side location, the pulp needs only a single drying. *But the fact that we wish, for technical reasons, to locate two processes together does not require joint ownership.* Pulp and paper manufacturers located side by side might be owned by different firms. In order to understand when joint ownership is advisable, we need to look much more closely into the workings of the firm. Technology is relevant, but it is not all that matters.

The principles governing an organization's decisions as to how to structure its transactions or how deeply to vertically integrate were first articulated in 1937 by Ronald Coase in a landmark article.[5] In this article, Coase argued:

> The operation of a market costs something and by forming an organization and allowing some authority (an "entrepreneur") to direct the resources, certain marketing costs are saved. The entrepreneur has to carry out his function at less cost, taking into account the fact that he may get factors of production at a lower price than the market transactions which he supersedes, because it is always possible to revert to the open market if he fails to do this.

Coase's central argument is that, by vertically integrating, a firm opts to make its resource decisions internally using whatever management mechanisms are available, as opposed to using the market to direct resources.[6]

What are the advantages to the firm of using internal versus market allocation mechanisms? Let us look at the cost of using the market. If a firm enters the market to purchase supplies, it must undertake the costs of searching for the best price and quality goods, arranging delivery in a prompt and reasonable way, and ensuring that all terms of the transaction be met. These are the transaction costs associated with using the market.

A nonintegrated firm experiences search and contracting costs in dealing with buyers and suppliers.

If the firm instead internalizes the transaction and buys and sells within the firm, it bears a quite different set of transaction costs. Now the firm must bear the costs of coordinating buying and selling activities within the firm, organizing and motivating workers, and the like. An optimal strategy will involve trading off the costs of using each of the available methods of organizing transactions. Or, stated more formally:

Firms tend to structure their transactions in ways that will minimize the costs of using the transactional apparatus.

Let us return for a moment to the pulp and paper example. The proposition we are arguing is that pulp and paper manufacture is vertically integrated not because of technical considerations involving the water content of wood, but because of the relative ease of coordinating pulp and paper within the firm as opposed to coordinating pulp transfer across disparate firms. As we will see, the technical linkage across pulp and paper is relevant to the costs of coordination, but it is only part of the puzzle.

The broad transaction-cost principle articulated above is just that, a broad principle. But considerable work has followed since Coase's article that has tried to make this principle operational from the perspective of management. This work has tried to be more concrete about the kinds of situations in which a transaction-cost analysis favors one kind of organizational structure versus another. When is it easier to use markets, and when do internal transactions serve us better?

From a motivational point of view, there is much to be said in favor of buying inputs or distributing outputs on the open market. In so doing, the firm need not worry about how the producing agent organizes itself, how it compensates its workers, how it runs its R&D efforts, and so on. Nor does the firm need to worry about fluctuations in its input demand. It need only locate the organization with the lowest price for a given quality of input and contract for supply from that organization. Many of the problems of monitoring and motivation discussed in Chapter 8 would be avoided if the firm relied on the market for its supplies. If a presumption exists in favor of purchasing from the outside, what causes us to move against this presumption?

A concrete example may provide an answer. Suppose we have two firms engaged in different stages of the printing process. Press, Inc. produces a wide line of printing presses, which it leases and sells to printing shops, one of whom is Print Shop 1.[7] The two firms are free-standing units engaging in a market transaction. Press Inc. can produce a press for Print Shop 1 by undertaking an investment that would result in costs per press of $5500. Of these costs, Press Inc. would have operating costs of $1500, and per-press fixed costs in the amount of $4000. The resulting press would have numerous special features of value only to Print Shop 1; other printing companies would be willing to pay only $4000 for the same press. Would Press Inc. willingly make the investment necessary to enable it to produce the specialized press? In general, we would think that, in the absence of contractual assurances from Print Shop 1 to purchase or lease the customized press, Press Inc. would be foolish to make this investment. Once the investment is made, Press Inc. has only two choices: sell the press to the generic printing firm for $4000, or sell it to Print Shop 1. But Print Shop 1, seeing the choices open to Press Inc., has no incentive to offer more than just over $4000 for the press. Press Inc. will thus find it difficult to recover its investment.

The difficulty is that the firm producing printing presses has made a specialized investment, creating an asset with value only to a very limited number of users. Once the firm makes this investment, it puts itself in an adverse bargaining position vis-à-vis the buying firm. To the extent that a transaction requires one of the parties to make a specialized investment, the possibility of bilateral bargaining problems arise. Under these conditions, transactions are rarely carried out in a pure open-market setting. The arm's-length transaction allows for no protection for the party who makes the original specialized investment.

In the example of the printing press, what would we expect to happen? There are several possibilities. First, the press manufacturer and the printing shop might merge. In practice, this is not often done in the publishing area as a consequence of other factors. Another possibility is that the two parties might sign a long-term contract, specifying the conditions under which the specialized press will be supplied. Or the two parties might set up a **joint venture,** organized with the sole intent of producing this press. In each of these cases, a closer relationship between the buyer and seller is forged with the intent of avoiding later bargaining difficulties.

The possibility of productive investment in assets specific to a transaction encourages vertical integration.

We see that firms will abandon the anonymity of the market in order to allow themselves to reap benefits from specific investments, without ending up at the mercy of a supplier or buyer. Williamson suggests four particular instances in which such investment specificity is most likely to occur:[8]

1. *Site specificity:* the asset is located in a particular area that makes it useful only to a small number of buyers or suppliers and it cannot be easily moved.

2. *Physical-asset specificity:* the product design makes it especially useful to a small number of buyers; the printing example given above has this characteristic.

3. *Human-asset specificity:* the transaction requires specialized knowledge on the part of the parties to the transaction.

4. *Dedicated assets:* the expansion in facilities is necessitated only by the requirements of one or several buyers.

In each of these cases, the specter is of an organization that makes an expensive, specialized investment in order to serve a particular limited market, and then finds itself in a tenuous bargaining position vis-à-vis that market. Once the specialized investment is made, possibilities for a "hold up" are created. These possibilities can make a particular transaction unattractive at the preinvestment stage, unless there is some way to guard against the hold up. Some form of vertical integration provides this assurance.

The same argument that we just made about the incentives to vertically integrate in the presence of specific assets also pertains to cases in which competition is absent in general in the supplier industry. With low levels of competition in the supplier industry, firms are again faced with the prospect of hold up and vertical integration may secure lower prices and more stable supplies. Of course, if there are important structural reasons for the low levels of competition in the supplier industry, a firm's ability to vertically integrate may be hampered. Nevertheless, the incentive to do so remains.

Low levels of competition in supplying industries encourage vertical integration.

Patterns of vertical integration within industries often change over time as the technology and market environments in which they are embedded change. The soft drink industry provides a cogent example. Historically, the industry has relied heavily on independent bottlers. Beginning in the 1970s, Coca-Cola and Pepsi-Cola began acquiring their larger bottlers and creating captive bottling capacity. Muris, Scheffman, and Spiller argue that this change can be attributed to changes in the transactions costs of negotiating with independent bottlers in an environment in which industry maturity has increased the importance of advertising and new product introduction, and technology has increased the scale of bottling operations.[9]

Incentives to Integrate: Information Access

As we look across a variety of manufacturing operations, we can perceive patterns of *partial* vertical integration. The Natural Resources Division of Scott Paper Co., one of the largest paper-products companies in the United States, produces pulp to supply to its own paper-products division, and also to the open market. IBM produces some of the chips it needs for the computers it produces itself, and others it buys on the open market. What advantages might we see from such a mixed system?

In some cases, having two suppliers—one inside the firm and a second outside—can improve the information available to the central organization. Consider a firm that is trying to negotiate a contract with an outside supplier in a circumstance in which only one such outside supplier is available. In order to negotiate, it would be quite useful for the buyer to have some information about the production costs of the supplier. Maintaining a small division internally that has some, though limited, ability to produce this input can help provide relevant information.[10] In this case, partial integration improves an organization's ability to bargain with its suppliers. In recent years, given the tendency of U.S. firms to narrow their range of outside suppliers in emulation of their Japanese rivals, the control afforded by a small amount of vertical integration may be of increasing value.

In the example above, we focused on the advantages of backward integration. But firms may also gain informational advantages from forward integration. Firms which produce consumer goods need to be sensitive to changes in their consumers' preferences. Partial vertical integration can provide manufacturers with a channel through which market information can travel. Increasingly, firms are recognizing the value of this channel.

A mixed system of reliance on outside versus inside suppliers may also improve the information-gathering process within the organization.[11] As indicated in Chapter 8, one of the central implementation problems facing an organization resides in its inability to monitor the behavior of individuals and groups within the firm. In a divisionalized paper firm, if the pulp division experiences high costs and passes those on to the paper division, senior management may not easily be able to determine whether the high costs are a function of mismanagement in the pulp group or bad luck. If that same organization, however, gets some of its pulp from an outside supplier in the spot market, this supply will provide yardstick competition for the pulp division.

Partial vertical integration can improve the information of the firm.

For several reasons an organization may wish to engage in some vertical linking. Regulatory rules may favor integration. The possibility of investing in productive assets specific to the joint activity of the two organizations may encourage some integration. Finally, vertical links may be sought as a way to improve information. But what *kind* of vertical relationship do we choose? As we indicated earlier, there are a variety of vertical relationships possible. Indeed, the potential contracting institutions that can mediate transactions span a broad range from vertical integration to modest contracting or even repeated buying relations. The mode chosen to reduce hold-up problems or to improve the firm's information access depend on a complex set of characteristics of the transactions themselves and the parties engaging in those transactions. We explore these further below.

How Much Vertical Linkage and What Form Should It Take?

We have thus far argued that the existence of transaction-specific investments and the need for better information tend to move organizations out of the spot market and into some form of either contractual relationship or vertical integration. But how do we explain the choice among various arrangements? When do we choose contract? When do we vertically integrate? We turn now to this set of issues.

An excellent example of the variety of arrangements possible between two firms in vertically related markets is provided by IBM's recent forays into the computer chip market. IBM, in its computer production, uses a considerable number of application-specific integrated circuits, customized for IBM use. Producing these chips requires specialized investment; arm's-length market purchases by IBM would thus leave suppliers in an adverse bargaining position. IBM has sought to alleviate the bargaining problem in several ways. First, it produces a number of these chips itself; thus it is vertically integrated in the traditional sense. But it also seeks outside suppliers. It has, for example, an agreement with General Electric for the development and production of customized chips through the 1990s. Under this agreement, IBM has committed itself to long-term purchase of the chips, and it has been involved in the design process. Thus G.E.'s risks from undertaking a specialized investment have been reduced by IBM's long-term commitment and its sharing of design costs.

IBM has a second contract, involving technology exchange, with Intel, the third largest merchant semiconductor producer in the United States. Earlier, IBM had experimented with partial integration with Intel. In sum, we see in this market a clear example of specialized investment and a range of experimental solutions *even within* a single firm. What sense do we make of these institutional choices?

A matrix based on one developed by Williamson is helpful in sorting out the forces that govern the choice of transaction structure.[12] One prime need for some closer relationship between buyer and seller to limit opportunistic behavior is created by the existence of specific investments associated with the transaction. In the matrix in Figure 11.2, investment specificity is one element governing the choice of degree of vertical linkage. Investment specificity increases as we move from left to right. The greater the asset specificity, all else equal, the tighter the buyer-supplier link will be. The closest buyer-seller relationship is complete ownership integration. Joint ventures, in which units maintain financial integrity, but share a facility, is a less bonded mode of integration. Contracts of one sort or another move us closer to the market.

A second relevant characteristic of transactions that determines the optimal extent of a vertical link is how often these transactions occur. A one-time transaction will typically not support an elaborate contractual arrangement; in these cases the loss from a possible hold up is not sufficient to induce firms to go through either a complex contracting arrangement or full financial integration. On the vertical axis of the matrix, we

| | Assets | | |
	General	Mixed	Specific
Occasional	Market transactions		Contracts often with arbitration
Frequency of transaction			
Frequent	Market transactions	Bilateral contracts	Vertical integration

Figure 11.2 Organization of transactions: governance matrix investment characteristics. *Source:* Reprinted with permission of The Free Press, a Division of Macmillan, Inc. from *The Economic Institutions of Capitalism* by Oliver E. Williamson. Copyright © 1985 by Oliver E. Williamson.

have thus placed frequency of transaction, with frequency decreasing as we move up the matrix. The more frequent the transaction, the more likely it will be that the transaction is internalized. Within the matrix we can then place each of the various organizational modes.

We see that vertical integration is most common when transactions between the two parties are frequent and the optimal investment strategy involves highly specific assets. In this case, the firms will find it worthwhile to bear the costs of monitoring and motivating activity inside the firm, rather than face market bargaining. As either the frequency of transaction diminishes, and/or the specificity of the investment falls, we move toward some form of contracting. Finally, for nonspecific investments market transactions are most common.

Thus far we have ignored the role of market uncertainty in shaping organizational boundaries. But uncertainty will play a role as well, as we indicated earlier.[13] Suppose we have a situation in which, as in the printing-press case, I will need to make some specific investment in order to supply you with your needs. Suppose further we are led by this asset specificity to write a contract governing the terms under which the transaction will occur. If we are operating in a fairly predictable market, writing such a contract and carrying it out may be fairly simple. But suppose the market is quite uncertain: Demand varies considerably, for example, so the needs of the buyer in terms of volume are highly variable. Or perhaps the supply costs depend on the weather or on the availability of some natural resource. Writing a contract to cover all contingencies will be difficult. If conditions change drastically, it may be hard to enforce a contract. Vertical integration will generally prove to be a better alternative under these conditions. We are thus more likely to see vertical integration in situations in which it is too costly and cumbersome to specify all of the contingent classes. Vertical integration is a way of obtaining residual rights, unspecified, in a linked operation.[14]

In the example above, uncertainty was symmetric: No one could predict what was happening to prices or demand. Another possibility is that one of the parties to the transaction has better information about the uncertain event than the other.[15] If the information is important in terms of the strategic decisions of the unknowledgeable partner, then a vertical merger may occur simply as a way to transmit information. In cases in which two firms are bargaining with each other in a thin market, the possession by one agent of private information may give that agent a strategic advantage. Vertical integration can reduce the strategic use of information, as we suggested earlier.[16] In this situation, partial vertical integration may be adequate, since our primary interest is in integration for its informational value. Notice in this instance, too, a coincidence of uncertainty, specific investment, and some frequency of transaction contribute to vertical integration.

We have thus far seen that uncertainty often increases the potential gains from vertical integration. There are exceptions to this rule, how-

ever. In particular, in markets in which there is rapid technical change
with its attendant likelihood of technical obsolescence, vertical integration
tends to be less effective.[17] In the 1980s when Hewlett-Packard moved to
launch its first laser printer, it chose to buy the engine for that printer
from Canon, a Japanese firm. Using an outside vender allowed HP to
concentrate its efforts on the software. HP now dominates this large market, and many attribute their success to the Canon partnership that allowed it to produce a high-quality product faster than the competition.
The complex network of vertical alliances in high technology industries,
which extends even across national boundaries, is summarized well by a
recent remark of John Scully, CEO of Apple: "We can't do without the
Japanese and they can't do without us."[18]

> **The right level of vertical linkage depends on the opportunities for spe-
> cific investment, the frequency of transactions across vertically linked units,
> and market uncertainty.**

Some Examples of the Role of Transactions Costs
in Contracting and Integration

We can now turn to look at several markets in which asset specificity and
asymmetric information appear to have given rise to closer relations between buyer and seller. We will again see in this discussion more of the
complexity of the buyer-seller relationship.

U.S. electrical utilities have for some time bought considerable amounts
of coal to provide power.[19] Indeed, the electric-power industry accounts
for more than 80 percent of domestic coal consumption. This coal is sold
to power companies on the spot market, and through contracts of varying
duration; in some cases, power companies have vertically integrated
backward into coal production. Why do we observe such large differences
in the institutions through which coal is purchased?

Joskow has argued that differences in the extent of vertical integration
of coal mines and power companies can be attributed to differences in
asset specificity involved in particular coal/power transactions. In our earlier terminology, both *site specificity* and *physical-asset specificity* may be important. Most electric power plants purchase coal from a mine and have
it transported to the plant. However, a small number of plants have located right next to the coal mine, in anticipation of using that coal supply.
These plants are known as "mine-mouth" plants and are a prime example
of site specificity. Joskow finds that mine-mouth plants are much more
likely to be vertically integrated than other kinds of coal mines; moreover,
for mine-mouth plants that are not vertically integrated, the average power
plant–mine contract is about 16 years longer than the contract for a more
distant mine. Locating a power plant adjacent to a mine offers the possibility of cost savings; to realize these savings, however, requires some *ex
ante* negotiation.

Physical asset specificity also plays a role in determining the nature of the relationship between power plants and coal mines. Most power plants are designed to burn a particular kind of coal, that is, coal with a specific BTU and moisture content. Coal mined in the western regions of the United States varies in type considerably more than does that mined in the east. Therefore western plants tend to be more often at the mercy of few suppliers than are eastern plants. And, in response, we find that contracts with eastern coal producers are on average three to five years shorter than western and midwestern contracts. Again we observe the role of specific investments and the fear of being held up in creating the design of the contract.

Another interesting example of the role of asset specificity is provided by the auto industry. Originally, autos were constructed of open wooden bodies. By about 1919, however, closed metal bodies were being manufactured using giant presses to stamp the body parts. Making closed bodies required stamping dies that were in large measure specific to the particular requirements of the model to be produced. In the early period of the auto industry, the producers of the dies were independent of the auto manufacturers themselves. Soon after the shift toward closed bodies, which entailed a large specific investment on the part of the die manufacturers, long-term contracts appeared. In 1919, for example, General Motors and Fisher Body entered into a 10-year contract according to which G.M. agreed to buy virtually all of its closed bodies from Fisher. This clearly protected Fisher from being held up by G.M. But now opportunities were created for Fisher to take advantage of G.M. At what price would G.M. buy? How could quality be assured? The contract negotiations became increasingly complex, until by 1926 the two firms merged, again as a final attempt to mitigate bargaining difficulties.[20]

In the modern automobile industry, considerable numbers of parts are made in-house, while others are purchased on the open market. Teece and Monteverde have argued, along the lines of the Fisher Body–G.M. case described above, that today's make-or-buy choice reflects the specificity of the physical assets required to manufacture particular parts.[21] Monteverde and Teece examined 113 automotive components, ranging from bumpers and seat belts to steering columns and wheels, and found that production was typically brought in house whenever the engineering effort required in the development of the component was substantial. In these conditions, if the development is done outside the firm, the developers will have an advantage in bargaining relative to the auto firms who need the part. Thus backward integration into components is a way to protect against overpowerful suppliers.

A similar study of the make-or-buy decision in the automobile industry was done by Walker and Weber.[22] Managers in a division of a large U.S. automobile firm were charged with authority for deciding whether to make or buy components. Walker and Weber evaluated a number of these managerial decisions, using both interviews and objective data about the characteristics of the component markets. They found that the role of uncertainty in determining the extent of vertical integration was affected by the level of competition in the market. For uncompetitive markets, in which volume fluctuations were expected, firms typically vertically integrated. In the absence of insurance provided by competition, firms chose to insure by producing their own parts. Technological uncertainty, on the other hand, led to vertical integration most forcefully when competition in the supplying industry was high. Under these conditions, it is possible that firms integrated in order to protect their innovations, even though competition would have led to low costs in a "buy" decision. Again, in the Walker-Weber study, we see the role of both uncertainty and competition affecting the decision to vertically integrate.

Summary

We have now seen the broad principles that help to determine the optimal vertical shape of an organization. It should be clear from the discussion that the optimal scope of the firm will vary as technological, social, and economic factors alter the possibilities for transactions across firms. Thus scrutiny of vertical relations forms a continuing function of strategic management.

To the extent that an organization decides to lengthen its vertical chain, it can do so in one of two ways. First, the firm can begin to build new capacity in the market it wishes to enter. Alternately, it can acquire an existing buyer or supplier. This latter case, known as a vertical merger, is considered in Chapter 12.

12

Mergers, Acquisitions, and Strategic Alliances

In Chapters 10 and 11, we explored some of the reasons an organization may wish to expand either in a horizontal or vertical direction. In many circumstances, firms will wish to accomplish these changes by investing in new capacity. In other circumstances, however, firms will find it more attractive to move into new areas via the acquisition of a firm that is already in the desired new market.

In 1991, there were $98 billion worth of merger transactions in the United States. These deals cut across industry and national boundaries. Ten percent of the 1991 merger deals involved acquisitions of U.S. firms by non-U.S. acquirers, and these deals comprised 20 percent of the value of all U.S. mergers and acquisitions. In 1991, for example, Matsushita Electric acquired the U.S. entertainment firm of MCA for $6.8 billion. In Europe, the pace of mergers and acquisitions has increased in response to the attempts to create a more unified Europe. BSN, Unilever, and Nestle have all been active buyers in the 1990s in the food industry. A Scandinavian company has purchased a number of mobile home companies in the United Kingdom. Daimler-Benz, the large German firm, bought 34 percent of the French computer services group of GAP Gemini-Sogeti. Mergers are a very prominent part of the industrial landscape globally and one of the most common routes firms use to reshape their corporate portfolios. But not all of these mergers turn out to be successful. For every 100 acquisitions recorded in the period 1970–80, there were 40 divestiture transactions.[1] In 1991, in the United States, there were 2117 merger deals and 1007 divestitures. Some of these divestitures represent attempts by firms to slim down, to reinforce a shaky core business. R.H. Macy's divestiture of its credit department to G.E. is a good example of this. A number of divestitures appear to have been the result of failed attempts to incorporate the new unit into the existing organization. Merger activity, while common, is by no means without difficulties. In this chapter, we explore some of the reasons firms may choose the acquisition route and some of the difficulties they may encounter along the path. We also discuss joint ventures, an alternative to mergers, which have become increasingly popular in the 1990s.

The Methods of Effecting a Merger or Acquisition

Broadly speaking, there are three types of mergers. In a **horizontal merger,** two or more direct competitors, producing in the same market, are joined. A **vertical merger** links firms that are in different stages of production within a particular market. Finally, **conglomerate mergers** are unions of firms that are neither direct rivals, nor produce in the same production chain. In this chapter, we will focus on the latter two merger types, since both of these are used to substantially alter the shape of the corporate portfolio.

Once an organization decides to join with another firm, it can do so through several different mechanisms. In some cases, the management of the two firms considering the union are actively and cooperatively involved in the negotiations. In other situations, stockholders play a more active role and management may be in a more defensive position. Often the form of the union will have both tax consequences and, at times, antitrust consequences. It is well known that the nature of a merger and acquisition negotiation can have a profound effect on the ability of the new management team to work together post-merger.[2]

In this chapter, we will refer to any union between two or more firms as a merger, although the formal definition of a merger is more narrow. A **merger,** in formal usage, occurs whenever all of the assets and liabilities of the acquired company are absorbed by the buyer. Acquired assets and liabilities need not be specified separately; *all* assets and liabilities are automatically assumed to be the responsibility of the acquiring firm. Traditionally, a proposal to merge is made to the board of directors of a firm, and the board approves the proposal and submits it to the stockholders. Since management normally holds significant membership on the board, most mergers are undertaken with management approval. In addition, in order for a merger to occur, the stockholders of the acquired firm must agree to it. The fraction of stockholders who must agree varies by state, but a two-thirds majority is commonly required.

Mergers are typically friendly unions between the management and stockholders of two firms. A rather different way to merge two firms is for the acquiring firm to purchase the stock of the selling firm. The 1991 takeover of NCR by AT&T for $7.5 billion took this form. The takeover typically begins with the purchase, in the open market, of a fraction of the stock of the sought-after firm by the potential buyer. Acquirers generally wish to engage in such stock purchases quietly to avoid bidding up the stock price. When any acquirer has purchased 5 percent of a firm, however, SEC rules require that this purchase be announced within five days. Within these five days, the acquirer can purchase up to an additional 5 percent of the firm. Thus 10 percent of the sought-after firm's stock may be bought on the open market before the announcement of a takeover. Once the acquiring firm (or individuals) announces its intention to take over, it will typically make a **tender offer** to outstanding stockholders, offering to purchase their stock at some premium over the market price. If enough stock is purchased, a merger can be forced.

In 1960, fewer than 1 percent of all the mergers and acquisitions in the United States were accomplished via the tender offer. In 1977, this figure had risen to 15 percent.[3] While more recent figures suggest that the proportion of tender offers has fallen somewhat since the late 1970s, this procedure is now very much a part of the financial environment facing a firm.

The increase in the proportion of unions accomplished through takeover rather than merger is not entirely understood. Nevertheless, there is some indication that part of the lure of the takeover is its tendency to *discipline* the management of acquired firms and to help align managerial behavior more with the interests of stockholders.[4] In the case of a union effected through the tender offer, the cooperation of the target firm's management is not required. Indeed, in recent years, many takeovers effected through the purchase of stock have been **hostile takeovers,** accomplished over the protest of management. In cases in which management has been lax or misdirected, such takeovers may improve the performance of the firm. Even the simple threat of a takeover may have felicitous consequences for the earnings of the firm. In a later section, we will discuss some of the reasons for managerial resistance to takeovers and some of the devices that have been developed to fight takeovers.

A third possible way in which a firm can move into a new area without *de novo* investment is to purchase the assets of a firm already in the market. For example, a firm might acquire the productive plant and equipment of a firm in a market it wishes to enter. An acquisition of this sort can be accomplished through negotiations between the management of the two firms and would not necessarily require stockholder approval.

We can see as we look at the various ways in which a union between two firms can be effected that an important distinction is *which* agents from the two firms are party to the negotiation. In the case of a merger, both the management of the two firms and the directors are actively involved. In the case of a takeover involving a tender offer, the management of the target firm is often not involved. In the case of an asset acquisition, management alone may make the relevant decisions. Seemingly small differences in the mechanics of mergers then may reflect much more profound differences in the underlying character of those mergers. As we explore some of the differences among mergers as background for our discussion about the motives for mergers, we will learn that, just as there are substantial differences in the ways in which mergers are accomplished, there are also differences in the underlying motives for merger and the success rate of those mergers.

The Diversity of Mergers

Broad differences exist among mergers. Some flavor of the magnitude and nature of those differences can be seen from the experience of one merger participant, Tom Wyman, CEO of first Green Giant and later CBS.

In the years 1975–79, when Wyman ran Green Giant, it was a $500 million company, with low margins but with an excellent reputation among consumers. Wyman and his team analyzed the problem and realized that Green Giant's narrow product line, frozen vegetables and its consequent poor bargaining power vis à vis its retailers, was one of the keys to its modest performance. Wyman believed that without the ability to exploit economies of scope in distribution, Green Giant would find it impossible to raise margins substantially.

At the same time, Pillsbury (like Green Giant, a Midwestern firm, albeit a much larger one) was casting about for a new line of business to take advantage of some of its fixed assets in distribution. Pillsbury had one set of strong consumer products—the Pillsbury Dough Boy line—and a rather marginal product—cake mixes. Clearly, there was some excess capacity both in distribution and marketing at Pillsbury that could be used to support another product. Thus both Green Giant and Pillsbury sought diversification as a way to exploit scope economies. The vehicle used for this diversification was a merger between the two firms. Wyman and the Pillsbury management, working together, moved Green Giant into the Pillsbury family, with Green Giant stockholders receiving a considerable premium over stock price. Wyman himself joined Pillsbury to run the Consumer Division and Green Giant is today a successful part of the Pillsbury group.

Contrast this scenario with the experience of Wyman a decade later at the Columbia Broadcasting System. Wyman left Green Giant in 1980 to become president of CBS. By early 1985, it had become apparent that CBS was the object of attention of several people interested either in merger or in a potential takeover. One of CBS's suitors was Laurence Tisch, and by the fall of 1986, Tisch had acquired in open-market transactions 24.9 percent of the company's stock. At this point, Tisch joined forces with William Paley, the Chairman of the Board of CBS and a large stockholder, and took over control of the company from existing management. In contrast to the Green Giant experience, this takeover was a hostile one, accomplished with great resistance from existing CBS management. While the Green Giant–Pillsbury merger involved relatively large premiums over market price paid to existing Green Giant stockholders, the CBS deal was largely accomplished through open-market stock purchases. After the takeover, the changes in CBS were dramatic. Wyman was dismissed in a dramatic boardroom scene, and layers of management disappeared along with considerable personnel. The magazine publishing division was sold off to a group of inside managers; the textbook group was sold to Harcourt Brace Jovanovich; and CBS Records was sold to Sony.[5] Changes occurred in the management and deployment of resources at Green Giant as well, but they were considerably more modest than the changes at CBS.

The Green Giant and CBS cases make an interesting contrast, at least in part because the same man headed each organization before changes occurred. The differences between these two situations are vast. In the United States, in the period before 1970, most mergers were "friendly," as in the Green Giant–Pillsbury union, and were accomplished with the cooperation of the senior management of the two firms. In the 1980s, the hostile takeover was more prevalent, with many more post-merger changes. Mergers and takeovers typically involve some restructuring of the new entity, in part to take advantage of economies of scope and risk management properties that motivated the change in the first place. Management changes following mergers are also common. In a survey of 1300 executives who had been dismissed from their jobs, 32 percent were let go as a consequence of a merger.[6] But the extent of the restructuring can vary considerably, with Green Giant on one extreme with rather modest changes, and CBS on the other.

Mergers then can be effected in a variety of ways and are quite diverse in their effects. But why enter a new business using mergers at all? Why not simply develop new businesses *de novo*? As we turn now to this issue, we will learn that the motives for mergers may be as varied as the form.

The Motive for Mergers

We begin our discussion by examining some of the data on mergers and acquisitions. Our first observation is that the popularity of mergers appears to vary considerably over time. Indeed, in the United States, mergers appear to move in waves.[7] In Figure 12.1, data are given on trends in the number of mergers accomplished from 1895 to 1980 and the asset values of those transactions.

As we can see, the first surge in merger activity occurred around the turn of the century.[8] Many of the mergers in this period were horizontal in nature, and many of the large industrial concerns we see today were formed during this period. Over the years 1897–1903, almost three thousand mergers occurred, many of them involving multiple partners. If we recall the relatively primitive state of financial markets and the overall smaller number of firms in the economy, we can see that this early merger wave was a very profound movement indeed. It was, in fact, responsible for many of the large manufacturing firms we see today. U.S. Steel, for example, was created during this period from the merger of a variety of

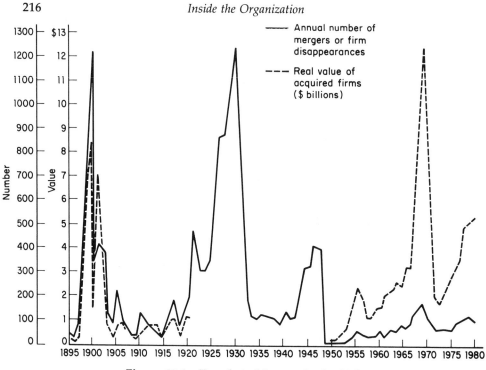

Figure 12.1   Trends in Mergers in the U.S.

smaller firms as were American Tobacco, International Harvester, Du Pont, and numerous other large and powerful U.S. firms.

Between about 1905 and the 1920s, the level of merger activity in the United States had declined in response to economic recession and World War I. The second great merger wave occurred in the late 1920s. In this wave, the vertical merger became more prominent, and conglomerate mergers also began to appear for the first time. This second movement, which was larger than the first, finally ended in the Depression of the 1930s.

Figure 12.1 dates the third merger wave from about 1955 to about 1970. From 1960 to 1970, more than 25,000 mergers were recorded. By this time, horizontal mergers between large firms with substantial market shares were largely prohibited under the antitrust laws. Instead, mergers in this period were more often conglomerate in nature. Approximately 70 percent of the value of assets acquired in the 1960s were in conglomerate mergers. In this period, U.S. Rubber Co. became Uniroyal, for example—a name change that reflected a fundamental change in the production of the firm.

The 1980s saw a fourth merger wave.[9] In the early 1980s, six multibillion dollar corporations in the energy sector alone were acquired by other firms: Cities Services, Conoco, Marathon, Gulf, Getty, and Superior.[10] The banking sector, reeling under several decades of major regulatory change, also experienced a surge of merger and acquisition activity. Chemical Bank's 1991 acquisition of Manufacturers Hanover is one example of this increased activity. Like the previous merger wave, the 1980s wave involved considerable conglomerate mergers. On the other hand, many of the recent takeovers have involved post-merger restructuring, in which an acquisition has been followed by substantial sell-off of a target company division.[11] Table 12.1 shows the volume of merger and acquisition activity from 1982–91, and clearly shows the slowing of the wave at the end of the period.

Merger waves are by no means unique to the United States. A large increase in merger activity occurred in Europe from the mid-1950s to 1970. Indeed, it has been argued that a substantial portion of the increase in British industrial concentration in the 1960s was due to merger activity.[12] In the late 1970s, merger activity again increased. As in the United States, recent mergers in Europe have been heavily conglomerate in nature. In 1981, L. M. Ericsson, the large Swedish telecommunications firm began diversifying into office information systems, with acquisitions of Data-Saab and Facit. Hanson Trust, a large British conglomerate, bought a battery maker, a footwear company, a retailer, and a food manufacturer during the decade between 1975 and 1985 to increase its sales over sixfold. Many of the European mergers have occurred across country boundaries, adding a new dimension to the ability of merger to expand the bounds of a firm.[13] As trade walls in Europe have begun to crumble, European mergers have increased. French companies have been particularly aggressive, consummating 83 European deals in 1991 alone, one-quarter of which represent acquisitions in the United Kingdom. Daimler-Benz, a German firm, has engaged in a number of large acquisitions across product and country boundaries. The opening up of Eastern Europe to the West has encouraged mergers across these borders as well. In 1992, Volkswagen Germany acquired Skoda of Czechoslovakia, for example. Foreign acquirers have also become increasingly active in the U.S. market, accounting for 20 percent of the U.S. acquisitions in 1990 and 1991.[14] British Petroleum, for example, paid $7.6 billion for the remainder of Standard Oil of Ohio in 1986. The Dutch firm Unilever purchased Chesebrough-Pond's for over $3 billion.

What accounts for the fluctuations in merger activity? In the early data, there appears to be some tendency for the overall level of merger activity to rise with the level of stock prices.[15] More recent work in the United States and abroad has been less successful in explaining the timing of mergers,[16] and indeed some work suggests that the merger waves may be generated by a simple random-walk process.[17] In any case, none of the traditional theories of motives for mergers seems to help us explain their wave-like quality. If we look at particular mergers, however, managerial and stockholder motives become more apparent.

We begin our discussion by asking ourselves, Why merge? Might not firms find it more effective to enter a new business by developing it them-

Table 12.1   Recent merger activity

Year	Value of U.S. acquisitions (billion)
1982	$ 55.7
1983	48.9
1984	121.1
1985	141.3
1986	200.7
1987	171.5
1988	232.4
1989	244.1
1990	164.3
1991	98.0

Source: *Mergers and Acquisition Almanac,* May–June,
1992.

selves rather than through merger or acquisition? In order for a merger
to occur, there must be one party—the buyer—who is willing to pay more
for the acquired entity than it is worth to the seller. A simple desire on
the part of a firm to enter a new market is thus not enough to induce a
merger. If the new market is a lucrative one, the target firm will require
a high price to induce it to sell.

**In order for a sale or merger to occur, it must be the case that the acquirer
expects to make more from the assets of the target firm than the target firm
can itself.**

Several factors, however, cast doubt on the acquiring firm's ability to
better exploit the target firm's assets. First, the organizational design and
resource configuration of the target firm's assets are not likely to fit perfectly with the acquiring organization. If an organization develops its own
new entry into a business area, the new unit can be designed to ensure a
better fit with the existing organization. Some of the difficult issues of
matching personnel styles across different organizations, which we will
discuss later in this chapter, can be minimized by *de novo* development
and are exacerbated in merger circumstances. An appreciation for the
realities of bargaining also suggests that mergers and acquisitions might
be an overly expensive way to enter a new business. In trying to buy an
existing company, the buyer typically knows a good deal less about the
future earnings prospects of that firm than does the seller. It is hard for
a buyer to get a bargain in this information environment. Indeed, the
evidence suggests that the prices that buyers pay to former owners typically exceed the book value of the purchased firm's assets and market
value of the stock holdings. Such premiums have been estimated at between 10 and 50 percent and may in part reflect differences in information
available to buyer and seller.[18]

Nevertheless, despite the seeming advantages of *de novo* investment, many mergers take place, and at least some of them make sense from the buyer's perspectives. In a sample of 33 large U.S. companies, Porter found that 70 percent of the diversification of these firms was accomplished through acquisition.[19] Surely all of these acquisitions were not mistakes. What factors counterbalance the design and information considerations discussed above and make mergers a preferred way to expand the product line in some instances? Under what circumstances might a buyer be able to generate enough surplus funds from a firm to more than offset the premiums necessary for acquisition and make this acquisition preferable to a new entry? Added value is likely only if the acquiring firm owns an asset or several assets that enhance the earnings capacity of the target firm but would not be equally valuable in a *de novo* entry. On occasion, that asset might be a physical one—perhaps a distribution network or a research lab; in other circumstances, managerial capacity may be the asset that the acquiring firm hopes to share with the target firm. We consider below specific examples in which mergers may dominate *de novo* entry.

Development of Market Power as a Merger Incentive

Traditional analyses of horizontal mergers emphasize the importance of the quest for *market power* as a motive for merger. If, for example, two potential merger partners are among very few firms in an industry, a merger might allow the new unified firm to raise prices after merger. The early merger wave has been described as one in which "approximately 71 important oligopolistic or near competitive industries [were converted] into near monopolies."[20] To the extent that market power is at issue, it is clear that *de novo* investment is not a substitute entry mechanism, since a central element in the strategy is the elimination of one of the competitors in the industry.

The pursuit of market power can be a powerful incentive for mergers, and it is one of the reasons the Department of Justice has relatively rigorous restrictions on the merger activity that firms in the same market can pursue. Given these restrictions, however, few current mergers can really be seen as attempts to increase market power. Indeed, in the case of a conglomerate merger, no additional market power typically results from the merger since merged firms inhabit different original markets. Even in the case of a vertical merger, instances in which such mergers eventually increase the market power of the firm are quite limited and typically come as a result of market efficiencies.[21] Thus in the instances of both conglomerate and vertical mergers, we must look for other explanations for a firm using mergers and acquisitions rather than *de novo* investment.

Entry Time Considerations

In Chapters 10 and 11, we explored some of the reasons a firm might wish to expand either through diversification or through vertical moves.

On occasion, a firm may be willing to pay a premium by using a merger or acquisition to speed up the entry process. As we have learned, entry into a new area is a complex matter. A variety of resources must be assembled and combined effectively: production labor, management labor, plant and equipment, and so on, and assembling these necessary assets can be a time-consuming activity. This is particularly true in the case of plant and equipment investment in industries with complex technologies. If an organization is interested in entering a market quickly, then merger or acquisition with an existing player may prove to be an effective strategy. In this case, it will be worthwhile for a buyer to pay a premium to the seller in order to expedite a quick entry.

Merger or acquisition of an existing firm typically speeds up the entry process.

In the early 1980s, rapid changes resulting from deregulation in the telecommunications area opened up the yellow-pages directory market. The $2 billion directory market has extremely high margins. Long dominated by local telephone companies who used revenues from the business to cross-subsidize local telephone rates, the market also included a number of small firms producing neighborhood directories in different areas of the country. As the market began to change, large firms—like Donnelly Publications, a subsidiary of Dun and Bradstreet, and L. M. Berry—began moving into it, but it became clear very early that the market would not sustain a large number of new entrants. After all, how many directories are most people willing to have? As a result, in the directory market, quick entry was needed, in part to preempt the entry of others, and widespread acquisition occurred of the smaller directory firms.

In 1992, the Coca-Cola Company entered the East German market. This market entry, too, was accomplished through widespread purchases of assets of existing bottling operations, rather than building anew. Here, again, speed was considered essential.

In the examples above, entry speed was an important factor in determining the eventual *profitability* of the new markets. At other times, management may be interested in the speed of new entry even if speed is not an important determinant of profit. In particular, in some instances—perhaps as a result of the structure of compensation in a firm—management may be primarily interested in the growth of an organization, rather than its returns. Mergers and acquisitions are a much faster way to expand than strictly internal investment. Thus mergers can serve as an instrument in the growth strategy of an organization.

Industry Capacity Issues

Merger can also be a preferred entry strategy in cases in which a firm wishes to enter a market but expansion of industry capacity is undesirable. If an organization enters a new business by *de novo* investment, the result will be an increase in the capacity of the industry. If there are substantial economies of scale in the new product, and the entering firm wishes to produce at minimum efficient scale, then a new entry will expand capacity appreciably in the industry. The result will typically be a fall in the market price, unless demand is also rising rapidly. A merger or acquisition will allow an organization to enter a new area without adversely affecting the market price.

Merger or acquisition may be a preferred entry strategy if demand and cost conditions make industry capacity expansions unwise.

In the petrochemical industry, for example, most of the new entrants into this capital-intensive market have come in through merger activity. U.S. Steel chose to purchase Marathon Oil as a way to enter the petrochemical industry, rather than build its own capacity. When Armstrong Tire decided in the early 1980s to move into the auto parts industry, it did so via acquisition of Dayco and Blackstone, two specialized companies, at least in part because it was reluctant to add new capacity to this slow growth industry. In 1987, Chrysler purchased American Motors for $1.6 billion as a way to expand in the mature auto market.

Mergers as a Way to Enter Foreign Markets

As we have already suggested, in the late 1980s and 1990s, we have begun to see an increased volume of cross-border mergers. U.S. acquisitions abroad have increased, as have Asian and European acquisitions both in the United States and in Europe. Mergers and acquisitions play a pivotal role in globalization strategies pursued by a number of firms. For a variety of reasons, it appears to be easier to enter a new country market through an acquisition than through *de novo* investment.

Entry considerations clearly play some role. The complexity of entering a new market is exacerbated by the task of entering a new country at the same time. The right acquisition can ease the entry process. In the case of the recent surge of European investments within Europe, it has clearly been important for firms to stake out a territory early, and mergers allow firms to move faster than new investments.

Politics play an even larger role. We have seen in our earlier discussion of barriers to globalization the role that indigenous management can play in encouraging governments to limit foreign competition. By acquiring a local firm, the foreign entrant can diffuse some of this opposition. As we will see later, setting up joint ventures across national boundaries serves a similar function. At the same time, governmental impediments to the free flow of capital can have the effect of artificially limiting the extent of cross-border acquisitions.

Undervalued Assets or We Can Do Better

A fifth incentive to use mergers rather than internal investment to enter a market occurs when a firm seeks *undervalued assets* in a market. If the stock price of a firm is less than its "true" market value, it will clearly be a good acquisition for a firm considering entering that market. Managers involved in mergers will often cite the ability to find a bargain as a reason for a given merger. Roll argues that managers are often misled by hubris, or pride in their managerial acumen, into overestimating the value of what they buy, believing they can do more with a set of assets than existing managers.[22] Economists who study market processes are less ready to believe in the proliferation of undervalued stocks than are the managers who seek such acquisition targets. Perhaps the most prominent theory of stock prices in finance, the **efficient market hypothesis,** argues that stock prices reflect the underlying value of a firm. Indeed, the theory argues that the stock price is nothing more than the present discounted value of the expected future stream of earnings of the firm. If this is the case, then stock acquisitions are not likely to represent a cheap way to move into a new business. A firm with a low stock price is one in which canny stock buyers have rather poor expectations of earnings. We explored this proposition earlier in Chapter 2, when we argued that there were few $20 bills waiting to be plucked.

Mergers are sometimes seen as a way to acquire undervalued assets.

Of course, not everyone believes in the efficient market hypothesis.[23] A competitive theory argues that stock prices also contain an element that is unrelated to the true value of the firm and more connected to the collective enthusiasms and despair of the trading community. According to this view, fads for one type of stock or another often develop in the trading community, which then causes those stocks to be overvalued, while others are undervalued. Stocks of the biotechnology firms in the early 1980s might be a good example of the operation of a fad. To the extent that fads do play an important role in the setting of market prices, it is possible that undervalued stocks exist in some appreciable number to be picked up by the savvy new entrant.

It is beyond the scope of this text to treat at length the fascinating and heated debate on stock valuation now current in the finance community. On the point at hand, however, it is worth noting that at least in the early years, merger activity appears to have been positively correlated with stock prices.[24] This fact does not lend support to the view that mergers are a way to pick up undervalued stocks. Moreover, the evidence of large premiums paid to the stockholders of acquired firms cited earlier also speaks against the bargain theory of mergers.

The acquisition of another firm's stock may be a good way to enter a new business if that stock is undervalued. Undervaluation of this sort, however, does not appear to be common.

The proposition that an active merger or takeover market may serve to discipline managers is another version of the undervalued assets theory of mergers. If current managers are not acting in the best interest of the shareholder or, in other words, if the assets of the firm are not earning up to capacity, a takeover can enhance firm performance.[25] Indeed, many senior managers who initiate merger or takeover activity argue that they are doing so because of a superior ability to manage the target firm's assets. This same motive underlies many takeovers by existing firm managers in **leveraged buyouts,** in which large amounts of debt are used by current managers to buy out a company or one of its parts. The recent takeover of IBM's typewriter keyboard division by its managers is a good example here.

In the case of a hostile takeover, a raider or a second company bids directly for the shares of the target firm. The negotiation is between the bidder and the shareholder. A bidder who gains control can then replace management. What do such raiders typically do to increase the value of the firm? Many targets of hostile takeovers are older firms in declining industries.[26] In these firms, managers have often failed to shrink operations rapidly enough, to deploy resources to more profitable ventures, or to pay out cash in dividends. By streamlining the operation, the raider hopes to increase the earnings of the target firm. It is often easier for new managers to restructure corporate assets than older managers, in part by violating some of the trust engendered by those older managers.[27] In some instances, a takeover also provides an opportunity to reduce wages to unionized labor. In the case of the Icahn takeover of TWA, for example, the premium paid to TWA shareholders in the takeover appears to have come largely from wage losses to the labor unions.[28]

A final possible source of gains from merger associated with undervalued assets comes from the change in capital structure that typically accompanies a merger. This view is sometimes called **free cash flow theory** of mergers.[29]

In some operations, typically mature ones, cash is generated in excess of that required to fund profitable ventures; this cash is known as free cash flow. To maximize firm value, such cash should be returned to stockholders. But shrinking the business in this way is often not in the interest of managers. So free cash flow often creates conflicts between managers and stockholders. Creating debt, through merger, can be helpful in resolving this conflict, by reducing the cash flow available for managers to spend. Mergers, by changing the capital structure of the new firm in favor of debt, can increase firm value.

One drawback of the "discipline the managers" merger motive is the difficulty of the acquirer in capturing the benefits associated with the management change. Once a shareholder realizes that a takeover is likely, he or she will have an incentive to hold on to shares until the price rises to reflect the earnings capacity of the firm under new management.[30] As a result, the acquiring firm or entrepreneur will typically reap only a portion of the benefits from a change in management.

While the acquiring firm can capture only part of the benefits of a merger, it bears most of the costs. And those costs may be substantial, particularly in instances in which the target firm opposes the merger. Evidence suggests that managers tend to resist the sale of firms, even when substantial premiums are involved, perhaps as a way to protect their own nonfinancial investment in the firm.[31] Indeed, in recent years we have observed a variety of defensive tactics by target firms that substantially increase the cost of takeovers.[32]

As the popularity of hostile takeovers has grown, so has the sophistication of managerial defensive tactics. A **poison pill** is any one of a variety of defenses that reduces the value of the target firm to the bidder if the target is "swallowed." The pill itself can consist of a large increase in corporate debt or stock dilution. One recent survey identified almost 400 poison pills adopted by firms seeking to avoid takeover, with the bulk occurring in 1986.[33] Another prominent tactic to avoid a hostile takeover is the payment of **greenmail**—the repurchase of a potential acquirer's shares at a premium by current management. The poison pill increases the costs of takeovers. Greenmail provides some incentive to initiate takeover action, but reduces the probability that a takeover will be consummated. Both tactics probably reduce the overall completed takeover activity.

A rather different kind of managerial defense against takeover is the **golden parachute.** The golden parachute is a clause in managerial contracts to operate in case of severance, usually under conditions of a shift in corporate control. Tom Wyman received over $11,000,000 in a golden parachute from CBS when Tisch took over control, including bonus, long-term compensation, and annuities. Tom Macioce of Allied Department Stores received over $13 million in the Campeau takeover.[34] Such contracts are generally thought to increase incentives of managers to develop stable and productive ties with a firm and to provide a kind of insurance that may well enhance managerial efficiency. From the perspective of the raider, however, these contract provisions reduce potential takeover gains. It is interesting to note that federal regulators have recently prohibited the payment of these substantial severance contracts in troubled Savings and Loan banks.

Tax Considerations

A final incentive to use the merger route to move into a new market may come from the tax system. Under the U.S. tax code, corporations may use past losses to shield current income. For organizations with few current earnings, these tax-loss carryforwards may be of little worth, for their earnings are too negligible to be worth shielding. But profitable firms may find the tax losses an extra incentive to use the merger and acquisition route—even though the Internal Revenue Service may challenge a merger engineered strictly to take advantage of tax losses. Under recent tax code revisions, carryforwards may also have diminished value. It is also worth noting that the value of the tax-loss carryforwards is likely to be at least somewhat reflected in the price of the acquired firm, assuming that there are other potential bidders for the firm.

Tax considerations may incline a firm toward merger as a way to enter a new business.

We have thus far looked at several reasons for a firm choosing to enter a new market via merger rather than through internal investment. In practice, speed of entry seems to be the most compelling reason for using mergers rather than *de novo* entry. We will now consider some of the performance results of mergers.

Merger Performance and Problems

The evidence on the performance effects of mergers and acquisitions is considerable, both in the finance literature and in the economics and strategy literature. Despite the volume of literature, however, there is little consensus on the effects of mergers and acquisitions on performance. The typical finance study, an **event study,** examines the stock market performance of acquired and acquiring firms around the time of the acquisition. In general, these event studies find positive abnormal effects on stock price of the acquired firm and little effect on that of the acquiring firm.[35] Strategy studies, which examine a longer period of time, have found more mixed results.

Part of the difficulty in coming to a general conclusion about the performance effects of mergers and acquisitions lies in the tremendous variation in their form. Over time, the average merger has changed, for example, in its degree of relatedness, the methods of financing, the initial health of the buyer and seller, the average size of the acquisition, and the mode of acquisition. And the literature suggests that each of these factors, as well as some others, may well influence the relative success of the merger.[36] Nevertheless, as we look at the results of the literature as a whole, and we examine particular mergers, it is clear that the failure rate for this activity is relatively high. During the period 1960–72, the 14 largest pharmaceutical firms made 116 domestic U.S. acquisitions, for an average of just over eight acquisitions per firm. Twenty-one, or 18 percent of these units were liquidated or divested in their entirety in the following 13 years. During the same period, the six largest tire manufacturers made 31 acquisitions, or about five per firm. Ten of these acquisitions, or 33 percent, ended in subsequent divestiture. At least some fraction of these divestitures may have been planned from the start. But in others, it appears that not willing divestiture, but failed merger was the case. How do we account for the prominence of this phenomenon?

Recent work by Scherer and Ravenscraft is quite illuminating on the topic of the failed merger and complements work done in the broader strategy literature.[37] Scherer and Ravenscraft examined 15 business acquisitions that later led to sell-offs. In all but two of the cases, the acquired firm was viewed as a potential star, not a firm in trouble. The large majority of the cases (13 or 15) were friendly mergers. Yet they all failed within a decade. In these failures, there were two problems that frequently emerged: the *inspection problem* and the *interaction problem*. Both problems have been described in the organizational literature as well.

The Inspection Problem

A merger requires that the buyer attach a higher value to the firm than the seller does. Yet the seller is typically the party with greater information about the prospects of the firm. In some cases, the buyer places a higher value on the firm because the buyer has the complementary assets needed to exploit the true value of the acquired firm. But, in other cases, the higher valuation placed on the firm by the buyer simply reflects the poor information of that buyer.

We have here a classic example of what is known in economics as the **lemons problem.**[38] In a situation in which a buyer and seller have asymmetrical information, potential buyers generally will make price offers that reflect the average quality of the product in the market. In the absence of good specific knowledge, buyers are expected to assume that the particular sample they are looking at is about like the rest of the market. But sellers are most likely to be willing to accept a particular price offer by a buyer if they have a product that is inferior to the market average—a lemon. Thus more lemons enter the market than high-quality products, the average quality of the product in the market falls, and so does the offering price of buyers as they learn of the deteriorating markets. A vicious cycle is set up in which only lemons are left in the resale market.

In the acquisitions market, the lemons model would tend to suggest that, on average, firms that are in the market to be acquired are worse in terms of earnings prospects than the average firms in their markets. Sellers wish to sell because they know their firm is not as good as the buyer believes. (Forecasting a high frequency of lemons in acquisitions markets is another example of a result that follows from understanding equilibrium market interactions.)

Of course, not all firms on the auction block are lemons, and acquiring firms spend considerable effort trying to identify the earnings prospects of potential acquisitions. Nevertheless, it will be impossible for potential buyers to learn everything about the new acquisitions and, once the purchase is made, some unhappy surprises are likely. If the surprises are sufficiently large, sell-off may be the best alternative. Along these lines, there have been a number of studies suggesting that organizations with prior acquisition experience have better post-merger performance than do neophytes.[39] In these cases, the lemons problem is lessened because firms have become more effective at inspection.

Hints of the inspection problem appear both in the pharmaceutical and tire industries described earlier. In both industries, acquisitions in the 1960–72 period were of the horizontal, vertical, and conglomerate types, but *the vast majority of the sell-offs were in the conglomerate area.* It is easy to see that the informational asymmetry between buyer and seller is likely to be largest in the conglomerate acquisition. In the pharmaceutical area, 38 percent of the unrelated mergers (or 16 of 42) ended in divestiture, as contrasted with only 7 percent (or 2 in 28) of the horizontal mergers. In the tire industry, 85 percent of the unrelated acquisitions were divested, while only 16 percent of the horizontal and vertical acquisitions were sold off. For both of these industries, sell-offs were most likely for unrelated units where the inspection problem is likely to be the most striking. The strategy literature similarly documents the superior performance of related over unrelated acquisitions, in a number of settings, a result that could be attributed to differences in the severity of the inspection problem in the two circumstances.[40]

An interesting example of the inspection problem comes from the 1986 takeover of Kidder Peabody, one of the top U.S. investment banks, by General Electric. Less than one year after the takeover, one of Kidder's former directors faced criminal charges for insider trading. Jack Welch, the CEO of General Electric, remarked: "We would not have touched Kidder Peabody with a 10-foot pole if we had known there was a skunk in the place. Unfortunately, we did and now we've got to live with it."[41] In this example, the acquiring firm, G.E., seems to have turned Kidder Peabody around, but the merger clearly brought with it many unforeseen problems. The problem of inadequate information is exacerbated by the human dynamics of the acquisitions process. Once merger fever begins, it may be hard to take a coldly rational view of the deal. Warren Buffet, chairman of Berkshire-Hathaway, noted that in merger activity "the thrill of the chase blinded the pursuers to the consequences of the catch."[42]

The Interaction Problem

Some organizations turn out to be lemons when acquired. Others quickly deteriorate under the new management of the acquiring firm. While economists have primarily focused on the inspection problem as a source of merger failure, organizational theorists have looked more closely at the fit between firms as a *source* of good or bad merger performance.[43] One survey found that as many as one-third of all merger failures were due to integration difficulties.[44] Incorporating a new unit into an organization is considerably more difficult than arranging the financing deal, and a failure to integrate can destroy an otherwise successful organization. The recent example of Peugeot in its acquisition of the European operations of Chrysler is instructive on this point. Peugeot engineered this acquisition in 1978, just three years after its acquisition of Citroen. The firm soon found that it lacked the infrastructure needed to fully absorb these two large acquisitions. Marketing people in particular were stretched beyond their abilities, and the increased debt charges from the acquisitions led some to worry that the firm would not survive the downturn in the industry.[45]

What determines the extent to which integration of two firms will be successful? To the extent that a merger represents an attempt to exploit interdependencies between firms, the management of these interdependencies will be critical.[46] Cultural fit between the two firms is thus important, particularly in the context of the kinds of subgoal pursuit we described in Chapter 8. Dissimilar cultures can reduce the commitment and cooperation of employees of the acquired firm.[47] In a very interesting study of merger results, using a combination of stock market data and interview results, Chatterjee et al. suggest that cultural fit has a profound effect on firm performance post-merger. They argue that "the management of a buying firm should pay at least as much attention to issues of cultural fit during the pre-merger search process as they do to issues of strategic fit."[48]

For many of the reasons just described, the relative size of the acquired and acquiring firms may also affect merger success. Large differences in the relative size of the acquired and acquiring firms may make it difficult for the acquiring firm to understand the problems of the target firm, and at the same time reduce the commitment levels of dwarfed target employees.[49] Evidence on the effects of size, however, has been mixed.[50]

When a merger occurs, there are clearly varying levels of coordination required. For mergers that are based on motives of synergy, coordination needs are relatively high. For conglomerate mergers, coordination is less essential and this factor may be one advantage of these types of mergers. There are also differences among firms in how much coordination is attempted post-merger. Chatterjee et al. suggest that firms that tolerate multiculturalism after the merger and avoid excessive control outperform less tolerant buyers.[51] Similar results come from Scherer and Ravenscraft. Interference from senior managers of the acquiring firm is likely to be viewed as just that—interference from a group with less knowledge of the market. We can look again at the General Electric–Kidder Peabody merger. In this example, corporate style differences were enormous between Kidder's investment bankers and G.E.'s manufacturing managers. One Kidder Peabody manager who joined a number of his fellows in leaving the firm after the merger asserted, "The G.E. people were clods; they broke two-thirds of the china in the shop."[52] But if the acquiring firm were to maintain an arm's length perspective on the new firm, we might wonder whether the merger had any point at all! Creating a new cohesive corporate culture with tolerance for group differences is a difficult task. It is no wonder that many mergers fail in the attempt.

Another source of post-merger difficulty comes from the financial side. The larger size of the merged organization and its more diverse nature, both consequences of a merger, may exacerbate the organizational agency problems described in Chapter 8 and reduce managerial incentives to work for stockholder value. The tendency of many of the sell-offs to involve leveraged buy out (LBO) by management testifies to the severity of the incentive problem in newly merged entities. In 1986, going-private and LBO transactions represented 39 percent of all public transactions.[53] Leveraged buy outs are often thought of as a way for management to regain its ownership incentives. In the typical LBO, top managers hold disproportionate amounts of equity in the firm.

Finally, the acquisition process itself may influence how well the firms are subsequently integrated.[54] Top management turnover is higher after a merger, and particularly high after a hostile or contentious merger. In a study of 102 mergers, Walsh found that management turnover reached 61 percent five years after a merger. For tender offers (hostile takeovers), management turnover is especially high.[55] Of course, in some cases, one of the motives behind the takeover was to purge the organization of "incompetent" managers. It may also be the case, however, that poorly executed mergers may end up depleting one of the hidden assets of a target firm—its managers.

In sum, we have seen that the obstacles to successful mergers are formidable. In a world of canny managers, it is hard to find a bargain. Even if one finds a solid organization at a good price that seems to fit well with the existing organization, actually engineering the melding process is a large task. It is no wonder that we observe a high failure rate for mergers. More recently, as the pace of mergers has slowed, we have seen an increase in **strategic alliances** among firms. As we will see in the next section of this chapter, there are costs and benefits to this attempt at reorganization as well.

Strategic Alliances

As we have seen, mergers are often used by firms as a way to move into new areas. Another method that firms have increasingly used to broaden their capabilities is the **strategic alliance.** The evidence suggests that there has been a dramatic increase in the number of alliances since the early 1980s. Between 1980 and 1990, Japanese firms alone signed over five hundred alliances with American firms. Presently there is no major U.S. steel firm without a partner in Japan. More recently, there has been a surge in Europe, particularly in alliances between Western and Eastern Europe. Volkswagen AG from Germany has a major alliance with Skoda of Czechoslovakia. Pilkington Glass, a major British glass firm, has formed an alliance with HSO Sandomierz in Poland.

Strategic alliances take a number of forms. We can define a strategic alliance quite broadly to include any arrangement in which two or more firms combine resources outside of the market in order to accomplish a particular task or set of tasks. The central defining feature of the alliance is that for a period of time, and for a defined set of operations, firms agree not to operate through the market place. This interfirm agreement can be long lived and broad purposed or it can be quite narrowly construed. Some alliances involve sharing of equity. In a **joint venture,** for example, a separate entity is set up and the contributing firms each transfer resources to the partnership and receive ownership rights over the common property. General Motors and Toyota currently run a joint venture in Fremont, California producing cars. British Steel and Avesta of Sweden have combined forces in a joint venture producing and marketing stainless steel. In some alliances, firms purchase minority interests in each other. British Telecom, for example, has a sizeable minority interest in McCaw Cellular Communications. Nippon Steel owns almost half of Oracle Systems. There is evidence that both joint ventures and minority interest ownership have grown quite rapidly in the mid-1980s and 1990s.[56]

Strategic alliances may also be forged without new equity sharing. Licensing agreements are a particularly common form of alliance, in which the firms agree to carry on a set of transactions through contracting rather than through the market place. Cray Research signed a marketing agreement with Digital Equipment in 1992 to allow DEC to market the Cray supercomputer, for instance. In the pharmaceutical industry, it is common for small firms to license distribution of their products to larger rivals.

In fact, in most situations, we see a combination of equity and nonequity forms of alliance within the same pairing.[57] Compaq Computer owns a 15 percent share in Silicon Graphics and also licenses a considerable amount of Silicon's technology. Dai-Ichi Mutual has a minority interest in Lincoln National Bank and also runs joint projects with Lincoln in producing pension instruments. Walker, Kogut, and Shan find a similar pattern in the biotechnology industry. In that industry, the formation of new alliances is heavily conditioned by the pattern of alliances in the past, as firms learn from current partners and based on this learning reconstruct their alliances.[58] Walker et al. argue that the social capital built up in alliances assists the partners in the formation of new relationships, both with each other and with close analogues.

Strategic alliances vary in terms of their duration as well their form. The typical joint venture lasts somewhat less than five years, although in the survey of biotechnology firms by Walker et al. most of the alliances lasted longer.[59] In some cases, dissolution dates are set in the original contract; in other cases, dissolution occurs once a project goal is reached. In joint ventures, it is typical for original contracts to specify buy-out mechanisms for the two parties. Licensing agreements almost always contain time limits and typically specify conditions under which recontracting occurs.

In order to understand why we have strategic alliances, we need to understand their place as an organizational form. In creating a strategic alliance, two or more firms are choosing to create an organizational form that is, in Powell's terms, "neither market nor hierarchy."[60] In the alliance, resources are combined across organizations, but the two organizations themselves maintain separate identities. The alliance, because it involves only an incomplete merging of the different organizations, is typically more flexible and easier to dissolve, when conditions no longer favor the particular resource combination, than would be the division of a firm. At the same time, the alliance creates more incentives for cooperation among the parties than a strictly arm's length market transaction. Under some conditions, then, the alliance provides advantages of both the market and the hierarchy.[61] Of course, alliances have some of the defects of each as well. The question is where alliances fit most naturally.

In trying to explain markets in which strategic alliances arise, we then look for two things. First, an alliance represents a new configuration of resources. Thus we find them arising when an opportunity has been created that is not currently exploited by firms embodying existing resource mixes. Joint ventures are common between pharmaceutical companies and small biotechnology labs because technological opportunities in the latter field opened up opportunities that required both the marketing and distributional assets of the large pharmaceutical companies and the research expertise of the smaller biotechnology firms. The technology created a new opportunity. But we have other questions to answer as well: Why it is that the new combinations are not created either through the intermediary of a market or through the creation of new firms, which embody the needed new combinations? What advantage does an alliance have in filling the new need?

The evidence suggests that in the last decade there have been two prime forces creating demand for new resource combinations: globalization of markets and new technology. Both of these trends encouraged firms to look for partners as a way to adapt to changing markets. Moreover, in both situations forces existed favoring alliances over more permanent resource reconfiguration.

We have already seen in Chapter 6 the way that technology and government policy have opened up global markets. But operating in different national markets requires country-specific resources as well as industry-specific resources. Alliances are a relatively rapid way for a firm to acquire country knowledge, as it tries to move into new markets.[62] These alliances may also be a politically easier way to enter a new country than either merger with a local company or new entry by the foreign firm. In our earlier discussion of global strategies, we have already seen the way in which Coca-Cola's strategic alliance with Kirin, the Japanese brewer, facilitated its entry into the Japanese soft-drink market. Historically, most international strategic alliances involved firms from developed countries using firms in less developed areas as marketing partners. More recently, the scope for alliances has broadened, both in terms of the character of the firms involved and the number and range of activities involved in the alliance. Prime examples of the role of globalization in creating a demand for alliances include the recent moves by West European firms into Eastern Europe and, in an earlier period, Hewlett Packard's entry into the computer market in Japan via a joint venture with Yokogawa Electric.

Second, strategic alliances have been particularly common in high-technology industries. These industries have a number of features favoring alliances. When technology changes, new combinations of assets are required, and firms will be induced to look outside their own boundaries to find these assets. Alliances are particularly helpful when there is a risk that the current combinations are valuable only for the current generation technology. Here the flexibility and lower termination costs of alliances will be favored over the classical merger or new investment. High-technology industries also favor speed and alliances as one way to move more quickly. Powell argues that the networks created by alliances are not only faster in adopting current ideas but enhance innovation by "bringing together different logic and novel combinations of information."[63] Finally, the high risk element in high-technology firms may favor alliances over mergers. Meyer, Milgrom, and Roberts have argued that firms may wish to keep risky ventures separate, to avoid managerial tendencies to throw good money after bad, when and if the venture starts to fail. The more separate the venture, the less likely its failure is to contaminate the rest of the organization.[64]

We have thus far seen several advantages to alliances. Relative to mergers or internal expansion, alliances tend to be fast and flexible, easier to start or stop. In high-technology industries, this is a particular advantage. Alliances have some political advantages in globalization, and speed is an advantage here too. But there are disadvantages as well in strategic alliances and the record on success has not been all positive. In a large-scale study of joint ventures over the period 1924 to 1985, Harrigan suggests that just under half of the ventures were considered a success by the partners.[65] This figure puts alliances on about the same plane as mergers and acquisitions. In exchange for the flexibility of alliances, we lose some of the goal congruity we usually find with activities brought more firmly inside the firm.[66] There is also considerable learning as partners begin working together and this, too, has its costs.[67] Dissolving partnerships can be very difficult, as partners struggle to make sure they are protected in the post-partnership period.

Antitrust Issues

As in most other areas of modern corporate life, mergers carry with them a public-policy aspect. In particular, the ability of a firm to effect a merger will depend in part on the policies of the U.S. Department of Justice and the Federal Trade Commission, the agencies charged with carrying out the U.S. antitrust laws. Let us now briefly review the current U.S. antitrust position on mergers.

Horizontal Mergers

The bulk of U.S. antitrust activity in the merger area is directed at the horizontal merger. Pepsico's attempts to purchase 7-Up would have been a horizontal merger, had it been successful. The merger of LTV and Republic was a horizontal merger in the steel industry. Both of these mergers came under antitrust scrutiny. Indeed, the Pepsico–7-Up deal was prevented by the Department of Justice. In general, horizontal mergers by large firms come to the attention of antitrust authorities.

Why has the horizontal merger received so much antitrust scrutiny? As we have indicated earlier, horizontal mergers can potentially increase the market power of an organization and thus lead to higher prices for the consumer. It is to prevent such increases in market power that horizontal mergers are sometimes outlawed by the courts. Consequently, standards on mergers are couched in terms of potential to increase market power. Current Department of Justice guidelines on horizontal mergers are written in terms of allowable Herfindahl indexes. The **Herfindahl Index** is a measure of the share of top firms in the industry. In particular, it is equal to the sum of the squares of the shares of the firms multiplied by 10,000. Current merger guidelines suggest that, in a market with a Herfindahl in excess of 1800, a merger that raises that index will not be permitted without considerable scrutiny.

The probability that the merger will be denied increases as the Herfindahl rises. In other words, firms most at risk in terms of their ability to effect a horizontal merger are those in concentrated industries with substantial pre-existing market power. In the soft-drink market, for example, the Herfindahl before the proposed merger was 2362. The Pepsico–7-Up merger would have increased this index considerably and thus was barred by the Department of Justice.

In some cases, mergers may be permitted even in quite concentrated markets if one firm is failing. This is known as the *failing-firm defense*. In practice, such a defense may be difficult to mount.

Conglomerate Mergers

The courts have also blocked a number of proposed conglomerate mergers. In the late 1960s, the FTC successfully blocked Procter & Gamble's attempt to enter the bleach market with the acquisition of Clorox.[68] In the early 1970s, the acquisition of Peabody Coal by Kennecott Copper was also blocked.[69] In more recent years, however, opposition to conglomerate mergers by antitrust enforcement agencies appears to have diminished considerably. Indeed, under recent Department of Justice guidelines, conglomerate mergers appear to be susceptible to challenge only if they have some well-defined adverse effect on competition in a well-specified market. Thus, if the merger eliminates one of very few potential entrants into a concentrated market with high entry barriers, it may be challenged in the courts. In other cases—indeed, in most instances—conglomerate mergers will not be challenged in the courts.

Vertical Mergers

In the area of vertical integration, as in most areas of firm strategy, the antitrust laws are of some relevance. Section 7 of the Clayton Act governs the possibility of mergers among organizations, including vertical mergers. In particular, Section 7 forbids mergers "where in any line of commerce or in any activity affecting commerce in any section of the country, the effect of such merger may be to substantially lessen competition."

As we indicated earlier, in applying this provision in recent years to horizontal mergers—that is, mergers among firms in the same industry—the Department of Justice has created some fairly concrete guidelines. There is considerably less specificity in the application of the Clayton Act to vertical mergers.

The primary judicial concern in the case of vertical mergers has been to avoid possibilities of **market foreclosure.** In particular, the court has on various occasions been concerned that if a manufacturer is permitted to acquire its supplier, that supplier will then be prevented from offering its supplies for sale to another manufacturer. If suppliers are few in number, it was feared that the merger would "foreclose" supplies to rival manufacturers. Hence, virtually all of the vertical merger guidelines and cases have turned on the question of how many alternatives are available in the merged sector. One set of Department of Justice guidelines, for example, asserted that a merger would be challenged "when the supplying firm accounts for more than 10 percent of the sales in its market and the purchasing firm accounts for 6 percent or more of the total purchases in that market."

In recent years, the number of vertical cases has declined, and judicial hostility toward such mergers also appears to be declining. In part, the new judicial attitude reflects the diffusion of the theory, articulated in Chapter 11, concerning the transactions efficiencies sometimes associated with vertical mergers. Then, too, it has proved to be a rare case in which supplies are really substantially foreclosed by a merger. Indeed, one prominent scholar and judge, Robert Bork, argued that foreclosure is "never a threat to competition . . . and in the absence of the most unlikely proved predatory power and purpose, antitrust should never object to the verticality of any merger."[70] While Bork is perhaps more conservative than the judiciary at large, overall concern with vertical mergers appears to be considerably diminished. For most firms considering a vertical merger, antitrust issues will not loom large.

III

RIVALRY

In Parts I and II we considered industry structure, issues of organizational structure and design, competitive advantage, and corporate diversification. In Part III, we proceed to another element in the strategic management process: the effect of rival behavior on an organization's ability to compete.

Let us return to our familiar schematic, introduced in Chapter 1.

In the chapters to follow we will explore the box on the left-hand side of the schematic. Chapter 13 looks at issues of rivalry among organizations, using primarily the apparatus of game theory. Chapters 14 through 17 then apply a broad set of tools, including but not limited to game theory, to explore the dynamics of rivalry in several diverse arenas: marketing, pricing, research, and regulation.

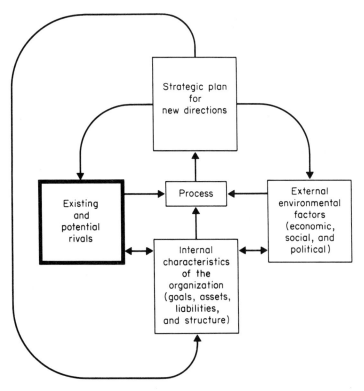

Figure III.1

13

Understanding Rivalry:
Game Theory

Chapter 3 described factors that influence the overall level of rivalry inside an industry. But industries differ not only in their overall level of competition, but also in the complex ways in which the particular interactions among firms are played out. In some industries, the entry of a new firm is greeted by large price cuts by incumbents; in other industries, product branding or changes in the distribution network is the prime response to new entry. In still other industries, there is little reaction at all. In some industries, there is considerable signaling of intentions across firms, both to existing firms and to new entrants. In other industries, firms pay little attention to one another.

Quite often the results of our decisions—both managerial and personal—depend not only on what we do, but on what everyone else does. The success of my bunt in a baseball game depends in part on whether the 3rd baseman and catcher have successfully anticipated the bunt and moved accordingly. The success of a bluffing strategy in poker depends on whether you fold your cards or recognize my bluff and stay in the game. Coca-Cola's profits from a new diet drink depend in part on whether Pepsi-Cola produces a copy-cat brand. The success of a Walk-A-Thon run by the Muscular Dystrophy Association depends in part on whether the March of Dimes is running a similar event at the same time in the same city. Clearly, in each of these situations, if we wish to make the right decisions ourselves, we need to anticipate the decisions of others.

Game theory is helpful in developing our understanding of the variety of firm interactions. The formal analysis of conflict and cooperation among intelligent and rational decision makers, game theory is an especially useful way to trace the likely reactions of organizations to the competitive moves of other firms. In this chapter, we will explore some of the techniques used in game theory.[1] As we will see, the applications of game theory in the areas of managerial strategy, defense, and public policy are large and rapidly growing.

The theoretic game models we will be discussing typically assume a fairly high degree of rationality on the part of the agents, and some researchers in the strategic management area have criticized these models on this basis. On the other hand, many of the conclusions reached by these models do not depend on assumptions of hyperrationality, but are much more loosely coupled to the theory.[2] In any case, I will try to indicate as we proceed how sensitive the conclusions we reach are to the level of reasoning employed by the agents involved.

Some Tools and Techniques

A first distinction that is helpful to make in adapting some of the tools of game theory to understanding strategy formulation focuses on the structure of the moves in the interaction we are examining. In particular, do the two or more agents in the interaction move *sequentially* or *simultaneously*? Chess is a sequential game. Good chess players, thinking ahead, will have to make some judgments about what their opponent will do. And these judgments will be updated each time the opponent makes a new move. The children's game 1-2-3- Shoot is a simultaneous game in which children choose, *at the same time*, whether to put out one or two fingers to create an odd or even sum. The kind of decision making that is helpful in these two circumstances may differ because the game structure differs. I will start with simultaneous games and move on to sequential games.

The Payoff Matrix

Suppose you manage a firm in an industry and are considering undertaking a particular action—for example, introducing a new product. The benefits of introducing the new product are likely to depend on whether any other firms in the industry introduce a similar new product at the same time. Thus there are typically several alternative possibilities that might result from your action. It is often useful to summarize the alternative contingencies in a **payoff matrix** in which each cell represents one alternative possibility (Figure 13.1). Suppose in the problem we are looking at, there is only one other firm likely to match your new product offering. There are then four logical possibilities, depending on whether you or your rival produce one or both of the possible products. Each of these four possibilities carries with it some payoff in terms of the profits you and your rival might earn. After some analysis of the figures, you might summarize the possible outcomes as follows:

Each cell represents a different outcome, with resulting payoffs. The columns represent my available strategies; the rows are my rival's avail-

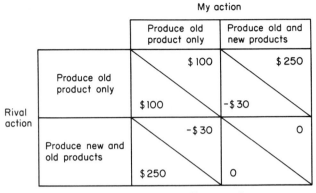

Figure 13.1 Payoff matrix I

able strategies. In each cell, the upper right number represents the payoff to my own action; the lower left number represents my rival's payoff. Suppose that both firms are producing only the old product; we are thus both in the upper left box of the matrix, usually referred to as cell 1. In this example, we begin with a symmetrical situation: Both firms are earning $100 in profits. If either firm introduces the new product, industry profits will rise to $220 from the original $200, with the introducing firm gaining substantially at the expense of the other; these two options are given in cells (2) and (3) of the matrix. In this example, the firm that remains with a single product finds itself so dominated by the other firm that it actually loses money. Finally, if both firms broaden their lines simultaneously, both will break even (i.e., payoffs = 0), as shown in cell (4).

We use the simple payoff matrix to represent games involving *simultaneous moves* with no communication. In the example at hand, we might imagine that the two firms must simultaneously make product-planning decisions, without knowledge of one another's moves. For the time being, we will also assume that the two players make only this single decision and are not concerned about future interactions in the market. Thus we are looking at a *single-period simultaneous game*.

Arranging the data in a payoff matrix provides us with insight into likely results. For instance, the ideal situation from my perspective is that I should introduce a new product, and you should not. This would allow me to increase my profits from $100 to $250. However, it is quite unlikely that we will end up at this point because both of us will be motivated by the prospect of being dominated by the other into moving on our own. Introducing a new product is thus the **dominant strategy** for each of the two firms. The fear of being outmaneuvered by a rival, held by each of the two firms, leads the industry into a position in which total industry profits are actually minimized, as the product space is cannibalized. We end up in the lower right cell, which is the only noncooperative equilibrium in this game—that is, the only place the two firms will end up without some cooperation. In this cell, each firm is maximizing its payoff given its belief about what the other will do. Neither the upper right cell nor the lower left cell are stable equilibria. The industry will not settle down to either of these situations.

A dominant strategy is one that is optimal, regardless of what one's rival does.

The example above belongs to a general class of games known as **prisoners' dilemmas.** In this situation, the payoffs are such that both players have individual incentives to choose strategies that together give both players a worse outcome than if both players had simultaneously chosen the other strategy. The name derives from a simple game in which two prisoners are separated and told that if either one confesses to a joint crime, both prisoners will be convicted, but the confessor will get a light sentence, perhaps a year in jail, while the other prisoner will receive a 10-year sentence. If neither confesses, both will likely be convicted of a lesser charge and have to serve two years.[3] The individual incentives are to confess—in the example above, to produce the new product—while the joint best is to keep quiet—produce only the single old product. Indeed, even if the two parties could discuss matters in advance, each would have an incentive to defect from a cooperative agreement.

In situations in which both firms have dominant strategies, as in Matrix I, it is easy to see what the eventual outcome will be. Suppose, instead, we have a situation in which one player has a dominant strategy while the other does not. What happens then? In this case, we would expect the firm without a dominant strategy to put itself in its rival's shoes and decide what the rival will do. The firm without a dominant strategy would be expected to choose its action based on the assumption that its rival will follow its dominant strategy. Here, too, the logical outcome of the competitive situation is easy to see. One firm chooses its dominant strategy while the second firm chooses its strategy to maximize its payoff given that choice.

Of course, the payoff matrix need not be configured as in the example above. An alternative possibility is presented below in Figure 13.2.

In this situation, each firm again would prefer to produce the new product itself and have its rival maintain a narrowed product portfolio. As before, the new introduction raises profits for the firm, but in this situation, brand proliferation is sufficiently costly that product duplication is less likely. In this example, new product introduction is not a dominant strategy, given the high losses of simultaneous introduction.

The case in Matrix II is a more complex one. Here neither firm has a dominant strategy. Under these circumstances it is harder to predict outcomes, and we require a richer description of the rival's situation in order to proceed.

Clearly many different numerical configurations are possible. Examining the particular payoff matrix—even if one has only limited informa-

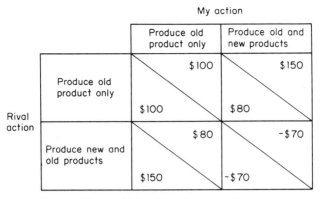

Figure 13.2 Payoff matrix II

tion on the actual numbers involved—is often quite useful in indicating how stable particular scenarios are. In the situation described above, for example, identifying whether you were in payoff Matrix I or II would be very important in helping you to decide likely results from a new product innovation.

Repeated Games

In the discussion above, we looked at interactions between rival firms ignoring industry history. That is, we looked at one interaction in isolation. But it is clear that in many contexts organizations face one another again and again. Firms repeatedly set prices in competition with other firms; products are introduced more than once; companies negotiate with each other over licensing terms and nations over armament issues many times. As we indicated in our earlier discussions, the history of an interaction and its future can have profound effects on current interactions.

Consider the prisoners' dilemma situation again. Each prisoner (firm) is concerned over the possible betrayal of the other. In a one-time interaction, there is no protection against such betrayal. *If organizations or individuals face each other repeated times, the prospect of future retaliation may discipline current actions.*

A study of **repeated games** can help us understand the development of some measure of cooperation in industrial settings.[4] The level of cooperation one can expect in the repeated-event setting, however, depends heavily on the kind of interaction expected.

Suppose we know that we are going to face one another in a set of product introductions for some specified period in the future, with payoffs configured as in Matrix I. In other words, we face a prisoners' dilemma structure *with a set ending period.* For example, we might know that the market in question has room for only five or six more products over the next year or two. How does this multiperiod (as opposed to single-

period) context alter our conclusion about the likelihood of product proliferation?

It is usual to analyze such a situation by working backward. We start
by looking at what firms will do in the last period in which they interact,
move to the penultimate period, and so on.[5] Suppose we are in a prisoners' dilemma as indicated, with a specified life to the interaction. There
is no incentive to cooperate in the last period: Since it is the last period,
there is no possibility of threatening future discipline. But if there is no
cooperation in the final period, then there will be no incentive to cooperate in the penultimate period, and so on. Indeed, according to this logic,
the repeated game unravels into the one-period prisoners' dilemma. In
other words, adding the prospect of future retaliation does not increase
cooperation, *if the end of the game is specified and known*.

But, of course, most interactions have an indefinite future. I don't know
how many times we will face the possibility of introducing new products,
changing our prices, negotiating licenses, and so on. Under these circumstances, the prospect of a continued threat can create cooperation among
firms, so long as the prospect of continued relations is large enough. Uncertainty about the preferences of rivals can also lead to cooperation.[6]

An interesting look at the dynamics of repeated games comes from
Axelrod.[7] Axelrod was interested in understanding how cooperative behavior emerged under a variety of natural circumstances, ranging from
animal behavior in the wild to human behavior in the boardroom. To look
at cooperation, Axelrod began with a standard noncooperative setting,
the prisoners' dilemma problem we examined earlier. He then developed
a series of computer tournaments to try to see which strategy is most
successful in repeated-game situations of the prisoners' dilemma type. In
Axelrod's game, each participant could either cooperate or defect in a
series of encounters. In each of the tournaments, economists, mathema-
ticians, and political scientists were asked to suggest rules for playing a
particular repeated Prisoners' Dilemma game. These strategies were coded
and played on the computer for several hundred moves. In Axelrod's
tournaments, **tit for tat**—if you hit me, I will hit you next time—turned
out to be the strategy producing the greatest benefit to the player in the
long run. None of the rather sophisticated strategies offered by the diverse
set of players dominated this simple reciprocation strategy. Even though
in any single encounter there were strategies that could beat tit for tat,
this simple strategy won the Axelrod competition because it always came
close to the competition. In practice, this strategy is effective because it
encourages cooperation and cooperation typically pays off in a prisoners'
dilemma.

The way tit for tat encourages cooperation is by retaliating in cases in
which your rival fails to be cooperative. But in practice, it is not always
so easy to tell if your rival is being cooperative or not. As a result, firms
that follow a tit for tat strategy will sometimes end up punishing their
rivals wrongly and thus beginning a chain reaction of punishments. Dixit

and Nalebuff argue that one of the flaws in this simple strategy is that it is too rigid in when and how it retaliates.[8] Their alternative strategy is to cooperate until your rival engages in relatively sustained noncooperative behavior and then retaliate by reverting to a tit for tat strategy.

The general observation that emerges from the literature on game theory is that cooperation is indeed possible, albeit fragile, in prisoners' dilemma situations. What creates cooperation is the threat of retaliation, either now or later, in this market or another. Indeed, it has been argued that one of the advantages of multiproduct firms is that these firms can discipline their rivals more effectively by virtue of the multiplicity of targets which they control.

Sequential Games: Trees

The payoff matrix summarizes outcomes associated with a particular event and describes outcomes in which the players move *simultaneously*. This visual representation is quite useful in some circumstances, particularly if one allows for the added complexity of repeated, simultaneous moves. But in other circumstances, the players move *sequentially* rather than simultaneously. One firm lowers its prices, and a second must consider whether or not to follow. The decision by the first firm is, in turn, a function of what it thinks its rival will do in further moves.

The main rule of strategy in a situation of sequential moves has been succinctly summarized by Dixit and Nalebuff[9] and is well known to chess players.

Look ahead and reason back.

In choosing whether to move my Bishop or my Knight in a game of chess, I must look ahead to what my opponent will do in subsequent moves in response to my move. I then go through a familiar thought experiment: "If I do this, he will do that, then I will do this," and so on. Based on this analysis, I decide what to do now. Similarly, in deciding a product strategy or a pricing strategy, a manager needs to anticipate what others in the market will do and then *based on that information* decide what is best for him or her to do.

This rule, while simple to articulate, is not so easy to follow in practice. The difficulty arises because in most situations there are a large number of possible responses that could be made to each of my moves and analyzing each of them or even thinking of each of them is not always possible. It is here that some of the formal structures of game theory are helpful for they allow us to systematically set out the possibilities and give us some clues about which possibilities need to be further examined and which can safely be ignored.

The central device used in game theory in analyzing sequential move interactions is the **decision tree** or **game tree**.

A game tree is a graphical representation of the sequence of moves or choices available to the agents in a particular situation and the outcomes associated with those moves. A decision tree spells out the options of a particular decision maker at various junctions.

We can return to the example posed in Matrix I to see how a game tree or extensive form of the game works. In that situation we had two players, firm 1 and firm 2. In the original game, we specified simultaneous moves by the two firms. Suppose now that firm 1 has the first move; in other words, we are looking at the problem from firm 1's perspective, trying to decide if a particular action should be taken. The action we are considering is a new product introduction. The **extensive form** of this game, which captures all the possibilities and includes the sequence of events, is given in Figure 13.3.

Each node in the tree marks a decision point for one of the players. In this game, firm 1 moves first and can choose either to continue producing only the original product or to add a second one. In either case, firm 2 can respond with its own product move. On this tree, the nodes are marked F1 (for firm 1) and F2. Branches of the tree represent possible moves by one of the players. Final outcomes are marked as O_1 to O_4. We can see on the tree that O_2 and O_3 are inconsistent with rational behavior on the part of both firms. Consider O_2, in which firm 1 produces the single old product and firm 2 broadens its product mix. Under these circumstances, firm 1 loses $30. But it can do better than that under the product-duplication strategy of O_4. Here firm 1 at least breaks even. Thus if firm 1 were initially to consider not introducing a second product, it could, by looking at the tree, immediately see that firm 2 *will* introduce the new product. This realization will force firm 1 to introduce the new product in the first instance.

The tree described above represents a simple game, with only one move per firm and no uncertainty. Most business decisions require a considerably more complex extensive form. In Figure 13.4, we have enriched the Figure 13.3 game by allowing firm 1 to respond to firm 2's move with another set of moves.

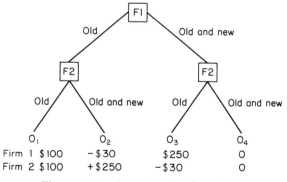

Figure 13.3   An extensive form tree

In constructing Figure 13.4, we have assumed that products cannot be withdrawn, once introduced. This limits the number of moves firm 1 can engage in. Notice that the element of time increases the number of possible outcomes. First, both firms can continue to produce a single product throughout the history of the game (O1). Another possibility is for firm 1 to broaden its product line mid-game in response to firm 2's move to either maintain its single product (O2), or expand it (O3). Firm 1 might also continue to produce a single product as 2 expands (O4). If firm 1 initially chooses a broad line, it must continue with that strategy in the face of 2's single product choice (O5), or broad choice (O6). We can then attach numerical values to O1 to O6 to help evaluate likely outcomes.

In the two figures constructed above, uncertainty was not introduced. Yet in many business situations chance plays a critical role. Although it is impossible to account for all uncertainty, one can make some provision for it. One way to do this is to act as though luck were another player in the game. In the case above, the uncertainty may well arise over the question of the second firm's ability to introduce a new product. One treats this case by trying to assign reasonable probabilities to the uncertain events and then following that uncertainty down the tree. (We explored the role of uncertainty in the formation of decision trees in the Hmong example in Chapter 4.)

It should be clear that there is a strong relationship between the extensive form of a game and a firm's *strategy*.

A strategy is a complete specification of what action to take at every contingency. It specifies actions at every information point.

A strategy follows through the extensive form of the game, tracing the moves the player intends to take. The close relationship between the extensive form and the strategy makes the extensive form a useful tool for the planner, for tracing the extensive form of a game encourages decision makers to think through all of the logical possible reactions to a move

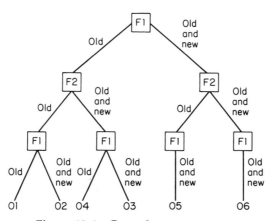

Figure 13.4 Game 2: repeat moves

they are contemplating. And, as we have stressed throughout this text, strategies can only be evaluated in the context of the expected reactions of the other players in the market place. In this respect, strategic planning in the market is very much like strategic planning in the defense area— where many of the original ideas were born.

The Core

The final concept in game theory that I wish to discuss is the **core**. The core consists of all solutions to a game for which no one in the game, acting either alone or in a coalition, can do better. This idea has turned out to be both very simple and very powerful as a tool for understanding competitor reactions.

Suppose I wish to engage in a trade with someone else. Based on the terms specified, I calculate the value of the trade to me and to the other party. Suppose it turns out that the trade benefits me, but does not benefit the other party. In this case, we would say that the particular trade, or the solution to this game, *is not in the core.* My potential trading partner would be better off not engaging in the trade. Since this is an option he can unilaterally exercise, the trade cannot be in the core. Since the trade is not in the core, unless there is coercion involved, the trade is not likely to occur. In Matrix I, outcomes 2 and 3 are not in the core of the game specified, since either party can do better with a unilateral action. In each case, breaking even dominates losing money, *and* each firm can at least break even without any cooperation from its rival. In Matrix II, on the other hand, outcomes 2 and 3 are in the core.

The idea of the core becomes both more complex and more useful when we introduce multiple players. Suppose there are three people interested in dealing with one another. Suppose further that there is some deal which leaves each of the three better off than any of them would be alone. Is that enough to say the deal is in the core? The answer is no. It must also be the case that the deal is better than any coalition of two parties can achieve without the third. Otherwise, the smaller coalition will have an incentive to go off and deal on its own.

A simple example may be useful here. Suppose a small firm has developed a new product. The firm itself lacks full resources to adequately market and distribute the product, and so it is in the market with the idea of selling the patent. Two firms are interested. If the small firm produces the product itself, the outcome will be $50,000 for it. If rival 1 buys the patent, it is likely to earn $75,000 on the product; if rival 2 purchases the patent, it will earn $100,000. What patent prices are *in the core?* There are four possible coalitions in this game: Small firm/rival 1; small firm/rival 2, small firm/rival 1/rival 2; and rival 1/rival 2. The best outcomes each of these coalitions could realize on its own are given in Table 13.1.

Suppose the initial product bidding consisted only of rival 1. The core would then consist of all bids between $50,000 and $75,000. Below $50,000,

Table 13.1 Coalition outcomes,
patent game

Small firm/rival 1	$ 75,000
Small firm/rival 2	$100,000
All three	$100,000
Rival 1/rival 2	0
Small firm alone	$ 50,000

the small firm would go it alone; above $75,000, purchase is not wise for rival 1. Interestingly, if the small firm had no production capability of its own, the core would lie between 0 and $75,000. Having an ability to produce on its own improves the negotiation position of the firm.

What happens to the core with the entry of rival 2? Now bids in the range of, say, $60,000 are no longer viable. A coalition of small firm and rival 2 can do better, acting alone. In fact, now the core lies between $75,000 and $100,000, and this is the region in which we would expect to find the price. Notice that the ability of self-production is no longer critical in setting the bid, since this option is dominated by the outcome of one of the coalitions. The small firm can use its opportunity to produce with rival 1 to ensure that rival 2 does not bid below $75,000. Thus the threat of self-production for $50,000 is no longer needed.

Identifying the core is an important feature in understanding the course of a negotiation or a set of competitive moves. Indeed, if we understand all solutions to a problem that are in the core, we have simultaneously described the set of **credible threats** available to the participants of the game. If two firms are negotiating, for example, either one can credibly threaten to take particular unilateral moves. For cooperative behavior to ensue, each of the participants must do as well as he or she could do on his/her own. The payoffs associated with alternative opportunities available to each of the parties to a negotiation are sometimes called the **threat points** of the bargain.[10] As we'll see in the illustration that follows, understanding points in the core can considerably improve one's negotiating strategy.

Pricing Strategy in Contract Negotiations: An Illustration

The case discussed below illustrates some of the complexities of pre-entry threats in the context of a negotiation in the pharmaceutical industry. The case illustrates the use of the core or threat points in understanding the progress of a negotiation.

In 1980, Farma, Inc., a medium-sized pharmaceutical company, obtained a patent on a new anti-inflammatory drug.[11] At the time of its innovation, Farma had limited marketing experience, and since it expected the drug to earn a fairly substantial market, it turned to Miller

Drugs for help. Licensing new drugs is a common procedure in the pharmaceutical industry. Miller, Inc., was a large diversified pharmaceutical company which in 1980 had no significant entry in the anti-inflammatory market. Given the demographic profile of the United States, it was viewed as strategically important to have some coverage in this area.

After considerable negotiation, Miller and Farma agreed on an exclusive license for Miller to market the new drug. Miller would undertake all production, marketing, and distribution costs. In return for the exclusive license, Miller would pay Farma 10 percent of the gross revenues from the drug. The contract had a five-year duration, at which point renegotiation would occur. Under the terms of the contract, Farma was required to allow Miller to continue to market the anti-inflammatory drug after the five-year period, but could revoke the exclusive part of the deal. Should Miller market under a nonexclusive license, it was required to pay royalties of 4 percent.

In 1984, senior executives at Farma began to evaluate the anti-inflammatory market in preparation for contract negotiations with Miller. The market for Farma's product had proved to be even better than forecasted. In 1984, the total sales of the product were $150 million, and sales were projected at $200 million for 1985 and thereafter. Operating profits realized by Miller on its sales hovered around the 60 percent level. Thus on sales of $200 million, Farma received $20 million—given the 10 percent royalty rate—while Miller earned returns of $120 million.

In addition to evaluating the current financial picture, Farma executives were also interested in the longer run prospects in the market. As indicated, the anti-inflammatory market had grown dramatically over the contract period. The Farma product was viewed very favorably by the medical market, and the patent was still viable. While other firms were interested in finding products in this market, there were no new close substitutes likely to appear for some time. Given the long FDA testing time, pharmaceutical companies often have considerable advance notice of the entry of a new competitor into the market. In this case, while there were several drugs currently under testing, none was expected to be ready to enter the market for at least five years.

Finally, the Farma executives were concerned about the strategic implications of the contract negotiation, both from the point of view of their own firm and from the perspective of Miller. As indicated, Miller was earning substantial profits from the new drug. Miller was also currently testing an alternative anti-inflammatory, but it had no ready alternative. Moreover, anti-inflammatory drugs were increasingly viewed as an important component in a firm's product portfolio. So the Farma product was of some strategic importance to Miller.

On the other hand, things had changed somewhat for Farma over the five years. The firm was in the process of building up its distribution network, and it had recently hired a large number of "field" salespeople. In the pharmaceutical market, field salespeople visit hospitals, clinics, and offices to show new and existing drugs to doctors. Typically, salespeople are trained to sell drugs in a particular area—that is, heart disease, obstetrics, pediatrics, and so on. Since 1980, Farma had launched new products in areas related to its anti-inflammatory drug, and part of its field staff was devoted to selling these new products. But Farma now perceived that there was some excess capacity in the selling staff, and moreover, that having their staff also market their well-known and respected anti-inflammatory drug would provide important benefits to the sales of their other products. In sum, in the last five years Farma had grown to view its contract with Miller somewhat less favorably.

So the stage was set for a rather complicated renegotiation. Renegotiations of this sort tend, in general, to be complicated, since the positions of both parties tend to have changed as a result of the initial contract.[12] In this case, Miller had invested less in its own anti-inflammatory as a result of its exclusive license, and it had simultaneously developed a skilled sales force with a good deal of knowledge about Farma's drug. Miller had thus made some strategic investments as a consequence of its contract with Farma. At the same time, Farma had adapted itself to receiving a rather large royalty stream, without any capital investment. Bargaining was likely to be somewhat more complex than it had been in 1980. As one might have expected, the original contract had anticipated that Miller might have to invest in some assets specific to the anti-inflammatory market in requiring that Farma not be permitted to revoke the contract entirely when it came up for renegotiation.

After their analysis of the current situation, the Farma staff held a meeting of the finance and planning groups to develop some idea of what kind of contract they would really like with Miller. The groups as a whole began by trying to understand the *threat points* of Farma versus Miller in the negotiation. What options could each firm accomplish on its own, and what payoffs could each expect from the unilateral action? Put another way, what solutions were in the *core* of the game?

Should negotiations break down, Farma could begin to market the anti-inflammatory drug in competition with Miller. The most aggressive approach for Farma to take would be to use an undifferentiated product strategy with price cutting. Farma's planning group believed that it could capture 30 percent of the $200 million market this way. Under this low-cost scenario, margins on $60 million of sales were expected to run about 60 percent for Farma. Gross margins on Farma's own sales would thus be $36 million per year. In addition, Farma would earn the 4 percent royalty rate on the $140 million in sales, as written into the earlier contract for a nonexclusive license to Miller. Royalty revenues would thus be $5.6 million, for a total of $41.6 million per year. This strategy was viewed by the Farma group as the most serious action it could unilaterally take against Miller. It was the firm's threat point.

What would Miller earn under this scenario? It would be left with 70 percent of the market, on which it would also earn about 64 percent margin, or 60 percent after royalty payments. This would amount to $84 million. Miller could be expected to accept only a deal that would earn it at least $84 million.

The option $41.6/$84 million was thus in the core of the negotiation game. It served as a basis from which all negotiations could proceed.

In the negotiations, Miller was interested in preventing entry by Farma. Using our threat points, we can now ask, What royalty rate would be sufficient to keep Farma out of the market? A current royalty rate of 10 percent is clearly insufficient: On sales of $200 million, the current rate yields only $20 million for Farma, well below its threat point. Of course, Miller would be pleased with this rate, but Miller has no power to enforce a bargain at the 10 percent rate. Indeed, simple arithmetic shows us that the royalty rate must be at least 20.8 percent to be as financially worthwhile to Farma as the full-entry option ($200 (.208) = $41.6).

What is the maximum royalty Miller will pay? Remember, if Farma enters, Miller will still be able to earn $84 million. So the royalty rate must yield earnings for Miller in excess of $84 million. If Farma does not enter, Miller's preroyalty margins will be 70 percent, somewhat higher than they would be under the entry scenario. Entry cuts margins, as we would expect. On a revenue base of $200 million, with gross margins of $140 million, Miller can "afford" to pay $56 million in royalties without going below its own threat point. In other words, as long as the royalty rate is less than 28 percent, Miller will benefit from deterring entry by Farma. So there is room for a deal. Any rate between 20.8 percent and 28 percent would be preferred from a financial perspective by both parties. This provides the range within which the negotiation can proceed. The three columns below summarize the negotiation space:

Option 1	Option 2	Option 3
Farma enters	No entry	No entry
4% royalty holds	Royalty = 20.8%	Royalty = 28%
$41.6	$41.6	$56
$84	$98.4	$84

Options 2 and 3, and all deals between, are preferred relative to the threat outcome. This is the *core* within which a deal can be struck.

Of what use is this calculation to the Farma executives trying to grapple with a bargaining strategy? First of all, it shows the value of a credible entry threat on the part of Farma. Farma's primary threat in the negotiation seems to be that it will enter on its own; senior management thus needs adequate ammunition to convince the Miller staff that they can and will enter the fray. The analysis also shows the Farma staff how well Miller could do on its own. Management fantasies of 50 percent royalty rates are soon dissipated by the simple calculations above. Finally, the analysis shows us that *there is a deal to be made* between Farma and Miller. In fact, there are several deals that are preferable to the threat outcomes.

This latter proposition is an important one. In many circumstances, the core is empty: There are no gains from cooperation. All games of pure conflict—zero sum or constant sum games—are without cores. In a game without a core, conflict is the most likely outcome.

Conclusion

The three topics introduced here—payoff matrixes, extensive form games, and the idea of the core—are valuable tools in trying to understand likely behavior of one's rivals. Each of these tools forces the decision maker to ask the difficult "what-if" questions of management. If we think back to the schematic of the planning process we have referred to throughout this text, we can see that game theory forces us to open the important "box" of rival behavior and investigate the contents. What will my competitor do? How will my rival respond to my actions? How best can I respond to my competitors' likely actions? In the next few chapters, we examine competition more specifically in the areas of pricing, research and development, and marketing, using and expanding on game theory.

14

Product Positioning and Strategic Marketing

General Foods is a $9.5 billion subsidiary of Philip Morris. One of the largest processors and marketers of packaged grocery products in the world, it competes with numerous other firms in a broad range of markets ranging from coffee and desserts to breakfast cereal. In competing in these markets, General Foods relies in part on pricing policy. But in many of General Foods' markets, product development, promotion, and distribution play an even more important role in the competitive struggle. The packaged food industry—of which GF is a part—is one of the heaviest advertisers in the United States. In 1986, for example, before it was acquired by Philip Morris, General Foods spent $500 million on advertising on a revenue base of $9 billion. New product introduction is a vital part of the General Foods strategy. In the breakfast cereal market, for instance, in which General Foods is a large player, there were 194 distinct brands of cereal in 1985, up from 181 in the year prior. In the faddish children's segment of this market, new products last an average of only two years, making continuous product innovation essential. Finally, General Foods sells the bulk of its products through freestanding grocery stores with limited shelf space. The battle for shelf space is another major concern of the organization.

Managing new product development, promotion, and distribution is a complex task. In this chapter, we will concentrate on only one aspect of marketing strategy: the effect of existing and potential rivals on selection of strategy. How are an organization's decisions about the rate of new-product introduction, advertising expenditures, and optimal distribution channels influenced by the competitive environment? For example, can a firm use rapid product introductions as a way to deter entry into its industry? In 1972, the U.S. Federal Trade Commission issued a complaint against the four largest cereal producers charging them with using product-line expansions to deter entry into this market.[1] Under what conditions might this be a viable strategy? Does advertising serve primarily to expand markets or to realign shares? When General Foods increases the advertising budget for its Post Fruit and Fiber cereal, does this increase the total demand for fiber cereals or simply divert customers from Kellogg's Fruitful Bran? What role does distribution play in determining market entry and the eventual configuration of a market? Can retailers play an important role in shelf space decisions? These are some of the questions we will be addressing in this chapter.

Product Planning

In the case of most consumer products, we observe some range in the variety of goods offered.

> **Product differentiation is said to exist whenever we have a class of goods that consists of a variety of similar but not identical items.**

Hundreds of shampoos are sold in the market place, and dozens of brands of pea soup. No two brands are precisely the same, and yet all are similar enough for most people to recognize the product class to which they belong. Moreover, despite the differences among brands, there is clearly some competition across product categories.

As we look across industries and, indeed, even within industries, we see that firms have adopted rather different strategies in their product lines. In some markets, a range of competitive products is offered under one organizational roof. Procter & Gamble, for example, produces Tide, Cheer, Dash, Bold, and several other lesser-known laundry detergents, none of which are labeled with the P&G name. Coca-Cola produces a family of brands: Coke, Classic Coke, Diet Coke, Cherry Coke, and so on, all clearly labeled as Coke. Firms sometimes offer a product line across a wide spectrum of product types, following a strategy of *broad product differentiation.* All of the major auto companies, for example, produce a fairly broad line of cars, in different size and cost categories. Procter & Gamble's detergents span a wide range as well. In other instances, organizations produce multiple brands, but specialize in a narrow band of the product spectrum. Coca-Cola has traditionally followed a strategy of concentrated differentiation. In still other instances, particular firms specialize in one product type, and variety is produced by the abundance of specialist producers within the industry.

> **An organization's product line is the series of related products that it offers for sale. Organizations can offer broad or narrow product lines.**

What factors influence an organization's choice of product strategy? Which variety of a product should an organization produce? How many varieties of a product should a firm produce, and how different should those varieties be?

    In explaining product-line choices of firms, we require some under-
standing of the way in which consumers choose among particular brands.
Fundamentally, organizations wish to offer for sale only products that
consumers want to buy. For this reason, it is helpful to begin the discussion of product-line choice with a simple model of consumer decision
making. How do consumers choose among the plethora of toothpastes,
soft drinks, and shampoos? One useful way to model consumer brand
choice is to think of a product as the embodiment of a particular set of
characteristics that are desired in some proportion by various segments of
the population.[2] Kellogg's Corn Flakes, for example, is defined by its specific combination of sweetness, crunchiness, fiber, and vitamin content.
Coca-Cola is defined by its mix of sweetness, caffeine content, and fla-
voring. Individual products are defined by how much of each of the attributes they have. One cereal is very sweet, but has little fiber content; a
second is less sweet, but has more fiber, and so on. Consumers buy particular brands because the characteristics of those goods most closely match
their preferences, assuming prices are the same.[3]
    If we simplify the problem somewhat further and treat a product as
though it possessed only two salient characteristics, we could display
product types visually as in Figure 14.1 below. This **product map** displays
a few of the breakfast cereals currently on the market, focusing on sweetness and fiber content. In each case, the desired attribute is measured in
terms of characteristics delivered per dollar expended by the consumer.
A dollar spent on Marshmallow Krispies, for example, delivers considerable sugar to the consumer, but little fiber. Fiber One, a General Mills
product, provides fiber without sugar. Products are placed on the map
based on *consumers' perceptions* of the attributes of the various products.
For this reason, the product-space map is sometimes called a **perceptual
map.**

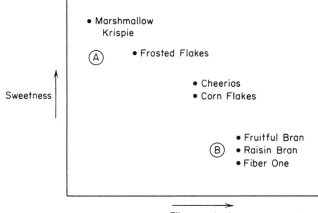

Figure 14.1   Product map for ready-to-eat cereals

A perceptual map is a visual representation of how consumers perceive products in a market based on the multiple attributes of those products.

How do consumers make choices among the cereals described in the product map? One model of consumer decision making is that the consumer computes implicit "distances" between his or her ideal point and the various brands in the market and then chooses the brand or brands closest to that ideal point. In Figure 14.1, for example, a consumer with ideal point A would choose Marshmallow Krispies, while B might choose any of the three high fiber brands.

In the perceptual map in Figure 14.1, we have focused on two specific attributes of breakfast cereals. But, as we have indicated, in practice consumers often care about multiple characteristics of products. Marketing managers use **multidimensional scaling** and **factor analysis** to try to compress the range of attributes identified by consumers. In most cases, a two-dimensional representation is sought. In what follows, we will continue to work with two-dimensional attribute space for ease of discussion.

Modeling products as bundles of characteristics is very helpful in delineating the competitive substructure in the product arena. In Figure 14.1, we can see that Fruitful Bran, Raisin Bran, and Fiber One occupy adjacent positions. They have similar product characteristics and thus, from the consumer's perspective, these products are close substitutes. Frosted Flakes, with a different mix of sugar and fiber, is a more distant substitute to these brands, but competes more directly with Marshmallow Krispies. As we can see, placement on the product map can be used to identify particular market segments and to indicate the source of major competitive pressures. And the map can also help us to identify attractive entry positions.

Products that are most similar to one another in the place they occupy in the characteristic space will provide the greatest competitive pressure on each other.

How does a firm decide what position to occupy in the product map, or, indeed, how many positions to occupy? The easiest case to begin with is a firm which is a monopolist in a market with blockaded entry. A monopolist is, by definition, the only firm in a particular market. That firm may nevertheless wish to produce a range of product brands. For this monopoly firm, the choice of product variety involves the following trade-off: If a firm can produce a product which most closely matches the *ideal points* of each distinct type of consumer, its revenues will be maximized. Each consumer will pay the most for a variety of good that most closely matches his or her preferences. The further a product is from a person's ideal point, the less he or she will be willing to pay for it. With a range of brands, the monopolist can charge a range of different prices.

Differentiated consumer preferences encourage product variety.

On the other hand, producing a wide range of brands may substantially increase production and marketing costs. If a market has a wide variety of brands, we expect the volume sold of each brand to be lower than in a market with fewer brands. While some market expansion undoubtedly results from brand proliferation, cannibalization of close markets is also expected in cases in which product characteristics partially overlap. Thus, in markets with multiple brands, the average production run per product falls, and this may impose costs on the firm if there are substantial economies to scale. Inventory costs also tend to rise with the number of varieties of a good.

To the extent that there are economies to scale in production, increasing product variety will be costly.

The existence of economies of scope may partially offset scale effects, also operating on the cost side of the equation. Economies of scope exist whenever it is cheaper to produce two product lines in one firm than to produce them separately.[4] Scope economies often arise in the marketing and distribution areas. The existence of multiple brands, for example, might allow a firm to pursue an advertising program which is uneconomical for the single product, but quite effective otherwise. Thus the minimum efficient scale may diminish as the number of brands increases, given possibilities for cost sharing.

The monopolist will choose a number of products to reflect this trade-off between holding down costs on the one hand and serving specialized consumer segments or exploiting scope economies on the other.[5]

Cost conditions and the existence of distinct consumer segments influence the choice of the length of the product line. Substantial economies of scale favor market aggregation. Economies of scope and the existence of distinct consumer groups favor market differentiation.

Suppose the monopolist decides to enter the market with multiple brands. Should it choose highly differentiated brands, or follow a strategy of producing multiple brands within a narrow span of the market? Should Coca-Cola produce only cola drinks, or branch into other flavors, perhaps even noncarbonated beverages? Demand side considerations suggest that the most effective product-line strategy for the monopolist will be one that covers a broad spectrum of products. Firms might produce one brand for the up-scale market and a second for the more price-elastic lower end of the market. In this way, the monopolist can meet a range of consumer preferences without excessively cannibalizing its own brands.[6]

When we look at the cost side, however, the message is not so clear. Economies of scope may reside primarily in products close to one another on the product map. For example, an organization may not be able to promote two diverse brands effectively in a single marketing effort, whereas related brands may be more easily packaged together. Indeed, in some products, producing a down-scale brand may tarnish the reputation of the up-scale version, creating a kind of diseconomy of scope. When brands are far apart on the perceptual map, firms sometimes avoid a common firm label. Thus P&G does not prominently display the firm name on its two diverse diaper brands, Luvs and Pampers. Hence economies of scope may encourage some narrowing of the product line.

For a monopolist producer, demand side considerations favor a broad product line. Considerations of cost sharing may, however, narrow the optimal line.

Thus far we have been treating the product strategy of a firm that has the market to itself. The question of product-line strategy becomes even more interesting when we consider the case in which a firm has numerous current and potential rivals. Now the firm must consider the effects of its product-line choices on the behavior of its existing and potential rivals. In this instance, the results of one's own product strategy will depend on the working out in the market place of everyone else's product strategy as well.

We can use a simple payoff matrix to examine the dynamics of product competition in television networking.[7] There are three major networks in the United States: ABC, CBS, and NBC. These networks do not appear to compete heavily in the prices they charge their customers—that is, the rates charged advertisers. Instead, competition among networks focuses on programming or product development. Since the overall program audience is fairly constant, programming competition aims to influence the division of that audience. In the language of game theory, this is a **zero-sum game.** Each customer won by ABC is a loss to either CBS or NBC.

In Figure 14.2, we have modeled this zero-sum game using two networks. The device each network has available to influence its market share is principally programming investment. In particular, each network can either spend a lot on program development and attract customers, or con-

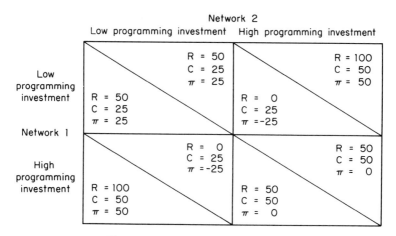

Figure 14.2 Network payoff matrix

trol costs by limiting program development. Each possible scenario has attached to it a revenue level, a cost level, and (by subtraction) a profit level for each of the networks. For example, if both networks have low programming investments, both will have modest revenues (50), low costs (25), and moderate profits (25). With high offsetting investments, revenues remain stable, but costs rise (50) and profits fall to zero. Extensive investments in programming increase the costs of the two networks without increasing overall industry revenues, since the networks are essentially splitting a fixed audience. The increased costs simply serve to move consumers from one network to another. This is the prisoners' dilemma introduced earlier. While both networks would be better off with symmetrical restraint in programming, neither can unilaterally exhibit restraint, or the other network will take over. The result expected is an escalation of programming competition. Competitive pressures have led to more product development than we would have expected if networks formulated product strategy in a vacuum.

The above discussion involves a simple game in which history and a fear of the future play no role, and competitive moves can be matched. In fact, the typical programming competition is more complex. As we suggested earlier, in games that are played over and over again by the same parties, prisoners' dilemmas are sometimes overcome. In television networking, there appear to be several devices that have been introduced to mitigate the pressures toward overprogramming. In particular, the major networks all follow the same rerun-frequency rule. That is, all networks share a common ratio of reruns to new shows over the year. This is clearly a device to reduce programming costs and appears to have been relatively successful over time in mitigating the prisoners' dilemma. On those occasions when one or another network changed its rerun policy, the occurrence was brief and chaotic.

A more complex way to look at product strategy in a competitive market place is to use the sequential-game framework introduced in Chapter 13. Entry into a market normally occurs not all at once, but one or two organizations at a time. As a new organization enters, it will position itself by looking at its costs, at consumer preferences, and at the position of other firms already in the market. It may also be important for firms to take into account the likely future product behavior of current and potential rivals in the market. Thus a new entrant looks at the behavior of firms already in the market and the behavior of those to come. Firms will wish to pursue product positions that are least destabilizing to the existing industry and most defensible against entry threats in the future.[8] In sum, a firm will take into consideration what it believes will be the final shape of the market in making its own product-line choices.[9] The most stable industry structures are ones in which firms follow segmentation strategies, each specializing in different bands of the product spectrum. New entrants, wishing to avoid direct confrontation with powerful incumbents, will aim for the "gaps" on the product map, as long as these gaps contain the right type and number of ideal points.[10] By occupying different areas of the map, firms can avoid the costs of direct confrontation and thus reduce the likelihood of aggressive price wars. Indeed, markets occupied by multiproduct firms appear to display somewhat less price competition than markets occupied by single-product firms.[11]

Concentrated differentiation strategies in which firms focus on bands of the product spectrum seem to reduce price competition within an industry.

Let us consider the New York museum market as an example of competitive strategy in product-line choice. On the perceptual map in Figure 14.3, I have focused on two characteristics of museums that seem to distinguish them in the eyes of New York consumers: the breadth of their collections overall and the depth of the collections in the area of modern art. With a given resource base, a museum can offer a wide collection with a few pieces representing each area, or follow a strategy of specializing in a more limited set of areas. As indicated on the map, the Metropolitan Museum of Art and the Brooklyn Museum own a broad spectrum of art, but have little depth in modern art. The Met, for example, has 19 different curatorial departments and over 2 million works of art. The Whitney and the Guggenheim, on the other hand, have less breadth, but great depth in the modern art area. The Whitney, which is considerably smaller than the Met, is the largest collector of American modern art in the United States, but has little else in its collection.

Each of the museums on the perceptual map constantly faces the strategic question of how much, if at all, it should change its product line. An organization's position on the perceptual map is a dynamic result of the strategic choices that organization has made. Should the Met expand further into modern art? Should the Whitney add branch museums or expand its scope to include European art? In the early 1990s, the Guggen-

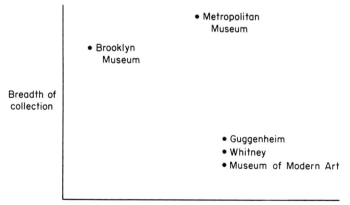

Figure 14.3 The New York museum market

heim began a major expansion, adding space to its classic, circular New York building, a new site in Soho, and additions in Europe. As it expands, the Guggenheim's position relative to its rivals also changes. Many factors will influence such decisions—factors relating both to curatorial objectives and to business concerns. In what way might the decision be influenced by the structure of the competitive environment?

Museums compete with one another for audiences, funds, and art. In the competition for audiences, in particular, a new local entry could have a substantial effect on existing players in the market. What would happen if a new museum entered the New York market? At present, we might broadly characterize the museum-going public as follows: Those who are interested in modern art go to the Whitney, the Guggenheim, or the Museum of Modern Art; patrons interested in a broad spectrum of work frequent the Metropolitan; and a number of people split their time between the two options. In short, people visit the museum closest to their ideal point. Now suppose a new museum entered in the modern art area, perhaps at a point next to the Guggenheim on the map. The new museum might house, for example, modern art plus a collection of Impressionist works. In this case, the new entrant would have its greatest effect on the patronage of modern art museums (possibly also on the donor pool at those museums).

> **A new entrant shares the consumers of the products closest to it on the perceptual map.**

In this situation, if existing modern art museums learned of a possible new museum, they might find it worthwhile to defend their fixed investments against the potential new entry by expanding their own product lines somewhat. This expansion might mean setting up a branch installation or expanding the target collection to prevent entry by an additional museum.[12] As we indicated in Chapter 13, however, entry deterrence is not always a successful strategy. A firm contemplating such a route must ask itself two questions: Will the product expansion in fact deter entry? And how expensive will it be to do so? (Recall the earlier discussion of the diseconomies of scale created by having too many brands.)

Suppose a new entrant sees a profitable gap in the perceptual map. Will it be deterred from entering that gap if it learned that an incumbent currently operating in another position as well had already entered it? Can the incumbent *pre-empt* new entry by an introduction of its own? Let us return to the example of the new museum seeking to serve an audience interested in modern art plus a bit of traditional exposure. Suppose this museum believes that it needs a specified audience size to justify its existence. How will it be influenced in its entry decision by an expansion in the scope of the Whitney's collection? *The answer depends critically on the way in which the Whitney expansion affects the entrant's expectations about the level of post-entry competition.* If the new entrant believes that if it broadens its scope the Whitney will intensify its competitiveness, then that entrant will be dissuaded from entering. Perhaps the new entrant might expect a broad-based Whitney to increase its advertising or the number of its blockbuster exhibitions to protect itself against new competition.[13] Is such behavior on the part of the Whitney likely? Whenever a multiproduct firm launches an aggressive campaign against an entrant, this depresses the demand for its line of related goods. If the Whitney, for example, opens a new wing devoted to the Impressionists, it will draw audiences from other of its own exhibitions as well as from the new entrant. Other exhibits at the Whitney may get a very limited audience. The Whitney may hurt its core product with this strategy more than it hurts its new rival, in the sense that it is diverting the audience from one of its exhibits to the new exhibit. The closer the Whitney's new product is to its old, the more its new product will affect the old, and thus the less credible will be a threat to launch an aggressive competitive campaign. The multiproduct firm has more to lose from aggressive competition than does the single-product new entrant, and the closer its products are to one another, the less aggressive it is likely to be. Thus it is easier to deter entry if you have a broad product line than if you market a concentrated narrow line. A broad product line leaves fewer holes to be filled by a new entrant.

How can an incumbent use a new product offering to convince an entrant of its aggressive intentions? It can do so only by investing heavily in irrecoverable capital to support the new product, thus raising barriers to exit from the new product.[14] Of course, this is a risky and expensive way to deter entry.

> **Product-line expansions can deter entry by a new rival only if they involve substantial specific investments so as to make the incumbent's commitment to the new line credible. Product-line expansions that are most different from the existing product line of the firm are most likely to deter entry.**

We can see here an interesting result. Concentrated market segmentation by organizations serves to promote industry stability by reducing the possibility of price wars. A policy of pursuing broader product-line choices may help to deter entry by leaving fewer profitable holes to be filled.[15]

As we have seen, using a product-line strategy to deter new entry is not a simple matter. This brings us to a second point, which is that such a strategy may also be expensive. In many industries, launching a new brand involves a substantial investment. The average cost of a new branded consumer product, looking across a range of markets, was between $50 and $100 million in 1985 with a 70 percent failure rate.[16] In the cereal industry, for example, the average costs to introduce a new brand range from $10 to $20 million. Major expansions in the scope of a museum are also very expensive, particularly as competition for art intensifies. In many markets, developing new products also requires considerable time. Even after a massive reorganization designed to help it compete with the Japanese, Xerox required two years to produce a new copier.[17] New product development is thus often not a readily available strategic weapon. It is also hard to justify such major expenditures for new product development on the grounds of entry deterrence alone, though the prospect of discouraging entry may certainly play a role.

Table 14.1 summarizes the various factors that affect product strategy. As we can see, the right strategy in this important area depends on conditions at the organizational level and in the market place overall. As we turn now to look at advertising strategy, we will see that here, too, no single strategy will suffice.

Advertising Strategy

In the United States, advertising expenditures comprise approximately 2 percent of the Gross National Product. Many companies spend more than 5 percent of their sales revenues on advertising, and in organizations, brand managers and marketing managers spend a substantial part of their time deciding on the level and mix of advertising. We discussed in Chapter 7 the way in which advertising may contribute to the pioneering-brand advantage of a firm and thus protect that firm against new entrants. In the discussion which follows, we focus on a second important aspect of the advertising decision: How can advertising be used to influence the competitive positions of firms already in an industry?

Return for a moment to the model of consumer choice presented in the earlier section. We argued that consumers choose among products by evaluating the mix of attributes found in various brands. But how do consumers know what characteristics particular brands have? Sometimes information is conveyed to consumers visually: We can easily see the color of a shirt or its size. Products whose characteristics can be determined fairly accurately on inspection are sometimes called **search goods**. But other products are less easily judged.[18] Products with many qualities that become apparent only with use are known as **experience goods**. One way that consumers learn about product characteristics, including quality, is

Table 14.1   Product strategy

Conditions favoring a broad line	*Conditions favoring a narrow line*
Economies of scope across multiple brands	Blocked entry with multiple current producers
Threat of entry by newcomers	High product-development costs
Distinct consumer tastes	Economies of scale in production and/or distribution

through advertising. Indeed, even the fact that a firm chooses to advertise at all reveals some information about the quality of the product it offers, with high advertisers on average offering higher quality goods than low advertisers.[19] Moreover, while it is clear that advertisers have some self-interest in minimizing the negative qualities of their products, there is some evidence that competition in advertising leads to the provision of relatively full information in many instances.[20]

By serving to inform consumers, advertising can play two different roles. First, advertising can help to expand the overall market for a product. This effect is particularly pronounced in the early stages of a product's life cycle when advertising serves to inform consumers of the existence and usefulness of the particular new product. Under these conditions, advertising by one firm may actually serve to increase demand for the entire industry.[21] Indeed, in an interesting study of French television advertising it was found that advertising by the dominant firm in an industry in a period just after television bans on advertising were lifted increased the profits of smaller firms in the industry.[22]

In the early stages of a product, there may be substantial spill-over effects from advertising.

As an industry matures, however, advertising comes to serve primarily a second role, to influence the brand choice of consumers and thus to influence the market shares of competing firms.

Advertising evolves over the life cycle of a product. Early in a product's life, its primary roles are to build product awareness and provide information to the consumer. At this point, advertising may serve as a **public good:** It expands the market, and thus all producers of the product may gain from it, and it informs the public of the product's existence and function. In the mature phase of the industry, advertising is used to differentiate a product from its competitors.[23] In this phase, advertising serves as a **private good,** and indeed, advertising by one firm may diminish sales of a second.

In many industries in their mature phases, advertising is related to the fight over market share.[24] In the soap and detergent industry, firms spend approximately 10 percent of sales on advertising that primarily serves to vitiate their rivals' messages.[25] Similarly strong competitive effects are typical in the cigarette industry.[26] A variety of other consumer goods are also competitively advertised.[27]

An interesting example of the role of advertising in the market-share battle is found in the brewing industry.[28] The brewing industry is at present a relatively concentrated one, with a six-firm concentration ratio of 92 percent. In the last several decades, this industry has undergone considerable concentration, as local breweries have dropped out or been merged into national operations. There has also been some reshuffling of industry leaders. Fifteen years ago, Anheuser Busch, Schlitz, and Pabst were the "Big 3" brewers. Today, Miller and Anheuser Busch lead the pack. At present, heavy advertising seems to be essential to support a viable brand.[29] In 1991, Anheuser Busch spent $722 million on marketing. At the same time, overall demand has been virtually constant since 1980. Clearly the heavy advertising expenditures in this industry are primarily used to fuel the battle for share. And the evidence suggests that advertis- -ing has indeed influenced market position substantially, with Anheuser Busch's gain in share very significantly influenced by its advertising bud- get.[30]

Is there anything special about the kind of competition we see in in- dustries characterized by heavy advertising and those in which advertis- ing is less prevalent? As we have indicated, advertising in the mature stage of a product often serves to differentiate products from one another, to position products on the consumer's perceptual map. By accentuating the differences among products, advertising can help to lower the cross elasticity of demand among them. Thus 7-Up and Coke and Tylenol and Aspirin become only imperfect substitutes in part as a result of advertis- ing messages. Since cross elasticity of demand is reduced by advertising, the effectiveness of price rivalry also declines.[31]

In industries characterized by heavy image advertising, price rivalry tends to be muted.

In other circumstances, advertising serves primarily an informational role. Here consumers may be made more aware by advertising of the presence of various products scattered throughout the perceptual map. When regulations prohibiting the advertising of retail drug prices and op- tometric services were lifted, for example, increased advertising helped to inform consumers of new competitors. In these cases, advertising actually increased price competition.[32]

How does advertising competition compare with price competition? Advertising competition is frequently more complex than price competi- tion because imitation in the former is more difficult. Procter & Gamble may be able to match the financial investment Kimberly-Clark makes on advertising without matching the impact of that advertising. Indeed, even matching the financial outlays may be difficult in the short run, since most advertising campaigns take an appreciable time to launch. Similarly, a particularly successful advertising campaign may be harder to match than simply matching advertising expenditures. There is some evidence, for example, that Anheuser Busch's advertising is more productive than that of its rivals in the brewing industry.[33] Winston cigarettes seem to benefit more from advertising than other brands.[34] Even within particular products, creative new ideas seem to pay off more than simple budget outlays, or more repetitions of the same message.[35]

Advertising message strategy is harder to match than changes in prices.

While there is often a presumption that advertising competition is sof- ter than price competition, this may not be the case in all markets. If market shares are perceived to be very sensitive to advertising, then competition in this arena may be aggressive indeed.[36] In the disposable-diaper market, for example, advertising competition appears to be quite intense.

We turn now to a discussion of the last element of the competitive marketing strategy of an organization, its distributional strategy.

Distributional Strategy

Very few manufacturers can carry out all of the activities involved in the distribution of their products themselves. Most rely at least to some extent on intermediaries—retailers, sales agents, brokers, and the like. These intermediaries are organized into a **channel system**—a system of organizations that move the product from producer to consumer. Channel systems vary considerably from one industry to the next. In some cases, firms are completely vertically integrated. In others, products move from manufacturer to retailer to customer. And yet in other markets, wholesalers play a role, as do sales agents and brokers. We inquired in Chapter 11 about the broad principles that motivate a firm to internalize distributional functions rather than rely on outside agents. In this chapter, we focus on the role of distributional channels in affecting the nature of competition within an industry.

In many industries, distributors appear to have substantial power over manufacturers. For goods marketed through retail grocers, for example, adequate well-positioned shelf space is essential to sales. In its ability to control shelf space, the retailer has a powerful lever over the manufacturer. On the other hand, manufacturers have the power to withhold goods from the retailer, a power that may be quite substantial in cases of very popular goods. A grocery store that does not carry General Foods' products is not likely to survive for long. We can see, then, that there is considerable interdependence among channel members.

Members of a distribution chain are interdependent.

One way in which this interdependence among channel members is manifest is in the extent of specific investments made by members of the system. How much information about the use and quality of a product needs to be provided at the point of sale? Selling cameras is obviously harder than selling soap flakes, because sales agents must acquire specific information about the technical superiority of, say, a Leica over a Nikon. Why should they make such an investment? Some products require demonstration in order to be sold. Electric trains are harder to sell than dolls, for example. Cosmetics require a more elaborate display than tennis balls. Why should a retailer design space to accommodate a particular supplier? These questions become more puzzling when we recognize that, while there is considerable interdependence among channel members, their objectives may differ. Manufacturers are often interested in national sales, while retailers care primarily about sales within their own territory. As a result, manufacturers may wish to increase the number of outlets carrying their products, while retailers might prefer exclusive licenses. Retailers often carry a variety of brands of a product, whereas manufacturers prefer to have their own brands highlighted. Manufacturers may wish retailers to carry their whole line of products, while retailers are perhaps interested in only a small band of products. Thus we have interdependence without perfect consonance in objectives. As a consequence, we need some mechanism for aligning the objectives of these potentially cooperative members in the channel system.

The objectives of various members of a distribution chain may not be the same.

As we indicated in Chapter 11, the more specific the investment needed in a distribution chain, the more we will need some safeguard to protect the investor. What safeguards are available?

In Chapter 11, we stressed the role of vertical integration and long-term contracts in protecting investors against hold-ups by their buyers.[37] In other situations, manufacturers provide the service offered on the distributor's premises themselves. Cosmetic demonstrators in retail stores are generally employed by cosmetic firms, not by the retailers. Major manufacturers often employ agents to arrange shelf displays at retail premises. In these cases, the manufacturer is actually undertaking the investment itself, simply using the retail space. In some cases, retailers and manufacturers run cooperative advertising campaigns as a way to exploit their interdependence. In still other cases, manufacturers "pay for" investments made by their dealers through the use of practices like **resale-price maintenance** (RPM). In resale-price maintenance, manufacturers direct retailers as to the prices that can be charged to customers for their goods. Retailers are not permitted to charge prices below those specified by the manufacturer. Levi Strauss, Florsheim Shoes, and numerous other well-known firms have used resale-price maintenance at one time or another in their histories.[38] By protecting the margins of retailers who promote the manufacturers' products, RPM can induce investments by those retailers.[39] RPM is especially useful when retailers' efforts affect the sale of a good in the broader market place. Under these conditions, the retailer's conventional incentives to promote manufacturer's products are reduced.[40] When there are no public-good problems, the normal competition *among* retailers can help to assure manufacturers of ideal customer representation, and RPM guarantees will be less useful. In part, the choice depends on the monitoring ability of manufacturers.[41]

A variety of contracting and facilitating devices are available to increase cooperation among channel members.

If we look within particular channel systems, we see that the relative power of manufacturers, retailers, wholesalers, and agents varies considerably. If manufactured products are quite similar, and competition is strong in the manufacturing end, distributors tend to gain in power. Using distributors to help stimulate demand is known as a **push strategy.** Avon is a company that has historically emphasized a push strategy, using relatively little advertising and instead relying on the distributors of its cosmetics to "sell" the products. Under these conditions, distributors can play off one manufacturer against another.[42] If products are highly substitutable, independent marketing middlemen can help to reduce the price competition among the manufacturers.[43]

Thus a complex and important relationship exists between a manufacturer and its distributors. To what extent can the distributor relationship be used to substantially alter the competitive structure in an industry? In earlier discussions, we noted the power of both product development and advertising in affecting entry and competitive dynamics. Can a manufacturer use its relationship with its distributor in a similarly powerful way?

Consider the following description of the relationship between Procter & Gamble, a large multiproduct consumer-products firm, and its distributors: "Aware of its strength, the company can force retailers to stock its Tide, Crest, Pampers, Crisco, and other brands. 'When they enter a market with an item, you've got to carry it,' declares a leading wholesaler."[44]

Clearly many retailers believe that manufacturers—especially large ones—have some power to leverage their existing products to acquire shelf space for new goods. But how substantial is this leveraging power? An arrangement by which a manufacturer requires that, in order to sell one product, dealers must agree to carry a second is known as **tying.** In one antitrust case, several Subaru dealers claimed that Subaru tied the supply of their new cars to the sale by the dealers of Subaru's transportation services.[45] *Formal tying arrangements are illegal under Section 3 of the Clayton Act.* Nevertheless, some manufacturer leveraging across product lines appears to be common. What functions are served by such leveraging?

Suppose P&G has market power in one of its products—say, Pampers diapers. It has two choices. It can use that power to reduce margins to retailers by increasing the wholesale price, thus capturing more of the final market price of the product for itself. Or it can be fairly generous on retailer margins but use its power to push one of its less popular products throughout the retail line. These are clearly alternative choices. P&G cannot both cut margins to the retailer and force a poor product on those retailers or retailers will rebel and move over to Kimberly-Clark. Why might P&G choose to push a new product, rather than take high profits on the Pampers line?

There are several reasons that a firm might choose to use its market power in one good to induce retailers to carry a second. First of all, there may be some economies of scope in the production of the two goods. Firms may wish to tie goods together to reduce product uncertainty.[46] Regulatory constraints on profits in one line may encourage tying of a second, unregulated line. Tying may be a way of using the profits from a mature line to invest in the development of a new product. In all of these situations, the fact that a firm carries multiple products through the same retail chain complicates the bargaining process between retailer and manufacturer.

Summary

In this chapter we have explored some of the issues associated with competition in the marketing area, and we have observed that product development, advertising, and distribution can all be used to influence the competitive landscape. We have also seen the role of competitive pressures in influencing product positioning strategy. In the next chapter, we will turn to an analysis of competition in the pricing area.

15

Competitive Pricing

The price at which a good or service is offered for sale is clearly one of the main decision variables of a firm, along with its product-line choice and the size and configuration of its production facilities. The pricing decision has many different components. How do we set prices relative to costs? How often do we change them? What price relationships should we have among our products? In this chapter, we look at pricing primarily as a *competitive* weapon. In particular, we look at the range of issues a firm considers in trying to decide whether to use prices as a prime weapon in competing against existing rivals or attempting to affect the rate of entry of new rivals. The issue, a complex one, has received a great deal of recent attention in the literature of game theory and industrial organization. It is also obviously central in terms of the strategic management of many organizations.

The issues we wish to consider are perhaps best posed by way of a few examples. In many areas of the United States, advertising in telephone directories has historically been a monopoly market, served only by the telephone companies themselves. In the divestiture of AT&T, the directory business was given to the Bell Operating Companies (BOCs), several of which set up affiliates to run that line of business. There is considerable evidence that the directory business has been extremely profitable for the BOCs, with margins on the order of 50 percent or more. Since the divestiture, there has been in a number of areas of the country large-scale attempted entry into this market; clearly the high margins have been an attraction. To what extent should the BOCs try to protect their markets by significantly lowering their prices? The high margins suggest that the BOCs have "room" to give. Should they? If so, for how long? What strategy is likely to lead to the highest profit rate? What are the legal rules about lowering prices in response to potential competition? We can also turn this set of questions around and look at pricing strategy from the perspective of a new entrant. Should a new entrant in this market focus on pricing as a way to capture share? Or does an incumbent firm typically have a pricing advantage?

A second example of the kinds of question we will be exploring in this chapter comes from economic history and involves a classic case in anti-trust law. Under John D. Rockefeller, Standard Oil came to control approximately 90 percent of the petroleum-refining business in the United States. This extraordinary market share was achieved in part as a result of merger. Some contemporaneous observers, including the Supreme Court in a landmark 1911 decision, argued that Standard Oil weakened its rivals by cutting prices dramatically in markets in which those competitors operated, while leaving prices unchanged in other markets. According to this position, Standard Oil then offered to buy its weakened competitors at rock-bottom prices. Standard Oil's high market share was the ostensible result. Recent commentators have questioned whether this strategy would in fact have been a rational one for Standard Oil to have followed.[1] Is selective price cutting a viable way to eliminate competition in particular markets? Are competitors likely to leave in response to this pricing strategy? Would new competitors simply re-enter the market if Standard Oil later raised its prices, or would the fear of future price cutting by Standard Oil effectively deter entry? Is a price-cutting strategy "too expensive" relative to the gains from exit?

We will begin our discussion of these issues by focusing on the role of pricing in the struggle among a fixed set of competitors. We will then turn to a discussion of the use of prices as a device to alter the path of industry evolution by reducing the rate of entry of new rivals.

The Simple Pricing Story

Suppose you are a small pharmaceutical company which has just invented a new lotion to treat poison ivy more effectively than calamine lotion. Production costs are minimal, and the drug is not patentable. (Patents introduce an interesting complication that we will deal with in a later chapter.) In this situation, we might represent the potential demand for our new lotion as shown in Figure 15.1.

The demand curve reflects the value consumers attribute to the lotion, including their perception of its value relative to calamine lotion. Suppose your new lotion is considerably more effective per ounce than calamine lotion and that calamine lotion is selling for $2.00 per eight-ounce jar. At prices of less than $2, your lotion will win the full market, since it is more effective than traditional calamine lotion. At prices above $2, you will share the market with the calamine-lotion producers. Even in this case of a new product, price is likely to be constrained by the prices of other similar products. The more effective your own product is relative to the other products in the market, or the more different is its function, the less the existing products will affect your pricing strategy. So we can see that

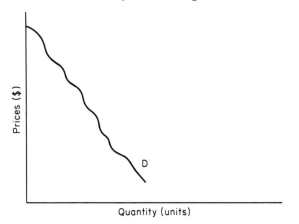

Figure 15.1 Demand for lotion

there are strong links between a firm's product strategy as discussed in the last chapter and its pricing strategy.

If we are faced with the demand curve shown in Figure 15.1, we might ask ourselves what price we should charge for our new lotion. As a first approximation, we might want to ask ourselves what price level will maximize our short-run profits from the lotion. To answer this, we need to look at both costs and demand. To be concrete, let us suppose that, forgetting the costs of inventing the lotion (which are after all sunk costs), all other costs amount to $.45 per eight-ounce jar, and that these costs are constant per jar—that is, there are no scale economies. Let us also suppose our marketing department has done some research based in part on existing calamine lotion sales and has come up with estimates of a demand schedule for lotion that reflect the demand curve in the figure. These are shown in Table 15.1.

The price that maximizes the firm's short-run profits is between $1.50 and $2.00 per jar. Below $1.50 you simply don't increase the customer base fast enough to warrant the price cuts. The market for poison-ivy

Table 15.1 Demand for lotion

Price	Customers per quarter (000 of jars)	Short-run profits (000)
$4.01	0	0
3.50	1500	$4575
3.00	3000	7650
2.50	4500	9225
2.00	6000	9300
1.50	8700	9135
1.00	9000	4950

cures is limited by its very nature, regardless of how low the price falls. On the other hand, raising prices above $2.00 has too large an effect on volume to be a profitable strategy.

So a first approximation might be to try to sell the lotion in the $1.75 range. Now let's make the problem a bit more complex to allow us to begin to see some of the underlying strategic issues involved in pricing. At a price of $1.75, if there is full information, you will take the full market away from traditional lotion producers. We might well expect those producers to respond in some way or other to your entry. In particular, we might think that these producers would lower their $2.00 price in response to your entry. In what way should your pricing *anticipate* this response? We might also note that, at a price of $1.75, you are making approximately $1.30 per jar over and above your costs, again ignoring the sunk-research costs. Suppose that to make this lotion requires no specialized equipment; the bottling and mixing assembly is available in standardized form; there is no patent protection, and shelf space in drug stores is easily found. Again, if we ignore R&D costs, our firm is making $1.30 per bottle on this lotion, and *this is a very attractive margin for other firms potentially able to copy our product and enter the market.* Should our pricing policy anticipate potential entry?

A strategic pricing policy should take into account the likely responses of existing and potential competitors to a particular set of prices. In the example above, the $1.75 price was arrived at assuming no response by rivals. Indeed, traditional demand curves, like the one in Figure 15.1, are calculated *holding prices of all substitutes constant.* But in real markets, producers of substitute goods often cut their prices in response to new product introductions. And, in real markets, high prices often induce entry. We return to the theme articulated again and again in this text: Strategy should be set with an appreciation for likely market responses to the organization's actions. The effects of pricing strategies emerge from an equilibrium that involves the interaction of strategies of all players in a market. Of course, at any point in time we will not fully know the strategies of rivals. And this makes pricing strategy even more complex.

A central ingredient in establishing a pricing strategy is a forecast of likely responses of existing and potential competitors.

We turn now to explore some of the complications involved in forecasting likely price responses of existing and potential rivals. We begin with existing competitors.

Complication 1: The Response of Existing Competitors

In 1976, Eastman Kodak entered the instant camera market, which had been dominated by Polaroid since 1942.[2] Indeed, instant cameras and Polaroid sunglasses were the *only* products produced by Polaroid. Kodak, a firm with approximately five times the sales of Polaroid, was a diversified firm operating primarily in the photographic market.

For ten years, between 1976 and 1986, Kodak and Polaroid battled in the instant camera market. Almost from the beginning, price cutting was a central weapon in the struggle. Polaroid's no-frills Pronto, for example, was priced at $79.95 in July 1976. The price fell to $59 in February 1977 and $39.95 by April 1977. While there were modest product changes along the way, it is fair to say that most of the price reductions appeared to be an aggressive response by Polaroid to the Kodak entry. Interestingly, Kodak was similarly aggressive in its prices. Its instant camera price fell by over $20 during this turbulent early year of rivalry, so that it too offered a $39.95 instant camera. Rebates to dealers by Kodak reduced the price of the camera even further to a point at which outsiders speculated that the firm might be losing money in this market.

In another type of competitor response, in the mid-1960s the U.S. steel industry was widely known for its conciliatory pricing strategies. At this time, the industry was dominated by seven firms that together controlled 75 percent of the market. Foreign competition was minimal, though growing, and the minimills were still few in number. Price increases were typically announced in advance, and price competition was often fought in the newspapers before the event, rather than in the market place. Consider the following sequence of headlines from a 1967 *Wall Street Journal*:

> January 5: Jones Laughlin to Increase Most Tube Item Prices on $\frac{1}{23}$; Net Effect a 2.7% Boost
> January 9: Smaller Makers of Steel Pipe Indicate They May Follow JL's Lead
> January 10: White House Reacts Mildly to Price Rises
> January 11: Republic and Pittsburgh Steel to Raise Prices 2.7%
> January 12: Steel Pipe Prices Raised by Four More Firms

The pricing minuet described by these headlines was carefully orchestrated with parts for both public and private partners. But the dance was a minuet, not a wild fandango.

And one more example: In the period before 1960, the U.S. motorcycle industry was dominated by U.S. and British firms.[3] By the mid-1970s, Honda—a Japanese manufacturer—dominated the U.S. market, and Yamaha and Suzuki had sizeable shares as well. In large measure, the Japanese firms gained share with an aggressive pricing strategy: In 1970, Japanese bikes sold for an average of $250, while American bikes were priced in the $1000 range. The bikes differed in size and power as well, but it is clear that pricing policy was a central element in the Japanese strategy.

How do we explain these differences? Why did we find heavy use of price cutting in the photography area, but much less in the steel industry in the 1960s? Why did the Japanese motorcycle firms use aggressive price cutting, but not the American and British firms operating in what would appear to be the same environment? On a spectrum of industry behavior, one would surely place the 1960s steel industry on the cooperative end of the spectrum and Kodak and Polaroid on the rivalrous end. Did this reflect rational strategy on the part of the various firms? Or are we just observing random choices made by idiosyncratic managers? Again we can ask ourselves, When does it pay to rely heavily on prices as a competitive weapon and when are other strategies more useful?

The first factor one needs to consider in defining the role of prices in the overall strategy of a firm is the reaction of the market to price changes. Do price changes primarily cause movement in market shares, or does the total market expand and contract with the price changes? The price responsiveness of the market clearly varies from market to market. Products with high elasticities of demand are ones in which deviations from the current price level elicit large changes in quantity demanded. In these markets, cutting prices induces a large positive response from customers, and raising prices causes large-scale desertion. Generally speaking, these are products for which customers have discretionary use: Either there are many good substitutes for the product, or the function served by the item is nonessential. For example, the elasticity of demand for personal computers for home markets appears to be relatively high.[4] As prices have fallen in this market, volume has rapidly expanded as many people entered the market for the first time. Products characterized by inelastic demand are ones for which price cutting has only a small effect on increasing the market. The elasticity of demand for local telephone service is fairly low; reductions in telephone rates have only a modest effect on increasing the market. The same is also probably true in the telephone directory market described earlier.

> **Price cutting is a more effective strategic weapon for goods with elastic demands.**

In markets in which demand is elastic, a price cut will both expand that market and take share from one's rivals. In the personal computer market, for example, price cuts have been a prominent feature of the landscape. In the telephone directory market, price cuts have been used less often, even in the recent turbulent times.

The role of pricing strategy often changes over the life cycle of a product, in part as a result of changes in demand elasticities. In the case of many products, price competition increases in importance as the market matures. One reason is that, as markets mature, more substitutes for the product in question enter the market, and the demand elasticity facing the firm tends to increase. Hence the firm experiences more response to its own price changes in a mature market. Strategic managers who could once soft-pedal pricing will now find it occupies a more central position.

In large measure, the efficacy of a price cut depends on whether that cut is matched by your rivals. Price cuts that are matched elicit much smaller volume changes than unmatched cuts. One influence on the speed of matching is the information environment. Industries vary considerably in the extent to which the transaction prices of particular firms are known. If pricing is made public quickly, price cuts are also likely to be followed quickly and thus will be less effective in the battle for market share. The steel industry example given earlier is an apt one. On the other hand, if there are opportunities for secret dealing, the payoff to modest price shading can be substantial.

Good information about prices—for example, through the public posting of prices—reduces the effectiveness of a price-cutting strategy.

The production environment also influences the ability of a firm to match a given price cut. Technologies vary considerably in how flexible they are. If it is easy to expand or cut production, on average we will see less price movement than under inflexible production conditions. Under these conditions, firms can vary output in response to demand fluctuations and thus rely less on prices.

Flexibility in production, all else equal, diminishes price competition.

Excess capacity also plays a role. If a firm has considerable excess capacity it will be easy to accommodate any increased volume from a price cut. Excess capacity thus favors price cutting. Holding excess inventories can also favor price cutting for similar reasons.[5] Of course, in excess capacity situations, there are considerable financial pressures moving prices down as well.

Excess capacity and large inventories favor a price-cutting strategy.

Firms that are small relative to the market leader are generally more likely to find that price cutting is a viable strategy. There are several reasons for this. First of all, if you are small and cut prices, you can often gain large increases in market share without having much of an effect on the major firms in the industry. A large market gain for you is still a small loss for the market leader. Price cuts by small fringe firms often go unnoticed and unmatched. Thus the dominant firms in the industry are less likely to retaliate for any price cut. Moreover, small firms often are more flexible than large, and thus can often sustain more price movements—both up and down—than a large organization. Finally, in a sustained price war, the losses suffered as a result of price cuts are directly proportional to the volume of the firm. This suggests that dominant firms in an industry often prefer weapons other than prices in the market-share battle, while we often see smaller fringe firms putting most of the pressure on prices. This reaction is another factor in the telephone directory market in which the telephone companies are big players relative to new entrants into the market.

Price cutting is generally a more effective strategy for small competitors than for a dominant firm.

Price cutting also tends to be a more favorable strategy for new entrants into a market than for incumbent firms. First of all, new entrants tend to be small relative to incumbents, and we have already indicated the advantage of price cutting to smaller players. Then, too, lower prices can help introduce consumers to a new product, particularly products that need to be used to be appreciated.

Price cuts are also more likely to be successful if you have a cost advantage in the market. The larger your cost advantage, the more likely it is that you can sustain price cuts when your rivals are no longer able, assuming that both firms have reasonable access to capital markets. While holding a cost advantage is not a sufficient condition to make price cutting rational, it is a necessary condition. High cost firms are not generally successful in price wars.

Price cutting is a more effective strategy for firms with a cost advantage.

Firms with broad product lines face a more complex pricing decision. For a multiproduct firm, considering a price cut in one market requires that it consider the impact this will have on the rest of its markets, particularly in terms of its reputation. Suppose a firm competes against another firm in two markets. In market 1, the firm in question is a small player. In market 2, the firm is the dominant player. In market 1, the firm may wish to shade prices somewhat. However, the fact that it faces the same competitor in market 2 may prevent the firm from using aggressive pricing in market 1. The firm may be afraid that its rival will engage in a **cross parry**—retaliate for a price cut in market 1 by starting a price war in market 2. In industries like pharmaceuticals, airlines, or paper products, for example, in which firms typically compete against one another in many markets, these cross-market considerations may play a very large role. There are other effects as well that result from participation by firms in multiple markets.[6] If sellers meet in multiple markets, they have a chance, for example, to learn one another's style and to practice getting along. They also may be most symmetrically placed. As we suggested in Chapter 3, both considerations may encourage coordination among firms.

Multimarket contact reduces the value of a price-cutting strategy.

Table 15.2 summarizes the factors that favor the use of pricing as a competitive weapon. Some of these factors, like demand elasticity, pertain to product characteristics. Others, like the flexibility of production, cost characteristics, and the extent of excess capacity, involve characteristics of the production technology. Finally, some important factors that influence pricing involve the market: the openness of transactions, size of competitors, and scope of product line.

Let us now return to the several examples of markets described above and see if we can make any sense of the pricing patterns we observe using our taxonomy. The steel industry in the mid-1960s did not rely heavily on pricing as a competitive weapon.[7] The demand for steel is

Table 15.2   Factors that influence the use of pricing as a competitive weapon against current competitors

Favor price cuts as weapon	*Discourage price cuts*
Elastic demand	Inelastic demand
Inflexible production	Flexible production with low fixed costs
Cost advantage	No cost advantage
Excess capacity	Tight capacity
Small competitors	Large dominant players
New competitors	Long history in the market
Single-product market	Rivals interact in many markets
Transactions are closely guarded	Public posting of prices

relatively inelastic: Price cuts have little effect on expanding the market. Also, steel firms face one another in many different markets: The market discussed above involved steel tubes, but in the 1960s virtually all of the same players faced one another in the can market, the auto market, and so on. Moreover, the steel firms differed substantially in the market shares they had in each market. So opportunities for cross parries abounded. While some firms in the industry appeared to have somewhat lower costs than others, these cost differences were not substantial. Interestingly enough, the industry leader, U.S. Steel, was not the cost leader. Finally, capacity utilization levels in the period were in the 85–90 percent level. All these factors discourage price cutting.

At present, pricing plays a more important role in the steel industry than it has historically, although it probably still does not occupy center stage as it does in some industries. Overall market demand is probably still fairly inelastic, although the availability of plastics and other materials has had an influence. New firms have entered the industry. Imports were 6–7 percent of the U.S. market in the 1960s; current levels are between 15 and 20 percent. Moreover, these new entrants appear to have a major cost advantage over domestic firms. Finally, capacity utilization levels have dropped considerably. All of these forces have led to more pricing competition in the market than was seen previously.

The instant camera market is rather different. Kodak was a new entrant in the market during the period in question. As we suggested, new entrants often find price cutting attractive as a way to induce trial use by consumers. Thus Kodak's strategy was understandable. Other forces were at work as well. The demand elasticity for cameras in general, and instant cameras in particular, was considerably higher than that of steel: Instant cameras are clearly a discretionary item. Thus price cuts could be expected to expand the market. Polaroid and Kodak did not compete with one another in other markets, thus ruling out cross-parry possibilities. Finally, there was evidence that both firms had considerable excess capacity in their markets, which also put pressure on prices. While the evidence is limited, there is a suggestion as well that Polaroid's long experience in the market gave it a cost advantage over Kodak. This might have led Polaroid to counter Kodak's low price with a cut of its own.

Finally, we return to the motorcycle industry. Before the Japanese entered the U.S. market, the motorcycle market was relatively small and characterized by high-commitment, relatively price-insensitive buyers. The Japanese tapped a new market, in which price elasticity was considerably higher. Honda had a cost advantage over traditional producers, an advantage developed in part as a result of the learning curve and scale economies effects of its large domestic market. The maturity of that domestic market had left the Japanese with an excess capacity problem. At the onset of its efforts, Honda was a small new player in the U.S. market. And, last, opportunities for cross-product parries were minimal. In the industry developed by the Japanese, and given their **comparative advantage,** price cutting was a logical strategy, in large part because they did not expect the United States and Britain to follow. In this industry, price cutting was a viable strategy for one group in the market.

We have thus far considered the kinds of forces that influence the viability of pricing as a weapon against current competitors. But the profitability of a market may also depend on the rate of entry into that market of new competitors. In what way might pricing policy influence this entry rate?

Complication 2: The Effect of Prices on New Entry

Let us return for a moment to our example of the pricing of poison ivy lotion. At a price of $1.75, with costs of $.45 per bottle, the innovator in the market would be earning quite substantial profits, and existing calamine lotion producers might cut prices to compete. But something else might happen in this market, for high profits might be expected to attract new entrants into the market. If other firms enter the market and increase the total supply of lotion, the price will fall. And so will margins. What can we do? In Chapter 4 we indicated that a potential entrant's expectations about future prices play a central role in influencing entry. Here we ask how incumbents can use pricing strategy to influence those expectations. Is there anything that can be done with *pricing strategy* to thwart this new entry and protect existing margins? Or is it better to rely on other weapons to protect a market position? (In all of this, we want to remember that new entrants into a market will have limited information about that market, and part of our strategy may be to try to use their uncertainty against them.)

Let us expand our earlier example a bit. Suppose the firm which invented the lotion has no particular advantage in its production. There are no scale effects and no learning-curve effects. The original price of the product was $1.75, as compared to costs of $.45. In the normal course of events, new firms would be expected to enter the industry as soon as the high margins were recognized and capacity could be installed. In anticipation of entry, an incumbent might try a **limit-pricing strategy.** Under a limit-pricing strategy the incumbent firm holds down prices in order to discourage new entry.[8] Rather than charge $1.75, which maximizes short-run profits but encourages entry, the firm might price in such a way that new entrants will be less attracted to the market.

Limit pricing involves restraint on current prices. Another possibility is to charge high prices now, but dramatically cut those prices whenever a new entrant appears. This strategy relies on the **reputation effect** that comes with aggressive pricing behavior by setting low prices.

A third possibility for the firm facing potential entry is simply to charge short-run maximizing prices now and adapt to the entry if it occurs. Each of these three strategies involves some expenditure of resources. The right strategy will depend on the circumstances in the market in ways we will now explore.

Limit Pricing

As we suggested in Chapters 3 and 4, expectations play a central role in the entry decision. Whenever a firm thinks about entering a new market, it is really less interested in the current price in that market than in what the price path will look like once entry is accomplished. Sometimes current market price is a good forecast of future price, if the new entrant is adding only a small capacity to the market, if current market participants are not retaliatory, and if demand and cost conditions are stable. In other cases, a new entrant must engage in a good bit of speculation, both informed and not, about what future prices might be. *One* of the ingredients in this speculation is an assessment of what the dominant firm is likely to do, an assessment that will depend on the new entrant's guess as to the costs of the incumbent and the reputation of the incumbent.

Decisions as to whether or not to enter a new market are predicated on forecasts of future prices in that market.

How does a limit-pricing strategy fit into this view of the entry process? A current low price will not necessarily discourage entry since it is *future* prices that are of concern. In order to discourage entry, the incumbent wishes to convince potential entrants that future prices will be low. One way to do this is to convince those rivals that the incumbent has low costs. By convincing entrants of its cost advantage, the incumbent will set itself up as an advantaged rival. No firm wants to compete against a rival who has a big cost advantage, since that cost advantage translates into the power to charge low future prices. One way to convince a rival of your own low costs is to charge a relatively low price. Thus limit pricing becomes a sensible strategy for incumbent firms to convey misleading information to potential entrants.[9]

Adopting a limit price can signal to potential entrants that the incumbent has lower costs than it actually does. This misleading signal will lead to forecasts of low future prices.

If the potential entrant believes the incumbent's costs are lower than its own costs, that entrant will be loathe to enter this market. In this way, the limit-pricing strategy can deter entry. Note that this interpretation highlights the value of secrecy about costs to a firm. It is only when costs are unknown that limit pricing emerges as a viable strategy.

In this context, it is interesting to speculate on the Yellow Pages example raised earlier. In that example, we asked whether local telephone companies should use low prices to discourage entry. But in telephone markets, which have been regulated for many decades, information about production costs—including directory production costs—is widely known. For this reason, limit pricing is probably not a good strategy in the directory market. Similarly, in our hypothetical example of a lotion producer, if the technology is as simple as portrayed, the market will probably have a good sense of costs. In this case as well, limit pricing is not likely to be effective.

Another consideration in deciding the viability of a limit-pricing strategy is the cost of providing the misleading signal to potential entrants. With a limit-pricing strategy, the incumbent has prevented entry only by charging lower prices than the market could bear. The cost of this strategy is thus the foregone profits associated with that lower price. And the size of the foregone profits will depend on the cost structure of the incumbent, as well as on the elasticity of demand facing the firm. If, for example, the incumbent's costs were in fact higher than those of the potential entrant, the profit-loss penalty from convincing the potential entrant that the incumbent's costs were lower would be substantial. If the incumbent's costs really are lower, but only by a little, limit pricing may be a way to convince potential entrants that the cost gap is considerably larger than it is, with only modest profit losses. Finally, if the incumbent's costs really are substantially lower than that of the potential entrant, limit pricing is unnecessary: Charging the market price that corresponds to those low costs will adequately convince potential entrants of the folly of entry.

Limit pricing is most effective as an entry deterrent when the cost advantage of the incumbent is moderate.

An additional factor in deciding whether or not limit pricing is a good strategy for dealing with an entry threat is how long entry would take to occur if prices were set at the monopoly level. If building production and/or distribution networks to compete requires a considerable period, then the dominant firm may find that, although its high prices do indeed ensure entry, this entry is so slow that it is financially better off earning high margins now and suffering the perils of competition in some distant future than moderating current prices. On the other hand, if the entry time is short, limit pricing will be more attractive. When entry time is very short, the threat of entry can hold prices down even in highly concentrated markets. These markets are known as **contestable markets.**[10]

Rapid potential entry favors limit-pricing strategies.

In this context, consider the situation faced by Upjohn several years ago when its patent on Motrin expired. In the early 1980s, Upjohn's largest selling product was Motrin, the brand name of ibuprofen, a nonsteroidal anti-inflammitant used to combat arthritis. Motrin was at that time available only by prescription and was protected by a patent. It accounted for about 10 percent of the firm's sales and nearly one-third of its profits. (This is by no means a unique situation. In the pharmaceutical industry, only 10 percent of the drugs that reach the clinical testing stage eventually reach the market. Drugs that succeed pay for the research on the many that fail.)

Prior to 1985, Upjohn was largely alone in providing ibuprofen, but in pricing Motrin Upjohn nevertheless faced some constraints: Aspirin and Tylenol are, for example, partial substitutes for ibuprofen. However, direct entry into Upjohn's market was not possible in the early years, for Motrin (unlike the poison-ivy lotion) was protected by effective patents. In the mid-1980s, the situation changed in two vital ways: The patent on Motrin expired, and new entry by imitative firms, *which did not have to face the R&D costs of Upjohn*, was imminent. And the Federal Drug Administration approved a version of ibuprofen for sale over the counter. Two of the barriers which had protected Upjohn's product were dismantled simultaneously. At this point, Upjohn faced the questions we asked in the lotion case. How do they fight new entry? In particular, should Upjohn use pricing to protect against entry?

Upjohn is a family-owned company with sales of $2.5 billion. Among the top 17 firms in the industry, Upjohn ranks number 12 in sales. The pharmaceutical industry has a large number of players, many of whom are larger than Upjohn. Moreover, for most drugs—including Motrin—there are few economies of scale or learning-curve effects in production. In the production of ibuprofen, Upjohn would not have an appreciable cost advantage over new entrants, despite its long dominance of the market. Moreover, information in this industry is sufficiently good that trying to convince potential entrants of a cost advantage would be very difficult. In this situation, limit pricing would not likely be an effective way to deter entry. And, in fact, limit pricing does not appear to have been the strategy followed by Upjohn. Of course, Upjohn prices did fall as new entry occurred and market pressures began to operate. But Upjohn's prices moved with the market; the firm did not try to use prices to keep out entry. And, indeed, as we indicated this would have been a quixotic venture.

Implementing a limit-pricing strategy can create interesting management issues in a complex organization. In the overall strategic management of an organization, cash-flow considerations at times become paramount. Clearly there are times when an organization needs the cash flow from a product, even if, when viewed as a single-product problem, limit pricing would be preferable. At other times, limit pricing may serve to build an area of the company at the expense of one product in that area. Limit pricing leads to management choices involving current versus future payoffs. In choosing to follow a limit-pricing strategy, a firm is opting to forego some current profits in favor of a longer time stream of protected profits. From the shareholder's perspective, one would want to consider the relative net present value of the two options. In other words, once we take account of the different time paths of profits associated with the two strategies, and fully account for the time value of money, which strategy yields higher net returns? As we suggested earlier, however, managerial objectives may not always perfectly coincide with those of the stockholder. We may have goal problems of the sort discussed in Chapter 8. In the current context, for example, a managerial-compensation plan tied to sales growth may encourage management to follow a limit-pricing scheme even when this strategy is overly expensive from a profit perspective. On the other hand, a compensation scheme tied to short-term earnings growth, at the expense of long-run profitability, may bias management against limit-pricing strategies.

Differences in managerial and stockholder objectives may affect the attractiveness of a limit-pricing strategy.

Limit pricing works as a strategy for deterring entry primarily by interfering with the information a potential entrant may have about incumbent firms—and thus affecting the forecasts entrants make of likely post-entry prices. We will see that information plays an important role in the second of our possible strategies as well, the strategy of cutting prices once entry has occurred.

Post-entry Price Cutting To Build Reputation

In forecasting what market prices will look like after entry, the potential entrant will use the information it has on costs of incumbent firms. We have already seen how limit-pricing strategies can distort this information. But the potential entrant will also have to make an assessment of how aggressive the incumbent will be if faced with entry. Will the incumbent cut prices dramatically, perhaps close to costs, as a way to protect its market share? Or is it more likely that the incumbent will accommodate the new entrant and the price-cost ratios will remain more or less stable? In this area, the institutional context, particularly antitrust laws, is especially pertinent, since many of the choices of incumbents are conditioned by those laws. In the discussion which follows we will lay out the strategic issues, without reference to the legal standing of various strategies. Legal issues will be touched on later in the chapter.

Post-entry price forecasts will be predicated on judgments as to the aggressiveness of incumbent firms.

Let us return for a moment to the Standard Oil case with which we began this chapter. In this early application of the Sherman Antitrust Law, the government argued (successfully) that Standard Oil had engaged in a practice of cutting prices in selected markets in order to drive out competitors. Once competitors were driven out—or actually bought out by Standard Oil—prices again were raised. More recent economists have argued that selective post-entry price cutting of this sort would not have been a profit-maximizing strategy for Standard Oil, and that draconian price cutting on entry is not generally a profitable strategy.[11] Post-entry price cutting is typically quite expensive for the high-volume incumbent, much more expensive than it is for the small competitor. Moreover, once one entrant is chased out, and prices are raised, new entrants will enter. The incumbent firm will find itself in an endless cycle of price-cutting adventures. Foreseeing this, incumbents will avoid price cuts.

But will new entry occur if powerful incumbents like Standard Oil cut prices and eliminate old competitors? If potential entrants observe past aggressive behavior on the part of incumbents, they might well expect future aggression. And if the entrant expects the dominant firm to adopt an aggressive position on prices in the face of entry, then entry will be less likely, particularly if exit costs are high. For under these conditions, making an entry mistake will be expensive.

Threats to cut prices will be most effective when exit costs are high.

From the point of view of the firm already in the industry, one's ability to influence the expectations of one's potential rivals is critical. Ideally, a firm would like to convince rivals as cheaply as possible that it will be a tough competitor. But how does it do so? As suggested above, one way to try to convince entrants that the dominant firm will aggressively defend market share is to cut prices whenever a new competitor arises.[12] The lost profits associated with such price cuts will represent an *investment* in developing a reputation for the incumbent. As such, the price-cutting strategy may be a good one, even if it is not profitable in the short run.[13]

Price cutting in one market may reduce entry elsewhere by creating a reputation for aggression.

We have seen how the incumbent can affect the new entrant's assessment of its likely response. Another uncertainty facing the new entrant is the actual consumer response to the product. New entry typically proceeds either with some product differentiation or a price cut. But consumer responses to these changes—the price or product elasticity—are unknown when the new entrant begins operations. Information about these matters is provided by the actual response of consumers in test markets and in final markets. But established firms can take unobservable actions that distort the information received by the new entrant. Secret price cutting and localized couponing are two examples. This strategy by incumbents of trying to interfere with information received by new entrants in entering a market has been called **signal jamming.**[14]

> **Incumbents may use unobserved pricing and marketing techniques to interfere with the marketing information generated by the new entrant in its market introduction.**

Using price cutting to develop a reputation for aggression or to distort the information received by the new entrant can involve a relatively large investment. A less expensive way to deter entry may be to keep current prices high, but to develop a threat strategy to convince potential rivals that, should they enter, prices will fall. If the threat strategy works well, the incumbent may never need to carry it through.

Of course, not all threats work because not all threats are believed. In order for threats to deter entry, they must be credible. In general, a credible threat is one which, if carried out, would generate reasonable profits for the threatening firm—assuming that the firm is a rational competitor.

We can use a payoff matrix to illustrate the principle of credibility. Suppose the payoff matrix associated with the potential entry of firm 2 into firm 1's market is configured as in Figure 15.2. Firm 1's strategic choices involving pricing are given in the columns, and firm 2's entry choice is shown in rows. Each box in the matrix has the payoff of the strategy pair to each of the two firms, with 1's payoff in the upper right and 2's in the lower left.

Thus, if firm 1 cuts price, it will earn $80 if firm 2 does not enter and $60 if it does. If firm 1, on the other hand, holds its price level, it will earn $120 without entry and $70 with entry.

Firm 1 can, of course, threaten that, if firm 2 enters, it will cut prices. Indeed, firm 1 might even cut its current prices, suffering a substantial profit loss ($120 to $80) as a way to deter entry. But if firm 2 is aware of

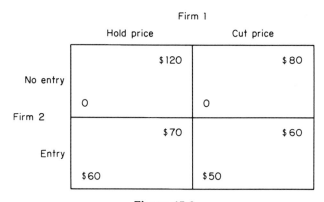

Figure 15.2

the costs of the incumbent and understands the way in which the payoffs are configured, then neither the entry threat nor the limit price will be successful as an entrant deterrent. In this example, it is *not credible* that firm 1 would choose a price-cutting strategy once entry occurs. If entry does occur, firm 1 earns higher profits ($70 vs. $60) by maintaining its prices not by cutting them. Without contrary information, firm 2 will expect firm 1 to behave so as to maximize its profits in the market in question. In this market, firm 2 will enter with an expectation that prices will remain high because holding prices is a dominant strategy for firm 1.

If an incumbent firm is in the position outlined above, in which maintaining prices is known to be the dominant strategy, the incumbent firm may still be able to deter entry. In particular, the incumbent firm needs to find a way to make a seemingly irrational move look credible. If the firm can figure out a way to do this, it may never in fact have to take the irrational move.

A credible threat to cut prices may deter entry.

In this context, there are a variety of ways to make threats credible, but they all share the core idea that one makes a threat credible by, in one way or another, "tying one's hands" vis-à-vis one's future action.[15] If you threaten an action that will *not* be profitable, for that threat to be credible you must somehow "guarantee" that you will follow through.

One way to establish credibility in price response is to undertake investments that have the effect of changing your payoff matrix. One form of investment which has been the target of considerable work along these lines has been the use of excess capacity as an entry deterrent.[16] Carrying excess capacity may deter entry if potential rivals believe incumbents will use all capacity if threatened. Holding excess inventories may have a similar effect.[17]

It is easy to construct an example of this effect. Suppose the firm begins with the earlier payoff matrix, in which price cutting was not a credible threat. Now the firm builds an extra plant, leaving it with some additional excess capacity relative to the current market. We might find, as a result, that the new matrix looks like Figure 15.3.

By building excess capacity, firm 1 has reduced the earnings it can expect with either strategy it pursues. For example, if no entry occurs and firm 1 maintains current price levels it will earn $100 as contrasted to the $120 specified in Figure 15.2. Thus holding excess capacity has a real cost for the firm. But the excess capacity also affects the *relative* payoff to various strategies. Now, cutting prices in response to entry *is* a credible response for firm 1 to make since it would earn more by cutting prices ($55) than by maintaining them ($45). We should remember that creating credibility has not been costless. In this hypothetical example, the firm reduces its profits in the no-entry case from $120 to $100 by building the excess capacity. Given how costly competition is for firm 1, building this excess capacity may nevertheless be an attractive strategy.

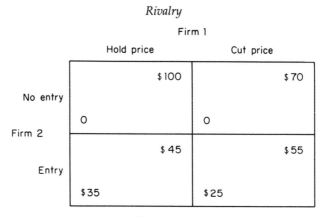

Figure 15.3

Entry deterrence may involve considerable expenditure of resources, and the dynamics of markets may further complicate matters. New firms are attracted to industries based on expectations of further profit. To the extent that current firms take actions that raise entry barriers to the industry, they are effectively increasing post-entry profits. These actions thus raise both the prize from successful entry and the risks of trying such entry. The overall effect of attempts at entry deterrence is thus ambiguous.[18]

Figure 15.4 summarizes the factors that influence the strategic choice of an entry-deterring mechanism. Of course, using any of these strategies involves spending some resources. Holding excess capacity and/or inventories or building a reputation for price cutting are all expensive ways to convince a potential rival of price-cutting intentions. Limit pricing is also expensive in terms of foregone profits. In many markets it will turn out

Limit pricing is most effective if:	1. Information about production and distribution costs is poor
	2. The true advantage of the incumbent is moderate
	3. Other barriers to entry are low
	4. The organization has a long horizon
A threat to cut price if entry occurs is most credible when:	1. Information, especially on the demand side, is poor
	2. The incumbent operates in many markets
	3. The incumbent is not substantially larger than its rival
	4. The incumbent has excess capacity and/or excess inventories

A threat to cut prices post entry is most <u>effective</u> at deterring entry when the cost of exiting a market is high.

Figure 15.4   Entry-deterring strategies

that the best long-run policy for the organization is simply to accommodate the new entrant. New entrants can help revitalize an industry, bringing in new product and process ideas and stimulating existing firms. In growing markets in particular, accommodation is often the best strategy.

Antitrust Issues Involving Pricing

In Chapter 3, I briefly reviewed the antitrust rules on coordination among firms, particularly in the pricing area. In this chapter we have been looking at the use of pricing as a competitive weapon, both against new entrants and against other firms already in the industry. Behavior in this area is also limited by the antitrust laws. Laws governing strategic behavior by firms are complex and change over time. All I hope to provide here and elsewhere in this text is an indication of the areas in which antitrust law and competitive strategy may clash.

The central statute governing the use of prices to affect rivals is the Sherman Act of 1890. The second section of the Sherman Act governs a firm's independent price-setting behavior (as well as other forms of behavior). Section 2 reads:

> Every person who shall monopolize, or attempt to monopolize . . . any part of the trade or commerce among the several states . . . shall be deemed guilty of a misdemeanor.

As we can see, this statute is very broad, and so we rely on case law for specific interpretations. The courts have applied a so-called rule of reason in using Section 2 of the Sherman Act. In order to prove attempts to monopolize, the court must prove both that there is a monopoly *and* that the firm engaged in overt acts to establish and maintain that monopoly position. The fact of monopoly is not an offense, only the pursuit of such monopoly. The Standard Oil case referred to earlier was litigated under Section 2 of the Sherman Act.

From the perspective of the pricing discussion in this chapter, the central antitrust concern of the firm from Section 2 of the Sherman Act is the issue of **predatory pricing.** Predation or predatory pricing is defined as deliberate aggression on the part of a firm against rivals, using prices or other business practices that would not be profit maximizing unless they had the effect of driving the affected rivals out of business. The spirit of this prohibition is clear. On the other hand, it has not been an easy one to enforce, for it is difficult to discern the intent of particular actions. Is a price cut simply a way to win new business, or is it a deliberate attempt to drive out a rival and establish monopoly? It is rarely easy to tell the difference.

In 1975, Areeda and Turner proposed a concrete rule for identifying predatory pricing.[19] The A-T rule is based on a simple principle of economics: A firm will never price below *average variable cost* if it seeks to maximize short-run profits. At times, a firm will operate with prices below average total costs: In periods of excess capacity, as long as incremental units are contributing to overhead it makes sense to produce them. But by selling at a price *less* than average variable cost, the firm loses incremental dollars for each unit produced. This, according to Areeda-Turner, can be sensible only if the firm views those prices as helping to maintain its monopoly position. But this is precisely what the Sherman Act seeks to avoid. Thus the A-T standard is that all prices below average variable costs are deemed predatory. In the last decade, the Areeda-Turner (A-T) rule has been applied numerous times in litigation, although it does ignore the possible benefits to firms and customers of below-cost pricing to build up firm experience.[20]

The U.S. antitrust laws are designed to try to create conditions that will lead to more competitive pricing patterns. As such, the primary targets of investigations are large firms with dominant market positions for it is these firms that are most likely to be able to garner long-lived market power through strategic moves. Thus dominant firms need to be somewhat more careful of the antitrust implications of their strategies than do smaller, less powerful firms. All those involved in setting organizational strategy need to be aware of possible conflict between the law and particular strategic initiatives.

16

Competitive Research and Development and Innovation

In the U.S. economy today, a considerable amount of growth is generated by firms in the high-technology area. Indeed, some have argued that developing and fostering innovation remains our nation's prime area of **comparative advantage.** Approximately 2 percent of the U.S. Gross National Product goes into research and development. For the average firm, R&D to sales ratios have been in the 3 percent range.[1] In some industries, expenditures on research and development are substantially heavier than this. In the cellular phone and microprocessor markets, for example, R&D can amount to 25–30 percent of firm sales.[2] In these markets, a fundamental managerial goal must be the fostering of an environment supportive of innovation. Moreover, if we think of strategic planning as a way to help an organization deal with rapid changes in its environment, we can see that in a high-technology organization planning will be especially important.

Creative management of technology is essential not only to the survival of individual firms in our economy, but also to its overall health. Hayes and Abernathy, in a critique of American management practices, argue that cutbacks in research and development have endangered America's economic position vis-à-vis its competitors abroad.[3] The short-run strategy of sacrificing R&D to cost-cutting efforts followed by a number of firms has had unfortunate effects at all levels. Indeed, in many markets, the United States is losing its technological lead, in part because of such short-sightedness. In this chapter, we apply the principles learned earlier in the text to the complex task of developing strategy in a rapidly changing technological environment.

The Strategic Question

The central strategic question facing an organization in a high-technology environment is, How rapid should the adoption and promotion of inno-

vations be? Should the organization invest resources to become the research leader in a market, or should it adopt a more conservative strategy? The answer to this question has implications across the firm: It helps
to determine the optimal level of research expenditures; it influences the
form of organizational structure which will be most suitable; it may even
influence management compensation. But what factors should guide the
firm in deciding its research strategy?

Research and development decisions involve more uncertainty than
many of the other strategic decisions of the firm, in part because the pay-
back period for a research expenditure is longer, say, than the payback
for a marketing program. The very fact that it takes longer to find out the
results of a research project, and during that period many other things
happen in the industry and economy, means that, from the perspective
of management, investments in research are risky.

**Strategic choices in the area of research and development involve substan-
tial uncertainty.**

An R&D decision involves three at least partially separable sources of
uncertainty. First, there is *technical uncertainty:* the answer to the question,
Can I make it at a reasonable cost in a reasonable time? Factors inside and
outside of the firm govern this aspect of the decision, with research people likely to provide important input. But technical uncertainty is only
one of our strategic concerns. There is also a *market uncertainty.* We can
think of this as the answer to the question, Will anyone want our product
enough to pay a reasonable price for it? Marketing people play a role in
helping to answer this question. Finally, there is *competitive uncertainty:*
the answer to the question, Can other firms make it cheaper and better?
To answer this, the planning department's competitor analysis will be of
central importance. As we can already see, developing a strategy for a
firm in a research-oriented environment will require the interaction of a
variety of people within the organization.

We can model the components of these questions about innovation
using a decision tree, as in Figure 16.1. This will allow us to focus our
discussion and structure the elements of a strategic-planning initiative.

The first question senior management needs to address is fundamentally a scientific one: Is this an industry segment in which there appear to
be large technological opportunities?[4] Technological opportunity is a measure of the base of innovation within an area. In part, technological opportunities arise from research in the basic scientific arenas. Most basic
research in the United States occurs in universities. The role of industrial
labs has been primarily to take those very basic scientific advances, further develop them, and finally commercialize them.[5] This suggests that
the opportunities available to industry will depend in part on the activities of the academy. The academy is, in turn, funded largely by the government, and this funding helps to determine its direction. To a consid-

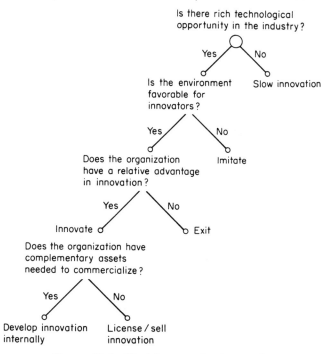

Figure 16.1   Decision tree for innovation

erable extent, then, the richness of technological opportunities facing a firm is exogenous to the firm, or outside its immediate control.

If we look at recent scientific history, we can see striking differences in the path of technological development across fields. In the immediate postwar period, chemistry and engineering were important sources of new technology. Later, perhaps beginning in the 1950s, electronics became more central. In the 1970s, biology assumed a larger role in stimulating industrial excitement and investment. Indeed, biological commercial innovation is still sufficiently new that industries whose technologies rest on biology seem to be closely tied to universities in their research.[6] Currently, there are hints that physics may be emerging as a new major source of a commercial technological spurt. The central question we ask in the first branching of our tree, then, is: Are we in an industry likely to feel the repercussions of a major new technical advance? There is good evidence that firms increase their research expenditures in response to improvements in technological opportunities, and this is a wise strategic move.[7]

A strategy that emphasizes innovation is favored in environments with fertile technological opportunities.

In the tree in Figure 16.1, I have suggested a yes or no answer to the question about technological opportunity in order to simplify the problem. In fact, technological opportunity in a market is a more subtle matter of degree. Ansoff, for example, characterizes industries as either low-technology industries, in which original technology is used throughout the demand cycle; medium-technology industries in which basic technology is constant, but there are some product changes; or high-technology industries, in which substantial technological change occurs.[8] Classifying the degree of opportunity in one's industry may not always be easy. Indeed, as we suggested in Chapter 7, a central task of entrepreneurship is to see new opportunities early. Nevertheless, having a sense for the source and extent of technological opportunities in one's industry is quite important as a first management task.

Once we get beyond the first branch of the tree, economy and market forces within the industry itself begin to play a larger role. If there is an opportunity for technological advance in an industry, the next question is, Is the environment favorable to innovators? Here, both market and competitive uncertainty play a role. In some industries in which there is rapid technological progress, firms that innovate thrive. In other industries, firms that invest heavily in research and development find themselves unable to recoup that investment due to the activities of imitative firms. In other industries, there is what appears to be uncontrolled product innovation, in which new products appear willy-nilly, well before firms can realize an investment on earlier products.[9]

The extent to which an environment favors innovators versus imitators will depend in part on the market place. How much, for example, do consumers value being first in the market? Will they develop brand loyalty to a first mover or wait for cheap imitations to crop up? Patents, labor practices, even antitrust laws play a role in the competitive environment. (We will discuss the environment for innovation at greater length below.)

If technological opportunity is rich, and the environment is favorable to innovation, then the potential innovator can advance to the third question on the tree: Does the firm itself have a relative advantage in developing innovations? This is essentially a matter of competitive position. As we indicated at length in Chapter 7, firms do well financially when they outperform their rivals. If a firm is in an environment with rich opportunities, that favor innovators, and if it does not itself have any specific assets that enable it to innovate, then that firm should not be in this part of the business. In this case, the *fit* between the assets and abilities of the firm and its environment is not good. We discuss below some of the literature on the management requirements for success in innovation.

There is one final branch to our tree. Does the firm have the management skills and assets needed to commercialize an innovation? Some firms are quite good at developing new ideas, but lack the resources to implement them. In this case, the firm may wish to sell its innovations or to license their use. We discuss this possibility later in the chapter.

Is the Environment Favorable to Innovators?

In most high-technology industries, production costs are a relatively small fraction of the total costs of the operation. The software industry is perhaps the most striking example. Macro, Inc., is a small company that sells a forecasting model of the U.S. economy for use on a personal computer. The model is provided to customers on several diskettes. To produce and mail out those diskettes and supporting literature requires costs on the order of $10 per customer. But the price of the final product is several thousand dollars. Marketing costs absorb part of the difference. But the bulk of the price-cost margin is used to defray the original investment costs of the project. For this firm, considerable costly investment in the product preceded the production period. A similar cost structure exists for most current producers of computer software. Production costs are small relative to development costs. But this cost structure has substantial strategic implications. For, unless firms have some prospect of earning high prices relative to production and distribution costs after production begins, they will have little financial incentive to invest in research in the first place. High margins are the only way to recover the fixed development costs.

> **We define an environment as favorable to innovation if price-cost margins are protected for at least some reasonable period after commercialization of the innovation.**

Speed of Diffusion

One ingredient in determining how favorable the environment is, is how fast *diffusion* of an innovation occurs once the innovation is introduced. The evidence suggests that on average information about a firm's decision to develop a new product or process is in the hands of at least some of its rivals within 12 to 18 months.[10] In early 1991, Compaq, one of the two largest personal computer manufacturers, introduced a product using the new Intel 486sx microprocessor. AST and Dell, two clone computer companies, announced that their new machines, with the same capabilities, would be on the market by early spring. In this environment of rapid diffusion, Compaq is having considerable difficulty sustaining its price premium. If imitation is inexpensive and not prohibited by law, as soon as a new product appears, other firms can copy it and drive the price down, thus quickly eliminating any return to the innovator. Pirating of new software programs and copycat versions of popular programs have rapidly driven down prices and profit margins in the software industry, for example.

The diffusion of ideas about technology shapes the industrial structure. But the rate of diffusion differs dramatically across industries. In the software industry as a whole, diffusion appears to be high, as it is in the computer market generally. In other industries, diffusion is much slower. One estimate is that while 60 percent of the capacity in the beer industry had converted to cans over bottles within one year of that innovation, it took 11 years for a similar adoption of diesel locomotives.[11] Clearly in the latter case, the innovator had a much longer time to amortize the research investment than in the former case.

The diffusion rate depends in part on the underlying value of the innovation: Profitable ideas are copied faster than marginal ones.[12] Given the underlying riskiness of innovations, those requiring relatively small amounts of specific investments will diffuse faster than innovations requiring large-scale specialized investments.[13] Innovations requiring concomitant changes in other institutions of the organization in order to be implemented will similarly be slower to catch on than more self-contained innovations. For example, innovations in equipment that require major changes in labor practices will move relatively slowly through a market. Many flexible production methods have been slowed down by the need for supporting labor changes.

Diffusion of new ideas is higher for profitable ideas requiring low levels of specific capital.

Another set of factors that influences the diffusion rate for an innovation is the technical character of the innovation itself. As we indicated in Chapter 7, innovations that are technologically "complex" in the sense that they are hard to capture in a simple formula, set of drawings, or slogan will be hard to copy even if there are no institutional barriers to diffusion.[14] Diffusion here is impeded by lack of observability. Other innovations may be easy enough to observe, but very hard to commercialize. This, too, may serve as a diffusion barrier.[15] There is some reason to believe that in the early life of a new technology, diffusion rates may be slower precisely because the innovation can less easily fit into the conventional ideas and styles of potentially imitative firms in the industry. For the same reason, process-development decisions by firms tend to leak out more slowly to their rivals than new-product decisions.[16]

Technologically complex, hard-to-articulate innovations favor innovators over imitators.

The value of some innovations depends on the size of the network over which the innovation is adopted. Telephone systems are the classic example here. For any individual consumer, the benefit of having a telephone increases with the number of phones in service. Thus there is a push on the demand side for more adoptions of an innovation as the size of the existing network increases. The same effect has been found for automated teller machines (ATMs) in the retail banking industry. For depositors, the value of an ATM system depends on the number of locations the network includes. As a result, banks with a large number of sites will earn more from adopting the ATM innovation than will banks with smaller networks. Saloner and Shepard find, for example, that in the period 1971–79, banks with more than fifteen branches had a probability of adopting an ATM of .545, while banks with only two branches had a probability over the same period of only .157. Clearly, in this case, network size is very important.[17]

For some innovations, network size has an important effect on profitability.

We can see that the particulars of an innovation influence how fast it will enter the mainstream in a market. But if we hold constant the particulars of the innovation, there are a number of features of the environment itself that help to determine diffusion rates.

Perhaps the most important environmental determinant of the speed of diffusion is the *patent rule*. Indeed, patents were expressly designed to reduce the rate of diffusion of new ideas so as to permit a return to the original inventive activity. In the United States, patent protection dates from colonial times and has been codified in the law since the late eighteenth century. In fact, the Constitution of the United States authorized patents in order "to promote the progress of science and useful arts, by securing for limited times to authors and inventors the exclusive right to their respective writings and discoveries."[18]

Patents create temporary monopolies, which result in higher than competitive prices to consumers, but also stimulate invention of new exciting products and cost-saving new processes. The right trade-off between the two objectives of encouraging the development of innovations versus encouraging the spread of those new ideas, once generated, continues to be debated. At present, for example, standard U.S. patent protection extends for 17 years; in 1984, however, patent life in the pharmaceutical industry was increased for up to five years to adjust for losses due to regulatory scrutiny of drugs.[19] The intent of this legislation was clearly to encourage further innovation in the pharmaceutical industry, and extending patent life was thought to be an important way of accomplishing this goal. In the computer software industry and the biotechnology industry, the 1990s have seen a series of Supreme Court decisions involving precisely what elements of a technology can be patented at all. Can new life forms be patented, for example? Can generic types of program improvements be patented (such as windows in computer programs), or must innovations be more narrow in scope? These are policy questions with enormous implications for the profitability of innovative firms inside these industries.

It is clear that a strong patent system will help protect innovators against potential imitators. The importance of patents for the earnings of a firm cannot be overemphasized. Empirical work clearly indicates that increases in the number of patents issued to a firm yield substantial increases in the market value of that firm.[20] But a strong patent system may also have the further effect of protecting a current innovator by allowing it to close off profitable opportunities for innovation by potential rivals through the device of pre-emptive patenting. **Pre-emptive patenting** is the patenting of an innovation by an existing firm with the express purpose of preventing the entry of a second firm into that industry. In some cases, a firm may patent a process or product and never put the patented item into commercial use; this is called a **sleeping patent.**

A large fraction of patents awarded are never put into commercial use. In the United States, Scherer has estimated patents in use to be 54 percent of the total.[21] In the United Kingdom, the use rate may be considerably lower.[22] Of course, some of the unused patents may simply be for products or processes that are not commercially viable. Some fraction of them, however, may be patents applied for in order to prevent their use by newcomers to a field, and deliberately not introduced into the market.

Pre-emptive patenting may serve to reduce entry into a market.

Consider the simple example of pre-emptive patenting depicted in Figure 16.2.[23] Products 1 and 2 are identical. The monopolist has two strategies available, as represented in the columns. If the monopolist produces product 1, it will earn profits of $100. The products are identical, so acquiring a patent on product 2 would not increase earnings from the market. As long as there are at least some development costs, the monopolist would never develop product 2, if it were in a protected market. Nevertheless, in an open market, the monopolist might patent product 2, since by doing so the entry of a rival into the market would be prevented. The two strategies available to the rival firm are given by the rows. Notice that, if entry occurs, the monopolist's profit will be reduced to $40. The benefit from pre-emption is thus $60. But the patent on product 2 is worth only $40 to the new entrant. In this case, we would expect the monopolist to patent product 2 as a pre-emptive move. Pre-emption is more valuable than the new entry.

Pre-emptive patenting may occur whenever products are related. A firm may wish to patent a product similar to its own to delay its entry

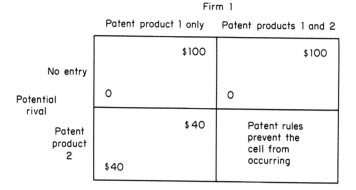

Figure 16.2   Original monopolist

into the market in order to prevent cannibalization of its original product. The higher the cross-elasticity of demand among products, the more valuable pre-emption will be.

In this example, the new rival has no advantage over the incumbent in developing the innovation. That is, either firm receives $40 from developing it. Thus the advantage to consumers of the new entry is strictly from the competitive pressure, and it is the loss of this competition that pre-emptive patenting causes. If a new rival had an advantage over the incumbent in developing the new product, we would probably see a patent transfer, for the original monopolist would earn more by sharing the rents with a more efficient rival than trying to develop it alone with less efficiency.[24]

In some countries, the anticompetitive effect of sleeping patents is lessened by compulsory licensing provisions in patent law. If the recipient of a patent does not use the patent innovation within a given time, licensing to other firms is required. The United States does not have such provisions.

We have seen that patents can be a powerful device for controlling entry into a market. In practice, however, it appears that the effectiveness of patents varies considerably across industries. In most chemical industries, including the drug industry, patents appear to be relatively effective in protecting an innovator against new entry. In many other industries, including highly research-oriented industries like computers, semiconductors, medical instruments, and aircraft, patents appear to be relatively ineffective.[25] In some cases, technology moves too quickly to be adequately protected by patents. The effectiveness of patents in particular areas also depends on the legal environment. In recent years, courts have been more liberal in protecting patentholders. Courts have also extended ideas of what products are patentable. In 1980, for example, the Supreme Court affirmed the right of firms to patent genetically altered life forms.

Under many circumstances, patents protect innovators against inroads made by rapacious rivals. But in other situations, patents may actually improve the position of imitators. In applying for a patent, an innovator must release some information about the new product or process—information that may be quite valuable to potential imitators. And, indeed, if there are rich opportunities for innovating around the patent, patent-application information may be disastrous from the perspective of the innovator.[26] Here innovators may prefer to avoid patents completely.

Patenting may reveal important information to rivals.

Value of a Head Start

Innovation gives a firm a head start on the market. We have already explored the importance of how much of a head start the innovator gets. But the value of any particular head start will also vary across markets.

In some markets a lead of one year may provide quite substantial incentives to innovate; in other markets, even five years is barely adequate. When it introduced the first ballpoint pen, Reynolds International Pen Co. earned backed its original investment a hundred times over in the 18 months it had a monopoly in this product.[27] In the pen market, the initial sales captured by the innovator was both large and lucrative. In other markets, product demand builds more slowly following an innovation, and entry may occur before the innovator earns back its investment.

The value of any head start of an innovative firm depends also on the underlying structure of the market in which it operates. Innovative gains may be preserved and enhanced by other first-mover advantages of the firm. For example, one factor that influences the value of a head start is the extent of learning-curve effects. If learning-curve effects are large enough, then the head start acquired by the innovator may permanently give an advantage to that innovator, in the sense that the innovator's costs will remain below potential rivals'. Similarly, if pioneering-brand advantages are important—in the sense that consumers are predisposed in favor of the innovator in the market place—then innovation can again create a more long-lived advantage. Consumers will tend to favor the original producer. Finally, if technological developments are connected—in the sense that innovating successfully today increases your chances of finding another good innovation tomorrow—an early innovation can pay off for a longer period.[28] Of course, previous innovations can also decrease the likelihood of future successes through the operation of a kind of complacency or "strategic myopia." Steven Jobs's early devotion to the Macintosh at Apple is an apt example of this.[29]

> To the extent that a market has other first-mover advantages, innovation can help a firm to exploit those advantages. Thus first-mover advantages on either the demand or supply side create a favorable climate for innovation.

The interaction between technological change and learning-curve effects is especially important. Learning-curve effects are important because they create an advantage for incumbent firms over potential entrants. If learning-curve effects are large, early entrants into an industry will have lower costs than potential rivals and these early movers will have an added incentive to gain market share to solidify that cost advantage. On the other hand, if diffusion rates are high and technological change uneven, learning will be either spread or made obsolete. Here it may pay to wait and enter an industry after early investments in technology have already been made. In some sense, we need to filter in information about the technology before we can appreciate the importance of learning-curve effects in a particular industry. In an interesting study of a broad range of chemical industries, Lieberman found that learning-curve effects at the firm level were almost entirely dissipated by rapid diffusion of technology.[30]

Learning-curve effects depend on the technological regime.

Innovative gains may be further cemented by the processes involved in the standardization of products. In many industries with rapid technological change, standardization is a common practice. In 1975, the National Bureau of Standards estimated that over 400 private organizations in the United States created standards. More than 20,000 standards have been produced by these organizations, a large number of which consist of firms within particular markets.[31] Thus firms themselves are creating the standards that govern entry into their industry. The Association of Home Appliance Manufacturers, for example, has promulgated several dozen standards applicable to home appliances. The standardization accomplished by these associations can formalize and extend any head start gained by an innovator.

Of course, not all standardization occurs through joint action. As many industries evolve, we see the emergence of a **dominant design**.[32] Once a dominant design emerges, other parts of the system often adjust to fit that design. At this point, competition focuses less on innovation and more on cost issues. It is clearly in a firm's interest to have its own design become dominant. Examples of the emergence of a dominant design without the intervention of government or industry standard-setting bodies include the typewriter keyboard and the RCA television standard.[33]

There are two primary benefits to consumers from standardization. If a product uses a complementary good, then standardization of the original product will allow uniformity in the complementary good and might therefore reduce the costs of that good. Computer software and video cassette recorders come most prominently to mind. A proliferation of incompatible computers and VCRs would impose large costs both in production and inventory in the secondary markets. A second gain to consumers from standardization comes from **network externalities**.[34] A network externality occurs when consumers value a good more highly as the number of compatible users increase. As we indicated earlier, telephone service is a ready example of a product exhibiting network externalities.

Inasmuch as consumers benefit from standardization, so too may producers. If standardization increases the value to a consumer of a product, producers should be able to sell more of that product, at a higher price. *But all firms will not gain equally.* Standardization reduces the product choice; in so doing it may favor some firms' products over others. Firms in high-technology industries in which standardization seems likely have an incentive to push for standards that promote their products over those of their rivals. Innovators in a market may be in the best position to promote standards that favor their product lines.[35]

Innovators may be able to shape a market to favor their strategic assets. Products for which standardization is important offer innovators opportunities in this area.

An interesting example of the strategic value of standardization can be found in the computer industry. In the late 1960s AT&T developed UNIX, a powerful new computer operating system. Recognizing the importance of standardization as a way of promoting the use of an operating system, AT&T from the start licensed the system to other firms. Over time, however, hundreds of versions of the UNIX systems developed. In 1987, AT&T and Sun joined forces to try to develop a common UNIX system, to impose standardization on the industry. A group of other industry giants, however, including IBM, DEC, and Hewlett-Packard, were concerned that standardization around the Sun-AT&T system would put them at a competitive disadvantage. These firms formed the Open Systems Foundation (OSF) with the goal of implementing standardization around the AIX system, an IBM product. While there have been talks of merging the two groups and moving to one true standard system, at present, these two "standard" systems compete, and, in doing so, reduce the attractiveness of the operating system as a whole. Although both groups clearly see gains from true standardization, strategic concerns in this increasingly competitive industry make the move to standardization difficult.

To the extent that a market has first-mover advantages, the early advantage of the innovator will persist over time. Typically, in order to capitalize on the early advantages of innovation, an organization needs the ability to grow rapidly. This growth requires access to capital—either internal or through capital markets—and some management flexibility and responsiveness.[36]

Markets in which resources for growth are available tend to favor innovators by allowing them to rapidly exploit their early lead.

Table 16.1 summarizes the environmental conditions that favor innovation.

Management Factors Leading to Success in Innovation

At the third branch of the research and development tree in Figure 16.1 we asked the question, Does the firm have a relative advantage in inno-

Table 16.1 Factors that create a favorable environment for innovation

---

Diffusion rate is slow
  Technological complexity of innovation
  Substantial specific assets required to implement
  Strict patent/ownership rules

Value of a head start is high
  Large, lucrative *early* market
  Large first-mover advantages in production, marketing, or R&D
  Product standardization important

Resources available to innovator for growth

---

vation? We now explore some of the managerial factors that help to make firms successful innovators. Unless an organization has the managerial infrastructure needed to carry out a research-intensive strategy, such a strategy will be a failure. Here, too, we see the relationship between the strategy of a firm and its structure.

Few companies succeed in the long run by virtue of a single idea, for imitation is inexorable and eventually erodes returns from a particular innovation. Firms we think of as being successful innovators take chances again and again on new products and processes at least some of which tend to be successful. At the highly successful 3M, for example, more than 25 percent of sales in 1987 came from products less than five years old. This performance requires continual dedication to innovation. Indeed, one vice president at Monsanto, another highly innovative firm, tells us that the "name of the game is to keep putting things through the pipeline."[37] When we look at highly diversified firms, we often see consistent high performance in research and development *across* a range of very different lines of business. Thus 3M has been innovative in sandpaper, tape, adhesive paper, and most recently, video discs. There are clearly firm-specific determinants of research style and intensity.[38] What common patterns do we observe in firms that have multiple successes in innovating?

We discussed above the forces that improve an environment from the perspective of a potential innovator. But it is clear that, in a given market, there is often no single winning strategy. Consider the personal computer market. In 1982, Compaq started operations with only $1.5 million in seed funding, hoping to cash in on the burgeoning personal computer market started by IBM and Apple. In large measure, Compaq took the position of an imitator, building computers that conformed precisely to the IBM-PC in terms of software and innovating strictly in the hardware area. This strategy was an astonishing success for Compaq in the early years. In 1988, after six years in operation, Compaq had over $1 billion in sales and a 7 percent share of the market. Contrast this with the experience of Digital Equipment Corporation (DEC). With its Rainbow, DEC, too, entered the market for personal computers in the second wave, taking a high-end, imitative strategy. For DEC, this strategy was a dismal failure, and DEC was forced to exit the market. Thus we have a single industry and two imitators—one a success and the other a failure. Moreover, when we look at Compaq in 1992, the picture is not so rosy. Companies like Dell and AST have emerged as imitators of Compaq, producing machines that are virtually identical to those made by Compaq. This imitation by lower-priced producers has threatened Compaq's market. So the strategy that worked for Compaq in the 1980s—high-end imitation—has been more problematic both for DEC in the 1980s and Compaq itself in the 1990s.

What are the necessary conditions for innovation to occur on a more or less regular basis in an organization? In order for there to be some innovative output, there must be some innovative input. If we are thinking about scientific advances of one sort or another, this suggests that some expenditures must be made on research and development. While the relationship between research and development effort and results is not a perfect one, there is in most areas some positive relationship.[39] If an organization seeks innovation in its structure or management practices, it must similarly devote some effort to that innovation. David Moore, a research manager at Compaq argues that, if you spend enough in the lab, "even with average management, you are going to get some commercially viable outcomes."[40] Of course, these ideas may be too expensive to execute from a business perspective. Nevertheless, it is equally clear that to develop new products and processes, some resources will need to be expended. Conspicuously innovative firms like Eastman Kodak and 3M have groups within the organization whose function it is to look at new ideas in a serious way, even at early stages of development and even if the ideas do not emerge from the formal R&D process.[41] These firms invest in the search process to promote R&D.

Successful innovators invest in creative search.

The need to actively seek new ideas and new ways of doing things is clearly articulated in the organizational literature on innovation. In most organizations, managers are preoccupied with everyday tasks. In this environment gradual changes are often ignored. Thus stimulating innovation becomes a task of capturing and holding the attention of management so that they will respond to changes in the environment before catastrophes strike.[42]

While resources are necessary to innovate on a consistent basis, there do not appear to be substantial economies to scale in the discovery of new ideas.[43] Thus small firms may well innovate where larger firms often fail. Apple and Compaq are cases in point. Indeed, some have argued that the management structure of small firms increases the likelihood of innovation.[44] The gains from innovation—both psychological and economic—may be higher in small firms. And fertilization across functional areas, an important ingredient in the innovative process, may also be easier in smaller organizations. Nevertheless, to commercialize and fully exploit a new idea may require substantial size.

In most technologies, the minimum efficient scale for innovation is moderate.

Highly innovative companies require entrepreneurial leaders. In this dimension, at least, organizations are reflections of the values and styles of top management.[45] Westley and Mintzberg's discussion of the forms of leadership highlight the several roles that top managers play in the innovative process.[46] For many innovative companies, the chief executive plays the role of *creative visionary*. Edwin Land, founder of Polaroid, is the classic example of this leadership type. Here the leader is the source of the original innovation, as well as the inspired and persistent champion of the innovation. A different role for the leader of an innovative company is provided by the Westley-Mintzberg portrait of Steven Jobs, cofounder of Apple. Jobs had little to do with the actual design or construction of the computer. His co-founder, Steve Wozniak, was the creative force behind the Apple. Westley and Mintzberg argue that Jobs's role in leading Apple Computer was to *proselytize* for the innovation, to show people, inside and outside the company, the value of the innovation. This is the second way in which the leader of a highly innovative company operates. Finally, leaders, by creating particular organizational structures in their companies, can also play an important role in stimulating innovative behavior throughout the organization. This task is in some ways the most difficult one, given the high risk of failure in innovations and the problems of goal congruence in large organizations.

Innovation is a very risky matter. Indeed, typically, the larger the innovation—in the sense that the new deviates from the old—the higher the risk. Large, successful innovators have strategies and structures that encourage risk taking by managers throughout the organization. In a large organization, the typical innovation requires the active support of the management team to get off the ground. But championing a new product or process is a risky activity. If the innovation succeeds, the owners of the firm (current stockholders) will reap the bulk of the rewards, in the sense that the stock price will rise to reflect the earnings generated by the innovation. The manager may get a raise or a promotion; in the likely event he or she owns stock, some value will be realized through this channel as well. *But the bulk of the rewards to the innovation will not devolve on the manager,* even at organizations like Monsanto, which rewards innovators handsomely. At Monsanto, a leader in chemicals and biotechnology, a scientist with the biggest commercial hit of the year receives a $50,000 prize. While this is substantial, it is nevertheless a small fraction of the value of the typical winning idea. Nor in most organizations, of course, will the manager face the full losses from an unsuccessful innovation. Here too the bulk of the effect will be on the stockholder. In most organizations, however, the costs of an unsuccessful launch to a manager far exceed the possible gains from a success.

> **Inasmuch as managers are agents in the firm and not owners, they will not face the right incentives to innovate. In most organizations, managerial reward structures discourage innovation by punishing failure more than rewarding success.**

Standard compensation programs offered to managers provide for a modest performance payment. Given the long gestation time for an R&D project, however, these standard compensation programs do not offer much financial incentive for innovation. As we indicated earlier, we will gain most from compensation schemes tied to some measure of performance when that performance measure most clearly reflects the efforts and abilities of the managers being compensated. But overall division profit is likely to have little to do with last year's R&D activity. In sum, the fact that the managers of a firm making the decisions on innovations do not typically own the firm leads to less risk-taking activity than would be ideal. Compensation programs in many organizations reinforce managerial risk aversion.

A restructuring of financial incentives can help to mitigate the incentive problem by increasing the ownership benefits that a manager will get from an innovation. 3M, for example, allows successful "product champions" to run new divisions based on an innovation.[47] Most successful large organizations have developed a set of small discrete units, resembling entrepreneurial start-ups, to commercialize new innovations. Financial rewards can then be at least in part keyed to the performance of that particular unit, rather than the organization as a whole. In this way, firms use financial incentives to make the manager react more like a firm owner. Another possibility is to increase the intrinsic rewards from innovation by improving the corporate spirit.[48] Here, too, the emphasis on smaller units can improve the incentives of managers to take risks by increasing control and opening self-management possibilities.

Creating financial and cultural ownership in the firm by managers will lead to more innovation.

Reducing the costs of failure is an essential part of creating an innovative environment in an organization.[49] One way of doing this is to subject new ideas to a multistage review process. At 3M, for example, a new proposal goes through a seven-stage capital-budgeting process before it is fully implemented; Eastman Kodak has a six-stage process. In both of these innovative firms, new ideas and proposals are welcomed at stage 1, and managers face no great failure risks from a rejected proposal. By the time substantial resources have been committed to a project, the product champion has been joined both in analysis and responsibility by a group of other senior managers who serve as the evaluation team.

Shared responsibility for projects encourages risk taking.

The focus of the discussion thus far has been on ways organizations can encourage risk-taking behavior on the part of management. But the composition of the management team may also play a role in how it responds to organizational incentives. Bantel and Jackson looked at the effect of composition of top management teams on adoption of innovations in the banking industry.[50] Innovations studied ranged from computerized retail customer applications to delivery systems to marketing and office automation. In this study, the composition of the management team was quite important in explaining the level of innovation. Innovation was greater in banks headed by more educated managers with diverse functional backgrounds. In a study of the building industry, Oster and Quigley similarly found that more well-educated managers were more likely to innovate.[51] There is also some evidence that younger managers are more likely to take risks and are thus more open to innovation.[52] Managers with more tenure in an organization are also likely to resist innovation, in part because of both psychological and economic commitment to the status quo and in part because long tenure tends to narrow one's perspective.[53]

The Bantel and Jackson article on banks, just cited, finds that heterogeneous management teams, encourage innovation. The effect of heterogeneity on firm performance has been debated at some length in the management literature, as we suggested in Chapter 7. Both Ouchi and Pfeffer argue that more homogeneous groups help teams to develop cohesiveness, and this in turn enhances firm performance.[54] For firms operating in environments with rapidly changing technology, however, the adaptability and receptiveness associated with diverse groups may be more important than goal congruence.[55] Diverse groups may also help in controlling the costs of failure in the process of innovation. All innovative firms have project failures. We suggested earlier that one task of an innovative firm is to encourage managers to risk these failures. But successful firms must also learn how to abandon projects and here group diversity can play an important role. Considerable work has been done in organizational behavior and politics on the problem of escalation.[56] Decision makers often persist in losing situations well beyond a reasonable period. Throwing good money after bad is a well-known problem from the individual to the organizational level. But evidence from both experiments and case studies suggests that dissent is more likely in diverse populations. Thus maintaining a diverse management team may help firms not only to adopt innovations but to abandon the failures of innovation.

Opening up the innovation process to a diverse group of people in an organization has other benefits as well. Important innovations typically require changes in a number of functional areas; Van de Ven refers to innovation for this reason as a "network building effort."[57] New ideas often come from outside the R&D team; indeed customers often stimulate innovation with new demands for service.[58] An innovative firm must have an open enough structure to reach out for ideas in and outside the organization.

Once an organization has developed an idea, it must commercially develop it. Under some circumstances, the innovator will choose to go it alone. Other times, innovators grant exclusive licenses to other firms. Many times, innovators develop new products themselves, but license others to produce as well. We turn now to a consideration of this choice, the last branch on our decision tree.

Licensing Innovations

Perhaps the easiest place to begin is with an innovating firm that decides *not* to commercialize the innovation itself. Clearly a firm will eschew production only if the earnings it expects from using the innovation itself are less than it expects from licensing fees paid by a second producer. Licensing fees, in turn, are likely to be more lucrative only if the innovator is a relatively inefficient producer in the market. Evidence suggests that licensors receive between a third and a half of the profits associated with the development of an innovation.[59] Innovators will agree to share the profits in this manner only if the licensing agreement substantially increases the total market returns.

But why should the innovator face such a substantial disadvantage in commercializing its innovation? If a firm thinks of a new product or process, why should it not be able to produce and market it? Increasingly, this will often turn out to be the case, for the innovator may lack the ability to acquire the complementary assets needed to commercialize an innovation effectively.[60] If we consider the pharmaceutical example given in Chapter 13, Farma, the innovator of a new anti-inflammatory drug, turned to Miller because Farma lacked the marketing expertise needed to commercialize its product quickly. The lack of a distribution network by an innovator may similarly be an important impediment to commercialization.

An interesting example of the difference in the abilities needed to create a new product and those needed to commercialize it is provided by the Snugli, a popular infant carrier.[61] The Snugli was developed in 1964 by a young ex-Peace Corps volunteer, Ann Moore. Sales began small, but grew by approximately 40 percent per year. By 1972, sales had reached $100,000. Shortly thereafter, *Consumer Reports* reviewed the product favorably, and by 1978 sales had reached $1,000,000. Moore converted her cottage operation to a factory, but soon began to face the problems of organizing labor, finding new distribution outlets to replace the original mail-order mode, and so on. By 1983, sales were at $5,000,000, but the business was in chaos. Moore sold the business to Huffy, an experienced firm in the toy and child-equipment market, and remarked later: "We simply didn't know how to run that kind of business."

In the Snugli example, the innovator, Ann Moore, began by developing the product herself but finally had to sell the innovation to a more experienced firm. In this case, growth outpaced the ability of the small entrepreneur. In other instances, early markets are large, and innovators turn to licensing as a way to increase the speed with which the innovation hits the market. The innovator may find that it would lose too much time in amassing the requisite complementary assets in order to begin production, and that in that time, a considerable opportunity to earn rents on the innovation would have been lost.[62] In this situation, it is often the case that the innovator will license a second firm.

> Innovators may license innovations to rivals who are expected to be more efficient in the exploitation of that innovation due to the presence of complementary assets. Licensing may increase the speed with which the innovation enters the market.

Scale conditions in the commercialization stage may also encourage licensing of innovation. There is considerable evidence that inventive entrepreneurs thrive in small operations. But commercializing innovations may require a larger scale operation. The *optimal plant scale* differs for the two stages in innovation. Some large organizations try to overcome this problem by simulating the small-firm environment through the establishment of **skunkworks,** small isolated operations with little hierarchy, designed to create new ideas. But in some cases, even the shell of a large bureaucracy may be too binding for entrepreneurial spirits. Licensing the innovation to a larger firm, and sharing the rents from the innovation with that firm, may be a way for the entrepreneurial inventor to ensure a future flow of creative output from his or her operation.

The above discussion focuses on the case in which the innovator licenses the innovation to a rival and abstains from using the innovation itself. In other words, we have thus far examined the granting of an *exclusive license* to a rival. Another strategy is for an innovator to simultaneously develop the innovation itself and license it to a second firm. In offering such a license to a rival, the innovator reduces its competitive advantage in the market. Why would the innovator ever do this?

Suppose the innovator faces some capacity constraints. It simply is unable to grow fast enough to serve the nascent market for its new product or to exploit fully a cost-reducing process innovation. In this case, the licensing may allow the innovator to expand the scale of the new technology or product, and thus reap at least a portion of the rents from this expansion.[63] Such licensing will be profitable for the innovator in cases in which the innovation is relatively small in terms of its cost-reducing ability or, in the case of a product innovation, subject to short-lived demand. If the innovation is major and more permanent, it will generally pay an innovator to lose a bit of time and profit now in order to maintain a monopoly position in the future.[64]

Innovators faced with capacity constraints will typically find it profitable to license small innovations to a rival.

An interesting example of the value of speed in some markets is the hula-hoop, developed in 1958 by Wham-O.[65] Millions of hula-hoops were sold the first year, but unsatisfied demand appeared to be substantial. Wham-O was a fairly small firm, however, without adequate production facilities. So the firm invested heavily in new capacity and churned out millions of new hoops. Unfortunately, by the time the new capacity was completed, the hula-hoop craze had ended. Wham-O was left with unneeded capacity and massive inventories. Its attempt to handle the market alone had simply taken too much time.

Licensing the hula-hoop to another firm with extant production facilities might have been a better strategy for Wham-O. We can see that a firm may wish to license its innovation in order to quickly develop and exploit a market. Of course, in this situation the innovator, if it later enters itself, will come in as a rival, not a monopolist, and indeed it may come in at a cost disadvantage relative to its own licensee, due to the experience in production amassed by the licensee.

In the case of a product innovation, the innovator may face a second, rather different incentive to license its innovation. Suppose the new product is one that requires some specialized investment by the user prior to use. One example might be a specialized microprocessor that requires particular hardware design in the computer. Another example of a product that requires specialized user adaptation is aspartame, an alternative to sweeteners like sugar or saccharine, currently used by soft drink and candy producers. In both of these cases, single supply by a monopolist will leave users "hostage" to unreasonable pricing demands by that monopolist. In this case, the innovator may need to license a rival in order to convince users to adopt the new product.[66] In effect, providing a second source through licensing makes credible an innovator's commitment to maintain quality and price levels.

Indeed, in the example of microprocessors, we have seen licensing to a second source by an innovator. Intel, for example, licensed its biggest buyer, IBM, to produce its 16-bit 8086 microprocessor for internal use.[67]

Licensing may be a way to credibly commit to users a moderate price path in order to encourage adoption of a new product.

Of course, licensing is not the only way firms may make credible commitments to their users. And it will not always be the least expensive. In the case of aspartame, G. D. Searle has given its buyers (largely soft drink producers) long-term contracts as a form of protection, rather than licensing rivals. Licensing rivals tends to be more effective when demand is growing, so that in some sense there is room for both the innovator and a rival. It may also be more common in areas in which there is considerable uncertainty about the demand or cost conditions involving the innovator and thus contracting is less feasible. It is also typical in this case that licensing is done with only a single rival.

Conclusions

In this chapter, we have explored competition in the area of technology. We have seen that creative management in a high-technology arena requires careful attention to the environment, the internal assets of the organization, and the competitive dynamics in the industry. In Chapter 17, we will introduce yet another player into the competitive game: the government regulator.

17

Regulatory Issues
in Strategic Planning

Virtually every modern organization in America is subject to at least some form of economic regulation. At the one extreme, we see the public utilities, whose rates, investment decisions, and pricing schedules are all subject to scrutiny by regulatory commissions. For these organizations, the formation of strategy is impossible to disentangle from the regulatory environment. Electric utilities, for example, would find it impossible to consider the choice of investing in a nuclear versus a coal-power plant without seeking regulatory advice. Local telephone providers, many of whom are currently diversifying into unregulated areas, must pursue their diversification strategies under the watchful eyes of state regulators.

For other organizations, regulatory scrutiny may come only at infrequent intervals and may involve only some of an organization's functions. In some instances, the regulatory focus may be on the production area. A steel firm, for example, might find itself unable to operate a particular coke oven as a result of regulations involving air pollution levels. For other organizations, the regulatory focus might be in the marketing and distribution area. Medical and legal practices in some states, for example, are not permitted to advertise their services. Employee relations are another important locus of regulatory activity; organizations are regulated in terms of the working conditions they must offer workers and the minimum wages they must pay.

Indeed, regulations are ubiquitous in the modern economy. Nor is this pattern unique to America. Most developed economies regulate in the areas of environmental health, occupational safety, and the like. How does the existence of a complex web of regulations influence the nature of strategic planning and management?

Many organizations see regulations as simply another impediment to strategic planning and management, another set of constraints on the options available to managers. And, indeed, sometimes regulations are precisely that. Managers may find themselves unable to implement specific investment decisions, for example, as a result of particular regulations. In other situations, however, regulations can open up opportunities for creative managers. In still other cases, forward-thinking managers can help to influence the path of regulation in ways that will benefit their own organizations. In this chapter, we will look at the regulatory environment that currently exists in the U.S. economy and ask what opportunities and/ or threats the presence of regulation in the environment creates for the modern manager.

A Look at the Scope of U.S. Regulations

Table 17.1 groups the vast array of regulations in the United States into four segments. The oldest form of regulation, and the one many consumers think of when one mentions regulation, is rate-of-return or entry regulation. The transportation industry, communications, and financial services are all heavily represented in this area. These organizations produce

Table 17.1   Incidence of regulation in the United States

Traditional rate-of-return/ entry regulation	Trade regulations	Enivironmental regulations	Health and safety
Transportation			
Railroads	Imports	1972, *Federal Water*	*Auto safety*
Motor carriers	Quotas	*Pollution Control Act*	(Seat belts, etc.)
Water carriers		Pulp and paper	
Airlines (growing less)	Tariffs	Heavy manufacturing	*Food and Drug*
		Chemicals	*Administration*
Pipeline	Anti-dumping legislation	Municipalities	Foods
Communications		*Clean Air Act*	*Occupational Safety*
Electric, gas, water		*(esp. 1976, 1977*	*and Health Act*
Telephone and telegraph		*amendments)*	*(1970)*
Radio and TV		Heavy manufacturing	Heavy manufacturing
		Autos	Textiles
Financial services		Mining	*Consumer Products*
Banks		*Resource Conservation*	*Safety Act*
Insurance companies		*and Recovery Act*	Toys
Securities		*(Toxics) (1976)*	Miscellaneous
		Chemicals	
About 11% of GNP		Machinery	
		Metals	
		Paper	

approximately 11 percent of current Gross National Product. Public-utility regulation, which often involves government intervention and an oversight at both the federal and state levels, is generally of a relatively "hands-on" sort.

Another important and traditional area of government regulation is in the trade area. All countries have some regulations governing the flow of trade in and out of their economies. In the United States we have at various times erected trade barriers to protect industries as diverse as tomatoes, motorcycles, and textiles. In many parts of the world, capital flow out of the country is restricted, and foreign investment is also curtailed. As more firms move into the global arena, understanding these trade regulations becomes an increasingly important part of the strategic planning process.

The late 1960s and early 1970s saw growth in a third regulatory area: the environment. As we see from Table 17.1, most of the regulations aimed at improving the quality of the environment were passed during this period. These regulations affect a much broader range of organizations than those influenced by rate-of-return regulation. The smokestack industries—steel, autos, tires, paper—were and are heavily affected by environmental regulations, and there have also been important effects on grain mills, dairy processors, semiconductor manufacturers, and health clinics. Municipalities themselves have been among the organizations most affected by environmental regulations, particularly in the water area.

Health and Safety, the last column in Table 17.1, has seen the most recent regulatory growth. As the population has become more affluent, regulators have come to pay more attention to matters of worker health, product safety, and even product quality. These matters are governed by a complex web of federal and state agencies, not all of which necessarily agree on objectives or procedures. These regulations, even more so than those in the environmental area, affect a very wide range of organizations.

Virtually all organizations are affected in one way or another by the regulations outlined in Table 17.1. For a larger organization, the regulatory scrutiny is typically more intense, but even small organizations will find their decision-making ability influenced by the regulatory process. Nor are public and nonprofit organizations immune from regulatory scrutiny. In the 1970s in particular, water-pollution and air-pollution regulations presented municipalities with enormous challenges. The problem of toxic wastes is currently testing the managerial limits of a number of public organizations. Nonprofit hospitals face the same kind of regulatory constraints on equipment purchases and patient reimbursement as do the for-profit hospitals run by Humana and the Hospital Corporation of America.

We have seen the prominence and diversity of regulations in the United States. But why do we have so many regulations? What forces create regulations? Why regulate in one area and not another? From the point of view of the strategic manager, the why's of the matter may be just as important as the how's. In particular, to the extent that a manager seeks to understand, anticipate, and perhaps even influence the regulatory process, an appreciation for the forces that lead to regulation is essential. We turn to this now.

The Sources of Regulation

Figure 17.1 is a schematic of the major players in the regulatory game. In the United States, regulations are typically developed on the basis of some legislation produced by elected officials either at the federal, state, or local level. Sometimes, the legislation passed by these policy makers is quite detailed and explicit. The Water Pollution Control Act of 1972, for example, specified how much pollution was to be cleaned up, by what date, and in some instances even by what method. Other legislation is rather vague, specifying an area of concern and a lofty objective, but containing little description of either rules or procedures. Legislation governing regulations in the area of food and drug safety is of this sort. Whether legislation is broad or detailed, the regulatory process is one by which the legislature directs the *bureaucracy* to intervene in some market process.

In the regulatory area, we see a partnership between elected officials and the bureaucracy. In virtually all cases, the bureaucracy has some power in interpreting the rules passed by legislators, and that power influences the extent to which the legislation is implemented. The degree of latitude varies considerably, although even in areas like water-pollution abatement, where the legislation is rather detailed, there appears to be sub-

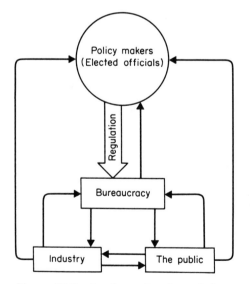

Figure 17.1   A schematic of regulation

stantial bureaucratic control. In the figure, arrows represent the interactive relationship between the two groups.[1] For an organization affected by a particular regulation, understanding the way the bureaucracy works in that area will be vital to anticipating changes in regulatory practice. Many heavily regulated organizations recruit personnel from regulatory agencies in order to learn more about the way that bureaucracy works.

The relationship between the legislature and the bureaucracy is another example of the principal-agent paradigm described in Chapter 8. Elected officials typically set objectives for the bureaucracy to meet. But it is often hard to tell whether the bureaucracy has met those objectives and even harder to ascribe blame if objectives have not been met. The bureaucracy (the agent in this example) may share the objectives of the elected officials, but equally well may not. At the federal level, for example, high level bureaucrats are appointed by the president who may not share the objectives of the legislators who passed the initial rules. The Environmental Protection Agency has operated under a fairly stable set of laws since its inception in 1970, but has done things quite differently under its various directors. In part these differences reflect underlying differences in the abilities and objectives of the bureaucrats themselves; in part they may be a response to changes in economic and political conditions.

The relationship between the rule makers and the bureaucracy is also akin to that of the corporate staff in an organization and line managers who must implement the ideas and strategies of that staff. While corporate staff can set objectives and at least try to monitor the line managers, such monitoring is imperfect. As with the bureaucracy and legislature, some delegation of authority must be made to the line manager.

Given the potential for differences between regulator and legislator in objectives, legislators often develop instruments to control those regulators.[2] Legislators may also take direct action in the form of passing new laws as a way to control bureaucrats. Nevertheless, in most circumstances control is imperfect.

The regulations that influence the economy are the result of a complex partnership between elected officials and the bureaucracy—a partnership in which one or another of the two parties has more or less power at any given time. What influences the kinds of regulations this partnership produces?

If we simply read Figure 17.1 downward, we see a simple mechanical story of the birth and effect of regulation. Regulations are born in the legislature, molded in the bureaucracy, and thrust on industry and the public. But this story is too simple. We need now ask ourselves some further questions. How is it that particular regulatory ideas come into the heads of legislators? Why are some regulatory initiatives pursued, while others die aborning? Why are some regulations nurtured by the bureau and others suppressed? The answers to these questions come from examining the boxes at the bottom of the figure.

Regulation is a product created by elected officials and agencies. To understand why particular products are produced—even products as arcane as regulations—we need to investigate the demand and supply for those products.[3] As Figure 17.1 makes clear, there are two groups which potentially express their demands for regulations of one sort or another: industry and the public. For both groups, regulatory demand is motivated at least in large measure by the forces of self-interest. We might suppose that the individual consumers who comprise the public seek regulations that encourage the production of desirable goods (including intangible goods such as clean water and air) at low prices. At the same time, we might expect industry groups to favor regulatory structures that have as little deleterious effect as possible on their profits. Indeed, industry groups might be expected to favor regulations which actually increase their profits.

So the first step in analyzing why we have regulations in a particular area is to understand the way in which regulations impinge on the public and on industry. To the extent that a new regulation has the potential to either increase profits to an industry or to improve the position of consumers, we will see some demand for that regulation. If a planner wishes to anticipate the drift of regulation influencing the organization, it will be important to investigate these underlying regulatory demands.

Regulations are produced in part as a response to demands for those regulations by groups in the economy.

In trying to influence the regulatory process, individual consumers and producers may ally themselves, forming **interest groups**. Interest groups are collections of people united by a common purpose or interest. In the regulatory process, interest groups may serve to inform regulators in ways which would be difficult for agencies to accomplish themselves.[4] At times, the desire to shape regulations in particular ways may create interest groups of quite disparate groups. One commentator calls this the Baptist-Bootlegger interest-group theory in a reference to coalitions in the southern states that, for widely differing reasons, supported the same restrictions on alcohol.[5] We are all familiar with the expression "Politics makes strange bedfellows!"

There is also a supply side to consider in determining the shape of regulations. Regulations are, as we have said, supplied by a partnership of elected officials making new laws, and agencies implementing and refining those laws. Each official has a limited amount of time and influence available to use in the pursuit of new legislation; bureaucrats similarly are limited in terms of time and resources. These limits constrain the supply of new regulations imposed. Within these constraints, officials and bureaucrats will respond to the demands of their constituents, both industry and consumers. Note in Figure 17.1 the set of arrows going *from* consumers and industry *to* the elected officials and agencies. The regulatory demands represented by these arrows are filtered through the structures of the agencies and the legislatures, tempered by the wishes and hopes of the officials themselves. The result is a regulatory pattern that broadly reflects often conflicting demands.

But what particular conditions cause consumers and/or industry groups to believe that regulations will improve their economic positions? Virtually all regulations interfere with the working of one or more markets. What characteristic of markets leads individuals to believe that suppression of economic forces in those markets gives rise to benefits? As we will see, consumer groups as a whole are most likely to benefit from regulation when there is a prior **market failure.** If markets are not currently working well, interaction is perhaps warranted. The larger the underlying market failure, the more likely it is that regulatory intervention will produce benefits.[6] So we need to ask ourselves what the central causes are of market failure? When do markets perform badly?

One prime form of market failure is the existence of **natural monopoly.** A natural monopoly occurs when we have a market in which the minimum efficient scale (MES) of operations is equal to or larger than the total size of the market (Figure 17.2).

The cost curve in Figure 17.2 represents the overall market demand for a product and the average costs of producing that product, using the best technology available. As we can see, in this example costs decline continuously over the relevant portion of the demand curve. This cost-curve shape tells us that a single production unit would allow us to achieve the lowest possible unit costs, noted as AC* on the graph. If this market was instead served by two producers, each with a market of 1/2 MES, we can see that each producer would have a cost considerably higher than AC*. Thus having only one unit in the area would best serve consumers by giving them access to goods produced in the most efficient manner

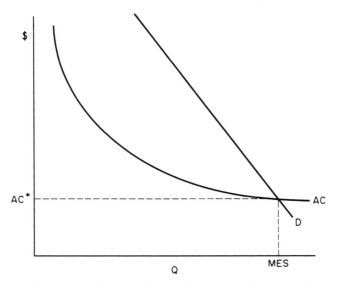

Figure 17.2 Cost conditions for a natural monopoly

possible. In this sense, a monopoly would seem to be the "natural" unit to serve the market. Many of the public utilities—telephone service, electricity, and the like—were regulated based on natural monopoly arguments.

There is one problem with allowing a monopolist to control the market, however. If we allow only one firm to produce in a market, we have created a monopoly. Our normal expectation would be that the monopoly would exploit its solitary position by charging excessively high prices. Thus allowing the monopoly would give us low costs—known as **technical efficiency**—but high prices—or **allocative inefficiency**. If the market were populated by many firms we would have price competition, but costs could be excessive.

One public-policy solution to this dilemma is to impose regulation. The regulation controls entry, permitting only one unit to supply local telephone service, or gas service, and at the same time controls the rates that these legal monopolies can charge, typically based on a set formula for rate of return on invested capital. In the ideal situation, this **rate-of-return regulation** is designed to allow us to achieve the best of both worlds: low production costs and moderate margins to producers.

From the consumer's side, demands for public-utility regulation come from a desire to be protected from the excesses of monopoly, while reaping the technical benefits of large-scale production. In the case of some public utilities, consumer demands for regulation are complemented by desires for regulation by the industry themselves.

The cost curve in Figure 17.2 represents a situation with considerable fixed investment, investment which is specific to the enterprise. In the face of competition, organizations already in an industry may find themselves unable to recover the large fixed costs which they undertook to enable them to serve the given market. The several firms competing in the market all face a situation in which they will be unable to recover their costs. Thus firms may themselves seek regulation that will protect them against new entry into their markets. In the late nineteenth and early twentieth centuries, many railroads sought regulation as a way to protect their considerable investments.

The existence of a natural monopoly is one form of market failure, and thus is one public interest argument in favor of regulation.

The existence of large fixed costs, and declining cost curves are thus one condition in which we see demands for regulatory intervention. A second condition favoring regulations is the existence of **externalities.** An externality occurs whenever an action taken by one economic unit results in an uncompensated benefit or cost to others. If the externality creates a cost for others, it is called a *negative externality*. A factory that emits smoke, thus increasing the costs of a neighboring laundry firm, is creating a negative externality. Externalities may also be *positive*, for example, when one economic unit creates benefits for a second. A honey farm creates positive externalities for the apple orchard by increasing the number of bees around and thus the rate of pollination.

Externalities create a market failure. The market failure occurs because economic agents will take actions without regard for the full consequences of those actions. The factory will emit more smoke than would be best if viewed from a system-wide perspective; the bee keeper, on the other hand, will have fewer bees than would be ideal when we view the apple orchard–bee farm together. The free working of the market will in these cases result in a "wrong" choice of output, at least from the view of society as a whole.

In the case of externalities, some intervention to enable agents to consider the full effects of their actions may improve social welfare. Thus demands for regulation are created when we have large externalities. Most of the regulations listed in the last two columns of Table 17.1 are responses to negative externalities. We regulate the production of air and water emissions to prevent pollution. We regulate the quality and efficacy of foods and drugs to prevent externalities in these areas.[7]

We typically think of the demanders of environmental protection as consumers, rather than industry groups. And, indeed, this has been primarily the case. Nevertheless, some negative externalities are created by industry and visited on other industries, as the factory/laundry example suggests.

Externalities form another class of situations in which regulatory intervention is likely.

We have thus far characterized the demand for regulation as arising from some market failure. And, indeed, this is often the case. Large market failures open up the possibility of regulatory benefits, by creating a role for government policy. In the case of market failures, private interests may benefit from regulations that on net have positive effects for the system as a whole. But we also observe regulations in areas in which the underlying market failure is really quite inconsequential, and the regulation produces losses on net. Under these conditions, there may *still* be demand for regulation inasmuch as some people may still gain from the regulation. Thus an industry group may seek to limit entry into its industry in order to protect profits, even if no particular social good will be served by such entry restrictions. A consumer group may wish to control prices, even if controls serve only to distort the market and create losses for stockholders. In these instances, the private interests of affected parties may demand regulation that is not in the overall interest of society. Nevertheless, *the language of regulatory lobbying is almost invariably the language of market failures and public interest.* Thus the industry group in the above example will seek to restrict entry, not by citing the gains this would yield for its private coffers, but by tracing through some consumer or public benefit. The consumer group wishing to control prices will also seek a public-interest cloak for its private-interest motives. Thus the manager seeking to understand regulations needs to understand the market-failure rationale for regulation, even if private interests are most prominent.

A cogent example of the public-interest language in which regulatory lobbying occurs can be seen in the current debate over interstate banking. At present, throughout the United States restrictions against interstate banking are being lifted. Thus regulatory change has the potential to influence dramatically the balance between small regional banks and big city operations, and bankers at all levels have been active in lobbying efforts on one side or another. But the debate has had an interesting public-interest quality, as this exchange between two bankers demonstrates:

> Do you care whether your Connecticut deposits are shipped out of the country to finance far-fetched deals in faraway places? Do you care if your personal banker suddenly becomes a computer terminal in New York City? Do you care whether your small neighborhood bank still is there five years from now? Sure you do, and so do I. That's why I'm against expanding Connecticut's New England regional banking Law to allow the New York City banks to enter Connecticut.
>
> James F. McNally
> *The Hartford Courant*
> March 8, 1987, Section C

And on the other side, we hear the following:

> Additional competition will bring lower prices (to keep existing customers), product innovation (to attract new customers), freer access to capital and higher budgets to develop new products and services. Additional competition also will benefit communities. Among the benefits: new jobs, increased business for suppliers, builders and other sub-contractors, and more tax revenues for Connecticut and its municipalities.
>
> David Evans
> *The Hartford Courant*
> March 8, 1987, Section C

If we ask ourselves which areas we expect to find regulated, one piece of the answer is that regulated areas tend to be ones for which some form of the market-failure story can be told. Again, this is not to say that all regulations are justified based on the public interest. I am arguing only that the legislative process typically requires there to be at least some reference to the public interest, as we have seen in the exchange quoted on banking rules. Arguments based on private gains associated with constraining otherwise efficient markets are not typically well received in the political arena.

There is, I think, another reason we find regulations in areas in which there is at least some market failure. If we attempt to regulate in what is otherwise an efficient market, that regulation will produce losses in excess of the benefits it confers. Of course, the losses and benefits will typically go to different people, so that we might still observe some groups asking for regulation, even though the regulation imposes considerable costs. But under these circumstances, there often will also be forces confronting the agencies and elected officials, lobbying *against* the proposed legislation. Thus regulatory programs with quite large efficiency losses tend not to emerge from the political arena. There will simply be too many regulatory losers who emerge to do battle with the potential beneficiaries of the proposed regulation.

Regulatory programs tend to emerge in areas in which there is at least some evidence of market failure.

In anticipating future directions for regulation, and in seeing how best to influence that direction, some attention to public-interest issues is clearly of importance. But as we've tried to indicate, public interest is not the whole story. Numerous regulations have been passed and strenuously enforced that were not in the overall public interest. Some groups benefit; others lose; and the net appears to be negative. How is it that such regulations are not squelched at their initial appearance by those who stand to lose from them?

One answer appears to lie in the distribution of benefits and costs from particular regulations. Lobbying legislators, even at an informal level, is a time-consuming and resource-intensive activity. So, too, are attempts to influence agencies. To justify intervention, an individual must perceive the potential losses or gains from a regulation to be fairly substantial. Suppose a new regulation has quite concentrated benefits, but rather diffuse losses. For example, a small group of firms and their stockholders might benefit via a price rise from tariff barriers that diminish foreign competition. The cost from the regulation is a small price rise, experienced by perhaps millions of consumers. Each consumer loses only a little, too little to justify intervention. Each firm gains a moderate amount, a sufficient amount to warrant lobbying. In this case, we might well see a greater *articulated* demand for regulation than against it, even though on net the program is a bad one.

Regulatory programs with concentrated benefits and diffuse costs tend to be favored by the regulatory process.

We have now seen that there is some systematic logic behind patterns of regulatory activity. But how will understanding the sources of regulation improve strategic planning in an organization? In Chapter 1, I argued that an early appreciation for changes in its environment is one way an organization can outperform its rivals. Simple economics tells us that, over a long period of time, most lucrative profit opportunities tend to disappear. Getting a head start on the market is thus particularly important. But as the economy becomes increasingly complex and government and business become more integrated, the extent to which regulatory changes create opportunities for firms, or threats to them, also increases. An organization that anticipates regulatory changes will find itself with an advantage over the field. Indeed, as we will see in the next section of this chapter, an organization that really understands the regulatory process can at times create some of its own regulatory opportunities.

Strategic Regulation

In the discussion thus far we have treated industry interests as though they were homogeneous. In fact, of course, they are not, and regulations may have quite different effects on some firms in an industry relative to others. Thus regulations may influence the *pattern* of competitive advantages within an industry. This opens up strategic opportunities for an organization. How can an organization anticipate and possibly even help to shape regulations in such a way as to improve its own position vis-à-vis its rivals?[8]

As long as differences exist among firms in an industry, some firms in that industry may call for regulations that increase the relative rate of return to their specific characteristics. Indeed, a firm may even encourage passage of a regulation that reduces industry demand or increases industry costs. The firm may desire such a regulation because it differentially damages its rivals, and thus rearranges market shares at the same time as it reduces the total market. To go one step further, the firm may even promote a regulation that lowers its short-term profits if that regulation simultaneously reduces the ability of its rivals to compete effectively.

Figure 17.3 provides a simple story of a variegated industry in which different firms have access to different production technologies. One set of firms, the A firms, uses a low-cost technique. For some reason, these

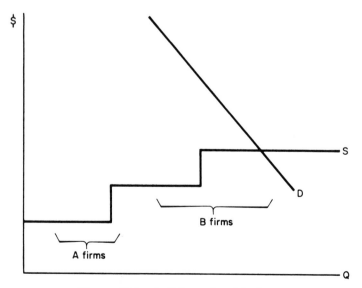

Figure 17.3   A differentiated industry

firms cannot expand to supply the entire market using this technique. Perhaps the technique requires an input that is in small supply. A second set of firms, the B firms, has two techniques available for producing the same goods the A firms are making: The high-cost technique has limitless capacity; the moderate-cost technique is limited, perhaps due to the same input constraints that affect the A firms. Under these circumstances, the supply and demand curves will look as we have pictured them in Figure 17.3. Both A and B firms are in the market, with A firms earning considerably higher profits than B firms. B firms are using both techniques, and all firms are operating at full capacity.

Now suppose the industry is subject to a new regulation that increases only the price of the high-cost technique. This regulatory change will shift the last segment of the supply curve in an upward direction. As a result, with stable demand, the market price will rise. Group A will clearly benefit from the regulation. Its costs are not affected, yet it gains from the new, higher market price.

At first, it may look as though the A firms benefit at the expense of the B firms. Group B, however, may also end up with higher profits as a result of the new regulation. For B, the central issue will involve a comparison between the price rise and its cost increase. We show in Figure 17.4 that in this case the B firms experience a cost increase on only some fraction of their production.

If we look at Figure 17.4, we can see that the B firms do not always gain from a cost-raising regulation. Sometimes regulations increase costs more than prices. Other times, cost increases influence only a fraction of the firm's production, and prices increase substantially. In general, the effect of the regulation will depend on the shape of the demand curve and the particular way in which the regulation influences costs. Two general principles emerge:

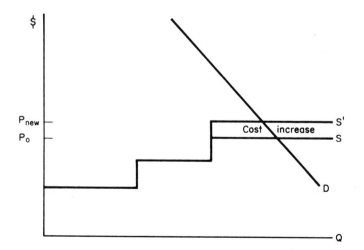

Figure 17.4 Regulatory change in a differentiated industry

The more inelastic demand is, the better, for supply decreases will have a larger price effect.

Optimal regulations from the firms' perspective are those that raise marginal costs more than average costs.

The more inelastic is demand, the larger will be the price rise associated with any cost increase. Inelasticity in the demand curve implies a lack of good substitutes for consumers. If no good substitutes exist for our product then we can effectively raise prices to cover new regulatory costs without losing customers. So demand inelasticity is obviously important in estimating the effect of a cost-increasing regulation.

The role of marginal versus average costs is more difficult to see. In Figure 17.4, prices are set in response to marginal cost—that is, the costs of the least efficient production units still in the market. But a firm's profits are determined by the difference between the market price and its *average* cost. Thus it is the relative shift in marginal versus average costs that is critical in determining regulatory results. Regulations that raise the costs of the marginal units significantly while leaving average costs relatively unchanged have the most promise for the regulated firm.

It is easy to see from Figure 17.4 that regulations may have differential effects on firms within an industry. In response to these differential effects, firms may have incentives to try to influence the regulatory process in some strategic way. In particular, firms may wish to lobby to influence the forms new regulation will take so as to favor themselves over their rivals. In this way, we may see competition develop in the political arena.

Three general conditions must be met before one would expect any rivalry in regulatory investments by firms to occur. First, the industry must contain differentiated subgroups of firms. This differentiation can come about either by firms producing different product mixes, or through differences in size, technology, levels of integration, or whatever. These differences create the possibility that a regulation can give a comparative advantage to some firms in the industry and lead to a shifting of market shares within the industry. In terms of Figure 17.3, cost differences often form a wedge between firms that can be enhanced by the regulatory process.

The second requirement for rivalry in regulatory investments to occur is that the firms in the industry must be fairly interdependent. That is, we must be dealing with groups within an industry and not with separate industries. In Figure 17.4, we characterized the two sets of firms as facing the same market demand curve. This is a high level of interdependence. As long as demand across products is related, some regulatory rivalry is possible. The essence of rivalry in investments is that a firm will try to exploit the differential effect of a regulation on itself versus its rivals; this differential effect is important only if firms are interdependent, though this interdependence can be either on the demand side or on the supply side.

Finally, if firms are to engage in strategic regulatory behavior, there must be some actual or potential barriers to entry to the industry and some barriers to mobility within the industry. Without barriers, any quasirents created by the firm's regulatory intervention will be dissipated. Barriers protect the return associated with the change induced by the regulation. This proposition is similar to the one articulated in our discussion of limit pricing. Without some entry barriers, neither limit pricing nor rivalrous investments are profitable strategies, since the rents accruing to the activity will be too rapidly dissipated.

If an industry meets these three requirements, then there is at least some potential for rivalrous regulatory investments to occur. Firms with different bundles of specific capital and hence different operating strategies can try to influence the regulatory process to increase the payoff to the particular strategies they have adopted.

In summary, for strategic regulation to be successful, we require several things.

Significant differences among firms, or groups of firms.

Interdependence among firms.

Barriers to entry and mobility that will allow excess profits from regulation to prevail.

In Figure 17.4, we showed a case in which a set of firms would favor a regulation that raised its costs. In considering why firms would support a regulation that seems harmful, the central issue is how the regulation affects the firm *relative* to the rest of the market against which the firm competes. Thus one needs to look at a firm's assets relative to those of its competitors, and its particular way of doing business. A capital-intensive firm may support unionization as a weapon against labor-intensive rivals; a high-quality firm may support labeling restrictions to keep out low-quality substitutes; old firms may push for grandfather clauses that reduce their obligations under the regulation relative to new firms, thus reducing entry rates.

We have thus far seen two important ways in which understanding regulation can improve the strategic position of an organization. First, it can allow the firm to anticipate regulatory changes and possibly get a head start on the market in responding to those changes. Second, firms may be in a good position to influence the regulatory process in a way that favors their own talents and assets.

On this second point, we might add a word about the broader social responsibility of a firm. In an earlier chapter, we discussed the issue of corporate objectives and suggested that in the modern U.S. corporation a *narrow* focus on profits is not common. Indeed, in many organizations, attention to the broader community and its interests is expected. The regulatory arena is one place in which we see much attention. In considering how the regulatory process might be influenced, many organizations concern themselves with the public interest as well as their own private interest. Firms in the so-called smokestack industries have, at times, worked with environmental regulatory agencies to reduce pollution, thus supporting public interests though perhaps not their own private interests. Of course, in the ideal situation a firm can serve itself while it serves the public. But one of the complex tasks of senior managers is to grapple with conflicts between public and private interests, and the regulatory area is one place in which such grappling occurs. We turn now to an interesting example of strategic regulation.

An Example of Strategic Regulation: The Pharmaceutical Industry

In January 1979, the Federal Trade Commission proposed a model Drug Product Selection Rule (hereafter, the Act). The history of this proposal provides a cogent example of the process of rivalrous regulatory investments. The Act was only one of many regulations affecting the pharmaceutical industry, but it reveals quite well the possibilities for strategic investments in regulation.[9]

Historically, physicians have often written drug prescriptions using the brand name of a drug, even if generic substitutes were available. In the 1950s and 1960s, many states passed *antisubstitution laws* requiring pharmacists to fill prescriptions with the exact brand-name drug prescribed by the physician. These laws appear to have been passed largely in response to pressure by drug manufacturers, who argued that the laws were necessary to ensure quality in the industry. Under these regulations, pharmacists were not permitted to substitute lower-priced generics for the brand-name drug prescribed. The market-failure argument made in support of the laws was that poor product choices by pharmacists acting on their own would endanger consumer health. Critics of these laws objected that they also raise barriers to entry in the industry, protect margins of innovative drug firms, and reduce the viability of generic drug houses.

In the 1970s a number of states began to repeal antisubstitution laws and to put in their place *generic-substitution laws*. These new regulations, which varied in form from state to state, were designed to encourage pharmacists to fill prescriptions with the lowest priced drug available. The Drug Product Selection Rule (the Act) proposed in January 1979 by the Federal Trade Commission was designed to be a model for the assortment of generic-substitution laws then existing in the states.

The Act has several provisions. First, substitution by the pharmacists is permitted but not required. A physician can *prevent* substitution by specifying on the prescription that the brand-name drug is "medically necessary." Pharmacists are also provided with a catalog indicating drug equivalences.

The reaction of firms in the drug industry to the Act reveals quite clearly the strategic elements we have been discussing. There are 1300 firms in the pharmaceutical industry. This large set of players is divided into two subgroups: large firms that specialize in the development and production of patented brand-name drugs, and smaller firms that specialize in the production of generic drugs. The former group, consisting of about 130 firms, accounts for about 90 percent of domestic pharmaceutical sales. These are the firms most of us associate with the industry: Bristol-Myers, Smithkline, G. D. Searle and so on. The generic houses constitute the bulk of players in the market in terms of numbers, but have a much smaller share of sales. These are firms with small research staffs, low marketing effort, and low visibility. At the same time, there are some firms that produce both brand-name and generic drugs, and there is clearly substitution both in consumption and in production in the two drug types. Thus one would consider the two firm types to be in the same industry using standard industrial organization criteria. They are clearly subgroups in the industry if we return to a distinction introduced in Chapter 5. The Pharmaceutical Manufacturers' Association (PMA)—an industry trade association—stresses the existence of subgroups in the industry:

> The U.S. prescription industry is made up of two distinct segments—"innovators" that research and develop new and improved drugs, and "imitators" (commonly referred to as generic houses) that produce only follow-on copies of the original version of a drug.[10]

Indeed, the PMA represents only the large innovative firms; the smaller generic houses have their own trade association—the National Association of Pharmaceutical Manufacturers. This is further evidence of the industry split and has provided a vehicle for strategic investments in the industry.

The easing of regulations on generic substitution threatened the major drug producers, who recognized the potential effect of the Act on the competitive structure of the industry. C. J. Stetler, past president of the trade association representing the large drug firms, argued that "drug firms that specialize in cheaper drugs and spend nothing on research may temporarily gain advantages here and there from a market artificially restructured in their favor by government." Encouraging pharmacists to dispense generic drugs, as the state and FTC rules did, clearly influenced the expected profits of the major firms. In this industry, the potential effect of the regulatory change appears to be large: the cross-elasticity of demand is high. Thus the substitution laws would be expected to reduce the payoff to branded drugs and reduce both the incentive for and ability to innovate.

What action did the drug firms take in response to this regulatory initiative? Led by the trade association, the firms tried to influence the new rules, and the trade association itself began to lobby legislators about the social costs of the proposed act. Individual firms made similar approaches to the FTC. Eli Lilly, one of the largest firms in the industry, argued, for example, that "repeal of the anti-substitution laws has regulatory implications when thought of as changing the environment upon which the current institutional structure of the pharmaceutical industry is based."[11] Armistead Lee, president of the PMA, used the language of the public interest in his lobbying efforts:

> Those in Government proposing the MAC and substitutions programs are using an Adam Smith model of perfect competition as a measure for maximizing consumer welfare. It is a static model, and it implies that departures from pure competition are contrived by producers through product differentiation based on advertising and promotion, which forces consumers to spend more than they should.
>
> We, on our side, are using a dynamic model—associated with the name of Schumpeter, even though most who share this philosophy may never have heard of that great economist. We recognize that competition is imperfect. We say that this is inevitable in an environment where one is dealing with a high-technology product, where quality differences are critical, where (admittedly) buyers or their agents are not perfectly informed on price, and where brand loyalties, as in so many other commodity areas, are very important. We would recall Schumpeter's assertion that under perfect competition one could not expect to find innovation.[12]

The generic firms were less vocal, though they too behaved as we would have predicted. The smaller drug companies, represented by their own trade association—the National Association of Pharmaceutical Manufacturers (NAP)—supported the repeal of antisubstitution laws, the FTC position. One of the major generic houses stated the position of this segment of the market: "There should be a substantial monetary saving if effective substitution laws are passed. . . . major companies will devote more time to research in order to maintain a lead in original pharmaceutical products and development."

Both types of drug company took predictable positions: The brand-drug companies emphasized the carrot as a way to encourage innovation; the generic firms placed their faith in the stick of competition. Both used the public interest to justify their positions.

At the same time as firms lobbied for regulatory changes, a number of the large brand-name producers began to increase their production of generic drugs. Indeed, the president of the trade association representing the large drug firms argued that the repeal of antisubstitution laws was bad precisely because it would "force" big companies to emphasize generics.[13] The large firms have been idiosyncratic in their use of this strategy. Eli Lilly, Upjohn, and Smithkline have been fairly aggressive in expanding into the generic market; a number of the other major firms have still not penetrated it. For some firms, regulatory change stimulated differences in strategic investments.

The attempt to use the regulatory environment strategically is most clearly seen in the response of the major firms to the requirements that they provide lists of equivalent drugs to pharmacists. Evidence indicates that substitution is increased substantially when the pharmacist is provided with such information. The major firms have argued that if such lists are to be developed more work needs to be undertaken to establish the equivalence—and that this research should take place within the traditional drug-testing channel.

Under existing FDA rules, all new drugs must eventually be tested in humans. On the other hand, chemical equivalents to new drugs made by other manufacturers after the original patent lapses require only an abbreviated testing procedure. In general, unless some problem exists, tests in vivo (in the body) are not required by copy-cat drugs; cheaper in vitro (lit. in glass) tests may be used instead. In order to assure therapeutic equivalency, the major research firms proposed that "each manufacturer of any multi-source product should meet monograph standards and hold either a full [test] that includes comparative bioavailability in man (in vivo)."[14] Had the FDA and FTC accepted this proposal, two effects would have followed: Our confidence in the bioequivalence of drugs in the equivalent list might have increased, and the testing costs to the generic houses would have risen substantially. As we can see, the proposed change would have improved the comparative position of major drug houses vis-à-vis the encroaching generics. It is a clear case in which one subgroup in the industry is attempting to use the regulatory process to change the structure of the industry—in this case to re-establish the old structure. Again, the discussion and lobbying language were in public-interest terms, and indeed there may well be a case that generic drugs require more testing for safety. But at least one side effect of this proposal would have been to improve the position of innovative firms by increasing imitation costs.

The major drug houses have also been active in trying to use regulation to shore up their position on the demand side. In particular, in early discussions of the various antisubstitution laws, it was argued that new regulations should be passed requiring that the manufacturer be identified on the package label for each drug product dispensed. The innovative drug firms are heavy advertisers, relative to the generic houses. Clearly, the advertised firms would gain more from product identification than would the smaller drug houses. This proposal too could be seen as a way to re-establish barriers between the two markets, and thus protect rents threatened by the regulatory change.

The regulation on the substitution of generic for brand-name drugs is but one of a complex list of regulations affecting the pharmaceutical industry. Nevertheless, in this example, we see each of the ways in which strategic planning interacts with the regulatory environment. First, the regulatory change opened up new opportunities and threats in the industry. In response, some firms changed their product mixes; others held firm. Second, lobbying against the new rules was carried on with a public-interest flavor. Finally, firms attempted to tinker with the new rules to reduce their impact on the major players in the industry.

Some Final Thoughts

In the American economy, regulation is ubiquitous. The modern manager as a result often spends a considerable time trying to influence decisions *outside* of the firm. In public utilities, the regulatory process is central to management. But even in free-market areas, the influence of government is large, and the possibilities for strategic management are substantial. We are reminded again of interdependence in the economic system, and of the importance of tracing interdependencies in developing and pursuing viable strategies.

IV

THE PLANNING PROCESS

18

The Strategic Planning Process

Strategic decision making is typically thought of as one of the jobs of top management within an organization.[1] The top management of an organization is expected to have the broad vision and perspective necessary to make decisions about where the organization should be going. But top management does not form this vision alone. Indeed, Quinn has argued that most strategic change occurs incrementally, step-by-step, as the result of actions taken by managers scattered throughout the organization and not as a result of a grand design emerging from the office of the CEO.[2] Formal planning groups form one of the building blocks of strategic decision making, but only one.[3] Indeed, in most organizations the functional units—particularly marketing, production, and finance—play roles equal to that of the planning division.[4]

The observation that strategic planning proceeds with input from a wide range of people within a firm comes naturally out of a theme we have pursued throughout this book concerning the implementation problems of the firm. We have argued, following the interesting and influential work of Williamson and others, that decision making in organizations proceeds under conditions of **bounded rationality**.[5] Put simply, decision makers attempt to do the best they can, given inevitable limits on their information-processing abilities. Conditions of bounded rationality imply that top management must rely on the cooperation of other agents in the organization in the strategic decision-making process. It is simply impossible that the leader of a complex organization could, without considerable cooperation, gather and process all the information needed for decision making. Nor could strategic decisions be implemented without cooperation.

Strategic decision making depends on cooperation from managers located throughout the organization.

The problems of bounded rationality are most acute in large, complex organizations. In very small organizations, the chief executive can often have a finger in most parts of the organizational pie. In larger organizations, this is not possible. Indeed, one of the difficulties that entrepreneurs often face as their organizations grow is learning to live with the fragmented information they come to possess. In a large organization, the task of the chief executive is not only to develop a broad vision for the company but to "manage a network of organizational forces that lead to the discovery, evolution and enrichment of that vision."[6]

Since strategic decision making requires the cooperation of a wide range of agents within an organization, it is important that the principles of strategic decision making be widely diffused in the firm. In some organizations, attempts at diffusion take on a highly formal, almost mechanistic form. Division managers are expected to use printed forms to guide their environmental analysis, for example, or other structured instruments on which the future prospects and plans of the division may be represented. Principles about what is or is not important in the business as well as the goals of the overall organization are embodied, more or less, in these forms. Diffusion is sometimes managed through executive retreats or broad-based planning sessions. Xerox runs a series of participatory activities for the top 15 managers in the organization as a way to diffuse the strategic decision-making process throughout the firm. One critical element in the Xerox process is a series of individual discussions with each of the top managers around particular strategic issues in an attempt to understand the goals and decision biases of each of these managers before the group process submerges those differences.

Principles of strategic decision making should be widely diffused in an organization.

A recent fascinating multiyear study of almost 100 Scottish firms by Reid provides insight into how strategic planning proceeds in many companies and how far practice is from the ideal we have been sketching.[7] Two-thirds of the senior managers in Reid's sample had not been involved in developing firm strategy and thought it to be someone else's job. In more than half the companies studied, there was no structured setting to facilitate cooperation from senior management. Instead, planning responsibilities were given to planning teams which often did not include top management. Even the chief executive of the firms in Reid's sample was often distant from the strategic planning process. Thus, while most of the chief executives of firms in Reid's sample claimed to have strategic objectives, fewer than half could actually list those objectives.[8]

Of course, wide diffusion of the principles of strategic decision making is not enough to ensure cooperation throughout the organization. For, as we have seen, individuals within the organization may have very different incentives and interests. And, as we also observed earlier, some individuals might exploit their information advantages in pursuing self-interests. **Opportunism,** indeed, can derail the most well-thought-out decision process. In a survey of several hundred middle managers, for example, Guth and Macmillan found significant tendencies for managers to intervene in broad organizational decisions in such a way as to protect their own self-interests.[9] In this case it was not that individual managers misunderstood the decision process, but that they had private interests to pursue that were not congruent with overall organizational objectives.

Participants in the strategic decision making process typically have quite different objectives.

The characterization of strategic planning as an activity which requires cooperation from a group of potentially opportunistic individuals leads us naturally to the view that this process is a highly political one. That is, the results of planning and the actual decisions made will depend not only on the analytical "facts" of the situation, but on the constellation of power within the firm.[10] In most important strategic decisions, we see the operation of **coalitions,** groups within the organization which bargain with one another for mutual advantage.[11] Thus one division may support an initiative of a second with the implicit understanding that the second will reciprocate. Indeed, in complex organizations reciprocity is often essential to accomplish anything.

Of course, as coalitions form in the strategic planning process, we will observe opposition among coalitions. As we suggested in Chapter 1, a strategy is a commitment to undertake one set of actions rather than another, and such choices almost inevitably redistribute power within an organization. It is this opposition that made it so difficult to implement the 1960s strategies of using funds from mature divisions to fund investments in other divisions of the firm: the "milking the cow" strategy. For, of course, managers in those mature segments—who controlled both information and decisions—often lost power as they lost resources. The likelihood of opportunistic behavior under these conditions is high.

When we have coalitions that differ in an organization, which coalition's voice is heard? Here we must return to the role of the chief executive, for it is typically the chief executive who ultimately decides in matters of strategic importance which course to take. The power of the chief executive is felt perhaps most by those in the strategic planning group itself, whose impact depends on how it is viewed by the chief executive. Polaroid is a good example of the power of the chief executive. Under Edwin Land, there was essentially no planning group; strategy was Land's job, and he accomplished it without very much staff aid. When William McCune took over from Land and became CEO in 1980, his goal was to diversify Polaroid and guide it into other high-technology businesses. To accomplish this, he developed and relied on a strong planning group. The planning group lost power when I. MacAllister Booth became Polaroid president in 1984, however, as diversification efforts were abandoned and the core photography business once again emphasized. Dependence on the good will and intentions of the chief executive makes planning something of a high-risk profession!

One role of the chief executive is to manage creatively conflicts that arise among various coalitions within the organization.[12] To the extent that there is a market place for ideas in an organization, it is more likely that all aspects of strategic decisions will be considered. Indeed, Selznick argues that coalitions with divergent ideas should be protected within an organization.[13] In the same vein, Winter argues that every large organization—public and private—should have a few divergent thinkers empowered to help the organization do its strategic worrying.[14]

There is strong indication as we look at various organizations that knowledge gives power.[15] Again, we recognize that bounded rationality characterizes the decision-making process. Access to information which others do not share confers influence. Power rests in part on the ability to resolve sources of uncertainty.[16] This is one reason that networks are often important sources of power and influence inside organizations, for networks help in disseminating information within the narrow group. It also helps to explain why groups shut out of particular networks—for example, women and minorities, in some instances—sometimes have difficulty in gaining influence.[17]

Organizations should create incentives for managers to work together in strategic decision making.

One way firms can try to monitor strategic decisions is by implementing a strategic control system. There is considerable agreement in the strategy literature that imposing controls is an essential final step in the planning process given the diversity of information and goals we have been describing.[18] And, yet, most firms, while they have operational controls, focusing on short-term budgetary objectives, typically do not have long-term strategic controls.[19] One result of the absence of strategic controls is that managers become myopic, focusing on short-term goals, to the detriment of the firm's long-term profits.[20] On the other hand, developing strategic controls that are functional in an environment in which change is ubiquitous is very difficult. We have focused throughout this book on the theme that strategy involves taking advantage of opportunities that typically last only a short time. Here the strategic frontier may be changing too fast for most control systems to have any salience. In a similar way, Gould and Quinn argue that in turbulent businesses, the value of a control system may be quite low.[21] We are left here, as we are in many management decisions, with a difficult trade-off: Without control systems, it is more difficult to judge and motivate managers. On the other hand, control systems may be overly rigid and thus prompt managerial behavior that is unproductive.

Strategic planning serves as a way both to create and to manage change in an organization, and change itself creates the most important opportunities for and threats to an organization. Recent interesting work suggests that organizations with the most vulnerable technologies—and thus the ones most sensitive to change—rely most heavily on the strategic planning process.[22] As Drucker put it, the "pertinent question [of management] is not how to do things right, but how to find the right things to do."[23] Finding the right thing to do is most difficult when the environment is changing and the organization is threatened by that change. And here strategic controls may be most needed but least helpful.

But strategic planning is not only most useful in times of change; strategic planning itself evolves over time in organizations. Mintzberg distinguishes between the *entrepreneurial planning mode* that characterizes young, rapidly growing organizations and the *adaptive* and *analytical planning modes* that typically develop as an organization matures.[24] In early stages of organizational life, the entrepreneur has the dominant role in planning. At this point, the organization is less likely to be hounded by problems of bounded rationality and opportunism. So centralized strategic decision making is more possible. Moreover, in this stage of the organization's life, there is often very little experience and data on which one can base analytical methods of planning. As an organization grows and the rate of change in its environment slows, more analytical and more decentralized planning typically emerges. In sum, the strategic planning process often has a life-cycle character to it as does the rest of the organization.

The strategic planning process changes not only within organizations as they grow and mature, but also over time, across institutions. In recent years, as we have gained an appreciation for the cooperation needed in planning, many organizations opened the planning process to the lower ranks in the organization. Multidivisional organizations like General Electric, Kodak, and Dial have slimmed down the corporate staff involved in planning and instead rely on managers in the various lines of business to take responsibility for much of the strategic planning. Welch, the CEO of General Electric, defends his attempt to streamline planning and management at G.E. in highly graphic terms: "Layers in highly layered organizations are like people who wear several sweaters outside on a freezing winter day. They remain warm and comfortable but are blissfully ignorant of the realities of their environment. They couldn't be further from what's going on."[25] Of course, such decentralization is usually undertaken with a global view of the objectives of the corporation. Nevertheless, decentralization reflects a growing awareness of the implementation problems described earlier in this book. And, as our knowledge of this area grows, we should expect other changes in the planning process as organizations begin the inevitable process of experimentation with and then imitation of others' successful management ideas. This is as it should be, for it is the process of experimentation, as tested in the crucible of the market place, that gives our economy its variety and vigor and gives to the management process much of its challenge.

APPENDIX 1

Some Case Suggestions

In courses on strategy, cases are an essential vehicle for learning the material. Many possible cases could be used with my text. Below are a few suggestions based on cases I use in my own teaching. Many of the cases listed are Harvard Business School products, noted HBS, and are available directly from HBS. Other cases are from the Yale School of Management, noted SOM, and may be obtained directly from me. In some instances, a case is listed in several places to reflect its broad content. As you use this text, I expect you will find many other suitable cases which will fit well with particular chapters.

Chapters 1–4: Industry Structure

The Soft Drink Industry in 1986 (HBS)
Note on the Electronic Component Industry (HBS)
The Disposable Diaper Industry (HBS)
Sierra Log Homes (HBS)
The Water Meter Industry in 1982 (HBS)
Molecular Genetics (HBS)

Chapter 5: Strategic Groups

U.S. Bicycle Industry (HBS)
SWECO, Inc. (HBS)

Chapter 6: Global Competition

The Global Semiconductor Industry (HBS)
Corning (HBS)

Chapter 7: Competing for Advantage

Levi Strauss in 1982 (SOM)
Note on Aluminum, 1983 (HBS)
The United Woodcutters Association (SOM)
General Electric in 1974 (HBS)

General Electric in 1984 (HBS)
The United Hmong Association (SOM)
Norton Co. (HBS)

Chapters 8–9: Implementing Goals and Organizational Structure

Speer Industries (HBS)
The United Woodcutters Association (SOM)
General Electric, 1984 (HBS)
First Federal Savings (HBS)
Waverly Community House (SOM)
People Express A (HBS)
Honeywell Information Systems: Culture Change, 1985 (HBS)
TRW Systems D (HBS)
Rockford Containers A (HBS)

Chapter 10: Diversification

Raytheon Corp, Diversification (HBS)
The U.S. Steel Industry in 1982 (SOM)
U.S. West, Inc. (HBS)
Norton Co. (HBS)
Sears, Roebuck in 1987 (HBS)
Gurney Seed (HBS)

Chapter 11: Vertical Integration

Toledo Gear (HBS)
EMP Corp.: Asbury Park, Plant A (HBS)
Sensorimatic Electronics Corp (HBS)
Fafco (Stanford Case)

Chapter 12: Mergers

Raytheon Corp, Diversification (HBS)
Volkswagen Group (HBS)
Gurney Seed and Nursery Corp. (HBS)

Chapters 13–15: Rivalry

Disposable Diapers in 1974 (HBS)
GE vs. Westinghouse: Large Turbine Generators (HBS)
Kodak Polaroid (HBS)
Du Pont Co.: Titanium Dioxide (HBS)

Chapter 16: Rivalry in Research and Development

Cray Research (HBS)
Fiber Optics (HBS)

Chapter 17: Strategic Regulation

U.S. West Inc. (HBS)
General Telephone of the Northwest (HBS)
Tiner Trucking Co. A (HBS)
Electric Utility Industry in 1982 (HBS)
Elscint (HBS)

APPENDIX 2

Financial Ratio Analysis

In Chapter 2, we stressed the difficulty of inferring organizational performance from one or two simple numbers. Nevertheless, in practice a number of different ratios are often calculated in strategic planning endeavors and, taken as a whole and with some caution, these ratios do provide some information about the relative performance of an organization. In particular, a careful analysis of a combination of these ratios may help us to distinguish between firms that will eventually fail and those that will continue to survive. Evidence suggests that, as early as five years before a firm fails, one may be able to detect trouble from the value of these financial ratios.[1]

In this appendix, the basic financial ratios are reviewed, and some of the caveats associated with using them are highlighted. The ratios tend to be most meaningful when they are used to compare organizations within the same broad industry, or when they are used to make inferences about changes in a particular organization's structure over time.

Liquidity Ratios

In order to survive, firms must be able to meet their short-term obligations—pay their creditors and repay their short-term debts. Thus the liquidity of the firm is one measure of a firm's financial health. Two measures of liquidity are in common

Current ratio = Current assets / Current liabilities
Quick ratio = (Cash + Marketable securities + Net receivables) / Current liabilities

The main difference between the current ratio and the quick ratio is that the latter does not include inventories, while the former does.

Which ratio is a better measure of a firm's short-term position? In some ways, the quick ratio is a more conservative standard. If the quick ratio is greater than one, there would seem to be no danger that the firm would not be able to meet its current obligations. If the quick ratio is less than one, but the current ratio is considerably above one, the status of the firm is more complex. In this case the valuation of inventories and the inventory turnover are obviously critical.

A number of problems with inventory valuation can contaminate the current ratio. An obvious accounting problem occurs because organizations value inventories using either of two methods, LIFO or FIFO. Under the LIFO method—Last

340

in First out—inventories are valued at their old costs. If the organization has a substantial quantity of inventory, some of it may be carried at relatively low cost, assuming some inflation in overall prices. On the other hand, if there has been technical progress in a market and prices have been falling, the LIFO method will lead to an overvalued inventory. Under the FIFO method of inventory valuation— First in First out—inventories are valued at close to their current replacement cost. Clearly, if we have firms that differ in their accounting methods, and hold substantial inventories, comparisons of current ratios will not be very helpful in measuring their relative strength, unless accounting differences are adjusted for in the computations.

A second problem with including inventories in the current ratio derives from the difference between the inventory's *accounting value*, however calculated, and its *economic value*. A simple example is a firm subject to business-cycle fluctuations. For a firm of this sort, inventories will typically build during a downturn. The posted market price for the inventoried product will often not fall very much during this period; nevertheless, the firm finds it cannot sell very much of its inventoried product at the so-called market price. The growing inventory is carried at the posted price, but there really is no way that the firm could liquidate that inventory in order to meet current obligations. Thus including inventories in current assets will tend to understate the precarious financial position of firms suffering inventory build-up during downturns.

Might we then conclude that the quick ratio is always to be preferred? I think not. If we ignore inventories, firms with readily marketable inventories, appropriately valued, will be undeservedly penalized. Clearly some judicious further investigation of the marketability of the inventories would be helpful.

Low values for the current or quick ratios suggest that a firm may have difficulty meeting current obligations. Low values, however, are not always fatal. If an organization has good long-term prospects, it may be able to enter the capital market and borrow against those prospects to meet current obligations. The nature of the business itself might also allow it to operate with a current ratio less than one. For example, in an operation like McDonald's, inventory turns over much more rapidly than the accounts payable become due. This timing difference can also allow a firm to operate with a low current ratio. Finally, to the extent that the current and quick ratios are helpful indexes of a firm's financial health, they act strictly as signals of trouble at extreme rates. Some liquidity is useful for an organization, but a very high current ratio might suggest that the firm is sitting around with a lot of cash because it lacks the managerial acumen to put those resources to work. Very low liquidity, on the other hand, is also problematic.

Leverage

Firms are financed by some combination of debt and equity. The right capital structure will depend on tax policy—high corporate rates favor debt, high personal tax rates favor equity—on bankruptcy costs, and on overall corporate risk.[2] In particular, if we are concerned about bankruptcy possibilities, the long-run solvency or *leverage* of the firm may be important. There are two commonly used measures of leverage, the *debt-to-assets ratio* and the *debt-equity ratio:*

> Debt-to-asset ratio = total liabilities / total assets
> Debt-equity ratio = long-term debt / shareholder's equity

As with liquidity measures, problems in measurement and interpretation also occur in leverage measures. The central problem is that assets and equity are typically measured in terms of the carrying (book) value in the firm's financial statements. This figure, however, often has very little to do with the market value of the firm, or the value that creditors could receive were the firm liquidated.

Debt-to-equity ratios vary considerably across industries in large measure due to other characteristics of the industry and its environment. A utility, for example, which is a stable business, can comfortably operate with a relatively high debt-equity ratio. A more cyclical business, like manufacturing of recreational vehicles, typically needs a lower D/E—a reminder that cross-industry comparisons of these ratios is typically not very helpful.

Often, analysts look at the debt-equity ratio to determine the ability of an organization to generate new funds from the capital market. An organization with considerable debt is often thought to have little new financing capacity. Of course, the overall financing capacity of an organization probably has as much to do with the quality of the new product the organization wishes to pursue as with its financial structure. Nevertheless, given the threat of bankruptcy and the attendant costs, a very high debt-equity ratio may make future financing difficult. It has been argued, for example, that railroads in the 1970s found it hard to find funds for new investments in piggybacking, a large technical improvement in railroading, because the threat of bankruptcy from prior poor investments was so high.

Rates of Return

We have indicated some of the main problems with traditional measures of return in the main body of the chapter. Thus, the discussion here will be brief.

There are two measures of profitability common in the financial community, *ROA*, or return on assets; and *ROE*, or return on equity.

$$ROA = \text{net income} / \text{total average assets}$$
$$ROE = \text{net income} / \text{total stockholder's equity}$$

Assets and equity, as used in these two common indexes, are both measured in terms of book value. Thus if assets were acquired some time ago, at a low price, the current performance of the organization may be overstated by the use of historically valued denominators. As a result, the accounting returns for any investment generally do not correlate well with the true economic internal rate of return for that investment.

Difficulties with using either ROA and ROE as a performance measure can be seen in merger transactions. Suppose we have an organization that has been earning a net income of $500 on assets with a book value of $1000, for a hefty ROA of 50 percent. That organization is now acquired by a second firm, which then moves the new assets onto its books *at the acquisition price*, assuming the acquisition is treated using the purchase method of accounting. Of course, the acquisition price will be considerably above the $1000 book value of assets, for the potential acquirer will have to pay handsomely for the privilege of earning $500 on a regular basis. Suppose the acquirer pays $2000 for the assets. After the acquisition, it will appear that the returns of the acquired firm have fallen. The firm continues to earn $500, but the asset base is now $2000, so the ROA is reduced to 25 percent. Indeed, the ROA may be less as a result of other factors, such as increased depreciation, of the newly acquired assets. *Yet in fact nothing has happened to the earnings of the firm.* All that has changed is its accounting, not its performance.

Another fundamental problem with ROA and ROE measures comes from the tendency of analysts to focus on performance in single years, years that may be idiosyncratic. At a minimum, one should examine these ratios averaging over a number of years to isolate idiosyncratic returns and try to find patterns in the data.

Stock-Market Ratios

Several ratios are calculated not from the income statements and balance sheets of organizations, but from data associated with their stock-market performance. The three most common ratios are *earnings per share (EPS),* the *price-earnings ratio (P/E),* and the *dividend-yield ratio:*

EPS = (net income − preferred dividends) / common shares outstanding
P/E = market price per share / earnings per share
Dividend yield = annual dividends / price per share

EPS is one of the most widely used statistics. Indeed, it is required to be given in the income statements of publicly traded firms. As we can see, the ratio tells us how much the firm has earned per share of stock outstanding. As it turns out, this is not generally a very helpful statistic. It says nothing about how many assets a firm used to generate those earnings, and hence nothing about profitability. Nor does it tell us how much the individual stockholder has paid per share for the rights over that annual earning. Further, accounting practices in the calculation of earnings may distort these ratios. And finally, the treatment of inventories is again problematic.

The P/E is another ratio commonly cited. Indeed, P/E's are reported in daily newspapers. A high P/E tends to indicate that investors believe the future prospects of the firm are better than its current performance. They are in some sense paying more per share than current earnings of the firm indicate is warranted. Again, earnings are treated differently in different accounting practices.

Finally, from the perspective of some stockholders at least, dividend policy may be important. The dividend-yield ratio tells us how much of its earnings the firm pays out in dividends versus reinvestment. Rapidly growing firms in new areas tend to have low dividend-yield ratios; more mature firms tend to have higher ratios.

Summary

In this appendix, we have briefly reviewed a variety of ratios commonly used in strategic planning. All of these ratios are subject to manipulation through opportunistic accounting practices. Nevertheless, taken as a group and used judiciously, they may help to identify firms or business units in particular trouble. Finding profitable new ventures requires rather more work.

APPENDIX 3

Using Statistics To Determine Advantage

If your organization has been operating in an industry for a long period of time, you probably have at least some idea of the sources of relative defensible advantage in that industry. On the other hand, firms moving into new ventures may have relatively little feel for which factors have the largest payoffs. In this appendix, I briefly review several methodologies that might be used to understand the determinants of profit in an industry.

The Problem

Suppose you are thinking about moving into an industry that currently has 15 firms. A quick look at the industry suggests that the firms appear to have taken rather different strategies in this market. Thus, you have some questions about what kind of entry strategy you might pursue. The first thing you might do is collect some basic data on the performance and structure of the firms already in the industry in order to figure out how well current firms are doing and why they are succeeding, or not succeeding. In this industry, suppose you already have a sense that size, advertising, and research are the core differences among extant firms. Some of the data you might collect are presented in Table A3.1.

We can see from the data that the firms in the industry differ considerably in their profitability.[1] Firm 3 earned a return of 32 percent, while Firms 5 and 6 earned only 4 percent and 3 percent. The firms also differ considerably in their size, research and development efforts, and advertising efforts. For example, Firm 3 has the highest profits in our hypothetical industry and is a high-share, high-R&D, high-advertising organization. Firm 1 has a modest share and advertising budget, a relatively high R&D budget, and earns relatively high returns as well. And so on.

If we look at the table and ask ourselves to identify the role of share, research, and advertising in this industry, a simple answer would not be forthcoming. Some of the high share firms do quite well, other less so. Some of the researchers do well, others badly. And, similarly for advertising. The pattern revealed in the data is not a simple one.[2]

Table A3.1   Constructed profit data

Firm	Returns %	Market share %	Advertising to sales ratio	R&D sales ratio
1	17	7	.017	.004
2	23	8	.021	.004
3	32	10	.020	.005
4	6	3	.001	.003
5	4	4	.005	.001
6	3	5	.004	.001
7	15	9	.016	.002
8	20	10	.018	.003
9	12	6	.015	.002
10	15	9	.021	.003
11	5	4	.010	.001
12	7	8	.010	.001
13	8	4	.013	.001
14	14	7	.010	.002
15	12	6	.009	.002

The Case-Study Option

One can take two approaches at this point: the case-study approach or the statistical approach.

Through a detailed study of each of the organizations in the industry, one might discern how their research and advertising budgets are allocated, for instance, and what their production facilities are like, and how coordination is accomplished across areas.

If the number of industry participants is small, a detailed investigation can help to sort out salient differences among firms and focus on strategic differences. But the ease with which one can gather such data varies tremendously across areas. For industries with a large number of participants, detailed information on a substantial portion of the group is probably beyond the purview of an investigation. For concentrated industries the task is easier. Publicly traded firms reveal more information about themselves than private firms. Regulated firms are often required to reveal considerable details of their cost and operating structures.

For any group of firms, there are a variety of legitimate sources of information about the way the organization runs. The business press is an excellent source of information on businesses, particularly those in the limelight. Several years ago, a firm in the Fortune 100, operating in a prominent industry, became interested in how good the quality of its competitor information was. To answer this question, they conducted a small experiment. A management student who knew nothing about the firm, but who had a modest knowledge of management and a great deal of energy, was hired for the summer. The student was given a corner office and a set of questions about the firm—the kinds of questions the firm typically tried to find out about its competitors. She was then told to answer the questions, using only public sources. At the end of the summer, she reported to her superiors. The correlation between her information and the facts as known by company insiders was excellent. The public image of the firm turned out to be quite accurate. This firm subsequently put more faith in the information it gathered about other firms—and developed a bit more reticence in its own dealings with the media.

Another often excellent source of information about an organization is its prior employees and the customers and suppliers of rival organizations. In this way, using public data as well as more private data, a new entrant can begin to put together a picture of successful strategies in the market.

If an industry is large, new, or out of the public eye, gathering detailed data may be difficult. Indeed, it may even be difficult to collect data such as that represented in Table A3.1. An alternative is to conduct a statistical study. (This approach, of course, can also serve as a complement to the case-study method.)

The Statistical Approach

Economists often try to account for differences across firms in profit patterns, by using regression analysis. Regression analysis is a statistical method that allows us to identify the extent to which a variety of factors influence some particular variable. In this case, for instance, regression analysis might identify the contribution of various firm characteristics to profitability.

Regression analysis begins with the specification of a *regression equation*.[3] Let us start with a simple model, in which firm profitability is expected to be related to market share, research patterns, and advertising. We can write this relationship as follows, assuming the simplest linear form:

$$1.\ P = a + b_1 MS + b_2 RD + b_3 ADV + u$$

Firm profits are hypothesized to be equal to a constant, plus a contribution depending on the market share *(MS)*, research budget *(RD)*, and advertising budget *(ADV)* of the firm. The actual values of a, b_1, b_2, and b_3 are determined from the data.

If we were to estimate equation 1, using the data given in Table A3.1, we would find the following:

$$2.\ P = -5.9 + 1.05\ MS + 3523\ RD + 226\ ADV$$
$$(2.03) \qquad (.82) \qquad (1.38)$$

The numbers in parentheses under the coefficients are the t statistics for each of the coefficients. These figures tell us how confident we are in our estimates. If the t statistic is over 2, we are generally confident in the sign of that relationship.

In the regression run on these data, we see that market share and research appear to have strong effects on profitability. For the case of market share, for example, a 1 percent increase in share yields approximately a 1 percent increase in profitability. In Figure A3.1, I have posted actual observations against those predicted by the three variables. As we see, predictions are quite close to actual. In fact, this equation explains approximately 90 percent of the variance in returns.

Regression analysis can be used to try to understand many economic phenomena at the firm level. One simple example is some early work I did on the Basic Oxygen Furnace (BOF) in the steel industry, a process described earlier in this chapter. I was interested in the speed with which various plants in the industry converted to BOF technology. My sample was 45 plants in approximately 20 firms

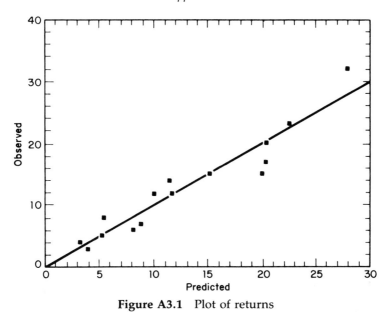

Figure A3.1 Plot of returns

in the industry. The hypothesis tested was that speed of adoption was determined by cost savings from the BOF, demand growth, and firm size.

This hypothesis was confirmed by the results in Table A3.2.

Plants for which the BOF would yield a large cost advantage—typically older plants—adopted relatively early. Growth in demand stimulated adoption of the innovation. All else equal, larger firms were more conservative than smaller in their investment strategies.

In order to employ regression analysis, one requires a reasonable number of observations. In our regression based on Table A3.1, for example, we used 15

Table A3.2 Adoption of the basic oxygen furnace by plants in the U.S. steel industry

Independent variable	Tobit estimate of years since adoption (1980 = 0)
Constant	−14.51
	(−.99)[a]
Cost advantage	3.75
	(2.15)
Growth in demand in region	.120
	(1.32)
Firm size (in tons)	−.293
	(−2.93)
Number of observations	45

[a] t statistics in parentheses.

firms. This is a rather small sample. In my work on steel, I used plant data and thus was able to find 45 observations, a respectable though still modest sample size. If we are using data on firms *within* an industry, it is often hard to build a sample; especially if there are not many firms in a particular industry. Moreover, in some industries all the participants are multidivisional firms who do not report much data on the relevant *line-of-business* or *LOB* level. In cases where organizations cannot learn much about an industry, they can turn to an outside organization that uses line-of-business data to generate statistical profiles of industries.

One of the foremost organizations using statistical methods at the line-of-business level is the Strategic Planning Institute, with its PIMS model (Profit Impact of Marketing Strategy). When a new client approaches the Institute, it submits data for a wide range of variables, all at the line-of-business level. Typical data include research budget, advertising expenditures, major buyers, market share, capital investment, and financial data. At the same time, the PIMS model has a good deal of data on the industry in which the LOB operates, for example, growth rates, concentration levels, and so on. In this way, the PIMS group builds up a data base, using information provided by clients at a very detailed level. This data base can then be used to examine the profitability of various management factors. At present, the PIMS data include observations on more than 2000 individual strategic-business units.

The PIMS group is not alone in undertaking analyses on the line-of-business basis. Some government data are also collected this way. In the mid 1970s, the Federal Trade Commission collected a rich set of line-of-business data from its large sample of businesses. For this period, government data are a sample on which LOB statistical work could be done. And, indeed, that data set has generated considerable analysis. In Table A3.3, we reproduce one sample of the profitability regression that has emerged from the FTC data.

The over-all methodology and results of the FTC regressions bear a strong family resemblance to PIMS work. In the case of both PIMS data and FTC data, profitability is explained by aggregating across a wide range of different lines of business and examining relations between profits and an assortment of plausible explanatory variables. As we see from Table A3.3, the explanatory variables include such important strategic factors as market share, integration, diversification, research and development, and the like. Explanatory variables also typically include some industry characteristics, such as import and export levels, market growth rate, and industry concentration.

In the regression we described early in this appendix on our 15 hypothetical firms, we generated estimates of the value of research, market share, and the like by looking at data only from firms in the industry in question. This gave us specific data, but few observations. Even in the PIMS data base or the FTC data, for many industries the number of LOB observations is extremely small, too small for statistical analysis. Instead, one can try to merge industries, control for salient differences among them, and use the information contained in a variety of LOBs across a set of industries to try to determine the impact of particular strategies. Thus, for example, rather than confine ourselves to the soft-drink industry to try to determine the efficacy of advertising, we might merge all beverage LOBs or even all food LOBs to look at the payoff to advertising.

In the past, considerable aggregation has been used in the PIMS analyses, as well as in work done on government LOB data. As mentioned earlier, in some cases, so little data are available on a particular LOB that one must rely on data

Table A3.3 Determinants of profits, FTC line-of-business data, 1975

Explanatory variables	Coefficient	(t-statistic)
Intercept	−.20	(−6.0)
Concentration ratio	−.02	(−1.77)
Market share	.15	(5.51)
Min. efficient scale	.18	(2.1)
Buyer concentration ratio	.05	(4.5)
Buyer dispersion	−.004	(−.64)
Suppliers' concentration	−.03	(−1.39)
Suppliers' dispersion	−.05	(−2.86)
Growth 76 v. of shipments		
72 v. of shipments	.04	(6.70)
% imports	−.04	(−2.23)
% exports	.065	(1.73)
Distance shipped	−.013	(−2.52)
Vertical integration, firm	.01	(1.55)
Vertical integration, industry	−.03	(−3.39)
Diversification, firm	.01	(1.65)
Diversification, industry	−.03	(−1.87)
Advertising/Sales, firms	−.02	(−.35)
Advertising/Sales, industry	.23	(2.29)
R&D/Sales, firm	−.47	(−3.68)
R&D/Sales, industry	−.25	(−1.51)
Assets/Sales, firm	−.02	(−2.82)
Assets/Sales, industry	.06	(4.98)
Capacity utilization, firm	.19	(11.44)
Capacity utilization, industry	.04	(1.25)
$R^2 = .12$		

Source: David Ravenscraft, "Structure-Profit Relationships at the Line of Business and Industry Level," *Review of Economics and Statistics,* February 1983, pp. 22–31.

from related industries—that is, trade off sample size against reliability of individual data points. Unfortunately, such aggregation has a significant cost. If we aggregate three industries, we are implicitly assuming that each of the strategic variables has the *same incremental* effect on profits across those three industries. But this will often not be true: Market share does not have the same effect in all industries, nor do research and development or advertising. Growth in demand increases profits rapidly in industries in which entry is slow and difficult and may have modest effects in more flexible industries. To the extent that strategic relationships differ across the industries we have aggregated, the true relations will be obscured.[4]

Recent work using the line-of-business information from the PIMS data base has tried to disaggregate the data somewhat. One study classified the PIMS line-of-business data into broad groups: mature, declining, export oriented, emerging, and so on. Separate regressions were run on each data set, arguing that particular strategies paid off differently in various environments.[5] Table A3.4 presents the

Table A3.4   Determinants of ROI by environment
type

Independent variables	Mature	Emerging
Receivables/revenue	.003	.203*
Inventory/revenue	−.165	−.126*
Investment intensity	−.257*	−.403*
Backwards integration	−.189*	.022
Towards integration	.053	−.069
Capacity utilization	.101	.112*
Labor productivity	.165*	.117*
Relative compensation	.035	.077
% purchase: 3 suppliers	−.065	−.039
Product breadth	−.108	.036
Product quality	.120*	.176*
Relative price	.169*	−.029
Relative cost	−.214*	−.074
Manufacturing exp/rev	−.302*	−.205*
R&D/revenues	−.054	−.150*
Adv/revenues	−.097	−.239
Market share	.220*	−.056
R^2	.58	.48

Source: J. Prescott, A. Kohli, and N. Ven Katraman, "The Marketshare-
Profitability Relationship: An Empirical Assessment of Major Assertions
and Contradictions," *Strategic Management Journal*, Spring 1986, p. 386.

results for two of the broad classes studied: the mature industries versus the
emerging industries. In many cases, the coefficients differ substantially. Market
share is positive and significant for mature industries, but insignificant for lines
of business in emerging settings. There also appear to be differences in payoffs to
integration, price cutting, and product breadth.

But the aggregation problem may be worse than even this literature recog-
nizes. Some of the underlying relationships may vary by *group within industries*.
In Chapter 5, I suggested some of the ways that strategic groups in an industry
might be differentially able to exploit profit opportunities and might find themselves with substantially different profit-payoff functions. In earlier work, Porter
found, for example, that advertising budgets had substantial payoffs for dominant
firms in an industry, but none for small followers, while industry growth had a
bigger impact on followers than on the dominants. It is in principle possible to
distinguish among industry groups in a PIMS-like regression, but again sample
size makes this difficult.

**In evaluating the output of PIMS-like regressions, homogeneity in the strategic re-
lationships of the aggregated units is essential.**

One must be cautious in other ways in using large-scale regressions to understand industry structure. In the regression I specified early in this chapter, the
model of profits was quite simple. Profits depended in a linear way on market
share and on last year's advertising and research budgets. Even PIMS regressions
typically rely on linear structures and *ad hoc* specifications. But the determinants

of profitability are often more complex. In understanding the results of the regression, it is important to think seriously about the variables in the equation and the way in which you interpret results. A few examples will help make this point clear.

In some early experiments with this model of profits, one of the determinants of profits used in the regression equation was the current research-to-sales ratio of the organization. The estimated equation then showed a negative coefficient on research: current research decreased firm profits.[6] If we look back at Table A3.2, we see this negative relationship from the FTC data. Table A3.3, using PIMS data, also indicates a negative return to research. How do we interpret this? Should firms reduce research expenditures as a way to increase returns? Most firms realize that current research spending reduces current profits. But research is expected to have a payoff in the future. Thus, the relevant question is how *past* research has affected firm profitability. In the regression, it is preferable to have past research expenditures, not current, for a careful analysis of the strategic role of research. In evaluating the impact of advertising, one might similarly be interested in the stock of advertising, rather than its current flow. In many cases, the explanatory variables used in a regression are not good representations of strategic choices.

A second problem crops up with the use of variables in the equation that are codetermined with profits. A good example is capacity utilization. High rates of capacity utilization clearly lead to higher profits. On the other hand, it may not help an organization very much to tell it to increase utilization rates to boost profits. What the firm really needs to know is *how* to raise utilization rates, and here the regression is less meaningful.

Summary

Statistical work can be extremely helpful in understanding the dynamics of an industry, particularly an industry relatively unknown to the firm. Case-study work can also be quite illuminating. In the appendix, methodological issues have been reviewed. One message of this appendix is that one needs to be careful in using statistics.

APPENDIX 4

A Discussion of Portfolio Techniques

In the practice of strategy at most large organizations, the BCG matrix discussed in Chapter 8 or a variant thereof is commonly used for corporate-portfolio analysis. These portfolio techniques are relatively simple to use, and they provide some clarity in helping an organization to picture its aggregate composition. As I have tried to indicate, however, there are difficulties in overly relying on these techniques, because a full-fledged portfolio analysis should embrace a variety of considerations not well captured in a simple matrix. Recent attempts to preserve some of the simplicity of the BCG approach better model the underlying complexity of the portfolio-choice problem. In this appendix, I review one of these alternative approaches, the G.E. matrix.

The G.E. Matrix

In the early 1970s, General Electric developed a portfolio matrix known as the Business Attractiveness Screen. As in the BCG matrix, the unit of observation was the particular business unit, but the G.E. matrix took into account the greater complexity of the causes of a business unit's profitability. Exhibit A4.1 below provides a sample G.E. screen.

On the horizontal axis of the G.E. matrix is placed the *industry attractiveness* of the unit. Attractiveness is measured in different ways by different organizations, but it typically includes some attention to the growth rate of the industry, the average margins in the industry, and so on. On the vertical axis of the matrix, units are ranked according to the *strength of the business unit*.

Exactly how are industry attractiveness and business strength measured? Industry attractiveness can be measured in terms of industry growth rates. In this case, the G.E. matrix resembles the BCG matrix. On the other hand, an assessment of industry attractiveness can involve an in-depth economic analysis of the industry, including an analysis of the levels of barriers to entry into the industry. In terms of our earlier metaphor, the firm might ask, What kind of a poker game is this unit engaged in?

On the vertical axis of the matrix, business strength can be regarded as synonymous with market share, and if it is the G.E. matrix will resemble the BCG

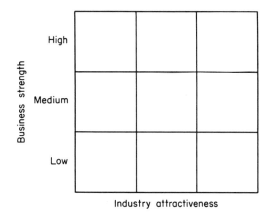

Figure A4.1 Sample G.E. Business Attractiveness Screen

matrix. Alternatively we can ask the kinds of questions about the business unit posed in Chapter 7. What are the key success factors in this industry? How does our organization do on these factors relative to our rivals? Can our organization protect its advantage in the face of the inevitable attempts at imitation? Units with a strong relative advantage on factors of key importance to the business, and which are defensible, are strong units. Units that currently have an advantage, but have no way to protect against imitation, are somewhat weaker in terms of future potential. Units with a defensible advantage in an area of modest importance to the success of the business are also in a weaker position. And so on.

Once the organization has analyzed its industry and the unit's strength, it can place all of its operations in the G.E. matrix. As with the BCG matrix, this provides one way of describing the range of business units in the organization. As we look at a G.E. screen, we see a "snapshot" of the organization, one view of a complex firm. Now we might ask: What are the strategic implications of placement in the G.E. matrix? What do we do once we see a particular pattern revealed in the screen? Typically, the prescription is to grow and develop units in attractive industries with unit strength; divest weak units in unattractive industries; and selectively develop the middle ground. Thus the G.E. screen is used to suggest portfolio evolution, just as the B.C.G. matrix did in an earlier period.

One of the interesting features of the G.E. matrix is that, while it is often characterized as one of the portfolio approaches, *it actually focuses not at all on the relationships among business units.* All of the units in the organization appear on the screen, but nowhere is it indicated how the pieces might fit together. The BCG approach, it will be remembered, focused on the cash-flow relationship among business units. In order to develop the "stars," the organization needed the cash from the cash cows. In the G.E. approach, however, there is no sense in which units from one cell will be used to fund growth in another cell. There is no sense in which having a unit in the upper left-hand quadrant of the screen affects the way we view the units anywhere else in the screen. Thus, while the matrix graphically describes the various units of the firm, it does not really provide the strategic function of helping us to *see our business units in the context of the organization as a whole.* Thus I would argue that, while the matrix is sometimes helpful in allowing an organization to organize and depict its analysis of individual business units in the way we described in Chapter 7, we need to go quite a bit further in helping to think about balance and integration among units.

The G.E. screen is a helpful tool in organizing information about the position of the units in an organization. It does not help us in understanding the portfolio issues of the firm.

NOTES

Chapter 1. Introduction and Overview

1. Henry Mintzberg, "Patterns in Strategy Formation," *Management Science*, 29, May 1978, pp. 934–938.
2. T. Mitchell Ford, *Long Range Planning*, December 1981, pp. 9–11.
3. H. Ansoff, *Corporate Strategy* (New York, 1965).
4. P.H. Grinyer, S. Al-Bazazz, and M. Yasai, "Toward a Contingency Theory of Corporate Planning," *Strategic Management Journal*, January–February, 1986, pp. 3–28.
5. P. Lawrence and J. Lorsch, *Organization and Environment: Managing Differentiation and Integration* (Boston, 1967); R. White and R. Hammermesh, "Toward a Model of Business Unit Performance," *Academy of Management Review*, April 1981, pp. 213–283.
6. S. Cray, *Chippewa Falls Herald Telegram*, May 1972. Quoted in F. Aguilar, *General Managers in Action* (New York, 1988), p. 188.
7. The control function has been stressed by P. Lorange in "Formal Planning Systems: Their Role in Strategy Formulation and Implementation," in D. Schendel and C. Hofer, eds. *Strategic Management: A New View of Business Policy and Planning* (Boston, 1979).
8. Reginald Jones, quoted in Aguilar, *General Managers*, p. 267.
9. J. Utterback and W. Abernathy, "A Dynamic Model of Product and Process Innovation," *Omega*, 3 (1975), pp. 639–656.
10. A compelling discussion of the early history of the automobile industry is given in R. Lanzilloti, "The Automobile Industry," in W. Adams, ed. *The Structure of American Industry* (New York, 1971), pp. 256–302.
11. M. Porter, *Competitive Advantage* (New York, 1985).
12. D. Teece, "Firm Boundaries, Technological Innovation, and Strategic Management," in L. Thomas, ed. *The Economics of Strategic Planning* (Lexington, MA, 1986), p. 187.
13. K. Andrews, *The Concept of Corporate Strategy* (Homewood, IL, 1971).
14. P. Haspeslagh, "Portfolio Planning: Uses and Limits," *Harvard Business Review*, January 1982, pp. 58–73.
15. A nice review of contingency theories is provided by G. Steiner, "Contingency Theories of Strategy and Strategic Management," in D. Schendel and C. Hofer, eds. *Strategic Management* (Boston, 1979), pp. 403–416.

Chapter 2. Efficient Markets

1. B. Malkiel, *A Random Walk Down Wall Street,* 4th ed. (New York, 1985), p. 175.
2. Recent work on this proposition has been done by P. Dybvig, "Inefficient Dynamic Portfolio Strategies or How to Throw Away a Million Dollars in the Stock Market," *Review of Financial Studies,* Spring 1988, pp. 67–80.
3. The Security Exchange Commission (SEC) has detailed rules on the use of inside information and has episodically prosecuted offenders in this area quite vigorously.
4. K. Eisenhardt, "Speed and strategic Choice: How Managers Accelerate Decision Making," *California Management Review,* 32 (1990), 1–16.
5. Markets in which entry and exit are easy are known as contestable markets. The importance of this market feature has been emphasized by W. Baumol, J. Panzer, and R. Willig, *Contestable Markets and the Theory of Industry Structure* (New York, 1982).
6. The proposition that marginal costs rise with volume has strategic implications. In particular, it suggests that it is unwise for a start-up firm to project its costs based on its experience with early units of production.
7. D. Graham, D. Kaplan, and D. Sibley, "Efficiency and Competition in the Airline Industry," *Bell Journal of Economics,* Spring 1983, pp. 118–138.
8. A. Kahn, "Airline Deregulation: A Mixed Bag but a Clear Success Nevertheless," *Transportation Law Journal,* 16 (1988), p. 236.
9. A comprehensive review of problems with using accounting numbers to infer economic performance, with particular reference to empirical economic work is G. Benston, "The Validity of Profits-Structure Studies with Particular References to the FTC's Line of Business Data," *American Economic Review,* March 1985, pp. 37–67.
10. Development of strategies-based changes in the market value of the firm are discussed by A. Rappaport, *Creating Shareholder Value: The New Standard for Business Performance* (New York, 1986).
11. S. Wheelwright and K. Clark, *Revolutionizing Product Development* (New York, 1992).
12. Jack Welch, 1991 *General Electric Annual Report,* p. 3.

Chapter 3. Industry Analysis

1. M. Porter, *Competitive Strategy* (New York, 1980), Chapter 1.
2. W. Knowlton, "Statement Before the FTC Symposium on Media Concentration," December 15, 1978. Cited in L. Coser, C. Kadushin, and W. Powell, eds., *Books* (New York, 1982), p. 48.
3. In all of these areas, antitrust issues are raised by the possibility of coordination. The issues will be briefly discussed later in the chapter.
4. This focus on the issues of coordination and cheating was initiated by G. Stigler, "A Theory of Oligopoly," reprinted in G. Stigler, *The Organization of Industry* (Homewood, IL, 1968), pp. 39–66.
5. There has been considerable recent work on the ability of a group of firms to collude successfully under conditions of uncertainty. See, for example, D. Abreu, D. Pearce, and E. Stacchetti, "Optimal Cartel Equilibrium with Imperfect Monitoring," *Journal of Economic Theory,* June 1986, pp. 251–269;

R. Porter, "Optimal Cartel Trigger Price Strategies," *Journal of Economic Theory*, April 1983, pp. 313–338; and P. Cramton and T. Palfrey, "Cartel Enforcement with Uncertainty About Costs," Yale Working Paper #37, 1987.

6. A. Fraas and D. Greer, "Market Structure and Price Collusion," *Journal of Industrial Economics*, September 1977. Another article on this topic is G. Hay and D. Kelly, "An Empirical Survey of Price Fixing Conspiracies, *Journal of Law and Economics*, April 1974, pp. 13–38.

7. Federal Judge Gerhard Geselle.

8. See T. Schelling, *The Strategy of Conflict* (New York, 1960).

9. W. Ouchi, *Theory Z: How American Business Can Meet the Japanese Challenge* (Reading, MA, 1981).

10. Asset specificity has received considerable recent attention in the field of economics. An interesting treatment is provided by O. Williamson, *The Economic Institutions of Capitalism* (New York, 1985).

11. The airline industry does, however, have other specific assets such as gates.

12. D. Mills and L. Schumarin, "Industry Structure with Fluctuating Demand," *American Economic Review*, September 1985, pp. 758–767.

13. See L. White, *The S & L Debacle* (New York, 1991).

14. See G. Douglas and J. Miller, *Economic Regulation of Domestic Air Transport* (Washington, DC, 1974).

15. United States v. Westinghouse Electric Corp., CCH 1960 Trade Cases.

16. An interesting discussion of facilitating devices which uses this distinction is S. Salop, "Practices that Credibly Facilitate Oligopoly Coordination," in J. Stiglitz and G. Mathewson, eds., *New Developments in the Analysis of Industry Structure* (Cambridge, MA, 1986), pp. 265–290.

17. Salop, ibid. Also T. Cooper, "Most Favored Customer Pricing and Tacit Collusion," *Rand Journal of Economics*, Autumn 1986, pp. 377–388.

18. An analysis of these provisions can be found in C. Holt and D. Scheffman, "Facilitating Practices: The Effects of Advance Notice and Best-Price Policies," *Rand Journal of Economics*, Summer 1987, pp. 187–197.

Chapter 4. Understanding the Impediments to Entry

1. Work on specific assets is associated with O. Williamson, *The Economic Institutions of Capitalism* (New York, 1985).

2. Adam Smith, *The Wealth of Nations* (1776), eds. R. Campbell and A. Skinner (Oxford, 1976).

3. F. Popper, *Industry Structure and Competitive Advantage* (Madison, WI, 1984).

4. A discussion of the motorcycle industry can be found in the HBS case, *A Note on the U.S. Motorcycle Industry*, 1974.

5. Capacity estimates were generated from the American Iron and Steel Institute, *Directory of Steel Works*, 1980.

6. K. Bhaskar, *The Future of the World Automobile Industry* (New York, 1980), and *Ward's Automotive Handbook* (Detroit, 1980).

7. The role of excess capacity in reducing entry has been highlighted by M. Spence, "Entry, Capacity, Investment and Oligopolistic Pricing," *Bell Journal of Economics*, Autumn 1977, pp. 534–544; A. Dixit, in "The Role of Investment in Entry Deterrence," *Economic Journal*, March 1980, pp. 95–106 pointed out that the role of excess capacity in deterring entry depended critically on demand

and cost conditions. Recent extensions have been done by S. Perrakis and G. Warskett, "Capacity and Entry Under Demand Uncertainty," *Review of Economic Studies*, July 1983, pp. 495–512, and J. Bulow, et al., "Holding Idle Capacity to Deter Entry," *Economic Journal*, March 1985, pp. 178–182.

8. S. Salop, "Strategic Entry Deterrence," *American Economic Review*, May 1979, pp. 335–338.

9. The application of the free-rider doctrine to the excess capacity tactic is discussed in R. McLean and M. Riordan, "Industry Structure with Sequential Technological Choice," *Journal of Economic Theory*, February 1989, pp. 1–21.

10. U.S. v. Aluminum Company of America, 148 F. 2nd. 416 (1945).

11. P. Milgrom and J. Roberts, "Predation, Reputation and Entry Deterrence," *Journal of Economic Theory*, August 1982, pp. 280–312.

12. The emphasis on transactions costs is best associated with Oliver Williamson. A good recent discussion is Williamson, *Economic Institutions of Capitalism*.

13. J. Stiglitz, "Introduction," *New Developments in the Analysis of Market Structure* (Cambridge, MA, 1986).

14. Such contract provisions are discussed at length in S. Salop, "Practices that Credibly Facilitate Oligopoly Coordination," in Stiglitz, ibid., pp. 265–290.

15. A review of literature on the way in which rent-seeking behavior dissipates profits from operating a regulated monopoly can be found in R. Tollison, "Rent Seeking: A Review," *Kyklos*, 35 (1982), pp. 575–602.

16. R. Levin, et al., "Survey Research on R&D Appropriability and Technological Opportunity," Yale University working paper, 1984.

17. Some of the earliest work in the area was done on airframes. See T. Wright, "Factors Affecting the Cost of Airplanes," *Journal of Aeronautical Science*, 13, (1936), pp. 122–128.

18. M. B. Lieberman, "The Learning Curve and Pricing in the Chemical Processing Industry," *Rand Journal of Economics*, Summer 1984, pp. 213–228.

19. R. Ghemawat, and A. M. Spence, "Learning Curve Spillovers and Market Performance," *Quarterly Journal of Economics*, 100 (1985), 839–857.

20. Nancy Stokey, "The Dymanics of Industry-wide Learning," in W. Heller, ed., *Essays in Honor of Kenneth Arrow* (New York, 1986).

21. R. Stobaugh, *Innovation and Competition: The Global Management of Petrochemical Products* (Cambridge, 1988.

22. M. B. Lieberman, "The Learning Curve, Technology Barriers to Entry, and Competitive Survival in the Chemical Processing Industries," *Strategic Management Journal*, September–October, 1989, pp. 431–447.

23. R. S. Bond and D. F. Lean, "Sales, Promotion and Product Differentiation in Two Prescription Drug Markets, *FTC Report*, 1977.

24. R. D. Buzzell and P. Farris, "Marketing Costs in Consumer Goods Industries," *Marketing Science Institute Report*, August 1976, pp. 76–111.

25. G. Brock, *The U.S. Computer Industry: A Study of Market Power* (Cambridge, MA, 1975).

26. "Intel's Powerful New Computer," *Business Week*, October 25, 1976, p. 74.

27. P. Nelson, "Advertising as Information," *Journal of Political Economy*, 81 (1974), pp. 729–754.

28. Work on the role of pioneering brands as entry barriers is provided by R. Schmalensee, "Product Differentiation Advantages of Pioneering Brands," *American Economic Review*, June 1982, pp. 349–365, and J. Farrell, "Moral Haz-

ard as an Entry Barrier," *Rand Journal of Economics,* Autumn 1986, pp. 440–449.

29. The central role of consumer information transmission on market structure is discussed in S. Salop, "Information and Monopolistic Competition," *American Economic Review,* May 1976, pp. 240–245, and B. Klein and K. Leffler, "The Role of Market Forces in Assuring Contractual Performance," *Journal of Political Economy,* August 1981, pp. 615–641.

30. Early work on the relationship between exit costs and entry can be found in R. Caves and M. Porter, "Barriers to Exit," in *Essays in honor of Joe Bain* ed. P. Qualls and R. T. Masson (Cambridge, 1976).

31. U.S. Small Business Administration, *The State of Small Business* (Washington, DC, 1986).

32. Industries characterized by no exit costs are known as contestable markets. The classic work on contestability is W. Baumol, J. Panzer, and R. Willig, *Contestable Markets and the Theory of Industry Structure* (New York, 1982).

33. M. Peteroff, "The Effects of Potential Competition on Market Performance in Airline Markets," Ph.D. Thesis, Yale University, 1988.

34. A review of the current state of airline deregulation is M. Levine, "Airline Competition in Deregulated Markets," *Yale Journal of Regulation,* Spring 1987, pp. 393–493.

35. An excellent discussion of the role of contestability in the airline industry is given by E. Bailey and W. Baumol, "Deregulation and the Theory of Contestable Markets," *Yale Journal of Regulation,* 2 (1984), pp. 111–138.

36. Even here, some use changes are possible, as one contemplates carrying other fuels through the line.

37. Bailey and Baumol, "Deregulation and the Theory of Contestable Markets."

38. An interesting experimental model of the role of entry is given in D. Coursey, R. Isaac, and V. Smith, "Market Contestability in the Presence of Sunk Costs," *Rand Journal of Economics,* Spring 1984, pp. 69–84.

Chapter 5. Groups Within Industries

1. Work in the area of strategic groups includes R. Caves and M. Porter, "From Entry Barriers to Mobility Barriers," *Quarterly Journal of Economics,* May 1977, pp. 241–261; M. Hunt, "Trade Associations and Self-Regulation," in R. Caves and M. Roberts, *Regulating the Product* (Cambridge, 1975; and S. Oster, "Intraindustry Structure and the Ease of Strategic Change," *Review of Economics and Statistics,* August 1982, pp. 376–384. A comprehensive review of the management literature in this area is J. McGee and H. Thomas, "Strategic Groups: Theory, Research and Taxonomy," *Strategic Management Journal,* 7 (1986), pp. 141–160.

2. W. Adams, "The Steel Industry," in W. Adams, ed. *The Structure of American Industry,* 4th ed. (New York, 1971).

3. In 1986, LTV filed for bankruptcy.

4. S. Oster, "The Diffusion of Innovation Among Steel Firms: The Basic Oxygen Furnace," *Bell Journal of Economics,* Spring 1982, pp. 45–56.

5. *Forbes,* January 1, 1968, p. 55.

6. *Business Week,* September 30, 1967, p. 46.

7. *Annual Report,* 1968, p. 7.

8. *Fortune,* January 1973, p. 27.

9. *Forbes,* October 1, 1968, p. 34.

10. There are numerous interesting discussions of the PVOs, including B. Landrum, *Private Voluntary Aid: U.S. Philanthropy for Relief and Development* (Westview Press, Colorado, 1982); and Brian Smith, "U.S. and Canadian Nonprofit Organizations as Translation and Development Institutions," PONPO Working Paper 70, ISPS, Yale University, August 1983.

11. Another distinction in the funding area is what share of the agency's budget is in food and kind rather than dollars. This distinction, too, carries with it substantial strategic implications.

12. Strategic mapping is a technique developed by M. Porter, *Competitive Strategy* (New York, 1980).

13. D. Mills and L. Schussman, "Industry Structure with Fluctuating Demand," *American Economic Review,* September 1985, pp. 758–767.

14. A. Chandler, *Strategy and Structure* (Cambridge, MA, 1962).

15. P. Geroshi and A. Murfen, "Entry and Intra-industry Mobility in the U.K. Car Market," ISF Conference, Boston, May 1987.

16. R. Miles and C. Snow, *Organizational Strategy, Structure and Process* (New York, 1978).

17. H. Mintzberg, "Ideology and the Missionary Organization," in J. Quinn, H. Mintzberg, and R. James, *The Strategy Process* (Englewood Cliffs, NJ, 1988), p. 345.

18. Miles and Snow, *Organizational Strategy.*

19. Mintzberg, "Ideology."

20. For an interesting discussion of this, see K. Arrow, *The Limits of Organizations* (New York, 1974).

21. An interesting survey of the functioning of nonprofits, including a discussion of goals, is E. James and S. Rose-Ackerman, *The Nonprofit Enterprise in Market Economics* (Chur, Switzerland, 1986).

22. G. Cubbin and P. Geroski, "The Convergence of Profits in the Long Run," *Journal of Industrial Economics,* June 1987, pp. 427–441.

23. L. Thomas, "Advertising in Consumer Goods Industries: Durability, Economies of Scale and Heterogeneity," *Journal of Law and Economics,* October 1988, pp. 243–263.

24. Oster, "Intraindustry Structure."

25. A. Fiegenbaum and W. Primeaux, "An Empirical Examination of Strategic Groups in Three Manufacturing Industries," working paper, University of Illinois, August 1985.

26. B. Mascarenhas and D. A. Aaker, "Mobility Barriers and Strategic Groups," *Strategic Management Journal,* September–October 1989, pp. 475–485.

27. W. Comanor and T. Wilson, *Advertising and Market Power* (Cambridge, MA, 1974), pp. 73–75.

28. Comanor and Wilson, ibid.

29. Mascarenhas and Aaker, "Mobility Barriers."

Chapter 6. Competing in Global Markets

1. P. Krugman, *Geography and Trade* (Cambridge, MA, 1993).

2. Krugman, ibid.

3. The original version of the theory of **comparative advantage** was developed by D. Ricardo, *Principles of Political Economy and Taxation* (London, 1817). The standard modern statement of the theory comes from E. Hecksher and B. Ohlin, *Interregional and International Trade* (Cambridge, MA, 1933).

4. T. Hout, M. Porter, E. Rudden, "How Global Companies Win Out," *Harvard Business Review*, September–October 1982, pp. 98–108.

5. S. Kobrin, "An Empirical Analysis of the Determinant of Global Integration," *Strategic Management Journal*, December 1991, pp. 17–31.

6. K. Ohmae, *The Borderless World* (New York, 1990).

7. Krugman, *Geography and Trade*.

8. Harvard Business School case, *The Global Semiconductor Industry*, 1987.

9. This example is taken from C. Baden-Fuller and J. Stopford, "Globalization Frustrated: The Case of White Goods," *Strategic Management Journal*, October 1991, pp. 493–507.

10. For a discussion of some of these issues, see B. Kogut, "A Note on Global Strategies," *Strategic Management Journal*, July–August 1989, pp. 383–390.

11. C. Prahalad and Y. Doz, *The Multinational Mission* (New York, 1987).

12. R. Gut, quoted in N. Bray, "CS Holding Girds for Global Competition," in *Wall Street Journal*, July 10, 1992, p. 4.

13. T. Levitt, "The Globalization of Markets," *Harvard Business Review*, May–June 1983, pp. 92–102.

14. Krugman, *Geography and Trade*.

15. These examples are developed by M. Mason, *American Multinationals and Japan: The Political Economy of Japanese Capital Controls, 1899–1960* (Cambridge, MA, 1991).

16. L. Franko, "Global Corporate Competition: Who's Winning, Who's Losing, and the R&D Factor as One Reason Why," *Strategic Management Journal*, September–October 1989, pp. 449–474.

17. R. Vernon, "International Investment and International Trade in the Product Cycle," *Quarterly Journal of Economics*, May 1966, pp. 190–207.

18. M. Porter, *The Competitive Advantage of Nations* (New York, 1990).

19. B. Kogut, "Country Capabilities and the Permeability of Borders," *Strategic Management Journal*, December 1991, pp. 33–47.

20. K. Pavitt, "The Nature and Determinants of Innovation: A Major Factor in Firms and Countries' Competitiveness." Paper presented at the conference on "Fundamental Issues in Strategy," Napa, California, November 29, 1990.

21. *Economic Report of the President* (Washington, DC, 1990), p. 125.

22. *Economic Report of the President*, ibid.

23. Krugman, *Geography and Trade*.

24. B. Scott, G. Lodge, and J. Bower, *U.S. Competitiveness in the World Economy* (Boston, 1985).

25. Porter, *Competitive Advantage of Nations*, p. 87.

26. Porter, ibid.

27. Pavitt, "Nature and Determinants of Innovation."

28. Krugman, *Geography and Trade*.

29. R. Nelson, *High Technology Policies: A Five Country Comparison* (Washington, DC, 1984).

30. Nelson, ibid., p. 70.

Chapter 7. Competing for Advantage

1. An interesting summary of the three sources of rent tied to both the economics literature and the management literature, is J. Mahoney and J. Padian, "The Resource-based View with the Conversation of Strategic Management," *Strategic Management Journal*, 13 (1992), pp. 363–380.

2. This use of the term *entrepreneurship* follows the classic in the field, J. A. Schumpeter, *Capitalism, Socialism and Democracy* (New York, 1950).

3. Literature on distinctive competence and its role in generating rents started with E. Penrose, *The Theory of the Growth of the Firm* (New York, 1959). A more modern application in the area of management practices is J. Tomer, *Organizational Capital: The Path to Higher Productivity and Well-Being* (New York, 1987).

4. R. Schmalensee, "Do Markets Differ Much?", *American Economic Review*, June 1985, pp. 341–351.

5. B. Wernerfelt and C. Montgomery, "What Is an Attractive Industry," *Management Science*, 32 (1986), pp. 1223–1229.

6. J. Cubbin and P. Geroski, "The Convergence of Profits in the Long Run," *Journal of Industrial Economics*, June 1987, pp. 427–442, and D. Mueller, "The Persistence of Profits Above the Norm," *Economica*, November 1977, pp. 369–380.

7. J. Scott and G. Pascoe, "Beyond Firm and Industry Effects on Profitability in Imperfect Markets," *Review of Economics and Statistics*, May 1986, pp. 284–292.

8. R. P. Rumelt, "How Much Does Industry Matter?", *Strategic Management Journal*, March 1991, pp. 167–186. Rumelt's work suggests that adoption of an intermediate focus, somewhere between the industry and the individual firm, would be fruitful.

9. Quoted in A. Thompson, A. Strickland and W. Fulmer, *Readings in Strategic Management* (Plano, TX, 1984), p. 152.

10. The winner's curse was first described in the context of bidding for oil leases by three Atlantic Richfield engineers, E. Capen, R. Clapp, and W. Campbell, "Competitive Bidding in High Risk Situations," *Journal of Petroleum Technology*, June 1971, pp. 641–653.

11. T. Peters and R. Waterman, *In Search of Excellence: Lessons From America's Best Run Companies* (New York, 1982).

12. Some interesting evidence on the persistence of high profits across firms is provided by D. Mueller, "Persistent Performance among Large Corporations," in L. Thomas, *The Economics of Strategic Planning* (Lexington, MA, 1986), pp. 31–62, and Rumelt, "How Much Does Industry Matter?"

13. J. Schumpeter, *The Theory of Economic Development* (London, 1934), pp. 129–132.

14. O. Port, "A Smarter Way to Manufacture," *Business Week*, April 30, 1990, pp. 110–117.

15. P. Shoemaker, "Strategy, Complexity and Economic Rent," *Management Science*, 36 (1990), pp. 1178–1192.

16. An interesting treatment of the evolutionary model in economics is R. Nelson and S. Winter, *An Evolutionary Theory of Economic Change* (Cambridge, MA, 1982).

17. The first two of these needed abilities are the focus of work in learning theory. For a review of this work, see R. Normann, "Developing Capabilities for Or-

ganizational Learning," in J. Pennings, *Organizational Strategy and Change* (San Francisco, 1985).

18. "Sun's Sizzling Race to the Top," *Fortune*, August 17, 1987, p. 88.

19. A nice statement of the evidence here is provided by M. Hannan and J. Freeman, "Structural Inertia and Organizational Change," *American Sociological Review*, April 1984, pp. 149–164.

20. R. Kanter, *The Change Masters* (New York, 1983).

21. T. Burns and G. Stalker, *The Management of Innovation* (London, 1961); and P. Laurence and J. Lorsch, *Organizations and Environment* (Homewood, IL, 1967).

22. C. Alderfer, "Consulting to Underbounded Systems," *Advances in Experiential Social Processes* Vol. 2 (London, 1980), Chapter 11.

23. C. Chandler, "Eastman Kodak Opens Windows of Opportunity," *Journal of Business Strategy*, Summer 1986, pp. 4–10.

24. C. Gersick and R. Hackman, "Habitual Routines in Task-Performing Groups," *Organizational Behavior and Human Decision Processes*, 47 (1990), pp. 65–97.

25. An early version of the decision-rule idea is contained in R. Cyert and R. March, *A Behavioral Theory of the Firm* (Englewood Cliffs, NJ, 1963). A recent discussion is in Nelson and Winter, *Evolutionary Theory*.

26. M. Zald, *Organizational Change: The Political Economy of the YMCA* (Chicago, 1970). An excellent review of organizational change in the nonprofit sector is given by W. Powell and R. Friedkin, "Organizational Change in Nonprofit Organizations, in W. Powell, ed., *The Non Profit Sector* (New Haven, 1987).

27. R. Miles, *Coffin Nails and Corporate Strategies* (Englewood Cliffs, NJ, 1980).

28. G. Dosi, D. Teece, and S. Winter, "Toward a Theory of Corporate Coherence," working paper, University of California, Berkeley, 1990; and C. Prahad and G. Hamil, "The Core Competence of the Corporation," *Harvard Business Review*, 90 (1990), pp. 79–91.

29. G. Rockhart, "The Chief Executive and Data Nerds," *Harvard Business Review*, March–April, 1979, pp. 81–93.

30. R. Rumelt, "Toward a strategic Theory of the Firm," in R. Lamb, ed., *Competitive Strategic Management* (Englewood Cliffs, NJ, 1984), pp. 556–570.

31. David Ricardo, *Principles of Political Economy and Taxation* (London, 1817).

32. Work on the limits on the size of the firm is extensive. The early classic in the area is R. Coase, "The Nature of the Firm," *Economica*, 4 (1937), pp. 386–405. Recent work has been done by O. Williamson, *The Economic Institution of Capitalism* (New York, 1985); B. Wernerfelt, "From Critical Resources to Corporate Strategy," *Journal of General Management*, 14 (1989), pp. 4–12.

33. Z. Griliches, "Hybrid Corn: An exploration in the economics of technological change." *Econometrica*, October, 1957.

34. S. Oster, "The Diffusion of Innovation Among Steel Firms: The Basic Oxygen Furnace," *Bell Journal of Economics*, Spring 1982, pp. 45–56.

35. S. Oster and J. Quigley, "Regulatory Barriers to the Diffusion of Innovation, *Bell Journal of Economics*, Autumn 1977, pp. 361–377.

36. See A. Chandler, *Strategy and Structure: Chapters in the History of the American Industrial Enterprise* (Cambridge, MA, 1962).

37. Chandler, ibid., p. 394.

38. Some early interesting work of the determinants of the speed of imitation is E. Mansfield, *Industrial Research and Technological Innovation* (New York, 1968).

39. New literature includes D. Mueller, "Persistent Performance," and J. Prescott, A. Kohli, and N. Ven Katraman, "The Marketshare–Profitability Relationship: An Empirical Assessment of Major Assertions and Contradictions," *Strategic Management Journal,* July 1986, pp. 377–394. Older literature is well represented by B. Gale, "Market Share and Rate of Return," *Review of Economics and Statistics,* November 1972, pp. 412–423.

40. D. Hambrick and I. McMillan, "The Product Portfolio," *California Management Review,* Fall 1982, pp. 54–68; R. Rumelt and R. Wensley, "In Search of Market Share Effect," *Proceeding of the Academy of Management,* Spring 1981, pp. 2–6.

41. Quoted in D. Ross, "Learning to Dominate," *Journal of Industrial Economics,* June 1986, pp. 337–354.

42. Work by Woo describes situations in which low shares are associated with high returns. See C. Y. Woo, "Market Share Leadership: Does it Always Pay Off?" *Proceeding of the Academy of Management,* Spring 1981, pp. 7–11, and C. Woo and O. Cooper, "Strategies of Effective Low Share Businesses," *Strategic Management Journal,* July–September 1981, pp. 301–318.

43. This line of argument has been made a number of places including most prominently by H. Demsetz, "Industry Structure, Market Rivalry, and Public Policy," *Journal of Law and Economics,* April 1973, pp. 1–10.

44. J. Scott and G. Pascoe, "Beyond Firm and Industry Effects on Profitability in Imperfect Markets," *Review of Economics and Statistics,* May 1986, pp. 284–292.

45. R. Levin, et al., "Survey Research on R&D Appropriability and Technological Opportunity," Yale University working paper, 1984.

46. Ross, "Learning to Dominate."

47. For an elaborate discussion of the role of ideology in the corporate culture, see H. Mintzberg, *Power In and Around Organizations* (Englewood Cliffs, NJ, 1983).

48. A nice discussion of this issue is given in J. Barney, "Organizational Culture: Can It Be a Source of Sustained Competitive Advantage?", *Academy of Management Review,* July 1986, pp. 656–665.

49. H. Itami, *Mobilizing Invisible Assets* (Cambridge, MA, 1987).

50. K. Iwai, "Schumpeterian dynamics: An Evolutionary Model of Innovation and Imitation," *Journal of Economic Behavior and Organization,* 5 (1984), pp. 159–190.

51. These distinctions are made in Nelson and Winter, *Evolutionary Theory.*

52. S. Winter, "Knowledge and Competence as Strategic Assets," in D. Teece, ed., *The Competitive Challenge* (Lexington, MA, 1987), pp. 159–184.

53. D. Teece, "Firm Boundaries, Technological Innovation and Strategic Management," in Thomas, *Economics of Strategic Planning,* p. 187.

54. G. Libecap, *Contracting for Property Rights* (New York, 1989).

55. In practice, most organizations transfer inputs at market prices which helps preserve the integrity of profit centers. The use of market prices is, however, inappropriate if the supplier has market power and/or economies of scope exist. For a discussion of this, see R. Eccles, "Transfer Pricing as a Problem of Agency," in J. Pratt and R. Zeckhauser, *Principles and Agents: The Structure of Businesses* (Cambridge, MA, 1985), pp. 151–186.

56. Nelson and Winter, *Evolutionary Theory.*

57. J. Sá and D. Hambrick, "Key Success Factors: A Test of a General Theory in the Mature Industrial Sector," *Strategic Management Journal,* July–August 1989, pp. 367–382.

Chapter 8. Organizational Goals: Politics and Power in the Organization

1. J. Pfeffer, *Organizational Design* (Northbrook, IL, 1978).
2. J. March, "The Business Firm as a Political Coalition," *Journal of Politics*, December 1962, pp. 48–73.
3. C. Perrow, *Complex Organizations: A Vertical Essay* (New York, 1986).
4. R. Cyert and J. March, *A Behavioral Theory of the Firm* (Englewood Cliffs, NJ, 1963).
5. G. Hansen and B. Wernerfelt, "Determinants of Firm Performance: The Relative Importance of Economic and Organizational Factors," *Strategic Management Journal*, September–October 1989, pp. 399–412.
6. J. Lorsch, "Managing Culture: The Invisible Barriers to Strategic Change," *California Management Review*, Winter 1986, pp. 95–109.
7. The earliest analysis of the extent of separation of ownership can be found in A. A. Berle and G. C. Means, *The Modern Corporation and Private Property* (New York, 1932).
8. S. Grossman and O. Hart, "Takeover Bids, the Free-Rider Problem, and the Theory of the Corporation," *Bell Journal of Economics*, Spring 1980, pp. 42–64.
9. This point was made in the context of the takeover market by Grossman and Hart, ibid. See Chapter 12 for further discussion.
10. T. Hammond, "The Agenda of the Term." Paper given at conference on "Fundamental Issues in Strategy," Napa, California, November 29, 1990.
11. A. Alderfer and K. Smith, "Studying Intergroup Relations Embedded in Organization," *Administrative Science Quarterly*, March 1983, pp. 35–65.
12. Alderfer and Smith, ibid. and P. McCain, F. O'Reilly, and J. Pfeffer, "The Effects of Departmental Demography on Turnover," *American Journal of Management*, December 1983, pp. 621–641.
13. J. March and H. Smith, *Organizations* (New York, 1958).
14. There is extensive literature on this problem. An early piece is S. Ross, "The Economic Theory of Agency: The Principals's Problem." *American Economic Review*, May 1973, pp. 134–139. An interesting more recent approach is S. Grossman and O. Hart, "An analysis of the Principal Agent Problem," *Econometrica*, January 1983, pp. 7–45. an interesting collection of articles on the subject is J. Pratt and R. Zeckhauser, *Principals and Agents: The Structure of Business* (Cambridge, MA, 1985). A review of agency theory from a broader organizational perspective is D. Levinthal," A Survey of Agency Models of Organization," *Journal of Economic Behavior and Organization*, 9 (1988), pp. 153–185. For a critical review, see R. Lane, *Market Experience* (Cambridge, MA, 1991).
15. The existence of opportunism is a central part of the work of O. Williamson, *The Economic Institutions of Capitalism* (New York, 1985). For an interesting discussion of opportunism in this context see G. Dow, "The Function of Authority in Transaction Cost Economics, *Journal of Economic Behavior and Organization*, March 1987, pp. 13–38.
16. See B. Holmstrom and P. Milgrom, "Aggregation and Linearity in the Provision of Intertemporal Incentives," *Econometrica*, March 1987, pp. 303–328.
17. W. Guth and I. MacMillan, "Strategic Implementation vs. Middle Management Self-Interest," *Strategic Management Journal*, July–August 1986, pp. 303–328.

18. A. Sloan, *My Years with General Motors* (New York, 1964), p. 49.
19. H. Mintzberg, *Power In and Around Organizations* (Englewood Cliffs, NJ, 1983).
20. This example is a disguised case.
21. V. Vroom, *Work and Motivation* (New York, 1964).
22. R. Porter, E. Lawler, and R. Hackman, *Behavior in Organizations* (New York, 1975).
23. G. Salancik, "Commitment and the Control of Organizational Behavior and Belief," in B. Stein and G. Salancik, eds., *New Directions in Organizational Behavior* (Malabar, FL, 1977).
24. J. Pfeffer, *Organizations and Organization Theory* (Boston, 1982).
25. Lane, *Market Experience.*
26. E. Trist and K. Bamfirth, "Some Social and Psychological Consequences of the Longwell Method of Coal Getting," *Human Relations,* Spring 1951, pp. 1–38.
27. G. Homans, *The Human Group* (New York, 1950), quoted in M. Olsen, "Group Size and Group Behavior," in H. Leavitt and L. Pondy, eds., *Readings in Managerial Psychology* (Chicago, 1973), p. 449.
28. "Executive Compensation, 1987," *Inc.,* September 1987, pp. 70–77.
29. Steven Cheung, "The Contractual Nature of the Firm," *Journal of Law and Economics,* April 1983, pp. 1–22.
30. Cheung, ibid., p. 11.
31. Interesting work in the area has been done by Williamson, *Economic Institutions of Capitalism.* Chapter 9, in particular, covers the historical evolution of work organization. B. Holmstrom and J. Tirole, "The Theory of the Firm," in R. Schmalensee and R. Willig, eds., *Handbook of Industrial Organization* (Amsterdam, 1989), survey much of the technical material in this area.
32. The simple model is based on one developed by Joel Demski.
33. "Executive Pay," *Business Week,* May 4, 1987, p. 58.
34. P. Diamond and R. Verrecchia, "Constraints on Short-Selling and Asset Price Adjustment to Private Information," *Journal of Financial Economics,* June 1987, pp. 277–311.
35. W. Thomas, quoted in E. Meadows, "New Targeting for Executive Pay," *Fortune,* May 4, 1981, pp. 176–182.
36. R. Antle and A. Smith, "An Empirical Investigation of the Relative Performance Evaluation of Corporate Executives," *Journal of Accounting Research,* Spring 1989, pp. 1–39.
37. R. Bauman, quoted in *Fortune.*
38. Yardstick competition or the use of rank order tournaments to reward relative performance was first studied by E. Lazear and S. Rosen, "Rank Order Tournaments as Optimum Labor Contracts," *Journal of Political Economy,* October 1981, pp. 841–864. An interesting follow-on which develops a more general theory of compensation along these lines is B. Nalebuff and J. Stiglitz, "Prizes and Incentives: Towards a General Theory of Compensation and Competition," *Bell Journal of Economics,* Spring 1983, pp. 21–44.
39. Porter, Lawler, and Hackman, *Behavior in Organizations,* p. 321.
40. "Executive Compensation, 1987."
41. Porter, Lawler, and Hackman, *Behavior in Organizations,* p. 343.
42. J. Rosenbaum, "Organizational Career Mobility," *American Journal of Sociology,* July 1979, pp. 21–48.
43. The discussion of promotions as a contest comes from Lazear and Rosen,

"Rank Order Tournaments." See also Nalebuff and Stiglitz, "Prizes and Incentives."

44. K. Abraham and J. Medoff, "Length of Service and Internal Labor Markets," *Industrial Labor Relations Review*, October 1984, pp. 87–97.

45. M. Granovetter, "Labor Mobility, Internal Markets and Job Matching," *Social Stratification and Mobility* (New York, 1986), pp. 3–39.

46. Perrow, *Complex Organizations*.

47. J. deLorean quoted in J. Wright, *On a Clear day you can see General Motors: John deLorean's Look Inside the Automotive Giant* (Grosse Pt., MI, 1979), p. 41.

48. G. Baker, M. Jensen, and K. Murphy, "Compensation and Incentives: Practice and Theory," *Journal of Finance*, 43 (1988), pp. 593–616.

49. Some of Ouchi's works are W. G. Ouchi, *Theory Z: How American Business Can Meet the Japanese Challenge* (Reading, MA, 1981), and W. Ouchi and A. Wilkens, "Efficient Cultures: Exploring the Relationship Between Culture and Organizational Performance," *Administrative Science Quarterly*, 28 (1983), pp. 32–57.

50. L. Bolman and T. Deal, *Modern Approaches to Understanding and Managing Organizations* (San Francisco, 1986).

51. H. Mintzberg, *Power in and around organizations*.

52. N. Lyons, *The Sony Vision* (New York, 1976), p. 110. Quoted in F. Aquilar, *General Managers in Action*, (New York, 1988), p. 26.

53. Pfeffer, *Organizations and Organization Theory*, Chapter 3.

54. Pfeffer, ibid.

55. Ouchi and Wilkens, "Efficient Cultures."

56. A. Edstrom and J. Galbraith, "Transfer of Managers as a Coordination and Control Strategy," *Administrative Science Quarterly*, June 1977, pp. 248–263.

57. E. Schein, "Organizational Socialization and the Profession of Management," *Industrial Management Review*, Spring 1968, p. 2. For a more recent discussion of the important role of socialization, see R. Pascale, "The Paradox of Corporate Culture: Reconciling Ourselves to Socialization," *California Management Review*, Winter 1985, pp. 26–45.

58. K. Weick, "Repunctuating the Problem," in P. Goodman and J. Pennings, eds., *New Perspectives on Organizational Effectiveness* (San Francisco, 1977).

59. T. I. Janis, *Victims of Group Think* (Boston, 1972).

60. T. I. Janis, "Sources of Error in Strategic Decision Making," in J. Pennings, *Organizational Strategy and Change* (San Francisco, 1985), pp. 157–197.

61. A. Schlesinger, quoted in Janis, *Organizational Strategy*, Chapter 2.

62. A. Murray, "Top Management Groups, Heterogeneity and Firm Performance," *Strategic Management Journal*, Summer 1989, pp. 125–142.

63. A. Stinchcombe, "Organizations and Social Structure," in J. March, eds., *Handbook of Organizations* (Chicago, 1965), pp. 153–193.

64. D. Carroll and J. Delacroix, "Organizational Mortality in Newspaper Industries of Argentina and Brazil," *Administrative Science Quarterly*, June 1982, pp. 169–198.

65. D. Carroll, "A Stochastic Model of Organizational Mortality," *Social Science Research*, December 1983, pp. 303–329.

66. J. Singh, D. Tucker, and R. Houn, "Organizational Legitimacy and the Liability of Newness," *Administrative Science Quarterly*, June 1986, pp. 171–193.

67. In F. Aguilar, *General Managers in Action* (New York, 1988), p. 13.

Chapter 9. Organizational Structure and Strategic Planning

1. This view of senior management as having a central integrating function is widespread, but perhaps best articulated by P. Drucker, *Management Tasks and Responsibilities* (New York, 1974): "There are a number of tasks which are top management tasks and . . . can be discharged only by people who are capable of seeing the whole business," p. 609. See also F. Aguilar, *General Managers in Action* (New York, 1988), Chapter 1.

2. In economics the characterization of inevitable limits on our ability to comprehend all facets of an operation has been termed the *bounded rationality* of the manager. This slant is closely associated with the work of H. Simon, for example, *Administrative Behavior* (New York, 1976); and O. Williamson, *The Economic Institutions of Capitalism* (New York, 1985).

3. This dual role for information in a complex organization is stressed by J. Demski and G. Feltham, *Cost Determination: A Conceptual Approach* (Cedar Rapids, IA, 1976).

4. J. Pfeffer, *Organizational Design* (Northbrook, IL, 1978), p. 25.

5. J. Bower, *Managing the Resource Allocation Process* (Boston, 1970).

6. A discussion of opportunistic behavior is contained in O. Williamson, *Markets and Hierarchies* (New York, 1975). By opportunism we mean self-seeking activity that takes advantage of information asymmetries.

7. Members of groups in conflict (an apt description for interdivisional capital competition in some organizations) perceive reality in ways that distort their own group's accomplishments. For a discussion of work in this area, see M. Sherif, ed. *Intergroup Relations and Leadership* (New York, 1962).

8. D. Hambrick and P. Mason, "Upper Echelons: The Organization as a Reflection of Its Top Managers," *Academy of Management Review,* 9 (1984), pp. 195–206.

9. An internal DuPont memo, quoted by A. Chandler, *Strategy and Structure* (Cambridge, MA, 1962), p. 69.

10. The classic account of the evolution of organizational structure in the U.S. is given in Chandler, ibid. The discussion which follows is based on that in Chandler.

11. See, for example, A. Chandler and H. Daems, *Managerial Hierarchies: Comparative Perspectives on the Rise of the Modern Industrial Enterprise* (Cambridge, MA, 1980).

12. T. Hammond, "The Agenda of the Firm." Paper presented at the conference on "Fundamental Issues in Strategy," Napa, California, November 29, 1990.

13. See, for example, P. Herbst, *Alternatives to Hierarchies* (Leiden, 1976) for a discussion of matrix organizations, or J. Galbraith, "Matrix Organizational Designs," *Business Horizons,* February 1971, pp. 29–40. A recent empirical look at the use of the matrix organization is E. Larson and D. Gobeli, "Matrix Management: Contradictions and Insights," *California Management Review,* Summer 1987, pp. 126–138.

14. For a discussion, see T. Peters and R. Waterman, *In Search of Excellence* (New York, 1982).

15. R. Christiansen, et al., *Policy Formulation and Administration* (Chicago, 1985), p. 407.

16. Quoted in R. Waterman, "The Power of Teamwork," in *Best of Business,* Spring 1988, pp. 16–33.

17. J. Pfeffer, *Organizations and Organization Theory* (Boston, 1982).

18. For an older view see W. Whyte, "Human Relations: A Progress Report," in A. Etzioni, ed., *Complex Organizations: A Sociological Reader* (New York, 1962), pp. 100–112. A more recent discussion of issues of span of controls is contained in C. Perrow, *Complex Organizations: A Vertical Essay* (New York, 1986), Chapter 1.

19. In fact, Blair distinguishes between what he calls "old-fashioned bureaucracies" with short hierarchies from "modern organizations" with tall hierarchies but considerable decentralization. P. Blair, "The Hierarchy of Authority in Organizations," *American Journal of Sociology,* January 1968, pp. 453–457.

20. This idea has been emphasized by J. Meyer and B. Rowan, "Institutionalized Organizations: Formal Structure as Myth and Ceremony," *American Journal of Sociology,* September 1977, pp. 340–363; and P. DiMaggio and W. Powell, "The Iron Cage Revisited," *American Sociological Review,* April 1983, pp. 147–160.

21. J. Coven and D. Stevin, "Small firms in Hostile and Benign Environments," *Strategic Management Journal,* January–February 1989, pp. 75–85.

22. The emphasis on the role of firm characteristics in determining structure is contained in J. Woodward, *Industrial Organization: Theory and Practice* (New York, 1965); and P. Lawrence and J. Lorsch, *Organization and Environment: Managing Differentiation and Integration* (Boston, 1967).

23. This is a theme developed by Chandler, *Strategy and Structure.*

24. J. Galbraith, *Designing Complex Organizations* (Reading, MA, 1973).

25. Transaction cost economics is most associated with the work of Ronald Coase and Oliver Williamson. Two accessible recent articles are O. Williamson, "Transaction Cost Economics," *Journal of Economic Behavior and Organization,* December 1987, pp. 617–625; and G. Dow, "The function of authority in Transaction Cost Economics," *Journal of Economic Behavior and Organization,* March 1987, pp. 13–38.

26. This principle was first formalized by J. Cremer, "A Partial Theory of the Optimal Organization of a Bureaucracy," *Bell Journal of Economics,* Autumn 1980, pp. 683–693. An earlier work which stressed the role of uncertainty in organizational design is T. Burns and G. Stalker, *The Management of Innovation* (London, 1961).

27. O. Williamson similarly describes incentives to vertically integrate as a need to deal with uncertainty of this sort in *Markets and Hierarchies* (New York, 1975).

28. This way of posing the situation is due to H. Simon, "Applying Information Technology to Organizational Design," *Public Administration Review,* May–June 1973, pp. 268–278.

29. The example which follows comes from Cremer, "A Partial Theory of the Optimal Organization."

30. This observation was first made by Woodward, *Industrial Organization.* It is an important part of the Aston studies of organizational structure. See, for example, D. Pugh, et al., 1 (1969) "The Context of Organizational Structure," *Administrative Science Quarterly,* 1 (1969), pp. 91–114; and D. Hickson, D. Pugh, and D. Pheysey, "Operational Technology and Organizational Structure," *Ad-*

ministrative Science Quarterly, 1 (1969), pp. 378–398. A more recent empirical study of the role of technology on organizational structure is M. Tushman and P. Anderson, "Technological Discontinuities and the Organizational Environment," *Administrative Science Quarterly*, September 1986, pp. 439–450.

31. The trade-off between the quality of information and its costs has been stressed by H. Simon, *Models of Man* (New York, 1957), and Simon, *Administrative Behavior*.

32. A. E. Pearson, quoted in Aguilar, *General Managers in Action*, p. 16.

33. The emphasis on limited computational abilities of individuals has been developed by Simon, *Administrative Behavior*, and Williamson, *Economic Institutions of Capitalism*.

34. The classic statement of this relationship is M. Weber. See H. Geith and C. W. Mills, eds., *From Max Weber Essays in Sociology* (New York, 1948).

35. This point is developed by M. Keren and D. Levhari, "The Internal Organization of the Firm and the Shape of Average Costs," *Bell Journal of Economics*, Autumn 1983, pp. 474–488.

36. T. Hammond and J. Horn, "Putting One Over on the Boss," *Public Choice*, 45 (1985), pp. 49–71.

37. This example is taken from Drucker, *Management Tasks*, p. 381.

38. Perrow, *Complex Organizations*.

39. Pfeffer, *Organizations and Organization Theory*.

40. Williamson, *Markets and Hierarchies*.

41. This focus has been developed formally in J. Geanakoplos and P. Milgrom, "A Theory of Hierarchies Based on Limited Managerial Attention," Cowles Paper #775, Yale University, 1986.

42. Quoted in R. Paulson, "The Chief Executive as Change Agent," in A. Thompson, A. Strickland, and W. Fulmer, eds., *Readings in Strategic Management* (Plano, Texas, 1984), p. 273.

43. A manager from Indsco, the disguised firm studied by R. Kanter in *Men and Women of the Corporation* (New York, 1977), p. 276.

44. See, for example, J. Galbraith, "Designing the Innovating Organization," in R. Lamb, ed., *Competitive Strategic Management* (Englewood Cliffs, NJ, 1984), pp. 297–318.

45. K. Eisenhardt, "Speed and Strategic Choice: How managers accelerate decision making," *California Management Review*, 32, 1990, pp. 1–16.

46. The term *influence costs* has been coined by P. Milgrom and is developed in "Employment Contracts, Influence Activities and Efficient Organizational Design," *Journal of Political Economy*, February 1988, pp. 42–60.

47. Perrow, *Complex Organizations*, p. 16.

48. Milgrom, "Employment Contracts."

49. The literature on this proposition is enormous. A sample includes S. Srivasts, *Job Satisfaction and Productivity*, (Cleveland, 1975); J. Bachman, C. Smith, and J. Slesinger, "Control, Performance and Satisfaction, *Journal of Personality and Social Psychology*, 4 (1966), pp. 127–136; Kanter, *Men and Women of the Corporation*, Chapter 10.

50. See J. March, "Decisions in Organizations and Theories of Choice," in A. Van de Ven and William Joyce, eds., *Perspectives on Organization Design and Behavior* (New York, 1981), pp. 205–244.

51. See, for example, A. Tannenbaum, *Hierarchies in Organization* (San Francisco, 1974).

52. R. Cole, *Work Mobility and Participation* (Berkeley, 1979).
53. The symbolic role of participatory decision making is highlighted by March, "Decisions in Organizations." The symbolic role of information collection is described in M. Feldman and J. March, "Information in Organizations as Signal and Symbol," *Administrative Science Quarterly*, June 1981, pp. 171–186.
54. See, for example, M. Ket de Vries and D. Miller, "Personality, Culture and Organization," *Academy of Management Review*, April 1986, pp. 266–279.
55. D. Miller and C. Droge, "Psychological and Traditional Determinants of Structure," *Administrative Science Quarterly*, December 1986, pp. 539–560.
56. This list of differences was culled from several sources, including J. Lincoln, M. Hamada, and K. McBride, "Organization Structure in Japanese and U.S. Manufacturing," *Administrative Science Quarterly*, September 1986, pp. 338–364; H. Itami, "The Firm and Market in Japan," in L. Thurow, ed., *The Management Challenge* (Cambridge, MA, 1985), pp. 69–81; and M. Aoki, "Horizontal vs. Vertical Information Structure of the Firm," *American Economic Review*, December 1986, pp. 971–983.
57. An interesting study using parallel U.S. and Japanese firms in a range of manufacturing industries and examining organizational structure is Lincoln, Hamada, and McBride, "Organization Structure."
58. M. J. Peck, "The Japanese Large Corporation: How Different and in What Ways Superior," Yale Working Paper, December 21, 1987.
59. See V. Pucik and N. Hatvany, "Management Practices in Japan and Their Impact on Business Strategy," in J. Quinn, H. Mintzberg, and R. James, eds., *The Strategy Process* (Englewood Cliffs, NJ, 1988), pp. 351–363.
60. R. Cole and T. Yakushiji, *The American and Japanese Auto Industries* (Ann Arbor, 1984).
61. Lincoln, Hamada, and McBride, "Organization Structure."
62. Lincoln, Hamada, and McBride, ibid.
63. R. Cole, "Target Information for Competitive Performance," *Harvard Business Review*, May 1985, pp. 100–109.
64. Aoki, "Horizontal vs. Vertical."
65. J. Abegglan, *The Japanese Factory* (Glencoe, 1958). Recent work which has questioned the certainty of culture in shaping the Japanese structure is C. Johnson, *Miti and the Japanese Miracle* (Stanford, 1982).
66. Peck, "The Japanese Large Corporation."

Chapter 10. Corporate Diversification

1. A recent thorough review of the strategic management literature on diversification is V. Ramanujam and P. Varadarjan, "Research Corporate Diversification: A Synthesis," *Strategic Management Journal*, November 1989, pp. 523–552.
2. R. Rumelt, *Strategy, Structure and Economic Performance* (Cambridge, MA, 1974).
3. See, for example, T. Levitt, "Dinosaurs among the Bears and Bulls," *Harvard Business Review*, January 1975, pp. 41–53; and Rumelt, *Strategy, Structure and Economic Performance*.
4. See, for example, B. Lamont and C. Anderson, "Mode of Corporate Diversification and Economic Performance," *Academy of Management Journal*, 28 (1985), pp. 926–934.
5. The term *Beta* refers to a symbol used in the capital-asset pricing model of

finance. Beta is the key measure of a firm's risk. It is the ratio of the covariance of the returns of the firm and the market to the overall variance of the market. A Beta of one implies that the organization's returns moved perfectly with the overall market. In other words, if Beta is 1, the firm is completely diversified in financial terms. Yale SOM lecture on competitive strategies, 1983. (The CEO wishes to remain anonymous.)

6. D. Jones, quoted in G. Stern, "Humana Considers Split of Hospitals and HMOs into Separate Companies," *Wall Street Journal*, July 10, 1992, a4.

7. R. Nielsen, "Piggybacking Strategies for Nonprofits," *Strategic Management Journal*, May 1986, pp. 201–216.

8. Rumelt, *Strategy, Structure and Economic Performance*.

9. M. Dubin, *Foreign Acquisitions and the Spread of the Multinational Firm* (New York, 1980).

10. O. Williamson, *Markets and Hierarchies: Analysis and Antitrust Implications* (New York, 1975).

11. G. Walter and J. Barney, "Management Objectives in Mergers and Acquisitions," *Strategic Management Journal*, January 1990, pp. 79–86.

12. The most extensive work on exit issues has been done by K. Harrigan. See, for example, Harrigan, "Deterrents to Divestiture," *Academy of Management Journal*, June 1981, pp. 306–323.

13. The proposition that the extent of diversification increases with age has been well documented. See, for example, Levitt, "Dinosaurs among the Bears and Bulls," and R. Chenhall, "Diversification Within Australian Manufacturing Enterprises," *Journal of Management Studies*, 21 (1984), pp. 23–60.

14. The first discussion of this possibility that I know of is M. Shubik, *Strategy and Market Structure: Competition, Oligopoly and the Theory of Games* (New York, 1959). For a more recent discussion of the theory, see J. Tirole, *The Theory of Industrial Organization* (Cambridge, MA, 1988).

15. D. Bernheim and M. Whinston, "Multimarket Contact and Collusive Behavior," *Rand Journal of Economics*, Spring 1990, pp. 1–26.

16. The original work was done by R. Caves, "Diversification and Seller Concentration: Evidence from Changes, 1963–72," *Review of Economics and Statistics*, May 1981, pp. 289–292. More recent work is C. Montgomery, "Product Market Diversification and Market Power," *Academy of Management Journal*, 28 (1985), pp. 789–798.

17. See, for example, J. Scott, "On the Theory of Conglomerate Mergers," *Journal of Finance*, September 1977, pp. 1235–1250.

18. C. Galbraith, B. Samuelson, C. Stiles, and G. Merrill, "Diversification, industry Research and Development and Performance," *Academy of Management Proceedings*, Fall 1986, pp. 17–20.

19. H. Geneen, "The Strategy of Diversification," in R. Lamb, ed., *Competitive Strategic Management* (Englewood Cliffs, NJ, 1984), pp. 395–414.

20. An early explication of the mean/variance trade-off among investors is provided by J. Tobin, *Essays in Economics*, Vol. 1 (Chicago, 1971), Chapter 15.

21. An early discussion of the proposition is H. Levy and M. Sarnat, "Diversification, Portfolio Analysis, and the Uneasy Case for Conglomerate Mergers," *Journal of Finance*, September 1973, pp. 79–96.

22. G. Baker, "Compensation and Hierarchies," HBS Working Paper, January 1986.

23. An early statement of this idea is J. March and H. Simon, *Organizations* (Chicago, 1958), Chapter 4.

24. See, for example, F. Herzberg, *Work and the Nature of Man* (New York, 1966), Chapter 6.

25. Some work along these lines is reviewed in B. Holmstrom and J. Tirole, "The Theory of the Firm," in R. Schmalensee and R. Willig, eds., *Handbook of Industrial Organization* (Amsterdam, 1989). A model of the use of diversification as a way to reduce managerial risk is contained in Y. Amihud and P. Lev, "Risk Reduction as a Managerial Motive for Conglomerate Mergers," *Bell Journal of Economics,* Autumn 1981, pp. 605–617.

26. G. Donaldson and J. Lorsch, *Decision Making at the Top: The Shaping of Strategic Directions* (New York, 1983).

27. Amihud and Lev, "Risk Reduction."

28. This line of argument was made by H. Demsetz, "Corporate Control, Insider Trading and Rates of Return," *American Economic Review,* May 1986, pp. 313–316.

29. A. Shleifer and R. Vishny, "Large Shareholders and Corporate Control," *Journal of Political Economy,* June 1986, pp. 461–468.

30. Early arguments on the bankruptcy gains come from Levy and Sarnat, "Diversification." A more recent discussion of the empirical world is I. Brick, R. Haber, and J. Weaver, "Financial Motives in Conglomerate Mergers," in D. Keenan and L. White, eds., *Mergers and Acquisitions* (Lexington, MA, 1982), pp. 75–96.

31. F. Black and M. Scholes, "The Pricing of Options and Corporate Liabilities," *Journal of Political Economy,* May–June 1973, pp. 637–651, and D. Galai and R. Masulis, "The Options Pricing Model," *Journal of Financial Economics,* March 1976, pp. 53–81.

32. A discussion of this possibility using the adverse selection model has been developed by H. Leland and D. Pyle, "Informational Asymmetries, Financial Structure and Financial Intermediation," *Journal of Finance,* May 1977, pp. 371–387. A model of informational gains from diversification of a different sort is contained in R. Kihlstrom, "The Informational Role of Mergers in the Context of a Complete Securities Market," in L. Thomas, ed., *The Economics of Strategic Planning* (Lexington, MA, 1986), pp. 171–186.

33. J. Crimmins and M. Keil, *Enterprise in the Nonprofit Section* (Rockefeller Fund, 1983).

34. P. Firstenberg, *Managing for Profit in the Nonprofit World* (Foundation Center, 1986).

35. For a discussion of this practice see E. Skloot, "Should Nonprofits Go Into Business?" *Harvard Business Review,* January 1983, pp. 20–23; Nielsen, "Piggybacking Strategies."

36. Smithkline, *Annual Report,* 1972.

37. For a discussion of this view, see M. Jensen, "Takeovers: Their Causes and Consequences," *Journal of Economic Perspectives,* Winter 1988, pp. 21–44.

38. A. O'Reilly, *Fortune,* April 15, 1988, p. 52.

39. G. Walter and J. Barney, "Management Objectives in Mergers and Acquisitions," *Strategic Management Journal,* January 1990, pp. 79–86.

40. S. Chatterjee and B. Wernerfelt, "The Link Between Resources and Types of Diversification: Theory and Evidence," *Strategic Management Journal,* January 1991, pp. 33–48.

41. See, for example, Rumelt, *Strategy, Structure and Economic Performance.* R. Caves, M. Porter, and M. Spence, *Competition in the Open Economy: A Model Applied*

to *Canada* (Cambridge, MA, 1980). R. Rumelt, "Diversification Strategy and Profitability," *Strategic Management Journal*, 3 (1982), pp. 359–369. R. Bettis and V. Mahajan. "Risk/Return Performance of Diversified Firms," *Management Science*, 31 (1985). K. Palepu, "Diversification Strategy, Profit Performance and the Entropy Measure," *Strategic Management Journal*, 6 (1985), pp. 239–255.

Chapter 11. Vertical Linkages

1. K. Harrigan, "Matching Vertical Integration Strategies to Competitive Conditions," *Strategic Management Journal*, November–December, 1986, pp. 535–556.
2. An interesting recent piece on the problem of transfer pricing is R. Eccles, "Transfer Pricing as a Problem of Agency," in J. Pratt and R. Zeckhauser, eds., *Principles and Agents: The Structure of Business* (Cambridge, MA, 1985), pp. 151–186. In a competitive market with no economies of scope across divisions, the right transfer price will be the market price.
3. Harrigan, "Matching Vertical Integration Strategies," pp. 535–556.
4. See T. Brennan, "Why Regulated Firms Should be Kept Out of Unregulated Markets: Understanding Divestiture in the United States vs. AT&T," *Antitrust Bulletin*, Fall 1987, pp. 741–793.
5. R. Coase, "The Nature of the Firm," *Economica*, 4 (1937), pp. 386–405.
6. O. Williamson has termed this the *markets vs. hierarchy distinction* and has written powerfully of it in *Markets and Hierarchies* (New York, 1975).
7. The example which follows is adapted slightly from the one in B. Klein, V. Crawford, and A. Alchian, "Vertical Integration, Appropriable Rents and the Competitive Contracting Process," *Journal of Law and Economics*, October 1978, pp. 297–326. Other work which takes a similar approach to vertical integration includes V. Goldberg, "Regulation and Administrated Contracts," *Bell Journal of Economics*, Autumn 1976, pp. 426–448.
8. O. Williamson, "Credible Commitments: Using Hostages to Support Exchange," *American Economic Review*, September 1983, pp. 519–540.
9. T. Muris, D. Scheffman, and P. Spiller, "Strategy and Transaction Costs: The Organization of Distribution in the Carbonated Soft Drink Industry," *Journal of Economics and Management Strategy*, Spring 1992, pp. 83–128.
10. K. Crocker, "Vertical Integration and the Strategic Use of Private Information," *Bell Journal of Economics*, Spring 1983, pp. 236–248.
11. See J. Demski, D. Sappington, and P. Spiller, "Managing Supplier Switching," *Rand Journal of Economics*, Spring 1987, pp. 77–97.
12. O. Williamson, *The Economic Institutions of Capitalism* (New York, 1985), p. 79.
13. See Williamson, *ibid.*
14. S. Grossman and O. Hart, "The Costs and Benefits of Ownership: A Theory of Vertical and Lateral Integration,"*Journal of Political Economy*, August 1986, pp. 691–719.
15. This case was analyzed by K. Arrow, "Vertical Integration and Communication," *Bell Journal of Economics*, Spring 1975, pp. 173–183.
16. Crocker, "Vertical Integration."
17. B. Wernerfelt and S. Balakrishnan, "Technical Change, Competition and Vertical Integration," *Strategic Management Journal*, July–August 1986, pp. 347–360.

18. J. Scully, quoted in G. Zachary, "High-Tech Firms Find It's Good to Line Up Outside Contractors," *Wall Street Journal*, July 22, 1992, p. 1.
19. The discussion which follows is based on the work on coal contracts done by P. Joskow and described in Joskow "Contract Duration and Relationship Specific Investments: Empirical Evidence from Coal Markets," *American Economic Review*, March 1987, pp. 168–185; and P. Joskow, "Vertical Integration and Long Term Contracts," *Journal of Law, Economics and Organization*, Spring 1985, pp. 33–80.
20. A fuller account of this case is provided in Klein, Crawford, and Alchian, "Vertical Integration."
21. K. Monteverde and D. Teece, "Supplier Switching Costs and Vertical Integration in the Auto Industry," *Bell Journal of Economics*, Spring 1982, pp. 206–213. Other empirical studies on integration and investment specificity are S. Maslem, "The Organization of Production: Evidence from the Aerospace Industry," *Journal of Law & Economics*, 27 (1984), pp. 403–418; and E. Anderson and D. Schmittlein, "Integration of the Sales Force" *Rand Journal of Economics*, 15 (1984), pp. 385–395.
22. G. Walker and D. Weber, "Supplier Competition, Uncertainty, and Make-or-Buy Decisions," *Academy of Management Journal*, September 1987, pp. 589–596.

Chapter 12. Mergers, Acquisitions, and Strategic Alliances

1. Cited in F. Scherer, "Mergers, Sell-offs and Managerial Behavior," in L. Thomas, ed., *The Economics of Strategic Planning* (Lexington, MA, 1986), pp. 143–170.
2. R. Fisher and W. Ury, *Getting to Yes: Negotiating Agreement without Giving In* (Boston, 1981) and J. Walsh, "Doing a Deal: Merger and Acquisition Negotiations and Their Impact upon Target Company Top Management Turnover," *Strategic Management Journal*, July–August 1989, pp. 307–322.
3. D. Austin and M. Jackson, "Tender Offer Update," *Mergers and Acquisitions*, 1984, pp. 60–69.
4. For a discussion of this view, see F. Easterbrook and D. Fischel, "The Proper Role of a Target's Management in Responding to a Tender Offer," *Harvard Law Review*, April 1981, pp. 1161–1204; and C. Knoeber, "Golden Parachutes, Shark Repellent and Hostile Tender Offers," *American Economic Review*, March 1986, pp. 155–167.
5. I am grateful to Tom Wyman for this account.
6. *Business Week* survey, cited in R. Walking and M. Long, "Agency Theory, Managerial Welfare and Takeover Bid Resistance," *Rand Journal of Economics*, Spring 1984, pp. 54–68.
7. Two good, early works on merger waves are R. Nelson, *Merger Movements in American Industry, 1895–1956* (Princeton, NJ, 1959); and S. Reid, *Mergers, Managers and the Economy* (New York, 1968). A more recent work is M. Blair, "Mergers," Ph.D. dissertation, Yale University, 1988.
8. The figure comes from W. Shugart and R. Tollison, "The Random Character of Merger Activity," *Rand Journal of Economics*, Winter 1984, pp. 500–509. The asset values are unavailable for the period 1920–1950.
9. See, for example, Shugart and Tollison, ibid., and L. White, "Mergers and Aggregate Concentration," in D. Keenan and L. White, eds., *Mergers and Acquisitions* (Lexington, MA, 1982), pp. 97–112.

10. Arthur T. Anderson, "Management Motives for Takeovers in the Petroleum Industry," *Review of Industrial Organization*, August 1987, pp. 1–12.
11. M. Scherer, "Corporate Takeovers," *Journal of Economic Perspectives*, Winter 1988, pp. 69–82.
12. L. Hannah and J. Kay, *Concentration and Modern Industry* (New York, 1977).
13. A review of recent European mergers is contained in Business International Report, *Acquisition Strategy in Europe* (Switzerland, January 1987).
14. *Mergers and Acquisition Almanac*, May–June, 1992.
15. Nelson, *Merger Movements*.
16. A. Beckenstein, "Merger activity and merger theories," *Antitrust Bulletin*, Spring 1979, pp. 105–128; and D. Mueller, *The Determinants and Effects of Mergers* (Cambridge, MA, 1980).
17. Shugart and Tollison, "Random Character of Merger Activity."
18. See, for example, J. Weston, "Determination of Share Exchange Ratios in Mergers," in W. Albert and J. Segal, eds., *The Corporate Merger* (Chicago, 1974), pp. 131–138. M. Jensen and R. Ruback, "The Market for Corporate Control: The Scientific Evidence," *Journal of Financial Economics*, April 1983, pp. 5–50.
19. M. Porter, "From Competitive Advantage to Competitive Strategy," *Harvard Business Review*, May 1987, pp. 43–59.
20. J. Markham, "Survey of the Evidence and Findings on Mergers," in National Bureau of Economic Research conference report, *Business Concentration and Price Policy* (Princeton, NJ, 1955), p. 180.
21. The traditional argument against vertical mergers has been one of *foreclosure*. Mergers of a vertical sort were thought to close off customers to other non-integrated suppliers. The current view of most economists and the Court is that such foreclosure is likely only in the most narrow of circumstances. Thus we see very little litigation in the area of vertical mergers today. A good reference on this area is R. Blair and D. Kaserman, *Antitrust Economics*, (Chicago, 1985), Chapter 12.
22. R. Roll, "The Hubris Hypothesis of Corporate Takeovers," *Journal of Business*, April 1986, pp. 197–216.
23. A leading dissident in this area is Robert Shiller. For a sample of his views, see R. Shiller, "Stock Prices and Social Dynamics," *Brookings Papers on Economic Activity*, December 1984, pp. 457–498.
24. Nelson, *Merger Movements*.
25. Early treatments of this role of the takeover are contained in R. Marris, *The Economic Theory of Managerial Capitalism* (New York, 1965), and H. Manne, "Mergers and the Market for Corporate Control," *Journal of Political Economy*, April 1965, pp. 110–120.
26. R. Morch, A. Shleifer, and R. Vishny, "Characteristics of Targets of Hostile and Friendly Takeovers," in A. Auerbach, ed., *Takeovers: Causes and Consequences* (Chicago, 1989).
27. A. Shleifer and L. Summers, "Breach of Trust in Hostile Takeovers," in Auerbach, ed., ibid.
28. For a discussion of this view see M. Jensen, "Takeovers: Their Causes and Consequences," *Journal of Economic Perspectives*," Winter 1988, pp. 21–48.
29. M. Jensen, "Agency Costs of Free Cash Flow, Corporate Finance and Takeovers," *American Economic Review*, November–December 1984, pp. 109–121.

30. This point was made by S. Grossman and O. Hart, "Takeover Bids, the Free Rider Problem and the Theory of the Corporation," *Bell Journal of Economics,* Spring 1980, pp. 42–64.

31. M. Jensen and R. Ruback, "The Market for Corporate Control," *Journal of Financial Economics,* 1983, pp. April 5–50; J. McConnell and C. Muscarella, "Corporate Capital Expenditure Decisions and the Market Value of the Firm," *Journal of Financial Economics,* September 1986, pp. 399–422.

32. A discussion of the effect of defensive tactics is contained in A. Shleifer and R. Vishny, "Greenmail, White Knights and Shareholder Interest," *Rand Journal of Economics,* Autumn 1986, pp. 293–309; and A. Shleifer and R. Vishny, "Value Maximization and the Acquisition Process," *Journal of Economic Perspectives,* Winter 1988, pp. 7–20.

33. M. Ryngaert, "The Effect of Poison Pill Securities on Shareholder Wealth," *Journal of Financial Economics,* January/March, 1988, pp. 377–417.

34. Cited in "Executives Pay: Who Got What in 1986?", *Business Week,* May 4, 1987, p. 51.

35. See, for example, Jensen and Ruback, "The Market for Corporate Control."

36. J. Kitching, "Why Do Mergers Miscarry?" *Harvard Business Review* November–December, 1967. pp. 84–101; and J. Hunt, "Changing Pattern of Acquisition Behavior in Takeovers and the Consequences, for Acquisition Processes," *Strategic Management Journal,* January 1990, pp. 69–78.

37. F. M. Scherer and D. Ravenscraft, *Mergers, Sell-offs and Economic Efficiency* (Washington, DC, 1987).

38. The lemons problem was first explored by G. Ackerlof, "The Market for Lemons," *Quarterly Journal of Economics,* August 1970, pp. 488–500.

39. F. Paine and D. Power, "Merger Strategy: An Examination of Drucher's Five Rules for Successful Acquisitions," *Strategic Management Journal,* 5 (1984), pp. 99–119, and K. Fowler and D. Schmidt, "Determinants of Tender Offer Post-acquisition Financial Performance," *Strategic Management Journal,* July–August 1989, pp. 339–350. For a divergent view, see J. Kusewitt, "An Exploratory Study of Strategic Acquisition Factors Relating to Performance," *Strategic Management Journal,* 6 (1985), pp. 151–169.

40. R. Rumelt, *Strategy, Structure and Economic Performance* (Cambridge, 1974), and M. Labatkin, "Merger Strategies and Stockholder value," *Strategic Management Journal,* 8 (1987), pp. 39–53. Empirical evidence on the effect, however, is mixed. See, for example, the review by A. Seth, "Value Creation in Acquisitions: A Reexamination of Performance Issues," *Strategic Management Journal,* 11 (1990), pp. 99–115.

41. J. Welch in "G.E.'s Costly Lesson on Wall Street," *Fortune,* May 9, 1988, p. 72.

42. W. Buffet quoted in D. Jemison and S. Sitkin, "Corporate Acquisitions: A Process Perspective," *Academy of Management Review,* January 1986, pp. 145–163.

43. See, for example, Jemison and Sitkin, ibid.; and S. Chatterjee, M. Lubatkin, D. Schweiger, and Y. Weber, "Cultural Difference and Stockholder Value in Related Mergers: Brand Equity and Human Capital," *Strategic Management Journal,* 13 (1992), pp. 319–334.

44. P. Shrivastava, "Post-merger Integration," *Journal of Business Strategy,* Summer 1986, pp. 65–76.

45. Shrivastava, ibid.

46. P. Haspeslagh and D. Jemison, "Acquisition Myths and Reality," *Sloan Management Review,* Winter 1987, pp. 53–58.
47. A. Dales and P. Mirvis, "Acquisition and the Collusion of culture," in R. Quinn and J. Kimberly, eds., *Managing Organizational Transactions* (New York, 1984).
48. Chatterjee, et al., "Cultural Differences and Shareholder Value."
49. Shrivastava, "Post-merger Integration," and G. Walter, "Culture Collision in Mergers and Acquisitions," in J. Frost, et al., *Organization Culture* (Belmont, CA, 1985), 301–314.
50. For a review, see Fowler and Schmidt, "Determinants of Tender Offer Post-acquisition Financial Performance."
51. Chatterjee, et al., "Cultural differences and Shareholder Value."
52. "G.E.'s Costly Lesson on Wall Street," p. 78.
53. W. T. Grimm, *Mergerstat Review* (Chicago, 1987).
54. Jemison and Sitkin, "Corporate Acquisitions," and Walsh, "Doing a Deal."
55. Walsh, ibid.
56. H. Hiller, "The Case for Strategic Alliances," *Salomon Brothers Report,* October 1991.
57. Y. Doz, "Technology Partnerships Between Larger and Smaller Firms," *International Studies of Management and Organization,* 17 (1988), pp. 31–57.
58. G. Walker, B. Kogut and W. Shan, "The Structure of an Industry: Cooperation and Embeddedness among Biotechnology Firms." Working paper, July 1992.
59. Walker, Kogut, and Shan, ibid. and K. Harrigan, "Strategic Alliances and Partner Asymmetries," in F. Contractor and P. Lorange, eds., *Cooperative Strategies in International Business* (Lexington, MA, 1988).
60. W. Powell, "Neither Market nor Hierarchy: Network Forms of Organization," *Research in Organizational Behavior,* 12 (1990), pp. 295–336.
61. Powell, ibid.
62. M. Porter, *The Competitive Advantage of Nations* (New York, 1990).
63. Powell, "Neither Market nor Hierarchy."
64. M. Meyer, P. Milgrom, and J. Roberts, "Organizational Prospects, Influence Costs and Ownership Changes," *Journal of Economics and Management Strategy,* Spring 1992, pp. 9–36.
65. Harrigan, "Strategic Alliances and Partner Asymmetries."
66. Doz, "Technology Partnerships" and Powell, "Neither Market nor Hierarchy."
67. B. Borys and D. Jemison, "Hybrid Organization as Strategic Alliances," *Academy of Management Review,* 14 (1989), pp. 234–249.
68. F.T.C. v. Procter & Gamble Co., 386 U.A. 568 (1967).
69. Kennecott Copper Corp. v. F.T.C., 467 F. 2nd 67 (10 Cir. 1972).
70. R. Bork, *The Antitrust Paradox* (New York, 1978), pp. 244–245.

Chapter 13. Understanding Rivalry: Game Theory

1. An engaging and readable discussion of the field of game theory is provided in M. Shubik, *Game Theory in the Social Sciences* (Cambridge, MA, 1985). See also A. Dixit and B. Nalebuff, *Thinking Strategically* (New York, 1991).
2. G. Saloner, "Applied Game Theory and Strategic Management." Paper pre-

sented at the conference on "Fundamental Issues in Strategy," Napa, California, November 29, 1990.

3. An extensive treatment of games of this sort is provided by R. Luce and H. Raiffa, *Games and Decisions* (New York, 1957).
4. A nice treatment of repeated games is given in P. Ordeshook, *Game Theory and Political Theory* (New York, 1986), Chapter 10.
5. Solving repeated games involves finding the *subgame perfect equilibrium* by identifying the optimal strategy for the last period, then the next to last and so on. Sequential equilibria are defined in D. Kreps and R. Wilson, "Sequential Equilibria," *Econometrica*, July 1982, pp. 863–894.
6. D. Kreps, P. Milgrom, J. Roberts, R. Wilson, "Rational Cooperation in the Finitely Repeated Prisoner's Dilemma," *Journal of Economic Theory*, August 1982, pp. 245–252.
7. R. Axelrod, *The Evolution of Cooperation* (New York, 1984).
8. Dixit and Nalebuff, *Thinking Strategically*.
9. Ibid.
10. A recent interesting treatment of threat points is K. Binmore, A. Rubinstein, and A. Wolinsky, "The Nash Bargaining Solution in Economic Modelling," in *Rand Journal of Economics*, Summer 1986, pp. 176–188.
11. The case described has been altered to protect confidentiality.
12. A great deal of recent work in economics has been done on the issue of contracting and bargaining in this kind of situation. See, most prominently, O. Williamson, *The Economic Institutions of Capitalism* (New York, 1985).

Chapter 14. Product Positioning and Strategic Marketing

1. FTC v. Kellogg et al., Docket No. 8883. A discussion of this complaint is given in Schmalensee, "Entry Deterrence in the Ready to Eat Breakfast Cereal Industry," *Bell Journal of Economics*, Autumn 1978, pp. 305–327. The FTC complaint was eventually dismissed.
2. The approach that follows in which products are defined by their characteristics is due to Kelvin Lancaster, and underlies much of the modern work in economics and marketing. Several good sources are K. Lancaster, *Consumer Demand: A New Approach* (New York, 1971); K. Lancaster, "Socially Optimal Product Differentiation," *American Economic Review*, September 1975, pp. 567–585, and K. Lancaster, *Variety, Equity and Efficiency* (New York, 1979). A treatment of the use of this model in marketing is given in G. L. Urban and J. R. Hauser, *Design and Marketing of New Products* (Englewood Cliffs, NJ, 1980).
3. Many techniques have been developed to elicit from consumers both the set of relevant product characteristics they see in a product class and how they map particular products to characteristic space. For a review of this literature, see J. Hauser and F. Koppelman, "Alternative Perceptual Mapping Techniques," *Journal of Marketing Research*, November 1979, pp. 495–506.
4. An excellent treatment of the economies-of-scope literature is given in J. Panzer and R. Willig, "Economics of Scope," *American Economic Review*, May 1981, pp. 268–272.
5. A discussion of product choice under these conditions focusing on the social optimality of monopoly choice is provided in Lancaster, *Variety, Equity and Efficiency*, and Michael Spence, "Product Selection, Fixed Costs and Monopo-

listic Competition," *Review of Economic Studies*, 1976, pp. 217–253. See also S. Moorthy, "Market Segmentation, Self-Selection and Product Line Design," *Marketing Science*, Fall 1984, pp. 288–307. Moorthy makes the point that quite apart from economies-of-scale considerations, concerns over cannibalization might favor market aggregation.

6. See Michael Spence, "Product selection;" and J. Brander and J. Eaton, "Product Line Rivalry," *American Economic Review*, June 1984, pp. 323–333.

7. The example which follows comes from W. Manning and B. Owen, "Television Rivalry and Network Power," *Public Policy*, Winter 1976, pp. 33–57. Reprinted by permission of John F. Kennedy School of Government.

8. An example of the use of positioning by an incumbent is provided in J. Hauser, "Theory and Application of Defensive Strategy," in L. Thomas, ed. *The Economics of Strategic Planning* (Lexington, MA, 1986), Chapter 5. See also S. Moorthy, "Product and Price Competition in a Duopoly," *Marketing Science*, Spring 1988, pp. 141–168.

9. This modeling of entrants with foresight has been fundamental to the literature in this area and is due to E. Prescott and M. Visscher, "Sequential Location Among Firms with Foresight," *Bell Journal of Economics*, Autumn 1977, pp. 378–393.

10. This result is quite different from the bunching result associated with the Hotelling model in which firms have no foresight. H. Hotelling, "Stability in Competition," *Economic Journal*, March 1929, pp. 41–57.

11. M. Gelfand and P. Spiller, "Entry Barriers and Multiproduct Oligopoly," *International Journal of Industrial Organization*, March 1987, pp. 101–113.

12. The classic treatment of entry deterrence via product line extensions has been done in the breakfast cereal market. See R. Schmalensee, "Entry Deterrence." Another treatment of this theory is B. Eaton and R. Lipsey, "The Theory of Market Preemption," *Econometrica*, 47 (1979), pp. 149–158.

13. The emphasis on the role of product-line choice on expectations of postentry competition is developed by K. Judd, "Credible Spatial Preemption," *Rand Journal of Economics*, Summer 1985, pp. 153–166.

14. See Judd, *ibid.*

15. This interesting result was articulated by J. Brander and J. Eaton, "Product Line Rivalry," *American Economic Review*, June 1984, pp. 323–334. The product line offered by a monopolist facing entry must be broader than one offered by a monopolist with no entry threats. Prescott and Visscher, "Sequential Location."

16. L. Thomas, "Advertising in Consumer Goods Industries," *Journal of Law and Economics*, October 1987.

17. "Speeding Up," *Wall Street Journal*, February 23, 1988, p. 1.

18. A formal analysis of the import of this difference among goods is given by P. Nelson, "Advertising as Information," *Journal of Political Economy*, July 1974, pp. 729–754. A similar distinction is made by M. Porter, using "shopping goods" versus "convenience goods," in M. Porter, *Interbrand Choice, Strategy and Bilateral Market Power* (Cambridge, MA, 1976).

19. The link between quality of product and advertising budget seems to be made both in the empirical literature and in the theoretical literature. P. Nelson, "Advertising as Information," provides a provocative model of the relationship. A more complete and formal model of this effect is provided by P. Milgrom and J. Roberts, "Price and Advertising Signals of Product Quality," *Jour-*

nal of Political Economy, August 1986, pp. 796–821, and R. K. Kihlstrom and M. Riordan, "Advertising as Signals," *Journal of Political Economy,* June 1984, pp. 427–450.

20. See, for a full model of this, P. Milgrom and J. Roberts, "Relying on the Information of Interested Parties," *Rand Journal of Economics,* Spring 1986, pp. 18–32.

21. W. Comanor and T. Wilson, *Advertising and Market Power* (Cambridge, MA, 1974), Chapter 5, provide some estimates of the demand elasticity of sales to advertising.

22. W. J. Adams, "Deregulation of Television Advertising in France: Impact on Product Market Power," paper presented at the A.E.A. meetings, December 1987.

23. Most marketing texts make this point. See, for example, P. Kotler, *Marketing Management,* 6th ed. (NY), Chapter 12.

24. An early formal model of excessive advertising resulting from competition among firms is given in A. Dixit and V. Norman, "Advertising and Welfare," *Bell Journal of Economics,* Spring 1978, pp. 1–17.

25. See F. M. Scherer, *Industrial Market Structure and Economic Performance* (Chicago, 1980), p. 389.

26. L. Telser, "Advertising and Cigarettes," *Journal of Political Economy,* October 1962, pp. 471–479.

27. A review of this literature and a more general econometric study of the competitive aspects of advertising is given in J. Netter, "Excessive Advertising: an Empirical Analysis," *Journal of Industrial Economics,* June 1982, pp. 361–373.

28. This example comes from C. Kelton and D. Kelton, "Advertising and Interbrand Shifts in the U.S. Brewing Industry," *Journal of Industrial Economics,* March 1982, pp. 292–304.

29. R. Weinberg, *Brewing Industry Research Program,* 1985 Report.

30. Kelton and Kelton, "Advertising."

31. Numerous economists have commented on the effect of advertising on price competition, including W. Comanor and T. Wilson, "Advertising, Market Structure and Performance," *Review of Economics and Statistics,* November, 1967; R. Schmalensee, *On the Economics of Advertising* (Amsterdam, 1972), and M. Porter, *Interbrand Choice, Strategy and Bilateral Market Power* (Cambridge, MA, 1976).

32. Lee Benham, "The Effect of Advertising on the Price of Eyeglasses," *Journal of Law and Economics,* October 1972, pp. 337–352; and J. Cady, "An Estimate of the Price Effects on Restrictions on Drug Price Advertising," *Economic Inquiry,* December 1976, pp. 493–510.

33. C. Kelton and D. Kelton, "Advertising."

34. L. Thomas, "Advertising in Consumer Goods Industries: Economies of Scale and Heterogeneity," *Journal of Law and Economics,* October 1987.

35. For an analysis of this proposition in the V-8 juice market, see J. Eastlach and A. Rao, "Modeling Responsiveness to Advertising and Pricing Changes for V-8 Juice," *Marketing Science,* Summer 1986, pp. 245–259.

36. See, for a discussion of this possibility, R. Schmalensee, "Advertising and Market Structure," in J. Stiglitz and G. Mathewson, eds., *New Developments in the Analysis of Market Structure* (Cambridge, MA, 1986), pp. 373–396.

37. A discussion of this principle specific to the distribution chain is in A. Jeuland and S. Shugan, "Managing Channel Profits," *Marketing Science,* Summer 1983,

pp. 239–272. See also S. Moorthy, "Managing Channel Profit: Comment," *Marketing Science*, Fall 1987.

38. For a series of cases, see R. Lafferty, R. Lande, and J. Kirkwood, eds., *Impact Evaluations of Federal Trade Commission Vertical Cases*. Report of the Federal Trade Commission, August 1984.

39. The classic article in this area is L. Telser, "Why Should Manufacturers Want Fair Trade?" *Journal of Law and Economics*, October 1960, pp. 86–105. Two modern treatments are H. Marvel and S. McCafferty, "The Political Economy of Resale Price Maintenance," *Journal of Political Economics*, October 1986, pp. 1074–1095; and G. Mathewson and R. Winter, "An Economic Theory of Vertical Restraints," *Rand Journal of Economics*, Spring 1984, pp. 27–38.

40. For an empirical survey of RPM in various industries, see T. Gilligan, "The Competitive Effects of Resale Price Maintenance," *Rand Journal of Economics*, Winter 1986, pp. 544–556.

41. R. Rey and J. Tirole, "The Logic of Vertical Restraints," *American Economic Review*, December 1986, pp. 921–939; and Rey and Tirole, "Vertical Restraints from a Principal-Agent View," in *Marketing Channels*, L. Pellegrino and S. Reddy, eds., (Lexington, MA, 1986).

42. For a discussion of this, see G. Butaney and L. Wortzel, "Distributional Power Versus Manufacturer Power," *Journal of Marketing*, January 1988, pp. 52–63.

43. A. Coughlan, "Competition and Cooperation in Marketing Channels Choice," *Marketing Science*, Spring 1985, pp. 110–122.

44. "Why P&G Wants a Mellower Image," *Business Week*, June 7, 1982, p. 60. Quoted in H. Assael, *Marketing Management*.

45. Chase Parkway Garage Inc. v. Subaru, June 16, 1982.

46. A nice review of the issues in tying is provided in R. Blair and D. Kasserman, *Antitrust Economics* (Chicago, 1985).

Chapter 15. Competitive Pricing

1. The classic article describing this case and debating the results of the court's findings is J. McGee, "Predatory Price Cutting: The Standard Oil Case," *Journal of Law and Economics*, October 1958, pp. 137–169.

2. For a detailed discussion of this situation, see Harvard Business Case 376–266.

3. A more detailed discussion of the facts of this industry can be found in Harvard Business School Case 9-578-210. An interesting perspective on the success of Honda in the U.S. market is R. Pascale, "Perspectives on Strategy: The Real Story Behind Honda's Success," *California Management Review*, Spring 1984, pp. 47–72.

4. This material is reviewed nicely in E. Mansfield, *Microeconomics* (New York, 1979), Chapter 5.

5. J. Rotemberg and G. Saloner, "The Cyclical Behavior of Strategic Inventories," *Quarterly Journal of Economics*, February 1989, pp. 73–98.

6. J. Scott, "Multimarket Contact and Economic Performance," *Review of Economics and Statistics*, August 1982, pp. 368–375.

7. For a more detailed discussion of competition in the steel industry, see S. Oster, "A Note on the Steel Industry," Yale SOM Case for Competitive Strategy.

8. An early classic discussion of limit pricing is J. Bain, *Barriers to New Competition* (Cambridge, MA, 1956).

9. This interpretation of the value of limit pricing was developed by P. Milgrom and J. Roberts, "Limit Pricing and Entry with Incomplete Information: An Equilibrium Analysis," *Econometrica*, 50, 1982, pp. 443–460. Another discussion of limit pricing using this interpretation is S. Salop, "Strategic Entry Deterrence," *American Economic Review*, May 1979, pp. 335–338.

10. See W. Baumol, R. Willig, and J. Panzar, *Contestable Markets and the Theory of Industry Structure* (New York, 1982).

11. Again, see J. McGee, "Predatory Price Cutting."

12. Two classic pieces make this point: P. Milgrom and J. Roberts, "Predation, Reputation and Entry Deterrence, *Journal of Economic Theory*, 27, 1982, pp. 280–312; and D. Kreps and R. Wilson, "Reputation and Imperfect Information," *Journal of Economic Theory*, 27, 1982, pp. 253–279.

13. Strictly speaking for this model to work, we need some uncertainty about, for example, the end point of the game. If the end point of the game is perfectly known, we get into the problems of repeated games described in the last chapter. In the last period of a finite, known game, the incumbent will not find predation worthwhile. But then in the penultimate period, predation is not a threat, and so on. This observation was pointed out by R. Selten, "The Chain Store Paradox," *Theory and Decision*, 9 (1978), pp. 127–159; and Milgrom and Roberts, "Predation, Reputation."

14. This model was developed by D. Fudenberg and J. Tirole, "A Signal-Jamming Theory of Predation," *Rand Journal of Economics*, Autumn 1986, pp. 366–376. A related article is M. Riordan, "Imperfect Information and Dynamic Conjectural Variations," *Rand Journal of Economics*, Spring, 1985, pp. 41–50.

15. The classic work in this area is T. Schelling, "An Essay on Bargaining," *American Economic Review*, June 1956, pp. 281–306.

16. M. Spence, "Entry Capacity, Investment and Oligopolistic Behavior," *Bell Journal of Economics*, Autumn 1977, pp. 534–544.

17. J. Rotemberg and G. Saloner, "The Cyclical Behavior of Strategic Inventories."

18. B. Bernheim, "Strategic Deterrence of Sequential Entry into an Industry," *Rand Journal of Economics*, Spring 1984, pp. 1–11.

19. See, for example, P. Areeda and D. Turner, "Predatory Pricing and Related Practices Under Section 2 of the Sherman Act," *Harvard Law Review*, February 1975.

20. See, for example, *International Air Industries and American Excelsior Corp.*, 517 F. 2d 714 (5th Cir., 1975); and M. Spence, "The Learning Curve and Competition," *Bell Journal of Economics*, Spring 1981, pp. 49–70.

Chapter 16. Competitive Research and Development and Innovation

1. For a broad discussion of R&D policy, see Z. Griliches, "Productivity, R&D and Basic Research of the Firm Level," *American Economic Review*, March 1986, pp. 141–154.

2. "New Profits from Patents," *Fortune*, April 15 1988, p. 188.

3. R. Hayes and W. Abernathy, "Managing Our Way to Economic Decline," *Harvard Business Review*, July–August 1980, pp. 67–77.

4. The answer to this question is not a clear yes or no, but a matter of degree. I

have tried to simplify matters here to focus on the central elements of the decision. N. Rosenberg, "Science, Innovation and Economic Growth," *Economic Journal*, March 1974, 90–108, has emphasized the scientific base to industrial innovation.

5. R. Nelson, M. Peck, and E. Kalachek, *Technology, Economic Growth and Public Policy* (Washington, DC, 1967). "Outside of the defense and space complex and the chemical and electronics industries (and to a considerable extent even within these) there is little basic research, and most applied research is not very far reaching," p. 56.

6. For a further discussion of this point, see R. Nelson, "Institutions Supporting Technical Advance in Industry," *American Economic Review*, May 1986, pp. 186–189.

7. A. B. Jaffe, "Technological Opportunity and Spillovers of R&D," *American Economic Review*, December 1986, pp. 984–1001.

8. H. Ansoff, "Strategic Management of Technology," *Journal of Business Strategy*, Winter 1987, pp. 28–39.

9. This possibility is discussed by Ansoff, in *ibid.*

10. E. Mansfield, "How Rapidly Does New Industrial Technology Leak Out?", *Journal of Industrial Economics*, December 1985, pp. 217–222.

11. E. Mansfield, *The Economics of Technological Change* (New York, 1968).

12. A careful look at the determinants of diffusion is given in Mansfield, *ibid.*

13. An early statement of this proposition is contained in Nelson, Peck, and Kalachek, *Technology, Economic Growth and Public Policy*, Chapter 5.

14. An interesting discussion of this point is given in S. Winter, "Knowledge and Competence as Strategic Assets," in D. Teece, ed., *The Competitive Challenge* (Lexington, MA, 1987), pp. 159–184.

15. For a discussion of this point, see D. Teece, "Firm Boundaries, Technological Innovation and Strategic Management," in L. Thomas, ed., *The Economics of Strategic Planning* (Lexington, MA, 1986), pp. 187–200.

16. E. Mansfield, "How Rapidly Does New Industrial Technology Leak Out?" *Journal of Industrial Economics*, December 1985, pp. 217–222.

17. G. Saloner and A. Shepard, "Adoption of Technologies with Network Effects," MIT Working Paper 577, April 1991.

18. U.S. Constitution, article 1, section 8.

19. H. Grabowski and J. Vernon, "Longer Patents for Lower Imitation Barriers: The 1984 Drug Act," *American Economic Review*, May 1986, pp. 195–198.

20. A. Pakes, "On Patents, R&D and the Stock Market Rate of Return," *Journal of Political Economy*, April 1985, pp. 390–409.

21. F. M. Scherer, "The Economic Effects of Compulsory Patent Licensing," N.Y.U. Monograph, 1977.

22. C. Taylor and Z. Silbertson, *The Economic Impact of the Patent System* (London, 1973).

23. The example and discussion is taken from R. Gilbert, "Patents, Sleeping Patents, and Entry Deterrence," in S. Salop, ed., *Strategy, Predation and Antitrust Analysis*, F.T.C. Report, 1981.

24. S. Salant, "Preemptive Patenting and the Persistence of Monopoly: Comment," *American Economic Review*, March 1984, pp. 247–250.

25. An interesting large-scale survey of R&D managers on the effectiveness of patents and other devices for controlling access to innovations is provided by R. Levin, A. Klevorick, R. Nelson, and S. Winter, "Survey Research on R&D,

Appropriability, and Technological Opportunity," Yale University Working Paper, July 1984. A brief summary of some of the survey results on the patent system is given in R. Levin, "A New Look at the Patent System," *American Economic Review*, May 1986, pp. 199–202.

26. I. Horstmann, G. MacDonald, and A. Sliviski, "Patents as Information Transfer Mechanisms: To Patent or (Maybe) Not to Patent," *Journal of Political Economy*, October 1985, pp. 837–858.

27. Scherer, "Economic Effects," p. 387.

28. R. Nelson and S. Winter, *An Evolutionary Theory of Economic Change* (Cambridge, MA, 1982) refer to this as "cumulative innovation." An interesting model of the effects of cumulative technology is given in J. Vickers, "The Evolution of Market Structure When There is a Sequence of Innovations," *Journal of Industrial Economics*, September 1986, pp. 1–12.

29. Ansoff, "Strategic Management."

30. M. Lieberman, "The Learning Curve, Technology Barriers to Entry, and Competitive Survival in the Chemical Processing Industries," *Strategic Management Journal*, September–October, 1989, pp. 431–448.

31. A review of the facts of standard setting in the U.S. economy is given in FTC, *Standards and Certification*, Staff Report, April 1983.

32. J. Utterback and W. Abernathy, "A Dynamic Model of Product and Process Innovation," *Omega*, 3 (1975), pp. 639–656; and J. Utterback and F. Suarez, "Innovation, Competition and Industry Structure," MIT Working Paper 29–90, June 1991.

33. Utterback and Suarez, ibid.

34. M. Katz and C. Shapiro, "Network Externalities, Competition and Compatibility," *American Economic Review*, June 1985, pp. 424–440.

35. J. Farrell and G. Saloner, "Standardization, Compatibility and Innovation," *Rand Journal of Economics*, Spring 1985, pp. 70–83, develop a model in which there are "bandwagon" effects favoring early innovators in standard choice.

36. R. Kihlstrom, "The Informational Role of Mergers in the Context of a Complete Securities Market," in L. Thomas, *The Economics of Strategic Planning* (Lexington, MA, 1986), pp. 171–185 argues that in a world of imperfect information mergers may help technological innovators to gain the capital and expertise needed to exploit an innovation.

37. S. Heininger, quoted in K. Labich, "The Innovators," *Fortune*, June 6 1988, p. 64.

38. J. Scott, "Firm vs. Industry in R&D Intensity," in *R&D, Patents and Productivity*, ed. Z. Griliches (Chicago, 1984), pp. 233–245.

39. An excellent survey of the relationship between innovation and firm characteristics is given in M. Kamien and N. Schwartz, "Market Structure and Innovation: A Survey," *Journal of Economic Literature*, March 1975, pp. 1–37. An interesting perspective on the traditional literature is contained in P. Dasgupta, "The Theory of Technological Competition," in J. Stiglitz and G. Mathewson, eds., *New Developments in the Analysis of Market Structure* (Cambridge, MA, 1986), pp. 519–547.

40. D. Moore quoted in K. Labich, "The Innovators," *Fortune*, June 6, 1988, p. 52.

41. The Eastman Kodak group is called a Venture Board. It is described by the CEO of Kodak, Colby Chandler, in "Eastman Kodak Opens Windows of Opportunity," *Journal of Business*, Summer 1986, pp. 4–9.

42. Andrew Van de Ven, "Central Problems in the Management of Innovation," *Management Science*, May 1986, pp. 590–607.
43. Kamien and Schwartz, "Market Structure."
44. See, for example, J. Quinn, "Managing Innovation: Controlling Chaos," *Harvard Business Review*, May–June 1985, reprinted in J. Quinn, H. Mintzberg and R. James, *The Strategy Process* (Englewood Cliffs, NJ, 1988), pp. 627–637.
45. An early expression of the importance of leaders in innovation comes from J. Hage and R. Dewar, "Elite Values versus Organizational Structure in Predicting Innovations," *Administrative Science Quarterly*, 18 (1973), pp. 279–290.
46. F. Westley and H. Mintzberg, "Visionary Leadership and Strategic Management," *Strategic Management Journal*, Summer 1989, pp. 17–32.
47. T. Peters and R. Waterman, *In Search of Excellence* (New York, 1982).
48. Sony's goals are stated to be a "free, dynamic and pleasant factory . . . where sincerely motivated personnel can exercise their technological skills to the highest level." Quoted in Quinn, "Managing innovation," p. 631.
49. For a discussion of the importance of this, see H. Stevenson and J. Jarillo-Morri, "Preserving Entrepreneurship as Companies Grow," *Journal of Business Strategy*, Summer 1986, pp. 10–22.
50. K. Bantel and S. Jackson, "Top Management and Innovations in Banking: Does the Composition of the Top Team Make a Difference," *Strategic Management Journal*, Summer, 1989, pp. 107–124.
51. S. Oster and J. Quigley, "Regulatory Barriers to the Diffusion of Innovation: Some Evidence from Building Codes," *Bell Journal of Economics*, Autumn 1977, pp. 361–377.
52. The classic paper from organizational behaviorists is V. Vroom and B. Paul, "Relationship Between Age and Risk-taking among Managers," *Journal of Applied Psychology*, 55 (1971), pp. 399–405.
53. J. Pfeffer, "Organizational Demography," in L. Cummings and B. Staw, eds., *Research in Organizational Behavior* (Greenwich, CT, 1983), pp. 299–357. B. Staw and J. Ross, "Commitment in an Experimenting Society," *Journal of Applied Psychology*, 65 (1980), pp. 249–260.
54. W. Ouchi, *Theory Z: How American Business Can Meet the Japanese Challenge* (Reading, MA, 1981), and Pfeffer, "Organizational Demography."
55. K. Weick, "Repunctuating the Problem," in P. Goodman and J. Pennings, eds., *New Perspectives in Organizational Effectiveness* (San Francisco, 1977).
56. For a good review of this literature, see B. Staw and J. Ross, "Behavior in Escalation Situations: Antecedents, Prototypes and Solutions," in Cummings and Staw, eds., *Research in Organizational Behavior*, pp. 249–260.
57. Andrew Van de Ven, "Central Problems in the Management of Innovation," *Management Science*, May 1986, pp. 590–607.
58. E. Von Hippel "Successful Industrial Products from Customers' Ideas," *Journal of Marketing*, January 1978, pp. 39–40.
59. R. Caves, H. Crookell, and P. J. Killing, "The Imperfect Market for Technology Licenses," *Oxford Bulletin of Economics and Statistics*, 1983, pp. 223–248.
60. D. Teece, "Firm Boundaries." See the discussion in Chapter 5.
61. See *Inc.* Magazine, March 1987, p. 58.
62. The idea that rents lost as a result of time needed to complete a transaction might influence the kind of bargain a firm makes has been made in the context of a labor negotiation in K. Binmore, A. Rubinstein, and A. Wolinsky,

"The Nash Bargaining Solution in Economic Modeling," *Rand Journal of Economics*, Summer 1986, pp. 176–199.

63. *Inc.* Magazine, March 1987, p. 52.

64. See M. Katz and C. Shapiro, "On the Licensing of Innovations," *Rand Journal of Economics*, Winter 1985, pp. 504–520; and N. Gallin and R. Winter, "Licensing in the Theory of Innovation," *Rand Journal of Economics*, Summer 1985, pp. 237–252.

65. Katz and Shapiro, ibid.

66. The treatment of this incentive to license is developed by A. Shepherd, "Licensing to Enhance Demand for New Technologies," *Rand Journal of Economics*, Autumn 1987, pp. 360–368. Another discussion of the role of second sourcing to credibly commit to buyers is J. Demski, D. Sappington, and P. Spiller, "Managing Supplier Structuring," *Rand Journal of Economics*, Spring 1987, pp. 77–97.

67. Shepherd, ibid.

Chapter 17. Regulatory Issues in Strategic Planning

1. The important role of the bureaucracy is modeled in M. Fiorina and R. Noll, "Voters, Bureaucrats and Regulation," *Journal of Public Economics*, April 1978, pp. 239–254.

2. Some interesting work on the control powers of legislators is B. Weingast, "The Congressional Bureaucratic System: A Principal Agent Perspective," *Public Choice*, 1984, pp. 147–191; and T. Moe, "Congressional Control of the Bureaucracy," Brookings Paper, 1985.

3. Two early classic pieces on the sources of regulation are G. Stigler, "The Theory of Economic Regulation," *Bell Journal of Economics*, Spring 1971, and Sam Peltzman, "Toward a More General Theory of Regulation," *Journal of Law and Economics*, August 1976, pp. 211–278. More recent pieces on the subject include S. Oster, "The Strategic Use of Regulatory Investment by Industry Subgroups," *Economic Inquiry*, October 1982, pp. 604–719; J. Kalt, "The Political Economy of Coal Regulation," in *The Political Economy of Regulation*, FTC report, March 1984; and R. Noll and B. Owen, *The Political Economy of Deregulation*, American Enterprise Institute (Washington, DC, 1983).

4. A discussion of the role of interest groups in the deregulation movement is contained in Noll and Owen, "The Political Economy of Deregulation: An Overview," in *The Political Economy of Deregulation*.

5. B. Yendle, "Bootleggers and Baptists," *Regulation*, May–June 1983, pp. 12–16.

6. The perspective that regulations are unlikely to emerge from the political process if they result in gross inefficiencies from unneeded intervention in the market may be found in Peltzman, "Toward a More General Theory of Regulation."

7. A classic early discussion of externalities is given in R. Coase, "The Problem of Social Cost," *Journal of Law and Economics*, October 1960.

8. Two good discussions of this effect are S. Oster, "The Strategic Use of Regulatory Investment," *Economic Inquiry*, October 1982, and Salop, Scheffman and Schwartz, "Bidding Analysis of Special Interest Regulation," in FTC report, *The Political Economy of Regulation*, March 1984. A review of the literature in this area is given in R. McCormick, "The Strategic Use of Regulation: A Re-

view of the Literature," in FTC report, *The Political Economy of Regulation,* March 1984, pp. 13–32.

9. A discussion of this regulation is contained in S. Oster, "The Strategic Use of Regulatory Investment."
10. Pharmaceutical Manufacturers' Association Press Release, January 9, 1979.
11. Eli Lilly, Comments on FTC Drug Substitutions Inquiry, April 1978.
12. Letter from Lee to James Mitchell, May 1979.
13. *Business Week,* November 6, 1978, p. 205.
14. PMA Press Packet, 8.

Chapter 18. The Strategic Planning Process

1. R. Paulson, for example, tells us that "there seems to be universal agreement among strategic planners that the key to strategic change is the chief executive." "The Chief Executive as Change Agent," *Management Review,* February 1982, p. 25.
2. J. Quinn, *Strategies for Change: Logical Incrementalism* (Homewood, IL, 1980).
3. This focus on the wide participation seen in the planning process is articulated well by Quinn, ibid.
4. W. H. Hegerty and R. Hoffman, "Who Influences Strategic Decision Making?" *Long Range Planning,* April 1987, pp. 76–85. An interesting early case study of the multiple agents in the strategic process is contained in J. Bower, *Managing the Resource Allocation Process: A Study of Corporate Planning and Investment* (Graduate School of Business Administration, Harvard University, 1970).
5. A recent interesting explication of Williamson's views is *The Economic Institutions of Capitalism* (New York, 1985).
6. J. Bower and Y. Doz, "Strategy Formulation: A Social and Political Process," in D. Schendel and C. Hofer, *Strategic Management: A New View of Business Policy and Planning* (Boston, 1979), p. 152.
7. D. Reid, "Operationalizing Strategic Planning," *Strategic Management Journal,* November–December 1989, pp. 553–567.
8. Reid, ibid.
9. W.. Guth and I. Macmillan, "Strategic Implementation Versus Middle Management Self-interest," *Strategic Management Journal,* July–August 1986, pp. 303–328.
10. The view that planning is a political process is a widespread one. A good discussion is contained in D. Jemison, "Organizational Versus Environmental Sources of Influence in Strategic Decision Making," *Strategic Management Journal,* January–March, 1981, pp. 77–89; and H. Mintzberg, D. Raisinghani, and A. Theoret, "The Structure of Unstructured Decision Processes," *Administrative Science Quarterly,* June 1976.
11. The focus on coalitions originated with R. Cyert and J. March, *The Behavioral Theory of the Firm* (Englewood Cliffs, NJ, 1963).
12. Bower and Doz, "Strategy Formation."
13. P. Selznick, *Leadership in Administration* (New York, 1957).
14. Sidney Winter, private observations.
15. See, for example, W. Hegerty and R. Hoffman, "Who Influences Strategic Decisions?"

16. Michael Crozier, *The Bureaucratic Phenomenon* (Chicago, 1964).

17. See, for example, R. Kanter, *Men and Women of the Corporation* (New York, 1977), Chapter 7.

18. See, for example, P. Lorange, *Corporate Planning: An Executive Viewpoint* (Englewood Cliffs, NJ, 1980); C. Roush and B. Ball, "Controlling the Implementation of Strategy," *Managerial Planning*, November–December, 1980, pp. 3–12.

19. J. Horovitz, "Strategic Control: A New Task for Top Management," *Long Range Planning*, 12 (1979), pp. 2–7; and P. Lorange and D. Murphy, "Strategy and Human Resources: Concepts and Practice, *Human Resource Management*, 22 (1983), pp. 111–133.

20. H. Hrebiniak and W. Joyce, "The Strategic Importance of Managing Myopia," *Sloan Management Review*, Fall 1986, pp. 5–14.

21. M. Gould and J. Quinn, "The Paradox of Strategic Controls," *Strategic Management Journal*, January 1990, pp. 43–57.

22. P. Grinyer, S. Al-Bazzaz, and M. Yasai-Ardekani, "Towards a Contingency Theory of Corporate Planning: Findings in 48 U.K. Companies," *Strategic Management Journal*, January–February 1986, pp. 3–28.

23. P. Drucker, *Managing for Results* (New York, 1964), p. 5.

24. H. Mintzberg, "Strategy Making in Three Modes," *California Management Review*, Winter 1973, pp. 44–53. A similar focus on the changing nature of strategic planning as organizations grow is contained in F. Gluck, S. Kaufman, and A. S. Walleck, "Strategic Management for Competitive Advantage," *Harvard Business Review*, July–August 1980, pp. 154–161.

25. J. Welch, in Stockholder letter, *General Electric Annual Report*, 1991, p. 2.

Appendix 2. Financial Ratio Analysis

1. W. H. Beaver, "Financial ratios and predictors of failure," *Journal of Accounting Research*, Spring 1966, pp. 77–111.

2. M. H. Miller, "Debt and Taxes," *Journal of Finance*, May 1977, pp. 261–276.

Appendix 3. Using Statistics to Determine Advantage

1. In all of this, we acknowledge the drawbacks of using return data based on accounting information.

2. The primary difficulty in drawing inferences without some careful analysis comes because of underlying correlations between explanatory variables.

3. Innumerable excellent texts on statistics cover this ground. The material that follows is intended as a cursory review.

4. Studies which have worried hard about the pooling of data across samples in the strategy area include M. Hatten and D. Schendel, "Heterogeneity in an Industry: Firm Conduct in the Brewing Industry," *Journal of Industrial Economics*, September 1977, pp.97–113; and L. Phillips, D. Chang, and R. Buzzell, "Product Quality, Cost Position and Business Performance," *Journal of Marketing*, Spring 1983, pp. 26–43.

5. J. Prescott, A. Kohli, and N.Ven Katraman, "The Marketshare-Profitability Relationship," pp. 377–394.

6. See the discussion in D. Abell and J. Hammond, *Strategic Market Planning* (Englewood Cliffs, NJ, 1979), pp. 271–290.

GLOSSARY

Adverse-selection problem Occurs when one party behaves opportunistically to lure a second into a disadvantageous contract.

Agency theory A theory which models the consequences of separation of ownership and managerial control in the context of imperfect information.

Allocative inefficiency A distribution of goods and resources in which a reallocation could make at least one person better off without harming anyone else.

Appropriability The extent to which the economic returns accrue to the innovating firm rather than to the market as a whole.

Asset turnover The ratio of net sales to average total assets.

Asymmetric information Information that is important to a bargain and is held by only one party to that bargain.

Average costs Costs divided by quantity produced.

Backward integration Input sources are moved into the organization.

Barriers to entry Industry characteristics that reduce the rate of entry below that which would level profits.

Barriers to exit Factors that impede exit from an industry. The major source of exit barriers are specific assets of the operation.

Barriers to mobility Factors that prevent the movement of firms across strategic-group boundaries in response to profit differences.

Beta A measure of market risk that comes out of the Capital Asset Pricing Model.

Bounded rationality The postulate that individuals attempt to be rational in their dealings, but do so subject to their own limited information-processing abilities. One of the central assumptions of transaction-cost economics.

Business Attractiveness Screen A matrix that arrays an organization's business units by a variety of factors in theory correlated with their attractiveness.

Captive production Producing for use within the same organization.

Cash cow A Boston Consulting Group designation for a mature industry with a cash flow in excess of its internal investment needs.

Channel system The distribution system that moves a product from producer to consumer.

Clan A group of individuals within an organization with shared social understanding; associated with the work of Ouchi.

Cognitive distortion Members of groups in conflict perceive reality in ways that distort their own group's accomplishments.

Comparative advantage The premier theory used to explain patterns of international trade. In this theory, countries come to specialize in areas in which they have an advantage relative to their rivals.

Competitive advantage Characteristics of an organization that allow it to outperform rivals in the same industry.

Competitor analysis Analysis of one's rivals designed to help answer the question, What is my rival likely to do in a given situation?

Complementary assets A group of assets that work together to mutually support a particular strategy. Teece focused on the importance of complementary assets in explaining superior performance of particular innovative firms.

Concentrated differentiation The production of a line of products all within the same general type.

Concentration ratio The percentage of industry sales or employment accounted for by the largest few firms in the industry. In the U.S., the concentration ratio is typically calculated for the top four firms, while in Britain, the top three firms are usually used.

Conglomerate merger Firms that are in unrelated lines of business join together.

Constant returns to scale Unit costs remain constant as output increases.

Contestable markets Markets in which exit and entry are sufficiently easy that entry threats hold profits down to the competitive level.

Contingency theory A theory of planning which argues that the right strategic moves depend on the circumstances of the organization and its environment.

Core All solutions to a game in which no one acting either alone or in a coalition can do better.

Cospecialized assets Assets that fit together and work together to support a strategic initiative. Associated with the work of David Teece.

Credible threats All actions which are believable to rivals in the sense that taking such action would increase the welfare of the acting agent.

Critical chance values Probability values that are critical to the decision made.

Cross elasticity of demand Percentage change in the demand for one good in response to a 1 percent change in the price of a second good.

Cross parry Action in one market is countered by rival action in a second market.

Culture The characteristic style and ways of doing things that influence an organization's perspective and operations.

Current ratio A measure of liquidity equal to current assets divided by current liabilities.

Decision rules Routine ways of doing things within an organization.

Decision tree A device developed by operations researchers to depict all of the actions and outcomes associated with a particular problem.

Decreasing returns to scale Unit costs rise as output increases.

Diffusion curve A curve showing the rate at which an innovation is copied by rivals over time.

Diversification The process by which a firm moves into new lines of business not directly related to its existing lines.

Dog A Boston Consulting Group term to denote a line of business with a small market share in a slow-growth market.

Dominant design An idea developed by Utterback and Abernathy that in many industries a technical product standard develops.

Dominant strategy A strategy that is optimal regardless of the action taken by one's rival or opponent.

Economies of scale Unit costs decline as output increases.

Economies of scope Costs of production of two lines of business run together are less than the sum of each run separately.

Efficient market A market in which prices reflect all information instantaneously or nearly so; often used to describe security prices.

Elastic demand Demand is very responsive to price changes; demand elasticity is greater than one in absolute value; total revenue increases with a price cut and falls with a price rise.

Elasticity of demand The percentage change in demand in response to a 1 percent change in the price of a good.

Entrepreneurship Taking risks by seizing new opportunities early.

Entry deterrence Any of a set of strategic moves that serve to reduce the rate of entry into a market.

Environmental analysis An analysis of the critical environmental factors that influence an organization's operations and the trends in those factors.

Equilibrium analysis The analysis of markets in which individual consumers, firms, and workers behave so as to maximize their own returns.

Equilibrium price A price at which quantity demanded by consumers exactly equals quantity supplied by producers.

Escalation A process by which individuals increase support of projects or activities based on prior commitments, even in the face of evidence that such support is not warranted.

Event study Econometric work common in finance and accounting in which consequences of a particular event are traced in stock market result.

Evolutionary economics A perspective on economic behavior associated with the work of Richard Nelson and Sidney Winter. The focus of the evolutionary model is on change. The central assumptions of the model are: firms satisfice rather than maximize, and rely heavily on routines and decision rules in doing so; the environment works to select out more successful routines from less successful ones; but, at any one time, the system is not likely to be in equilibrium.

Excess capacity The capacity to produce additional units without substantial incremental costs or additions to fixed capacity.

Exit costs Costs of leaving an industry; such costs typically depend on the amount of specific assets involved in the operation.

Expectancy theory A theory of worker performance developed by Victor Vroom. Vroom argues that worker job performance is directed towards achieving most-rewarded outcomes in an organization.

Expected value The value of a deal multiplied by the probability of getting that deal.

Experience curve See Learning curve effects.

Experience goods Goods whose value and characteristics can be determined only well after purchase and consumption has occurred.

Extensive form A description of sequential moves in a game in which the various moves are not suppressed.

Externalities An unpriced cost or benefit imposed on one agent by the actions of a second; costs are known as negative externalities and benefits as positive externalities.

Facilitating devices Practices that improve the ability of firms to coordinate their behavior.

Factor analysis A statistical technique designed to identify the major factors underlying particular phenomenon.

Filtering The keying of management compensation to the performance of an organization relative to other similarly placed organizations.

First-mover advantage A competitive advantage held by a firm by virtue of being first in a particular market or first to use a particular strategy.

Five Forces Model A model, developed by Michael Porter, that explains industry profitability as a function of current levels of competition, buyer power, supplier power, entry barriers, and availability of substitute products.

Focal point A solution to which like-minded individuals converge without any explicit discussion or cooperation.

Forward integration Output outlets are moved into the organization.

Free-rider problem The problem of eliciting true willingness to pay for a good, when that good is a public good that nonpayers cannot readily be excluded from enjoying.

Functional organization An organization structured into the traditional functional units—i.e., marketing, finance, production, and so on.

Game theory Formal analysis of conflict and cooperation among intelligent and rational decision makers.

Game tree A graphical representation of the choices available to an agent and the outcomes from those choices.

Global market A market in which the economics of operating in a particular area depend not only on what the firm is doing in that market but on its activities world-wide.

Golden parachute A clause in some managerial contracts which gives high termination payments in cases of takeover.

Greenmail The repurchase of a potential acquirer's stock shares at a premium to avoid takeover.

Gross national product The total market value of a final goods and services produced by factors of production owned by a nation's citizens.

Groupthink A tendency of individuals to adopt the perspective of the group as a whole.

Growth/share matrix A visual representation of divisions within an organization, arrayed by market share and market growth rate. The growth-share matrix was developed by the Boston Consulting Group.

Herfindahl Index Sum of the squares of the shares of the firms in an industry multiplied by 10,000; a measure of industry concentration.

Hit-and-run-entry Entry which can be accomplished quickly without substantial specific assets; associated with Baumol's theory of contestable markets.

Horizontal merger Two or more competitors in the same market are joined.

Hostile takeover One firm takes over a second without the cooperation of the management of that second firm.

Hurdle rate The minimum acceptable rate of return on a project; used by some organizations as an investment criterion.

Ideology A shared system of beliefs that distinguish one organization from others around it.

Industrial policy An affirmative encouragement of particular industries by government to foster macroeconomic growth and employment.

Inelastic demand Demand is relatively unresponsive to price changes; demand elasticity is less than one in absolute value; total revenue rises with a price increase and falls with a price cut.

Interest groups Collections of individuals coalesced around particular issues.

Joint venture Two or more firms set up a separate entity and share ownership rights in its product and profits.

Kanban The just-in-time system in Japan in which inventories of intermediate goods are minimized.

Key success factors Those assets which allow one firm to outperform its rivals in an industry for a sustained period of time.

Learning-curve effects Reductions in unit costs associated with cumulative, lifetime experience in an activity.

Lemons problem The tendency in some markets for bad products to drive out good as a result of the information asymmetries between buyers and sellers.

Leverage High debt ratio.

Leveraged buy-out The purchase of a firm or line of business by its managers using heavy debt.

Limit-pricing strategy Incumbent firms in a market hold down current prices in an attempt to discourage entry into the market.

Logistic curve An S-shaped curve.

Management by objectives A system under which groups within complex organizations are judged and compensated on the basis of a clearly specified, narrow set of objectives.

Managerial-hubris hypothesis A theory developed by Roll that managers seek acquisitions in part because they overestimate how much better they could manage the assets of the acquired firms.

Marginal costs The incremental costs of increasing output by a small amount.

Market failure A malfunction in a market mechanism that results in a misallocation or an unproductive use of resources.

Market foreclosure The cutting off of a portion of the market, typically accomplished through merger.

Market share The fraction of sales or revenues captured by a particular firm or set of firms.

Matrix organization A structure which contains reporting and authority relationships that move both across product lines and across functional areas within product lines.

Meeting the competition A clause found in some contracts in which a seller agrees that, if a second seller offers a comparable product at a lower price to the buyer, the original seller will either meet the price or release the customer.

Merchant production Producing for use and sale outside the firm.

Merger An arrangement in which the assets and liabilities of the seller are absorbed into those of the buyer.

Minimum efficient scale The smallest output for which unit costs are minimized.

Moral hazard One or more parties to a contract behave opportunistically to exploit an information advantage.

Most-favored-nation A contract clause in which sellers agree to extend any favorable offers made to the "most favored nation" buyer.

Multidimensional scaling A statistical technique that allows one to form clusters of related attributes identified as important by consumers.

Multidivisional organization An organization structured according to product lines with functional areas duplicated across those product lines.

National diamond A framework developed by Michael Porter to explain the location of economic activities among nations. The diamond represents those factors influencing this decision: factors of production, home demand, the presence of supporting industries, and the structure of home supply.

Natural monopoly A market situation in which the minimum efficient scale is equal or larger than the whole market.

Nenko A system used in Japan in which promotions are virtually guaranteed with age and seniority.

Network externalities The value to a consumer of a product increases as the number of compatible users increases.

Niche strategy A strategy of serving a specialized part of the market, often small.

Opportunism Opportunism occurs when an individual takes advantage of an informational advantage in his or her behavior. It is a central assumption of transaction-cost economics.

Opportunity cost The value of the next best opportunity which must be sacrificed in order to engage in a particular activity.

Organizational ecology Study of the birth and death of firms and industries.

Overbounded systems Organizations with rigid authority and reporting lines and considerable formal detail.

Pay-back period An investment criterion used by some organizations. The pay-back period is the length of time it will take a project to repay the cash invested in it.

Payoff matrix A visual representation of the results (payoffs) to a set of simultaneous actions by two agents.

Perceptual map A visual representation of how consumers perceive products in a market based on the multiple attributes of those products.

PIMS A regression model developed by G.E. and subsequently the Strategic Planning Institute which tries to model factors determining rate of return.

Pioneering-brand advantage Advantage which the first firm to introduce a product has over rivals; typically comes from informational problems in the consumer market.

Poison pill A device to defend against a hostile takeover which has the effect of reducing the value of the acquired firm if swallowed by the acquiring.

Portfolio management Management of resources across divisions within an organization.

Predatory pricing Deliberate aggression on the part of a firm against its rivals with the intent of driving those rivals out of business; in practice, often defined as pricing below average variable costs.

Pre-emptive patenting Patenting a product or process in order to keep it out of the hands of potential or actual rivals and thus protect one's current position in a market.

Principal-agent model A view that stresses the importance of the separation of ownership and control in the conduct of various transactions. The principal is the owner, or the controlling authority in the transaction, and the agent is the individual engaged to act for the principal.

Prisoners' dilemma A game in which the payoff configuration is such that both players have individual incentives to choose outcomes that together give both players a worse outcome than if both players had simultaneously chosen the other strategy.

Product champion A manager who takes a front position supporting a risky project and making sure it gets adequate resources.

Public good Goods for which one individual's consumption does not reduce the consumption of anyone else, and for which excludability is difficult. Defense is a classic example.

Push strategy Using distributors to stimulate demand; contrasted with pull strategy in which demand is pulled through, principally by advertising.

Quality circles Heterogeneous work groups charged with monitoring and improving product quality.

Quick ratio A measure of liquidity equal to current assets minus inventory divided by current liabilities.

Random-walk theory A theory associated with Burton Malkiel that fundamental analysis cannot yield an investor portfolio that dominates a buy-and-hold strategy in the long run.

Rate-of-return regulation A procedure by which a firm is regulated by overseeing the return it can earn on its invested capital.

Regression analysis A statistical technique of finding the best fit to explain patterns of a particular variable.

Regulatory evasion Attempts to exceed the regulatory allowed rate of return surreptitiously; often involves moving profits from a regulated to an unregulated line of business via transfer-pricing techniques.

Relative advantage The advantage of a firm over other firms in the same market.

Rent-seeking behavior The spending of resources to secure for oneself a position in a market in which excess returns are being generated; often used in the regulatory context.

Repeated games A competitive situation which occurs numerous times; in game theory, repeated games enhance the set of strategic options.

Reputation effect The constellation of past actions by a firm that condition views of expected future behavior.

Resale-price maintenance A practice by which manufacturers direct retailers as to the prices they can charge consumers.

Residual claimants Individuals who receive any value from the organization not due to creditors; in the for-profit firm, usually thought to be the stockholder.

Restructuring Selling off unrelated parts of a business in order to streamline operations and return to a core business.

Return on equity The equity earnings of a firm divided by the book value of its equity.

Return on sales The earnings of a firm divided by its sales.

Return to investors The price appreciation and dividend yield from a stock held for a specified period of time.

Risk aversion The preference for a certain deal over an uncertain one with equal expected value.

Risk premium The additional return investors expect for making a risky investment rather than a safe one.

Screening device A method for sorting out individuals of different qualities.

Search goods Goods whose value and characteristics are apparent upon inspection.

Secondary market A market in which one buys already issued goods; often used to refer to purchases of seasoned issues in the securities market.

Seniority wages A Japanese system in which wages rise over the worker's tenure with the firm, even if the job level does not.

Signal jamming Actions that interfere with the market information new rivals get when they enter a market; couponing heavily in a rival's test market is one example.

Skunkworks Small operations designed to push innovation with minimal hierarchy and formalism.

Sleeping patent A patent on a product that is never put into commercial use.

Span of control The number of subordinates under an individual.

Specific assets Assets which have value only in a very narrow use.

Spill-over effects The actions of one agent also influence a second agent.

Stakeholders Those individuals inside and outside an organization who believe themselves to have some residual claim on the output of that organization.

Strategic alliance An arrangement by which two or more firms combine resources outside of the market to accomplish a task.

Strategic groups Clusters of firms within an industry that share certain critical asset configurations and follow common strategies.

Strategic map A visual representation of the group structure within an industry.

Strategic piggybacking One line of business is operated using the resources of a second.

Strategic predisposition A tendency of an organization by virtue of its history and assets to favor one strategy over competitive possibilities.

Symmetrical solution A solution in game theory in which all parties end up with equal results.

Synergies The combined effect of two actions is greater than their sum taken separately.

Technical efficiency Use of resources in the most productive way holding most of final output constant.

Technological opportunity The base of innovation in an area.

Threat points Opportunities available to parties of a negotiation that do not require the cooperation of the bargaining partner.

Tit for tat A game strategy of "If you hit me. I'll hit you back." Lately associated with the work of Axelrod on cooperation in a variety of settings.

Transaction-cost economics A theory, developed by Ronald Coase and subsequently enlarged on by Oliver Williamson and many others, in which it is argued that contractual relations among and within firms are the result of efficiency-seeking behavior in a world of limited information and incomplete enforcement possibilities.

Transfer price The price at which a good is transferred across divisional boundaries within an organization.

Tying Conditioning the purchase of one good on that of a second.

Underbounded systems Organizations with very few structures in place and quite fluid relationships.

Vertical integration The process in which either one of the input sources or output buyers of the firm are moved inside the firm.

Vertical merger Firms that are in different stages in the production and distribution of a good are linked.

Winner's curse In bargaining, the winner often has overestimated the value of the deal.

Yardstick competition The measurement of performance for compensation or other purposes against all others in the same class.

Zero-sum game A game in which a gain by one player is exactly offset by a loss to a second.

INDEX